W9-BBO-874

CZARS

Also by James P. Duffy and Vincent L. Ricci:
Hitler Slept Late, and Other Blunders That Cost Him the War
Target Hitler: The Plots to Kill Adolf Hitler
The Assassination of John F. Kennedy: A Complete Book of Facts
Code Name . . . Military Operations of World War II

CZARS

RUSSIA'S RULERS FOR MORE THAN ONE THOUSAND YEARS

JAMES P. DUFFY
VINCENT L. RICCI

Facts On File, Inc.

AN INFOBASE HOLDINGS COMPANY

CZARS: RUSSIA'S RULERS FOR MORE THAN ONE THOUSAND YEARS

Facts On File, Inc.
460 Park Avenue South
New York NY 10016

Library of Congress Cataloging-in-Publication Data
Duffy, James P., 1941–
    Czars : Russia's rulers for more than one thousand years /
James P. Duffy, Vincent L. Ricci.
        p. cm.
    Includes bibliographical references and index.
    ISBN 0-8160-2873-7 (alk. paper)
    1. Russia—Kings and rulers—Biography. I. Ricci, Vincent L.
II. Title.
DK37.6.D87 1995
947'.0099—dc20
[B]   94-44654

Facts On File books are available at special discounts when purchased in bulk quantities for businesses, associations, institutions or sales promotions. Please call our Special Sales Department in New York at 212/683-2244 or 800/322-8755.

Text design by Grace Ferrara
Jacket design by Nora Wertz

Printed in the United States of America

MP FOF 10 9 8 7 6 5 4 3 2 1

This book is printed on acid-free paper.

To Michael Jackson

CONTENTS

ACKNOWLEDGMENTS

So MANY PEOPLE HAVE HELPED US IN so many ways to research the material in this book that it is impossible for us to list them without inadvertently leaving some out. Therefore, we have decided once again to simply express our appreciation to each of you as we did at the time you gave us your assistance.

Having said that, we would like to recognize the special help given us by the always patient and always professional staff of the Millbrook (New York) Free Library. They include Librarian Lois Rigoulot, Nancy Rogers, and Jo Hausam.

We also want to express our appreciation to Paula Ruffino for her conquest of the names, dates, and relationships required to prepare the genealogical tables used in this book. Her many hours at the keyboard have resulted in making it easier for readers to follow the long and often confusing line of Russian monarchs from the ninth century to the twentieth.

James P. Duffy
Vincent L. Ricci

INTRODUCTION

RUSSIA! THE NAME CONJURES IMAGES OF BROAD fertile steppes, the vast snow-swept barren expanses of the Siberian wilderness, and the opulent, mysterious lifestyles of autocratic rulers. Despite our strong historical ties to England, we Americans have a casual knowledge of more Russian emperors than British monarchs—from their jewel-encrusted sable robes and the exquisitely beautiful Fabergé eggs collected by the last czars, to their frequently brutal despotism. Peter the Great, Ivan the Terrible, Catherine the Great, and the last, most tragic Russian emperor, Nicholas II, and his wife, Alexandra, are as familiar to us as major characters in our own history.

Yet, these are merely four in a long line of sovereigns who ruled that mighty nation for more than a thousand years. In the following pages, we will come to know all the monarchs who helped to shape Russia's destiny. Little is actually known about the early princes who ruled the fledgling Russian nation because, until the arrival of Christian missionaries in the latter part of the 9th century, the Slavs had no written language with which to record their own history. Much of the history that survives was written centuries later in chronicles based on folk tales handed down from one generation to the next. It is probable that much information was diluted, lost, or embelished in the process, making the details less than certain. However, because those details are the only ones that are available, we are, in a sense, stuck with them without the ability to confirm or refute what they say, except in those rare instances when heroic deeds or the numerical strength of Russian forces appear out of place with the time and locale.

The history of the earliest years of Russia is thus a combination of Slavic myths, Viking tales, historical records kept by civilizations—primarily those of the Byzantine Empire of Constantinople—that came in contact with the earliest Russians, and stories passed down through the generations. In a general sense, its progress appears realistic, and until some unknown contemporary chronicles are discovered, this is the only history of Russia that exists.

Now, a word about spelling and dates. Russians use a different alphabet than the Roman one used in the West. Although some evidence exists of earlier forms of writing in the Slav lands, genuine literacy, including a common

alphabet, was first introduced by Christians. The Russian alphabet is called
Cyrillic, after its creator, St. Cyril. Because Russians use a different alphabet,
their language cannot be readily translated into English, but must be translit-
erated. This means that English words cannot be substituted for Russian words,
and that each Cyrillic character must be treated individually in the process. In
addition, the writer must choose from a wide variety of alternative methods of
transliteration. For example, a direct transliteration of the Cyrillic name for the
capital of Russia would be Moskva, yet we commonly call it Moscow. The same
problem arises with the popular Russian names Alexander (Aleksandr), Peter
(Petr), and Nicholas (Nikolai). In the case of Ivan, the direct transliteration is
Ioann, which becomes John. To preclude any confusion that could result from
a strict transliteration of Russian into English, we have elected to use the word
forms most commonly used in the West. Thus, instead of referring to one of the
most infamous Russian leaders as John the Terrible, we call him Ivan the
Terrible (to confuse the issue even further, a direct transliteration would
actually be John the Dread). Although some scholars and purists may disagree
with our method, we believe it contributes to an eminently more readable book.
We hope our readers concur.

Until the late 16th century, Europeans used the Julian calendar, which
was developed by the Roman emperor Julius Caesar. In 1582, the West converted to the Gregorian calendar, which was introduced by Pope Gregory XIII.
Russia, however, retained the Julian calendar until the Bolsheviks adopted the
Gregorian calendar in February 1918. As a result, the calendar used by the
Russians during the first 17 years of the 20th century lagged behind the Western
calendar by 13 days; by 12 days during the 19th century; and by 11 days in the
18th century. These discrepancies are important if one wishes to relate an event
that occurred inside Russia with another that happened elsewhere on the same
day.

The history of Russia covered in this book falls into four distinct periods.
The first is the ascendancy of Kiev, in what is now Ukraine, as the dominant
influence in a confederation of principalities that covered a large portion of
what would eventually become the Russian Empire. The grand prince of Kiev,
so designated because every prominent Russian settlement was governed by a
local prince who swore allegiance to him, was the leader of the Kievan realm
and the forerunner of the Russian emperors and czars. Kiev remained the seat
of Russian power and commerce until it was sacked and burned by a rival of the
grand prince in 1169. That defeat was followed by the second period, during
which the political center of Russia moved first to the northern town of

Vladimir, then to Moscow. During this era the mounted hordes of the Mongolian khan cut a wide swath across Russia, subduing the insular Russian princes and reducing them to vassals of the khan.

The third period of Russian history began with the reign of Ivan the Great in 1462. Ivan drove the Mongols from Russia, declared himself "autocrat" of all Russia, and began the initiative that finally united all the Russian principalities under one strong central government. The fourth and final period began in 1613, when the dynasty founded by the Viking prince Rurik was supplanted by Czar Michael I and the throne passed to the House of Romanov. This period ended in March 1917, when the last czar, Nicholas II, abdicated in favor of his brother, Grand Duke Michael, who refused to accept a throne that was by then all but nonexistent.

After the fall of the House of Romanov and the rise of the communist totalitarian dictatorship, the grand princes, grand dukes, and czars all but vanished from the official memory of Russia, although many older people secretly kept photos and other mementos of their czarist past in their homes. Since the collapse of the communist Union of Soviet Socialist Republics in December 1991, a surprisingly large number of Russians have been demonstrating a renewed interest in, and devotion for, their imperial past, even calling for Nicholas II to be made a saint of the Russian Orthodox Church.

Part One

THE
FOUNDATIONS
OF EMPIRE

CHAPTER 1

THE PEOPLE BEFORE THE RUS

NINETEENTH-CENTURY WESTERNERS CONSIDERED RUSSIA TO BE a nation with an "Asiatic" character. Most Europeans judged the Russians to be vaguely "Oriental" as opposed to European because Russia had been isolated from the progressive advances of western European civilization for hundreds of years by czars who had total control over every aspect of Russian life. Actually,

- - - Kievan Russia in 900 A.D.

Kievan Russia lands gained by 1054 A.D.

Kievan Russia

the people we now call Russians, and the nation we know as Russia, have European rather than Asian origins. Although the vast lands of the Russian Empire were inhabited by many peoples of varying heritages, the cradle of modern Russian society lies in the fertile lands of what is today southern European Russia and Ukraine. This territory, north of the Black Sea, is bordered by the lower Danube River in the west and the Don River in the east.

Seven centuries before the birth of Christ, Greeks colonized the northern shore of the Black Sea. They founded trading centers that attracted a multiplicity of tradesmen from the north and east. Many of these settlements, especially those in the Crimea, survive today, although little trace of their Greek origins remains.

The earliest inhabitants of southern Russia with a direct link to the modern Russian population were a diverse group. Known to the outside world by various tribal names, they called themselves Slovenes, the name evidently derived from "slovo," meaning "the word." The name later evolved to "Slavs." Little is known of the Slavs' origins, except that the first recorded families were nomadic cattle-grazers who eventually settled down and became the nucleus of the Russian agricultural population. The Slavs were a relatively peaceful people who organized themselves into tribes and clans, and for the most part they eschewed military and political organization.

The Slavs were tall and fair-skinned, with light-brown hair and slate-blue or gray eyes. Along the rivers that flow through European Russia, they built small settlements consisting largely of log homes grouped behind a protective wall that was actually little more than an earthen mound topped by a wooden stockade. From native trees they fashioned dugout canoes in which they traveled the river highways. These water routes were greatly superior to the land passages through the thick forests and all but impenetrable marshes.

Some tribes of Slavs migrated south, establishing settlements on the great flat plains known as steppes. Because there were few natural barriers to repel invaders, the Slavs were constantly at the mercy of warlike predators who regularly swept in from the east seeking grazing lands for their herds and plunder for themselves.

Among the earliest invaders were the Scythians, who were of Iranian origin. Nomadic warriors whose custom of using the scalps of slain enemies as articles of clothing was recorded by the Greek historian Herodotus in the 5th century B.C., the Scythians subjugated large numbers of Slavic tribes. They conducted a lively commercial traffic with the Greek Black Sea settlements as well as with the Mongol and Chinese centers far to the east. The Scythians were ultimately supplanted by the Sarmatians, another people of Persian origin. The Sarmatian occupation of the fertile steppes north of the Black Sea was a gradual process rather than the product of a bellicose confrontation. It began in the early part of the 4th century B.C. and was completed two centuries later.

The most powerful Sarmatians were members of a tribe of renowned horsemen called the Alans. Tall, blond-haired and fair-skinned, the Alans were also celebrated artisans who created elaborately decorated jewelry and weapons. Originally a nomadic people like their cousins the Scythians, the Alans gradually integrated with their Slavic subjects, and eventually several Alan clans established permanent agricultural settlements. Rudiments of the Alanic language blended with the language of the Slavs, and centuries later Slavic princes still bore names of Alanic heritage.

The origin of the name Rus, from which the name Russia is derived, remains contentious among historians. One school of thought holds that Rus originated with a clan of Alans who called themselves Rukhs-As, which means "the brilliant Alans."

Sarmatian domination of southern Russia lasted until the 3rd century A.D., when the Goth invasion that began rather obscurely in the 2nd century took hold. A Teutonic people prone to conquest, the Goths were more warlike than the Scythians or the Sarmatians. They traveled with entire families down the Western Dvina River from the Baltic Sea and made their way to the Dnieper, which leads to the Black Sea, and thence into the Mediterranean. With a more highly skilled military organization than that of the local populations, the Goths swiftly became the ruling class of the region bordering the Dnieper. Calling on their long experience in sea warfare, which they gained largely in the Baltic, the new rulers of Russia exploited their freshly acquired access to the Black Sea and the Mediterranean to raid and pillage other societies. In 267 they attacked Athens in a failed attempt to capture the Greek city.

The Goths' sole contribution of any significance to Russia's history was their creation of the region's first empire. During King Hermanric's reign, the Goths united the various races of Slavs, Scythians, and Sarmatians but left behind little of their own culture when they themselves were pushed west by the Huns in the latter part of the 4th century.

The Huns effected the first of the great Asian invasions of eastern Europe. An unholy composite of Mongolian and Tartar tribesmen ruled by a ruthless Mongolian aristocracy, the Huns drove west from central Asia in search of grazing land and conquest. After conquering Scythian and Sarmatian tribes, including the Alans, the Huns conscripted the defeated warriors for their war against the Goths. That campaign was consummated in the year 367, when 200,000 Goths were driven across the Danube River into the territory of the Greek Byzantine Empire.

Led by their famous king, Attila, the Huns pressed as far west as France before they were halted in 451 by an allied army consisting largely of Romans and Goths. Attila made Pannonia, now Hungary, the center of his newly established European empire. It was there in 448 that he received an ambassador from the Byzantine emperor, Theodosius II. Following Attila's death in 453, the Hun empire split into warring factions and quickly disintegrated. The legacy the Hun invaders left to the Slavs was to drive both the Iranian and Teutonic peoples from their land. Although woefully disorganized, the Slavs thereafter managed to retain control of their territory for more than two centuries. Invaders came and went, but as always the Slavs absorbed elements of each conquering force into their society and survived.

After the Hun empire collapsed, the Bulgars, another Asiatic group that included remnants of the Hun forces, crossed into Russia from Asia and ruled for a brief period. In 670 a Bulgar army invaded and conquered the territory now known as Bulgaria, but the Bulgars were so thoroughly absorbed by the local Slav population that their language and customs all but disappeared. The Bulgars were followed at the end of the 7th century by the Avars, who were themselves being driven west by the Altaic Turks. The Avars fought their way through a Slavic army to gain asylum in the Balkan peninsula where they, too, were absorbed into the Slav community living there.

Because of the Avars' reputation for cruelty, many Slavs abandoned their homes and fled in large numbers as this enemy approached. These Slavs migrated into sparsely settled or previously unoccupied regions, spreading their own customs and culture among more primitive populations. One group, the Eastern Slavs, keeping ahead of the Avar invasion, gradually made its way up the Dnieper River and eventually built along the river a settlement called Kiev, after a Slav prince named Kiy.

The result of these and future invasions was that the Slavs in different regions began to acquire slightly different characteristics through their absorption of other peoples. Soon there were Southern Slavs, Northern Slavs, and Eastern Slavs, all speaking a basically common language and having similar customs, but each group being slightly distinctive, reflecting the dialects and mores it had assimilated from its conquerors.

The next invading horde was the most unique in terms of its achievements. The Khazars were a homogenized amalgam of Bulgars, Huns, Caucasians, and Turks. By the middle of the 7th century, the Khazars had established a stable state along the northern shores of the Black and Caspian seas. Described as having a "curiously pacific military despotism," the Khazars were an extremely tolerant people, probably owing to the diversity of their background. Although some Khazars engaged in food production—including cattle breeding, fishing, and land cultivation—most were traders. Commerce was the lifeblood of the Khazar empire, whose capital was Itil, on the lower Volga River. With the growth of trade, Itil expanded from a primitive settlement of skin tents to a great commercial center boasting of superior baths and marketplaces. Khazar authority was concentrated in the hands of two men, the kagan, or great khan, and the beg. The great khan was the titular authority, but most historians agree that the beg, who controlled the army, owned the real power. The Khazar empire extended from the Volga River and the Caspian Sea to the Dnieper and the Black Sea, covering a large portion of the steppes.

Trade led to alliances, and soon the Khazar empire was allied with Byzantium. In the middle of the 8th century, this alliance led to the marriage of a Khazar princess to the Byzantine emperor, Constantine V. The progeny of that marriage, Emperor Leo IV, sat on the Roman throne in Constantinople from 775 to 780 and was known as the khazar.

During the 8th century, the Khazars came under tremendous pressure from a rapidly spreading Arab empire that coveted the productive fields of southern Russia. Although the Khazars failed to keep the Arabs from occupying the Caucasus and Armenia, they were able to prevent them from advancing any farther north.

Sometime around 740 the great khan, most of his court, and the upper reaches of Khazar society adopted the Jewish religion. This action appears to have been less a matter of faith than of political expediency. The Byzantines had been pressing the pagan Khazars to become Christians. At the same time, the Arabs, who were now close neighbors, were pressuring the Khazars to adopt the Muslim faith. By embracing Judaism the Khazars could remain neutral, desensitizing the competition between the two religions and thus neutralizing two powerful military forces.

The Khazars retained control of their empire as the first Russian state gradually came into existence. During the time of the Khazars, several Slav migrations took place, with many of the native steppe tribes moving north into the forests occupied by the Finns and Lithuanians and away from the danger of nomad tribes. The modern Russian population evolved from the Eastern Slavs, who settled along the Dnieper River and in its surrounding fertile country. The Western Slavs eventually made up the populations of the central European states, while the Southern Slavs, who settled in the Balkans, were subjugated by the Ottoman Turks. The Eastern Slavs gravitated north, building along river banks fortified settlements that were generally little more than military camps protected by earthen or wooden walls. The Eastern Slavs' primitive form of agriculture regularly depleted the soil, requiring periodic movement of entire communities to fresh, previously uncultivated land. Some Slav groups made frequent forays north into the great forested regions, where they captured Finns and Lithuanians as slaves and harvested fur and honey.

Because the Slavs did not mint money, they measured wealth by the number of slaves a family owned, or by its hoard of honey, furs, and agricultural products suitable for tribute to foreign rulers, such as the Khazars, or for barter with traders from Byzantium or the Arab world. An aristocracy of sorts developed, based on this assessment of wealth.

Most of the Slavs practiced a religion, similar in many ways to those of the ancient Greeks and Romans, that centered on the worship of nature-based gods. The most prominent of these was Perun, the god of thunder and lightning. Other important gods were Dazhbog (the god of heaven and light), Volos (the god of the underworld), and Striborg (the god of the winds).

The Eastern Slav communities coexisted peaceably as quasi-family entities with little formal governmental or military structure. That began to change during the 9th century with the appearance of new invaders from the north, the Vikings or Norsemen, and with the introduction of a common written language based on the Slavonic tongue. An alphabet was devised by Cyril and Methodius, two Christian missionaries from Byzantium, which at that time was still affiliated with the Roman Catholic Church. The two missionaries began their work in about the year 855. Cyril, for whom the Slav alphabet is named, preached the gospel among the Eastern Slavs as far east as the Crimea. Methodius concentrated his efforts among the Western Slavs in the area of Moravia. Cyril's success in spreading Christianity among the pagans was overshadowed by Methodius's calamity when the invading Magyars slaughtered Christians and drove the religion out of Moravia. Cyril died in 869, Methodius in 885.

Prince Rurik

CHAPTER 2

RURIK AND THE BIRTH OF A NATION

T HE BEGINNINGS OF THE FIRST RUSSIAN STATE are shrouded in controversy. Early Russian chroniclers recount that in the second half of the 9th century the Slav merchant families of the northern trading center of Novgorod who controlled the local population were weary of their vulnerability to outside marauders and sought the protection of a Viking band called the Varangians. According to this version, the families realized that they needed a strong central authority to govern their territory and maintain protective control over the river trade routes that were so vital to their economy. Unable to agree on a candidate for the princely position from among themselves, they recruited an outsider whose loyalty would not be influenced by allegiance to any one family. Whether by invitation or incursion, or by some other means, a Viking named Rurik became the Slavs' first monarch, the first ruler of what is now called Russia.

Most accounts of Rurik's ascent and ensuing reign rely on Russian chroniclers who wrote two or three centuries after the events. The accuracy of these accounts remains suspect, less for the time lapse than for their overemphasis on the "heroic" stature credited to Rurik.

❖ ❖ ❖

During the 9th century and into the next, Viking bands roamed along the coasts of Europe, raiding and pillaging. In 820, they conquered Ireland; in 874, Iceland; and in 911, Normandy. Marauding Vikings penetrated most of the rivers in western Europe, terrorizing the populations and the rulers alike. In the land of the Slavs the Vikings found the going easier than in the West. Although some Slav communities were willing to defend themselves, their primitive weapons and methods were no match for the Norsemen.

A versatile race capable of quickly switching roles from raiders to tradesmen, the Vikings discovered they could travel almost exclusively by water from their Baltic ports south through the Black Sea to the Mediterranean, where they could conduct a lucrative trade. Plying these water routes, they transported slaves, honey, and furs—all sought-after commodities in places like Constantinople—directly to their buyers. Most of these commodities were acquired as tribute from the Finns, Lithuanians, and Slavs whom the Vikings had conquered on their drive south. The large number of coins from Mediterranean cultures of this period that were discovered throughout Russia and Scandinavia during later centuries attests to the enormous volume of trade transacted by the Vikings.

Viking fortress-cities soon appeared along the shores of Russian rivers and lakes, and Slav villages grew up around many of them. The Viking invaders were not part of an organized Scandinavian force but members of a loosely connected network of roving bands that occasionally joined together for a specific expedition that might involve trade or war. In some cases, groups of Viking warriors sold their services as security forces to the merchants of trading centers. As such, they fought off bandits and invaders alike, not infrequently other Vikings.

Rurik led such a group of Vikings called the Varangians. Apart from a chronicler's account of aristocratic Slav families hiring Rurik to become their prince, a most unlikely circumstance, a second version of Rurik's ascendancy exists. The truth probably lies somewhere in between the two accounts.

The second account relates that the Varangians had hired themselves out as a protective guard to the Slav trading town of Novgorod, on the Volkhov River south of Lake Ladoga. When their agreed term of service ended, Rurik and his Varangians returned to Scandinavia and were replaced by another Viking band, but the latter was deemed unsatisfactory for the job and was sent away. A deputation from Novgorod visited Rurik and asked that he return to the city's employ. According to this tale, Rurik at first declined, complaining of the "savage habits" of Novgorod's population. Finally, he agreed to return, probably motivated by the promise of a sizable financial reward.

Rurik and his band returned to the land of the Slavs in the year 862. He settled on the shore of Lake Ladoga north of Novgorod while he continued to negotiate with the city's leaders. A dispute over the amount of money the city was to pay for Varangian protection prompted an attack on the Vikings by a rash young prince of Novgorod named Vadim. The Vikings annihilated the attackers and seized complete control of the city and the surrounding country-side. Rurik declared himself prince of Novgorod, founding a dynasty that would rule without interruption until the death of Theodore, the son of Ivan the Terrible, in 1598.

As was their custom, the Vikings brought with them their families and all their possessions, and were thus well equipped for a long stay. Rurik's two closest lieutenants, his brothers Sineus and Truvor, also accompanied him. With Novgorod firmly under Varangian control, Rurik's brothers set out with bands of warriors to expand their authority beyond the city and its environs. Sineus quickly captured Beloozero to the east, and Truvor annexed Izborsk on the Luga River to the west.

No completely reliable physical description of Rurik exists. Although there is disagreement about his heritage, as there is about almost every other aspect of Russia's beginnings, we can safely conclude that Rurik was a Dane with a long career as a trader-adventurer who led raids along the Atlantic coast of Europe. The name Rurik, sometimes spelled Riurik, is probably a Slavicized form of the Norse name Hrorekr. In the centuries since his rule, artists have portrayed him in conventionally heroic poses. He appears as a tall, stern-faced man with a flowing white beard. Rurik was doubtlessly a great warrior chieftain. With only a few exceptions, such as when he was compelled to leave Novgorod and travel west to defend his other holdings, he appears to have settled comfortably into the role of the permanent ruler of Novgorod. He evidently had no interest in extending his domain, allowing his brothers to rule their cities as independent fiefdoms.

Several years before Rurik's return to Novgorod, two Viking chieftains, Askold (Hoskuldr) and Dir (Dyri), had migrated south, traveling along the river routes until they reached Kiev. Kiev was then a small trading center on a hill overlooking the Dnieper River, which flows into the Black Sea. It was the last trading center in Russia's forested region before the river entered the broad plains of the steppes extending to the south. At the time, Kiev was nominally ruled by the Khazars, to whom the inhabitants paid a yearly tribute. Askold and Dir advanced on the town, quickly won the support of the Vikings employed by Kiev as a defense force, and assumed control without encountering any real opposition.

More ambitious and aggressive than Rurik, Askold and Dir led an army of Vikings and Slavs down the Dnieper River into the Black Sea, where they organized an assault against the capital of the Byzantine Empire. On June 18, 860, their Viking fleet of approximately 200 ships sailed from the Black Sea into the Bosporus Strait toward Constantinople. Whether by luck or design, the Kievan force struck while the emperor, Michael III, was campaigning in Asia Minor with his army, and while the Byzantine navy was busy battling Arab fleets in the Mediterranean, leaving the city all but defenseless.

Informed of the attack, Emperor Michael disengaged his troops and hurried to defend his capital. Meanwhile, the combined Viking and Slav force ravaged the countryside around Constantinople but failed to capture the city. Undismayed, the attackers laid siege to the city in the hope of forcing its citizens to yield. As the siege dragged on with little effect, the attackers began contemplating abandoning the effort and returning home. Their decision to do so was hastened by word that Michael, at the head of the Byzantine army, was rushing to the city's rescue.

The audacious aggression of the Rus against the capital of the last vestige of the Roman Empire brought them immediate notoriety among the Mediterranean nations and ushered them into European history. Askold and Dir returned to Kiev with their decimated army and continued to rule there with Rurik's approval.

Less than two years after the conquest of Novgorod, Rurik's brothers died. To secure his domain, Rurik annexed the territories formerly held by Sineus and Truvor, thus widening his own principality. Although the narratives of Rurik's rule are clouded by the politics and prejudices of the ancient Russian chroniclers, it would appear that Viking rule brought a time of peace and prosperity to northern Russia. Novgorod grew and prospered as the major commercial center of the region, and Rurik is generally acknowledged to have been a benevolent ruler with a keen faculty for conducting profitable trade.

By the time of Rurik's death in 879, Viking chieftains held sway over a vast stretch of land reaching from the Baltic Sea in the north to the southern steppes, but it was not yet united under one ruler. This territory included portions of today's western Russia as well as parts of present-day Belarus and Ukraine. The great rivers that traverse this area were the north-south trading routes that would connect the future Russian nation with the Greek Byzantine Empire and other Mediterranean cultures.

As they had done with every invader during several centuries, the Slavs at first submitted to Viking rule but eventually absorbed the Vikings into their own culture. Ironically, despite the fact that the Vikings are credited with founding the Russian state, except for a few archaeological sites, virtually no trace of the Vikings' presence remains.

Part Two

THE REIGN OF
THE GRAND
DUKES OF KIEV

CHAPTER 3

OLEG AND THE RISE OF CENTRAL POWER

WHEN RURIK DIED IN 879, HIS HEIR, an infant son named Igor, was too young to rule. The authority of the prince of Novgorod was entrusted to Igor's guardian, Oleg, who ruled in his place as regent. While Oleg's precise relationship to Rurik is not known, it is generally accepted that he was a kinsman and therefore a member of the royal family.

Oleg, whose Viking name was Helgi, proved to be a more aggressive empire builder than Rurik. In early 882 he set about bringing under his, and therefore Igor's, control the Varangian chiefs who had established princedoms along the Russian rivers. Each in turn swore allegiance to Igor or was eliminated as a potential rival. Arriving outside of Kiev late in the year, Oleg summoned Askold and Dir to a meeting aboard his ship. When the pair arrived they were murdered, and the city was informed that Oleg was its new ruler.

Oleg liked what he saw in Kiev and decided to move his capital from Novgorod. Ruling as regent for Igor, Oleg now controlled all of western Russia from the Baltic in the north to Kiev in the south. By unifying the autonomous cities and principalities into one alliance, he formed the nucleus of the future Russian Empire and, eventually, of the now defunct Soviet Union. Because of its proximity to Constantinople, Kiev had always been a more important trading center than its two closest rivals, Novgorod and Smolensk. As the new capital, it also became the center of political and military power.

Oleg now had before him three important tasks. The first was to consolidate the political and military power of his new capital; the second was to expand trade with the Mediterranean world; the third was to expand the territory under his domain. Because he dealt ruthlessly with those whom he considered traitors, Oleg's first task, consolidation of the power of the prince of Kiev, was the simplest of the three. By uniting the entire area under one ruler, he helped to maintain peace and forged military alliances that generally succeeded in fending off incursions from the semibarbaric tribes that roamed the Russian forests.

Control of the rivers at least as far south as Kiev insured the relatively safe collection of tribute from Slavic tribes, usually in the form of slaves, furs, and honey. Each year these were sent downriver to Kiev, where they were collected into one huge expedition that left Kiev in the spring, destined for Constantinople. Because the early princes of Kiev were never able to fully subjugate the steppes between Kiev and the Black Sea, it was necessary to provide a strong military escort for these trading expeditions to protect them from roving tribes of marauders.

Oleg's ability to expand his empire, the Kievan State, was limited by the lack of established settlements in the vast forests bordering his domain. These forests were inhabited by nomadic tribes that vanished as soon as his troops arrived. There was no one from whom to collect tribute, and settlers sent into these forests soon disappeared and were never heard from again. Several Kievan military campaigns were conducted across the steppes toward the east, one reaching as far as the Caspian Sea, but they enjoyed limited success.

Meanwhile, the trade agreement between Constantinople and Kiev had been fractured, prompting Oleg to launch a military expedition against the capital of Byzantium in 907. Leaving Igor in charge of Kiev, Oleg sailed for Constantinople with an army so massive that it required, according to the ancient chroniclers, 2,000 boats for transportation. Whether that number is accurate or not, it is generally accepted that Oleg hurled a formidable army against the Byzantines.

As Askold and Dir had done earlier, Oleg ordered his combined Viking-Slav army to lay siege to Constantinople while he ravaged the surrounding countryside. According to legend, the Greeks had closed the Bosporus gateway to Constantinople by stretching chains across the mouth of the strait. Oleg overcame this obstacle by outfitting his ships with wheels and "sailing" them across the flat peninsula east of the city. Palaces and churches were burned, local inhabitants were put to the sword or sent into slavery, and the capital of the empire was subjected to a siege.

Constantinople was stunned when Oleg attacked by land, having transported his men and supplies overland in the modified seagoing vessels. Stories of Vikings and Slavs slaughtering innocent villagers and farmers terrorized the Byzantines, who determined to find a way to appease the barbarians. Oleg, who now called himself the "Most Illustrious Grand Prince of Rus," agreed to receive a delegation from the Byzantine emperor, Leo VI. Because Oleg's motive for attacking Byzantium was to renegotiate the trade treaty, the delegation's gifts were graciously accepted and peace talks were opened.

The siege was lifted in 911 when Leo negotiated a second commercial treaty with Kiev. The new treaty guaranteed preferential treatment to Kievan merchants, thereby assuring an extended peace along the border between Byzantium and the emerging Russian state. Russian traders and merchants were assured of safe passage each summer to conduct their trade. Suspicious of the Russians' true intentions, however, the Greeks provided them with lodging, food, and baths in the Constantinople suburb of St. Mamo and restricted their access to the city proper to unarmed groups of less than 50 at a time. The merchants were required to leave immediately once their business was con-cluded, but no later than summer's end. As part of the trade agreement, Byzantine and Russian ships would help one another rescue the crews and salvage the cargoes of vessels imperiled by the frequent storms that plagued the Bosporus. Both sides also agreed to extradite escaped criminals and runaway slaves. The treaty was fair to both sides and effectively introduced Russian merchants to European commerce.

Russian aristocrats and merchants visiting Constantinople were awed by its splendor and pageantry. The richest and arguably the most beautiful city in the world at the time, it was the commercial hub of three continents, Europe, Africa, and Asia. Shopkeepers hawked treasures from every known civilization. Here a Russian nobleman could buy exquisitely crafted gold and silver jewelry, elegant silk and velvet garments, finely carved ivory boxes, and exotic fra-grances. The intoxicating attraction of this cosmopolitan, wealthy, and most civilized of cities so overwhelmed the Russians that for centuries they looked to Constantinople as a model for the great cities they themselves built.

The Byzantium Greeks called the territory ruled by Oleg the "Land of the Rus," which eventually evolved into "Russia." Historians offer different ac-counts of the beginnings of the Russian Empire. Slav historians, especially those writing during the Soviet period, insisted that the Slavs themselves created the empire, while others have credited Viking outsiders. A less biased and likely more precise view can be substantiated in the evidence recorded in Byzantine archives. The first commercial agreements between Kiev and Constantinople included the names of the Kievan merchants who received preferential treat-ment in the Greek capital. Although some names on the lists are obviously Slavic, most are unmistakably Scandinavian, including Farulf, Frithleif, Gun-nar, Injald, and Karl. These names clearly establish that most of the powerful merchant families in major Russian cities were descendants of a Viking heritage. In later commercial agreements, Slav names assumed greater prominence, reflecting an absorption of Scandinavians into Slav society that eventually erased almost all traces of the earlier Viking presence.

While Rurik deserves recognition as the first ruler of the Russians, Oleg must be credited with laying the cornerstone for what became the vast Russian Empire. Not only did he subdue the rival chieftains and consolidate his authority, he was also responsible for earning parity with what was then the most influential empire on earth, Byzantium. The Greeks no longer viewed the Russians as simple barbarians, but recognized them as equal partners in commerce, and even as allies against potential enemies.

In late 911, Oleg returned to Kiev triumphant, his ships laden with goods of such quality and beauty that he was acclaimed throughout the territories ruled by Kiev. The jewel in Oleg's budding dynasty, Kiev would for centuries be called the "Mother of Russian Cities," even after the Russian political capital moved elsewhere. For now, however, it was the capital of the grand prince to whom all other Russian princes paid homage. Each local prince was allowed to manage his domain unmolested, provided that he pay an annual tribute to Kiev, usually in the form of goods that could be bartered at Constantinople. These goods were still mostly furs, honey (widely used in Byzantium as a substitute for the rarer sugar), and wax (to make candles for the Greek religious ceremonies). Russia quickly became an important trading partner of the Byzantines.

Oleg governed in Kiev until 912, when Igor assumed his rightful place as grand prince. History is unclear about what happened to Oleg. According to some of the tales that have been passed down, after Igor reached manhood, Oleg stepped aside but remained faithful to Igor until his peaceful death. A more colorful account holds that the manner in which Oleg died was foretold by a wizard. According to this narrative, the wizard prophesied that Oleg's death would be caused by one of the prince's horses, which he identified by name. The superstitious Oleg never rode the horse after the prophecy was made, but he insisted that it be well cared for. When the horse died, Oleg rode to the open plain where the deceased animal's bones had been placed according to custom. Laughing, Oleg dismounted and exulted that he had cheated the death foretold in the prophecy. Approaching the pile of bones, he stomped on the horse's skull, not realizing that a venomous snake was nesting inside. As his foot crushed the brittle bone, the snake struck. Oleg died soon after receiving the snakebite. The tale, typical of ancient Scandinavian folklore, provides a heroic exit for Oleg and a dramatic entrance for Rurik's son and heir, Igor, who ascended the throne in 912, together with his strong-willed wife, Olga.

❖ ❖ ❖

From the little that is known of Igor, it can be safely assumed that he suffered from living in the shadow of Oleg's successes. Determined to outdo his predecessor the empire builder, Igor twice attacked Constantinople but never matched Oleg's success. Igor's reign was plagued by almost constant warfare against the nomadic tribes that regularly swept across the steppes from Asia in search of plunder and slaves. Russian settlements were routinely looted and burned, their inhabitants carried off to an unknown fate. When Russian armies occasionally encountered a raiding party, or were sent out after one, the fierce horsemen simply fled headlong from the superior force.

Possibly inspired by Oleg's success in a similar venture, Igor set out in 941 to conquer Constantinople. The Byzantine emperor, Romanus I, forewarned of the approaching Russian army by friendly Bulgars, prepared elaborate defenses to stop the invaders. Igor's fleet was turned back at the northern entrance to the Bosporus by Byzantine naval forces. Cut off from the direct water route to Constantinople, Igor landed his army in Asia Minor and marched toward the capital. According to the Bulgars, the Russians committed unspeakable atrocities, ravaging the provinces of Pontus and Nicomedia, dismembering some prisoners and using others for archery practice. Churches, monasteries, and entire villages were looted and burned. Whether true or not, the stories struck terror in the Greeks and spawned a resolve for revenge.

Revenge came in the form of "Greek fire," an advanced weapon for its time. A liquid mixture of unknown composition but probably petroleum-based, "Greek fire" burned intensely when it came in contact with water. Said to have been invented in Constantinople by a Syrian refugee in the 7th century, it was widely used by the Greeks for more than 800 years. Usually thrown with a hand-held device at an enemy, or fired from large syringelike weapons, it was especially frightful and effective in naval warfare, where the enemy had little chance of escape. "Greek fire" remained the weapon of choice until it was replaced by gunpowder in the 13th century

Having recently returned victorious from wars against the Muslim forces of the caliph of Baghdad and the Egyptians, during which some 12,000 Arab horsemen switched allegiance and joined it, the Byzantine army was well prepared for the Russian invasion. Two of Byzantium's greatest military leaders—John Curcuas and the naval commander Theophanes—directed the defense of Constantinople.

As Igor's army advanced on the capital, he encountered increasingly stiffer resistance until the Byzantine army stopped the Russian invaders and began to force them back. Soon the Russians were in full retreat, scrambling for their ships anchored along the Black Sea coast near Bithynia. After his army had embarked, Igor ordered a withdrawal, which was blocked when Theophane's navy launched a devastating attack that included the extensive use of "Greek fire." The Russian fleet was practically annihilated. Its ships were engulfed in flames and the sea itself blazed around them. Igor barely escaped with his own life.

Igor returned to Kiev less than triumphant, having lost most of his army and almost all of his fleet. The undaunted Slav chief spent the next few years stockpiling his tribute and preparing for another attempt to conquer Constantinople. To help rebuild an army for his second campaign against Byzantium, Igor negotiated an agreement with the Pechenegs. A ferocious Turkish tribe, the Pechenegs were originally natives of the territory between the Urals and the Volga River. Driven westward by the Khazars, they had settled along the lower Dnieper, where they continued to raid and plunder their neighbors. In the Pechenegs, Igor gained a potent military partner for his renewed assault against Constantinople in 944.

Spurning another perilous naval attack, Igor elected to march southwest toward the Danube, cross that river, and approach Constantinople from the north. Once again, the excellent Byzantine intelligence network functioned well and Emperor Romanus I was warned of the approaching Russian force. This time, however, Romanus shrewdly decided to appease the invaders rather than fight them. He sent a delegation to greet Igor before the Slav crossed the Danube. Igor, perhaps realizing that his second expedition had little chance of real success, wisely accepted the gifts Romanus had sent and agreed to negotiate a new commercial treaty with Byzantium. Ironically, Igor's treaty was much less favorable to the Russians than the pact negotiated by Oleg in 911. In the years since Oleg's treaty, a nuance had crept into the Russians' posture, and this did not go unnoticed by the Byzantine negotiators. When Oleg sealed his agreement with Constantinople, representatives from both sides had met to ratify its provisions. The Byzantine delegation had held aloft a cross of Christ, which was kissed in turn by each representative. Oleg's ambassadors had raised their swords and sworn allegiance in the name of their pagan gods. Many Russian nobles and merchants who traded with Constantinople during the intervening years had converted to Christianity, and a significant portion of Igor's negotiating team was drawn from this segment of Kievan society. Although their subtle influence on Russian society was not widely perceived at the time, the Christian doctrines issuing from Constantinople were gradually replacing the pagan beliefs held by many of the Slavs and Varangians. The first hint of this impending religious upheaval was manifested in the conciliatory posture that Igor's representatives brought to the conference table.

This time Igor's return to Kiev, although less triumphant than Oleg's, was a great improvement over his inglorious arrival following his defeat by the Byzantine navy three years earlier. The Pechenegs, more interested in plunder than trade and less enthusiastic about the treaty than their Russian allies, went off to make war on the Bulgars while a contented Igor settled down with the hope of ruling his domain in relative peace. His reign would prove to be short-lived.

One of the numerous Slav tribes that paid homage to the grand prince of Kiev was a primitive people called the Drevlyane. First brought under Kievan influence when Oleg had consolidated his domain, the Drevlyane paid an annual tribute to the grand prince but remained largely autonomous. In 945, Igor's nobles pressured him to exact from the Drevlyane a higher tribute because of the widespread belief that the tribe was much wealthier than it admitted. During that winter, Igor, along with his retainers and a large bodyguard, visited various princes to collect his tribute. The practice of the grand prince personally receiving the tribute had begun with Oleg, probably because it had helped him to maintain personal contact with the local princes and resulted in larger tributes.

In late winter 945, Igor visited Iskorosten, a Drevlyane town west of Kiev, and collected his tribute. With sledges loaded with goods paid as tribute, the party then set out toward Kiev. Several retainers commented to Igor that the Drevlyane men appeared better dressed and better armed than they themselves were. Igor brooded about this for a while, then decided to demand more tribute. Igor made the mistake of sending most of his bodyguard back to Kiev with the goods while he returned to the Drevlyane village with only a small number of men.

Hearing that the grand prince was dissatisfied with his tribute and would seek more, Iskorosten's leaders hastily consulted their prince, Mal. Citing an ancient proverb that said, "If a wolf gets the habit of coming among the sheep, he will carry off the whole flock unless he is killed," the prince sent an armed company to intercept Igor's party. Asked why he was returning, the grand prince foolishly confirmed his intention to collect additional tribute. The Drevlyane tribesmen swiftly attacked and killed Igor and his meager bodyguard, burying them where they fell.

Just as his father before him, Igor left a son too young to sit on the throne. The son, Sviatoslav, would not ascend the throne of Kiev for another 10 years. Meanwhile, his mother, Olga, would rule in his name as regent.

CHAPTER 4

ST. OLGA AND THE INTRODUCTION OF CHRISTIANITY

THE EASE WITH WHICH THEY HAD MURDERED Grand Prince Igor emboldened the Drevlyane chieftains, fueling their ambition to parlay Igor's assassination into a coup that would gain them control of the Kievan state. They decided to promote a marriage between Igor's widow, Olga, and their prince, Mal, thereby securing for him the Kievan throne. Sviatoslav would be killed, ending his claim to the title of grand prince.

The Drevlyane leaders faced far greater peril trying to coerce Grand Princess Olga into an unwanted marriage than they had when they murdered her husband. According to legend, Sviatoslav was born when Olga was 60 years old. Since Sviatoslav was 15 when Igor died, if the legend can be believed, Olga was 75 when she assumed the regency in her son's name. Her bold move to seize authority before any other prince could do so had been of vital importance because it guaranteed her son's succession to the throne at a time when no clear line of succession had yet been established.

Olga was a strong-willed woman with an innate passion for vengeance. She earmarked the Drevlyane nobles who had killed her husband for special retribution. Informed that a group of 20 Drevlyane officials had arrived by boat, asking for an audience to negotiate her marriage to Prince Mal, Olga sent word that she was honored by their proposal. She suggested that they rest on their boat overnight and in the morning she would have slaves carry them and their boat into the city, where they would be honored before the assembled citizens of Kiev. The Drevlyane accepted her suggestion and spent the night in their boat.

During the night, Olga had a huge, deep pit dug just outside her tower. In the morning, her servants made their way to the riverfront, where they shouldered the Drevlyane boat and carried it, with the 20 officials, to the pit. When they reached the palace, the grand princess gloated from atop the tower as the boat was thrown into the pit with everyone on board. The visitors screamed and cried for mercy as Olga's servants shoveled earth into the pit, burying them alive.

Not satisfied that Igor's murder had been fully avenged, Olga devised a plot to lure more Drevlyane victims to Kiev. She sent a message to the Drevlyane, stating that if they truly wanted her to marry their prince they should send an embassy of their most distinguished nobles to escort her to Iskorosten. The people of Kiev, she claimed, would consider it an affront unless she was extended this honor. Believing that this was their opportunity to claim the throne, the Drevlyane nobles complied, sending a high-level delegation to escort Olga to Prince Mal. When the nobles arrived in Kiev, she suggested a bath to wash away their travel grime. A bath hut had been warmed and prepared for them. The unwary travelers gratefully luxuriated in the bath until they realized that Olga's men had barred the exits. The diabolical grand princess ordered the hut set on fire, burning the occupants to death.

Still lusting for more revenge, Olga installed her son as leader of the Kievan army that ravaged Drevlyane towns and villages until all the outlying settlements either surrendered or were destroyed. Olga and Sviatoslav then laid siege to Iskorosten. The siege continued for several months, but the population of Iskorosten held firm, stubbornly resisting every attempt to dislodge them. Finally, Olga informed the town leaders that if they would surrender to her she would not extract a heavy tribute from the populace. She said she realized that the inhabitants were nearly destitute as a result of the siege, and asked only that each household pay a symbolic tribute of three doves and three sparrows. The Drevlyane gladly agreed and went about collecting the birds, which they dutifully delivered to Olga.

The grand princess then instructed the town leaders to have the people return to their homes; in the morning, she would withdraw her troops and leave the town in peace. The Drevlyane did as she ordered and waited for the morning. Meanwhile, Olga distributed the captured doves and sparrows among her soldiers with instructions to tie small amounts of smoldering kindling to each bird. During the night, the birds were released and quickly returned to their nests in the buildings of Iskorosten. Before the first morning light, virtually the entire town was in flames. Citizens fleeing the fires were either killed by Olga's soldiers or taken prisoner. After the town had been leveled, some inhabitants were allowed to return to begin rebuilding, a task made doubly difficult because of the heavy tax she levied on them.

Olga returned to Kiev and set about reforming its governmental structure. She had little interest in expanding the state, but she did dispatch expeditions to curb rebellious tribes and recapture lands lost during her husband's reign. By the time Sviatoslav reached maturity and took his rightful place on the throne,

Olga had restored his domain to roughly the same borders it had had when Oleg's rule ended. The only difference was that the grand prince now presided over a well-organized government. Olga had learned from Igor's murder that by personally collecting tribute the grand prince made himself vulnerable to angry taxpayers and disloyal local princes. She had ended this practice and had established regional depots called *pogosty*, where appointed officials, the precursors of the czars' tax collectors, collected the tribute for shipment to Kiev.

In 955, Sviatoslav was crowned grand prince of Kiev. Although no longer regent, Olga remained active in Kiev's affairs. Because of her son's lack of interest in government operations, and his preoccupation with expansion, much of the daily routine of governing was left to the former grand princess. Perhaps prompted by the urgings of palace officials who had adopted the Christian religion of Constantinople, and partly, we are told, because of the barren paganism of the Kievan people, Olga decided to embrace Christianity. She journeyed to Constantinople in 957, arriving in the Byzantine capital in September. Her reception by Emperor Constantine VII rivaled the pageantry normally reserved for visiting monarchs.

Olga told the emperor of her desire to become a Christian. Constantine arranged for the Byzantine patriarch, who was the Eastern Church's equivalent of the pope in Rome, to instruct her in the faith and baptize her. She took the Christian name Helena, which was the name of the reigning Byzantine empress. An often repeated account of Olga's visit to Constantinople exemplifies her legendary feistiness and independence. Although she was struck with the beauty and splendor of the Byzantine capital, she was evidently annoyed by the ritual and ceremony that caused long delays between formal audiences with the emperor and empress. Fully a year after her visit, she received a communication from Constantine VII, asking when he could expect the gifts she had promised him before she departed. She replied that when the emperor visited Kiev and waited around her palace as long as she had been forced to wait in his, he would get the gifts.

Once Olga had returned to Kiev, she resumed her duties as Sviatoslav's closest advisor and administrator of domestic affairs. Either unwilling or unable to dictate the religious practices of the Kievan population, Olga nevertheless made several attempts to persuade her son to convert to Christianity. Sviatoslav resisted her efforts because he feared it would diminish his stature with the majority of his nobles, who were pagans. He insisted that any of his subjects who desired to become Christians were free to do so.

Olga's conversion from paganism to the Eastern Christianity practiced by the Byzantines brought the religion new prestige among the people of Kiev. Conversions not only continued but actually increased. Having failed to convert her son, Olga concentrated her proselytizing on her three grandsons—Vladimir, Oleg, and Yaropolk—with what would later prove to be monumental results. Olga was later made a saint in the Russian Orthodox Church.

❖ ❖ ❖

Although Sviatoslav was of Scandinavian blood, he was the first grand prince of Kiev to have a Slav name (in English it means "of Holy Story"). Sviatoslav, who proved to be a strong leader with great ambitions to expand his rule, departed from his Viking heritage in other ways. Unlike his ancestors, he went to war without taking his family along, and traveled extremely light, foregoing the usual collection of baggage, tents, and cauldrons and kettles. Instead, he used his saddle as a pillow and his horse's blanket as his own when he slept. For sustenance he relied on what he could find in the districts in which he found himself.

While his mother managed the day-to-day operations of his growing empire, Sviatoslav concentrated on building a strong army for his conquests. He trained it to travel light, like himself, and to live off the land, so that it would not need to rely on a long and slow train of carts carrying its supplies.

Sviatoslav was an imposing figure who gave the appearance of a savage and gloomy man. Of medium height, he had a thick, muscular neck and a broad chest and shoulders. His blue eyes were partially hidden behind thick eyebrows that made his snub nose appear more prominent. Although he regularly shaved his beard, another divergence from Viking practice, he maintained a bushy mustache. Except for a lock of hair that hung from one side of his head as a symbol of his royal clan, his head was clean-shaven. A gold earring set with two pearls and a ruby hung from one ear. Perhaps because he was a soldier's soldier, or more likely for anonymity in combat, Sviatoslav dressed in the simple white garments of his troops. An approaching enemy could not single him out among his white-clad army.

As his predecessors had, and as his successors would also do, Sviatoslav looked south to expand his borders. Here were prosperous states wealthy in commerce and manufactured goods, with rich productive soil and access to the Black Sea. A warm-water port from which Russian ships could sail to any port in the world all year 'round would attract Russian leaders for centuries to come.

Sviatoslav chose the Khazar empire, the richest of the southern states, as the target for his first conquest. In 965 he led his finely honed army south from Kiev, determined to annex the Khazar lands to his growing empire. The kagan, the reigning prince of the Khazars, rode out with his army to meet the Russians in combat on the open steppes. Sviatoslav's troops killed the kagan and easily defeated his army, then marched against other nearby states, including those of the Ossetians, the Circassians, and the Vyatichi. In turn, each army fell and swore allegiance to the grand prince of Kiev, agreeing to pay him a handsome tribute as a sign of its loyalty.

By 967 the emerging Russian empire had almost doubled in size since Igor's murder. That year, the Byzantine emperor, Nicephorus, requested his Russian ally to make war on the Bulgarians, who had demanded that Constantinople pay them a tribute for their friendship. Sviatoslav was overjoyed to respond to the Byzantine request, for it opened to him new opportunities for conquest that had been closed by the Byzantine-Bulgarian alliance. The following year, Sviatoslav invaded the Bulgars' territory, capturing their king, Boris II, and several Bulgarian towns along the Danube River. Commerce on the Danube, one of the great trading routes between central and western Europe, had enriched the Bulgar trading centers along its banks, and Sviatoslav was captivated by the wealth he found there. In fact, he was so captivated that he shunned his capital in Kiev in favor of a new residence at Pereyaslavec, a Danube town also known as Little Preslav.

Nicephorus did not anticipate that Sviatoslav would take up residence in Bulgaria and append the title prince of the Bulgars to that of grand prince of Kiev. He quickly recognized that he had managed to replace one threat to his empire, the Bulgars, with another, the Russians. He set about contriving to dissolve his alliance with the Russians and reestablish the old alliance with the Bulgars, whom he would then encourage to drive Sviatoslav from their land. Nicephorus's plan eventually died with him when he was assassinated on December 10, 969, by members of a rival Byzantine faction.

Sviatoslav angered his mother and the people of Kiev by refusing to return to the capital after defeating the Bulgars. He also left much of his own territory poorly defended. With the grand prince and most of his army occupied in Bulgaria, the Pechenegs, who earlier had been allied with Sviatoslav's father, Igor, in his abortive campaign against Constantinople, mounted a treacherous revolt against Kiev in the summer of 968. Unable to take the city by force, they laid siege to it, hoping to force its capitulation before the Russian army could return. Inside Kiev, Olga directed the defenses and protected her three grandsons. The siege lasted several months and might have succeeded had it not been for the timely arrival of a small Kievan force that duped the Pechenegs into believing it was the vanguard of the entire Russian army returning under Sviatoslav's banner. The Pechenegs withdrew and were finally driven deep into the steppes when the grand prince, having learned of the siege, actually did return with most of his army.

The Pechenegs' attack on Kiev was in all likelihood a consequence of Sviatoslav's own earlier military successes. By defeating the Khazars he had removed a powerful deterrent to the continual onslaught of eastern nomadic tribes such as the Pechenegs, who regularly forayed across the steppes, plundering the prosperous towns that lay on or near these great plains, including Kiev. It is also likely that the Byzantines prodded the Pechenegs into attacking Sviatoslav's capital, hoping thereby to effect his withdrawal from Bulgaria. The Byzantine nobility apparently feared that the grand prince, intoxicated by his military success, was casting a covetous eye on Constantinople itself. Their concern was not unfounded.

To placate his mother as well as his own restive nobles, Sviatoslav returned to Kiev but stressed his eventual intention to move the capital to the Danube, which he viewed as the center of trade for his expanded empire. Olga solicited him to remain in Kiev at least until she died, and he agreed. When his mother died in early 969, Sviatoslav was freed of his promise and planned to return to the Danube and establish his new capital.

In the interim, the Bulgars had retaken possession of their territory. Sviatoslav mounted a new campaign to win back his former authority. By the middle of August 969, Sviatoslav, leading an army of some 60,000 Russian soldiers, recaptured Little Preslav, which he was still determined to make his new capital. He then turned south and took the Bulgar capital, Great Preslav, on the Ditzina River in the foothills of the Balkan Mountains. Before the year had ended, he crossed the mountains and seized Philippopolis, thereby achieving supremacy over all of eastern Bulgaria.

With Bulgaria defeated, the Hungarian Magyars newly allied with him, and many Bulgar formations solidly in his camp, Sviatoslav did exactly what the Greeks had predicted—he looked to Constantinople as his next objective.

While Sviatoslav was planning his campaign against Constantinople, an Armenian named John Tzimisces, whom many consider to have been Byzantium's greatest military leader, was crowned emperor of Byzantium on Christmas Day, 969. Tzimisces, the man who probably contrived the assassination of the former emperor, Nicephorus, had ascended the throne through a convoluted agreement of support from the patriarch Polyeuctus, who had established three conditions for the succession. The first was that Tzimisces had not personally inflicted the mortal blow on the dead emperor, which he had not, since the deed had been done by accomplices. The second was that Tzimisces exile Nicephorus's wife, Theophano, which was to his own liking because he had carried on a liaison with her to gain intelligence about her husband's plans and had no further use for her. The third condition was that he punish the assassin or assassins, which was also satisfactory because that would silence his accomplices concerning his own role in the murder.

The traitorous exchange of power in Constantinople had resulted in no change in policy toward the Russian occupation of Bulgaria, which itself had once been a Byzantine province. When Sviatoslav moved his army south from Philippopolis and proceeded against the Byzantine territory of Thrace, Tzimisces dispatched two of his most able generals, Peter Phocas and Bardas Sclerus, to stop him and contain the invasion. They stalled the Russian advance, and under relentless pressure from the Byzantine forces Sviatoslav withdrew to Bulgaria.

The newly crowned Byzantine emperor then attempted to buy off his former Russian ally with the gift of a large sum of money in exchange for the return of Bulgaria to Byzantium. Sviatoslav declined and instead sent word to Constantinople that if the "Romans" did not want to pay the enormous tribute he demanded of them, they would be better advised to abandon Europe and "retire to Asia." This was an affront no emperor of Byzantium could tolerate.

In early spring 971, Tzimisces sent 300 warships up the Danube from the Black Sea, effectively seizing control of the river. The Greek blockade of the Danube prevented supplies and reinforcements from reaching Sviatoslav and also severed his escape route. Leading most of the Byzantine army, Tzimisces marched north across the Balkan Mountains and on April 12, 971, attacked the Bulgar capital of Great Preslav. In less than 24 hours, the Russian defenders were either slaughtered or driven off.

When Sviatoslav learned that Tzimisces had overturned Great Preslav, he immediately set out to regain the city. The armies clashed on a plain 12 miles south of the former capital. The Russians and their allies proved no match for the armor-clad Byzantine infantry, and Sviatoslav retreated to Dorystolum, a fortified Bulgarian town situated on the banks of the Danube. The pursuing Byzantine troops pressed forward to the city's gates.

Sviatoslav was now hemmed in on land on three sides while a massive Byzantine fleet hurled "Greek fire" from the river at his back. The siege continued for several months while the condition of the Russian forces steadily deteriorated. On July 21, the desperate Russian garrison burst from the town in one final effort to break the siege. The ensuing battle raged for hours as first one side and then the other appeared to gain the advantage. The outcome remained in doubt until near the end of the day, when a sudden storm arose. Fierce winds blew sheets of dust into the Russians' eyes, blinding them and driving them back into the town. With less than 20,000 men left in his army, and most of them suffering from near famine, Sviatoslav had no alternative except to sue for peace. In return for safe passage back to Russia with enough supplies to make the journey, Sviatoslav pledged never again to make war against Byzantium. Anxious to presserve what remained of the Russian army as a potential future ally, John Tzimisces agreed to the terms and even conceded that Russian merchants would once again be welcome in Constantinople.

Soon thereafter, the ragtag Russian army began its long trek home. The journey proved more perilous than anticipated because the Russians had to negotiate territory swarming with hostile Pechenegs, their sometime allies who once again had become enemies. A series of running battles along the route cost many Russian lives, and finally, in the spring of 972, with only a small remnant of his army still intact, Sviatoslav was trapped near the great rapids of the Dnieper River several hundred miles south of Kiev. The Pechenegs massacred what was left of his army and hacked Sviatoslav to death. According to Pecheneg custom, the grand prince's severed skull was fashioned into a drinking cup for the Pecheneg leader, Prince Kurya.

Ironically, the first grand prince to bear a Slav name seems to have cared little for the Russia he ruled. Sviatoslav had left to others the routine operations of his domain while he devoted himself almost exclusively to conquest and expansion. After he had succeeded in adding new territory to his realm, especially that of the Bulgars, he had immediately decided to abandon Kiev, the "Mother of Russian Cities," in favor of a Bulgarian town. Except for his strong-willed mother's obstinate objections, Sviatoslav actually might have moved the administrative capital of Russia to Little Preslav on the Danube, a circumstance that would have invited certain disaster. If Sviatoslav had established the capital at Little Preslav, it doubtlessly would have been destroyed by the Byzantine army, possibly strangling forever the emergence of the Russian Empire.

Sviatoslav's demise triggered a series of bloody intrafamily feuds over the succession to the Russian throne. Before leaving for his second Bulgarian campaign, Sviatoslav had divided his realm among his three sons. The eldest, Yaropolk, had been seated on the throne of Kiev to assume the title of grand prince should his father fail to return. Little is known about Yaropolk's eight-year reign other than the endless turmoil between him and his brothers, Vladimir and Oleg. Surprisingly, both the Pechenegs and the Byzantines negotiated treaties with Yaropolk and paid homage to him as grand prince.

When his father was killed by the Pechenegs, Yaropolk had not yet reached political maturity and was still heavily influenced by court advisors. One of these, Svineld, held a personal grudge against Yaropolk's two younger brothers and convinced the young grand prince that they were plotting against him. Fearful of losing his throne, Yaropolk warred against his brothers and their allies. Outnumbered by the loyal Kievan forces, Oleg and Vladimir retreated northward. Oleg was killed in a skirmish just before the war ended, but Vladimir escaped. Traveling north along the Lovat River, Vladimir reached Novgorod, where he was surprised to find widespread opposition to Yaropolk.

With strong support from local Slavs and Vikings, Vladimir ousted Yaropolk's municipal governor and established himself as prince of Novgorod. As he was preparing a campaign against Kiev, he became infatuated with the daughter of Rogvolod, the Viking prince of Polotsk, a town on the Dvina River south of Novgorod. Vladimir sent an envoy to Rogvolod to ask for his daughter's hand. When the prince approached his daughter, Rogned, with Vladimir's request, she flatly refused, saying that she instead wanted to marry Yaropolk. Rogned added to the insult by making a disparaging remark about Vladimir being the illegitimate son of a slave woman. Vladimir, who had already earned a reputation as a lustful and vengeful hothead, marshaled his army and stormed Polotsk, killing Prince Rogvolod and both of his sons and carrying Rogned back to Novgorod, where he made her his wife.

By 980, Vladimir's army had grown sufficiently powerful to challenge Yaropolk. Although the bulk of his force consisted of Slavs and Varangians, he also recruited many hardy Finns and Estonians. That year, Vladimir laid siege to Kiev, but the campaign was short-lived. Yaropolk was betrayed and murdered by several of his advisors who probably recognized that the mild-mannered grand prince was no match for his ruthless brother. Vladimir entered the city and triumphantly declared himself grand prince of Russia.

Immediately after Vladimir had seized the city, a band of Varangian mercenaries hired for the campaign claimed credit for the victory and demanded a tribute of one pound of silver from every citizen of Kiev. Recognizing the Varangians' revolt as a serious threat to his throne, Vladimir persuaded the Vikings to shift their aggression to Constantinople, convincing them that it was a much more lucrative prize than Kiev.

Grand Prince Vladimir

CHAPTER 5

VLADIMIR AND THE OFFICIAL FAITH

WHEN VLADIMIR'S REIGN AS GRAND PRINCE ENDED in 1015, he was barely recognizable as the coarse heathen who had come to the throne 35 years earlier. Chroniclers of early Russian history described the young prince as a man of insatiable sexual appetite who kept as many as 700 concubines scattered across his realm, as well as a large number of wives who included Slavs, Czechs, Bulgars, Greeks, and Vikings. Nonetheless, the reluctant Rogned officially remained his royal consort. The chroniclers also portrayed a ruthless ruler who savaged his enemies and crushed all opposition to his authority.

Although he was born a pagan and grew up with the pagan rituals typical of the time, Vladimir was also profoundly influenced by his grandmother's Christian teachings. However, her canons were quickly abandoned by the new grand prince. Near the entrance to his palace, he immediately set about erecting statues of major pagan gods, including Perun, the god of thunder whose likeness included a head made of silver and mustache fabricated from pure gold. Svarog, the father of gods, and Stribog, the wind god, were given equal prominence. If there was any question of residual Christian influence over Vladimir, it was quickly lost when nearly a thousand human sacrifices were offered to these pagan deities to celebrate his coronation.

The sacrificial bloodletting aroused many factions of the Kievan populace, and there was widespread discontent about it. Because of the city's magnetism as a thriving trading center, people from many cultures and religions migrated to the capital. Pagans, Christians of the Byzantine faith, Catholic followers of the Roman pope, Muslims from the Arab world, and Jews from what remained of the Khazar khanate were all part of the mosaic that was Kiev. Vladimir frequently met with the elders of every religious persuasion to explore their various creeds, weighing one against the other, and especially against his own paganism. He soon recognized the imperfections and emptiness inherent in the pagan rituals and began a personal quest to find a religion that would be more fulfilling for himself and his subjects.

Religious reform was not Vladimir's sole concern. Constant revolts, especially among fractious tribes on the periphery of his empire, required unceasing attention, and his ambition to expand beyond the existing boundaries of Kiev occupied an enormous amount of his time. As did his predecessors, Vladimir looked south to the fertile lands and rich cities along the Black Sea coast. His interest focused on the Byzantine city of Kherson, a flourishing port on the Crimean Peninsula near present-day Sevastopol. However, the treaty between Kiev and Constantinople prevented Vladimir from menacing Kherson.

An unanticipated opportunity came in the spring of 988, when the Byzantine emperor, Basil II, invoked the treaty and requested that Vladimir provide troops to help him put down a rebellion by the Byzantine general Bardas Phocas. The would-be usurper's army occupied the Asia Minor side of the Bosporus and was threatening Constantinople itself. Vladimir responded that he would send 6,000 of his best warriors in return for the emperor's promise to give him the hand of Basil's sister, Princess Anne, in marriage. A hard-pressed

Basil anxiously agreed. The Russian troops that Vladimir sent were instrumental in crushing the rebellion.

With his throne again secure, Basil was reluctant to commit his sister to a marriage with a pagan ruler and found numerous reasons to delay. Finally, Basil told Vladimir that he would not permit the marriage unless Vladimir became a Christian. Vladimir seized on this insult to attack Kherson with a sizable force, and the city quickly capitulated.

In the meantime, Vladimir's envoys went abroad to learn about various alternative religions. He also continued his personal inquiries among foreign visitors of divergent religions. When word spread that Vladimir was seeking a new religion for his people, ambassadors from virtually every organized religion visited Kiev in an attempt to win him over. This influx of foreign missionaries became known as the "testing of the faiths."

The Khazars sent Jewish holy men to Kiev, but when they admitted that their God had driven them from their homeland of Jerusalem because he was angry with their ancestors, Vladimir chastised them: "You are trying to teach others, you whom your God has punished? He would not have done that if he loved you or your laws." The Jewish representatives were sent away. Next came spokesmen for the Muslim faith practiced by the Bulgars. Although Vladimir liked the promise that their prophet had presaged—that every worthy Muslim man would be attended by 70 beautiful women when he arrived in heaven—the Bulgars' cause was lost when they explained their religion's dietary restrictions on pork and alcohol. Vladimir dismissed them with the rationale that drinking was the chief pleasure of his subjects and he could not support a religion that forbade it. The Muslim envoys were followed by Catholic priests sent by the German emperor, Otto III. Early on, Vladimir expressed interest in their religion, which was closely related to Byzantine Christianity, but he balked when he was told that the pope in Rome was the supreme ruler to whom all Catholic monarchs were subservient.

Recognizing Vladimir's quest as an opportunity to reinforce its fragile alliance through a religious merger, Constantinople sent its own priests, who impressed Vladimir most with the doctrine that the nation's ruler was also the head of the Church.

To help him determine the best course of action, Vladimir consulted his nobles. They suggested that he send trusted representatives to observe the religions in practice and report their impressions. Not bothering to examine further the Jewish faith of the Khazars, the representatives traveled to Germany and Bulgaria but were not impressed with what they found. They told Vladimir that the Bulgars' mosques were unclean and "their religion is no good." Among the Catholics, they found "no glory there."

Everything changed when they arrived in Constantinople. Here the emperor had made elaborate preparations designed to win over the Russians with the pomp and grandeur of the Eastern Christian Church. Although pagans normally were not permitted to enter the great Cathedral of St. Sophia in the Byzantine capital, the Russian nobles were escorted in to witness a high mass sung by a magnificent choir while incense smoke drifted around the imposing marble church and upward toward its dazzling gold dome. To say the Russians were impressed would grossly understate their awe. When they returned to Kiev, they told Vladimir that when they entered the place where the Greeks worship their God, they did not know "whether we were in heaven or on earth. We only know," they exclaimed, "that God dwells there."

Vladimir, who had been leaning toward the religion of Byzantium since his grandmother had tutored him as a child, did not need much convincing, especially when one of the nobles emphasized that if the Greeks' religion had not been a good one, the great and wise Olga would not have adopted it.

The decision was made, and in 989 Vladimir was baptized a Christian. Shortly thereafter, Princess Anne, still reluctant to leave the splendor and comfort of Constantinople, crossed the Black Sea in a Byzantine war galley to become the barbarian ruler's new princess and live in his relatively primitive wood palace. For the Byzantines, a conversion of such enormous consequence could not be consummated without an accompanying miracle. According to an ancient chronicle, before his baptism Vladimir suffered from a severe eye disorder that caused him blindness. At the moment when he was baptized by the bishop of Kherson, when the bishop laid his hands on the grand prince's head and recited a prayer, the disease vanished and Vladimir's sight returned.

With Vladimir's baptism, the Eastern Christian religion became the official religion of the Russian Empire. Priests and holy men from Byzantium traveled across Russia, preaching the new religion and baptizing thousands of people. Generally, the transition to Christianity went smoothly, but when some pagans demurred, the sword quickly discouraged most of the resisters. Vladimir demonstrated publicly and emphatically that his conversion was sincere by removing the pagan statues that stood outside his palace. Every pagan image throughout the realm was destroyed or cast into the Dnieper River. Although some inhabitants wept at the destruction of their gods, most appeared indifferent. Few had actually idolized their nature-inspired deities, and the majority agreed to mass baptism rather than risk Grand Prince Vladimir's displeasure.

Less because of religious fervor, and more because of Vladimir's implicit threats, the Russian people became Christians.

The rapidity with which the empire was converted to Christianity attests to Vladimir's ability to draw from an ample reserve of Slavic-speaking priests to baptize the population. Since many Christians already lived in Kiev, and a Christian church had long been established there, the city had a nucleus of priests of Greek origin. Constantinople willingly supplied bilingual priests who understood the Russian language through their long association with visiting nobles and merchants. Bulgarian priests, whose language at that time closely paralleled the Russian dialect, volunteered to assist. By establishing Eastern Christianity as the official religion of the Kievan government, and by consolidating his realm into a unified state, Vladimir built on the foundation of Oleg's expansionist policies and his grandmother Olga's governmental organization to lay the cornerstone of the vast Russian Empire.

❖ ❖ ❖

Few early descriptions of Vladimir exist, only post-conversion illustrations that show a man aptly described by his contemporaries as Vladimir the Sunny. Some show him with a halo around his head, depicting his later canonization as a saint in the Russian Orthodox Church. Before becoming Vladimir the Sunny, or a saint, he was a heartless murderer who ruthlessly eliminated all who dared to challenge his authority.

Before his conversion, Vladimir had mounted savage campaigns against the Slav tribes who lived on the perimeters of his empire, in order to keep them under a tight rein. Through these forays he accumulated a large number of wives and hundreds of concubines throughout the empire. Consequently, wherever he traveled he had women to provide him comfort.

To safeguard his subjects from nomadic tribes such as the Pechenegs, who regularly raided poorly defended villages and towns, Vladimir constructed a series of fortified towns along the frontier between the forests and the steppes. For the most part, these strongholds succeeded in stemming the raids against his empire, earning him the grudging respect of his enemies and the gratitude of his people.

Vladimir's adoption of Christianity as the official religion of his empire had a profound effect on Russia and the Russian people, one more far-reaching than even he could have imagined. Although most Russians practiced their new religion in a perfunctory way, much as they had their pagan religion, the Greek influence on the architecture of churches was enormous. To preserve the

Russian identity, the grand prince insisted that religious services in the new churches be conducted not in the traditional Greek but in the language of the common people. Church scriptures were translated into Slavonic, and although the metropolitans of the Russian cities for the most part continued to be Greeks during the next five centuries, bishops and priests were increasingly appointed from among the Slavs themselves. In this way, the Greek religion gradually evolved into a distinctly Russian religion. Unlike the Eastern Christianity of Byzantium, which remained closely related to the Roman church, Russian Christianity was influenced by obscure rituals recalled from the people's earlier paganism. The result was a new religion, one loosely based on the Christian canons of Constantinople yet uniquely endemic to the Slav culture. Eventually, the Greek influence disappeared entirely and the Russian religion became thoroughly Slavicized.

Vladimir encouraged the establishment of schools and the publication of books in the Slav language, resulting in a highly literate urban population. Although inhabitants of some of the more remote sections of the empire resisted the new religion, the most enthusiastic converts were influential Russian nobles who perceived in Christianity a rationale for their lives as well as a bridge to the advanced civilizations of Byzantium and western Europe. They also realized that a universal literary language would solidify the Russian conversion to Christianity and advance the cultural development of their society. Many of these nobles had visited Constantinople and other European cities and desired that their own cities become a part of the European civilization.

In 996, the legal authority of the Russian Orthodox Church was solidly established when Vladimir decreed that a tithe (one-tenth of a person's income) be paid to the Church of Our Lady of Kiev to support the church and its religious activities. In 1010, statutes establishing ecclesiastic courts strengthened the Christian covenant by prohibiting secular courts from trying members of the clergy for civil offenses and instead making members subject to the special courts of the church. In addition, church courts were given jurisdiction over such matters as the relations between a husband and a wife, adultery, desertion, and a woman's right to inherit property. Under this enlightened jurisdiction, women's rights were greatly expanded, although murdering a woman still drew only half the punishment given for murdering a man.

Vladimir's conversion to Christianity did not diminish his determination to expand Russia's empire. He extended its southern borders closer to the Black Sea, thereby reducing the risk that pillaging nomads would attack Russian trade expeditions bound for Constantinople. In the west, he pushed the Polish army out of the Russian territory it had occupied since the war of succession that he had fought with his brothers. In the north, he gained a firm hold on a vital section of the Baltic coast by conquering and subduing the Lithuanians who lived there. By the turn of the century, Vladimir's empire was second in size only to the Holy Roman Empire, which was centered in Germany, and its population had grown to more than 5 million people.

Vladimir's conversion had a dramatic affect on his personal philosophy and lifestyle. According to the ancient chronicles, he invited his poorest subjects into his palace and lavished on them generous gifts from his private store of food, and money from his treasury. He also reportedly took literally the biblical caveat to "resist not him that is evil." As a result, the Kievan countryside became the haunt of criminal bands who attacked travelers virtually at will. Vladimir was finally persuaded to take appropriate action against these bandits when church leaders convinced him that he had been selected by God to "chastise malefactors." Unlike some of his successors, Vladimir viewed Christianity as a joy, not a grim religion to be used to control the lives of his subjects.

Satisfied with his territorial expansion, and pleased with the public's acceptance of Christianity, which he was convinced would enhance the lives of his people, Vladimir next set out to achieve political stability for Russia. He made each of his 12 sons a prince in the most important cities of his realm. Each was empowered to collect a predetermined amount of tribute from the local inhabitants. Two-thirds of these taxes were sent to Kiev and the remainder used for local expenses, such as the operation of the municipal government and the maintenance of adequate defenses.

Possibly because Vladimir's sons were only half-brothers, each born of different wives or concubines during his hedonistic days, or more likely because the temptation for the sons to usurp broader powers was too great, Vladimir's plan for stability failed. Two sons caused trouble almost immediately. The eldest, Sviatopolk, plotted continuously against his brothers, and Yaroslav, the prince of Novgorod, refused to pay his assigned tribute to Kiev. According to Kievan records, Yaroslav was authorized to collect from the citizens of Novgorod 3,000 *grivnas*, of which 2,000 were to be sent to his father in Kiev. (Although the precise value of a grivna is not known, the best estimates place it at about the equivalent of one-half pound of silver.)

During Vladimir's reign the Pechenegs launched two major offensives against Russian cities. The first, in 1007, was soundly defeated by Vladimir himself. The second offensive came in 1015, while Vladimir, who was gravely ill, was preoccupied with planning a campaign to chastise his rebellious son, Yaroslav. Another, more faithful son, Boris, drove off the invaders for his father.

On July 15, Vladimir succumbed to his illness with his empire intact. His death was kept secret for some time while his body was secretly moved from the death chamber to the Church of the Holy Mother of God in Kiev. When Vladimir's death was finally announced, the grand prince's bodyguards sought to name his successor from among the sons, much as the Praetorian Guards had occasionally selected the successors of the Roman caesars. Their candidate was Boris, the son of the Byzantine princess Anne, but Boris, realizing that his succession to his father's throne would involve warfare among his half-brothers, refused to take up arms against them and so declined the throne.

Sviatopolk, who coveted the throne, sent two groups of assassins who murdered Boris while he was at prayers. Next, they hunted down and killed Boris's full brother, Gleb. (Venerated as martyrs, Boris and Gleb were later canonized as the first saints of the Russian Church.) Sviatopolk then seized control of the throne of Kiev and became known as Sviatopolk the Accursed. Except for Yaroslav of Novgorod and Mstislav of Tmutorokan, Sviatopolk's remaining half-brothers lacked both the strength and the will to oppose him. Although Mstislav did not try to overthrow Sviatopolk, he did concentrate his efforts on consolidating his own domain and steeling his defenses against Sviatopolk's inevitable attack. Yaroslav, on the other hand, was determined to rule the empire of his father.

Grand Prince Yaroslav I

CHAPTER 6

YAROSLAV AND THE APEX OF KIEV

SVIATOPOLK KILLED HIS TWO MOST RESPECTED AND popular half-brothers, Boris and Gleb, but his logical target should have been his half-brother Yaroslav, the prince of Novgorod and the most dangerous obstacle to his possession of the throne. Anger over the treacherous murders of Boris and Gleb fueled Yaroslav's determination to gain the throne of Kiev and punish Sviatopolk. Yaroslav recruited a large army from among his subjects and augmented it with Viking mercenaries. Although the precise date is not officially recorded, it was during 1016 that Yaroslav's army sailed down the Lovat River toward Kiev.

Warned of the impending attack by Yaroslav's forces, Sviatopolk quickly negotiated a military compact with Boleslaus the Brave, the king of Poland, who also happened to be his father-in-law. The Poles had two compelling reasons for supporting Sviatopolk in the coming war of succession. The first was their desire to acquire Galicia, a neighboring Russian province. The second reason, and the one with perhaps the deeper significance, was that the Poles were Roman Catholics, and the Roman Church sought to replace the Eastern Orthodoxy of Constantinople as the official Russian religion.

Before the Poles could deploy their troops, Yaroslav attacked Kiev, driving Sviatopolk and his forces from the city. However, after rendezvousing with his Polish allies, Sviatopolk recaptured Kiev and expelled Yaroslav and his army. With the capital once more under his command, Sviatopolk agreed to quarter Polish troops in the homes of Kiev's citizens. The reluctant host families viewed the Poles as foreign intruders in a private war between rival brothers. Probably instigated by Yaroslav's agents, many Kievans murdered their Polish soldier-houseguests while they slept. The Poles prudently withdrew from the city when they realized the extent of the people's animosity toward them.

The Polish defection seriously weakened Sviatopolk's defenses, and in 1019 Yaroslav once again drove his brother from the capital. This time Sviatopolk appealed to Kiev's ancient nemesis, the Pechenegs, for help. Unwilling to risk Yaroslav's wrath, and convinced that he was destined to be victorious in the struggle for the throne, the Pechenegs betrayed Sviatopolk to his brother's troops, who promptly killed him.

When Yaroslav reclaimed the throne of Kiev, he inherited an empire far less extensive than the one his father had ruled. His brother Mstislav controlled the southeastern portion of the empire from his Black Sea capital of Tmutorokan and in fact began edging his borders north toward the forests held by Kiev. During the next two years, Yaroslav and Mstislav warred almost constantly. Mstislav's forces ultimately prevailed and Yaroslav was constrained to negotiate a truce with his brother, ceding to Mstislav the vast Kievan territory east of the Dnieper River.

The two rivals established a relative peace and in 1031 actually joined in a military alliance against Poland, reclaiming territory that had been lost earlier. Their combined Russian army scourged large portions of the Polish countryside and returned with vast numbers of prisoners. Five years later, in 1036, Mstislav died on a hunting trip. Yaroslav swiftly proclaimed himself monarch of the consolidated territories, which he promptly reunited under the Kievan mantle.

Achieving unchallenged sovereignty in Kiev apparently mellowed Yaroslav. After his successful Polish incursion with Mstislav, Yaroslav forcefully turned back another offensive by the Pechenegs, ending forever their capacity for military action against Kiev. A lackluster invasion of Estonia was quickly abandoned, and for the remainder of his reign Yaroslav devoted his energies to peaceful domestic pursuits. His domestic polices earned him the title Yaroslav the Wise. He ordered the translation of many Greek books, leading to the creation of the first Kievan or Russian library, which was housed in one of the many churches he built. These churches were augmented by the construction of monasteries and convents, and of the prized jewel in his crown, a magnificent citadel at Kiev. Yaroslav patterned his basilicas after the splendor of Byzantium. The Russian churches were as lavishly adorned with jewels, silver, and gold as those in Constantinople, except for the fine biblical mosaics that the Greeks exhibited in their churches. Because the skills to reproduce the mosaics were virtually nonexistent in Russia, Russian artists painted images of Christ and the saints and religious scenes on the church walls, beginning a proud Russian tradition of exquisite icon painting.

❖ ❖ ❖

Determined to end the blood feuds that pitted family against family, Yaroslav decreed that only designated close relatives could legally avenge the murder of a family member. If no qualified relative was available, the murderer would be forced to pay a large fine into the prince's treasury as compensation for his crime. Formal rules establishing legal procedures for courts were developed, based on Slav custom and Norman practices.

Yaroslav, determined that Kiev should rival Constantinople in its splendor, imported artisans and scholars from Byzantium to beautify his capital and educate the nobility. His beautification program made Kiev a model city that foreign travelers called the "glory of Greece." To his satisfaction they compared it favorably to Constantinople. Schools were established to educate the children of the *druzhina*, or princely retinue. Great markets flourished in Kiev, attracting merchants from Scandinavia, Arabs from the Muslim world, Catholics from Poland and the Holy Roman Empire, and of course Greeks from Byzantium. All were welcome to trade in Kiev, and the city and its prince grew increasingly affluent and influential.

With the riches came commissions for Greek architects to build elaborate homes for wealthy merchants and nobles. The absence of stone and Kiev's limited capacity to manufacture bricks, most of which were reserved for religious buildings, forced the Greeks to work with wood. Despite this handicap, they constructed ornate homes boasting finely carved entrances, windows, and porches that afforded their owners spectacular views of the bustling city.

No reliable census figures are available for 11th-century Kiev, but many historians estimate that the city's population rivaled Paris's 80,000 people during the same period.

It was during Yaroslav's reign, in 1051, that the character of the Church began to change with the appointment of the first Russian-born metropolitan, or head of the Church in all of Russia, Hilarion. Previously, many bishops had been Russians, but the metropolitan had always been a Greek. The grand prince was so convinced of the truth of his faith that he had the bodies of his uncles Oleg and Yaropolk disinterred so they could be baptized, thus ensuring the eternal salvation of their souls.

Yaroslav was the first Russian sovereign to employ royal marriages as a means of establishing and solidifying foreign alliances. Centuries later, Queen Victoria's foreign policy for England would be predicated on this same principle of royal marriages. Yaroslav himself married a Swedish princess; his sister married the king of Poland; his daughters married the kings of France, Hungary, and Norway. One son wedded a Byzantine princess who was a close relative of the emperor of Byzantium, while four others married the daughters of German princes.

Through strong matrimonial alliances and the continued growth of Christianity in the country, Russia entered a new era in which it was recognized as an equal by other European nations. Russia, and the Russians, were no longer considered barbarian. Anecdotal evidence of Russia's new enlightenment can be found in an engaging story about the marriage of Yaroslav's daughter, Anna, to the French king, Henry I. While Anna was able to sign her name to the marriage contract, the French king could barely manage an "X." Under Yaroslav, Kiev became the center of political power in Russia and one of the most beautiful cities in Europe. The foundations of Russian art, architecture, and literature were established during his reign.

❖ ❖ ❖

Under Yaroslav the Russian people enjoyed an exceptional degree of democratic freedom. Although Russia was ruled by a grand prince who possessed virtually absolute power and who sought advice only from a council of advisors composed largely of aristocrats, military leaders, rich merchants, government officials, and important landowners who were known collectively as boyars, democratic practices were firmly in place at the local level.

Each settlement was liable to the authority of a *veche*, a local assembly of all the free men residing in the district. The veche had extraordinary power. A local prince could be removed by order of the veche, and a new prince elected to replace him. Any member of the veche could call the assembly together merely by ringing the town's bell. A meeting might be called to settle a dispute between individuals, or a claim against a local official, or to decide if the prince who ostensibly ruled the town should be removed from his position and replaced. Because all decisions had to be unanimous, the assemblies frequently degenerated into violence. Nevertheless, they gave the local people a strong voice in how their government was run.

The influence of the veches varied from town to town. The most powerful assembly was in Novgorod, where the veche actually hired princes and quickly removed them if they failed to perform their duties satisfactorily. Novgorod's veche even conducted business with foreign countries, including negotiating trade agreements, as if the town were a sovereign state. The power of the Novgorod veche is apparent in the account of a delegation it sent to Kiev to tell the grand prince that the city refused to accept his son as its prince. The Novgorod veche remained a powerful force in the northern districts of Russia until it was crushed in the 15th century.

Yaroslav was Russia's first scholarly grand prince as well as its last ruler to maintain a link with his Viking heritage. He was also the last grand prince to attempt a military assault against Constantinople. Presumably in retaliation for the murder of a Kievan merchant in Constantinople, Yaroslav sent a fleet commanded by one of his sons to punish the Byzantine capital in 1043, but it was easily driven off and the affair quickly forgotten.

Contemplating his approaching death, Yaroslav wrestled unsuccessfully with the problem of the succession to his throne. Historically, the death of a grand prince had ignited a bloody dispute over the throne among his heirs. And as the royal family had grown, so too had the number of claimants to Kiev's crown and to control of Russia. The complex order of succession was to cause many of the calamities that would befall Russia after Yaroslav's death in 1054. The order of succession was not simply from father to son, as was the case in most other European kingdoms, but also from brother to brother, or uncle to nephew. The key factors were the age of each individual and his position in the princely genealogy. For example, the grand prince's eldest nephew was next in the order of succession after the youngest uncle, not the uncle's own son.

Adding to the confusion were the personal animosities and ambitions of individual princes who refused to wait their turn to become grand prince, and the power of several veches, especially the one in Novgorod, which was apt to reject a legitimate successor and offer the crown to another prince instead.

Yaroslav devised a plan that he hoped would avoid warfare among his sons after his death. The plan assigned each son a specific position in the line of succession. He gathered his sons together and told them he was dividing his realm into special principalities, with the distribution of land to be determined by seniority and the importance of the principality. The eldest son, Isiaslav, was designated prince of Kiev and Novgorod, the two most important Russian cities, and would succeed his father as grand prince. The second oldest son, Sviatoslav, was named prince of Chernigov, the next city in importance, and of two distant provinces. The third son, Vsevolod, was given Pereyaslav; the fourth, Viatcheslav, received Smolensk; and the fifth and youngest son, Igor, was made prince of the western district of Volhynia.

Yaroslav made each of the younger sons swear allegiance to Isiaslav and to accept him as grand prince when their father died. Isiaslav in turn promised to protect his brothers against all intruders. Yaroslav's system was simple. When Grand Prince Isiaslav died, the second brother, Sviatoslav, would take his place, and each brother would move up one step on the succession ladder, which meant physically moving his court to the next highest principality. Eventually, when all his brothers had passed on, the youngest, Igor, would inherit the throne and become grand prince.

This system might have worked if each brother had died in the order of his birth, which did not happen. To add further complication, the sons of these princes were unhappy to find that they would not inherit their father's throne if their father's younger brother, their uncle, was alive.

The result of this complicated order of succession was that when Yaroslav died in 1054, Russia was plunged into a prolonged period of civil strife as brothers, nephews, and uncles struggled for succession to the various principalities, and ultimately to the title of grand prince of Kiev.

Part Three

THE TIME OF THE MONGOL YOKE

CHAPTER 7

THE FALL OF KIEV AND THE
RISE OF VLADIMIR

O N YAROSLAV'S DEATH IN 1054, HIS ELDEST son, Isiaslav, became
grand prince according to his father's wishes. But the simple, kind-hearted
Isiaslav encountered trouble almost from the beginning of his reign. Two of his
brothers, Sviatoslav and Vsevolod, refused to honor their pledge of loyalty and
challenged Isiaslav's supremacy as grand prince. This challenge resulted in the
unified nation created by their father being displaced by a group of loosely
federated principalities, each ruled by one of his sons.

Compounding Isiaslav's troubles, there appeared on the steppes a Turkic
tribe called the Cumans, who replaced the now defunct Pechenegs as a constant
menace to the authority of Kiev. Isiaslav's forces waged frequent campaigns
against these ferocious nomads but failed to drive them off. As a result, the
members of Kiev's veche concluded that Isiaslav was not strong enough to
defend their interests, and in 1062 they expelled the grand prince from the city.
Finding an ally among the Poles, Isiaslav reentered Kiev the following year and
retook his place on the throne. Despite attempts by Sviatoslav and Vsevolod
to undermine him, Isiaslav managed to survive for the next 10 years, although
the trade route south to Byzantium on which Kiev relied for much of its wealth
was under constant harassment by the Cumans.

In 1073, Sviatoslav and Vsevolod declared that Grand Prince Isiaslav was
plotting to revise the order of succession and deny them their rightful ascent to
the Kiev throne. Although there was no evidence to support this claim, the
traitorous brothers nevertheless used it to enlist the support of local citizens,
and with their help they once more expelled Isiaslav. As the second oldest
brother, Sviatoslav assumed the title of grand prince and ruled as Sviatoslav II
until he died, evidently of natural causes, in 1076. Before Vsevolod, the next
brother in line, could be crowned, Isiaslav returned once again at the head of a
Polish army to recapture his throne. As the Poles approached Kiev, Vsevolod
retired from the city and decided to wait his turn to rule. Two years later, Isiaslav
died and Vsevolod became grand prince.

As internal jockeying for the Kievan throne continued, the great united empire gradually disintegrated. Yaroslav's fourth son, Vyacheslav, who was the prince of Smolensk, died. According to Yaroslav's formula, Igor, his youngest son, moved from Volhynia to Smolensk to become its prince. This did not please Vyacheslav's sons, who felt that they should inherit the principality. Three years later Igor died, leaving sons who also claimed a right to the Smolensk throne. More and more heirs saw themselves excluded from what they considered to be their rightful place in the line of succession, and they refused to recognize Yaroslav's plan for the princely sequence. Several of them began massing troops to forcefully support their claims.

When Yaroslav's last surviving son, Vsevolod, died in 1093, the throne passed to the eldest son of the eldest brother. This meant that the new grand prince was Sviatopolk II, the eldest son of Isiaslav. Many citizens of Kiev were unhappy with this succession and attempted to convince Vsevolod's eldest son, the extremely popular Vladimir Monomakh, who was living in Chernigov but had come to Kiev to be at his father's side at his death, to challenge Sviatopolk II. Not wishing to dispute the order of succession established by his grandfather, Yaroslav the Wise, Vladimir Monomakh declined to demand the throne and instead supported his cousin Sviatopolk's rightful claim.

The succession of Yaroslav's first grandson to the Kievan throne failed to reverse the deteriorating situation in Russia. Nomadic tribes, notably the Cumans, ceaselessly attacked merchant convoys and burned Russian settlements. The disunited princes seemed incapable of organizing themselves to curb the marauders. Instead, many plotted with foreign rulers, especially the kings of Poland and Hungary, soliciting support for their claims to one principality or another. Not since before the time of Oleg did the nomads have such a free hand in plundering Russian towns. Sviatopolk II proved to be too weak and too busy conspiring against his cousins to organize a genuine defense, so the task fell to Vladimir Monomakh. Vladimir was married to Gytha, the daughter of the king of England, Harold II, who was killed at the Battle of Hastings in 1066 by the forces of William the Conqueror.

Vladimir Monomakh wrote to his cousins, inviting them to attend a congress of princes for the purpose of settling their disputes and joining their forces to defend Russia against the nomads. When the congress convened, the main subject of discussion was not the defense of the realm, as Vladimir Monomakh had intended, but the reformation of the lines of succession to the various principalities. Most of those attending were Yaroslav's grandsons and great grandsons who resented the system he had created because it deprived them of succession to their fathers' thrones. They wanted the princely succession changed to a direct lineage from father to son. This was their price for peace.

Vladimir Monomakh, the nominal chairman of the congress, agreed to this demand in the interest of peacefully settling the disputes of the princes. Soon thereafter, though, the peace was violated when a young prince named David lured another young prince, the extremely popular Vasilko, to the palace of Grand Prince Sviatopolk II, where he was ambushed and blinded in a violent struggle. Under pressure from Vladimir Monomakh, Sviatopolk II banished David.

A second congress of princes, convened soon after the first, brought an agreement that enabled Vladimir Monomakh to marshal an army that would conduct three decisive campaigns against the nomads. The first was in 1101. The second, in 1103, struck into the heart of the Cumans' territory and took the lives of many of their leaders. The third, in 1111, drove the nomads from the steppes.

Grand Prince Sviatopolk II continued to engage in activities that brought him disfavor, not only from his princely cousins but also from the Kievan population. The Kiev veche charged him with conspiring with the Jews, moneylenders, and the monasteries to gain a monopoly on salt imports. Although the veche failed to depose him, the people's prayers were apparently answered when Sviatopolk II died shortly thereafter, in 1113.

According to the system of succession instituted by Yaroslav the Wise, the next man in line to become grand prince was Sviatoslav II's eldest son, but the Kievan population demanded that Vladimir Monomakh accept the throne. Reluctant to deprive his cousin of his rightful inheritance, Vladimir declined. Kiev was quickly swept by riots that became known as the "democratic revolution." An enraged population ransacked the homes of Jews, boyars, and government and military officials whom they suspected of plotting against Vladimir. The situation became so violent that the nobles and church officials beseeched Vladimir to accept the title of grand prince before the city was destroyed. Finally, and with reluctance, Vladimir Monomakh became the new grand prince of Kiev. His first actions were to institute sweeping changes in monetary practices, thereby relieving the population of the debt burdens that Sviatopolk's policies had placed on it.

Vladimir Monomakh, more widely known as Vladimir II, ascended the throne of Kiev when he was 61. He was a popular grand prince who always ruled with the interests of his subjects as a priority. Many historians consider him to have been the best leader available to the royal family at the time. Although Sviatoslav II's sons resented their cousin for taking the throne that rightfully belonged to them, there was little they could do against such a popular prince, and so they reluctantly accepted the people's choice.

Vladimir's last name, Monomakh, was a Slav rendition of the name of the royal family of Byzantium. Because Vladimir's father, Grand Prince Vsevolod, the third son of Yaroslav, had married a niece of the reigning Byzantine emperor, Vladimir was related by blood to the royal family in Constantinople and had taken his mother's family name as his own.

A pious man as well as a skilled organizer and military commander, Vladimir devoted most of the 12 years of his reign to traveling throughout his realm. He held meetings with local religious leaders, government officials, military commanders, and princes, preaching to them the importance of strengthening the religious beliefs of the people. He also effected an extensive reorganization of his armies, awarding commands to men who had demonstrated both courage and skill in battle.

One of Vladimir's greatest challenges upon ascending to the throne was to reestablish a cohesive empire and Kiev's central role in its government. His biggest problem was Novgorod in the north. Novgorod had grown in size and influence during the preceding decades, and had established its own trade agreements with foreign merchants. The proliferation of new trade routes between Novgorod and western Europe threatened Kiev's position as the commercial center of Russia. To make matters worse, the power of Novgorod's veche had grown commensurately, and many leading citizens of Novgorod considered the ever expanding territory over which the city ruled exempt from the direct authority of the grand prince in Kiev. They demonstrated their independence from Kiev by regularly rejecting the princes it nominated for the Novgorod throne and demanding the right to pick their own. Unlike the princes of most other Russian principalities, the prince of Novgorod had little real power; he was forbidden to own property within the city, and was little more than a figurehead who ruled at the will of the veche, which in turn was controlled by the city's wealthiest merchants. Fearful of going too far with their bid for independence, however, the members of the veche were always careful to select as their prince someone from Yaroslav the Wise's family so that they would not be accused of usurping the prestige of that large and powerful royal family.

Vladimir Monomakh worked diligently to solidify an alliance among the Russian princes. Although he achieved modest success, the rivalry between claimants to the Kievan throne, and the desire of many princes to be independent of Kiev, prevented Vladimir from achieving complete success.

Following Novgorod's example, other cities began to question Kiev's authority, although less forcefully than Novgorod. Among them were the towns located in the northeastern part of the empire, which formerly had been little more than a frontier populated mostly by Finns. The availability of tillable soil and the freedom from the raids of the steppe nomads had attracted countless peasants, each of whom had the right to move from one area of the empire to another. As this migration took place, a new center of power within the empire arose around the settlements of Moscow and Vladimir.

The growing influence of the principalities of Moscow and Vladimir presaged the decline of Kiev as the central power in Russia, but Vladimir Monomakh's succession to the throne of Kiev gave that city a reprieve that would last for another generation. Through the sheer force of his will and personal popularity, Vladimir Monomakh was able to stem the decline of Kiev.

Vladimir Monomakh is remembered as a great and talented grand prince who dispatched the steppe nomads and resolved disputes among the various princes without their resorting to warfare, which usually weighed heavily on the general population in terms of financial costs and lives lost. He is also remembered for the wisdom he passed to his children in a document called the Testament. In this document he implored his sons to never judge a man by his wealth alone, to be generous to the poor, to protect widows and orphans from the mighty, to shed blood only in battle, and to pray nightly. Vladimir's crown, which legend claims was a gift from the Byzantine emperor, was worn by every Russian ruler during the next 600 years, until Peter the Great. Vladimir himself reigned for more than a decade until his death in 1125, at which time the crown passed to his eldest son, Mstislav I.

Little is known about Mstislav's reign, which lasted until his death seven years later. He was a capable ruler who continued to protect Kiev from the nomads, but his efforts to forge a strong and lasting alliance of the Russian princes failed, as had his father's. Aside from his several campaigns against the Cumans, Mstislav maintained the peace by preventing a reoccurrence of the princely civil wars that had preceded his grandfather's reign and would plague Russia's future. In his only military campaign against another Russian, Mstislav swiftly removed the prince of Polotsk from his throne when he refused to join the Russian principalities in their war against the Cumans. Mstislav captured the prince, who was sent into exile with Mstislav's own mother's family in Constantinople.

Mstislav's death in 1132 signaled the beginning of the end of Kiev's central role in Russia. There followed in relatively quick succession four grand princes of Kiev before the city itself finally fell to invasion and was no longer considered the center of power in Russia.

Mstislav was replaced by his younger brother, Yaropolk II, who ruled from 1132 to 1139. His reign was distinguished by his military leadership of a Kievan force that repulsed a large invasion mounted by the Cumans. When Yaropolk II died in 1139, the veche of Kiev asked his younger brother, Viatcheslav, to become grand prince, which he did. But then the old rivalries flared up again.

It will be recalled that Vladimir Monomakh, the father of Mstislav, Yaropolk II, and Viatcheslav, had ascended to the throne at the insistence of the citizens of Kiev and over the objections of the rightful heir, the eldest son of Grand Prince Sviatoslav II. Now the descendants of Sviatoslav II demanded that the throne revert to their branch of the family. A similar demand came from Grand Prince Isiaslav's heirs, who claimed that the throne should have been passed to his sons instead of to his brothers, Sviatoslav and Vsevolod. Quickly, the tenuous alliances established and nurtured by Vladimir Monomakh and Mstislav crumbled and the violent civil wars resumed.

Vladimir Monomakh's third son, Viatcheslav, was grand prince for such a short time, probably only several weeks, that he is not recognized as ever having held the throne. Viatcheslav's right to the throne was immediately challenged by Vsevolod, the prince of Chernigov, who was the senior member of Sviatoslav II's branch of the royal family. Vsevolod claimed the throne as his birthright and demanded that Viatcheslav step down in his favor.

History records Viatcheslav's decision to abdicate if Vsevolod "does desire this throne," but not the reason for that decision. Viatcheslav may have wished to avoid a renewal of the violent bloodshed among cousins, or perhaps he viewed Vsevolod as too powerful to oppose in a military confrontation.

Having wrested the throne from Viatcheslav, Vsevolod II ruled as grand prince of Kiev until his death in 1146. He was succeeded by his brother Igor, who was ousted within a few months. Although before his death Vsevolod II had elicited from the leading citizens of Kiev their pledge of allegiance to his brother Igor, they failed to honor that pledge. Shortly after Vsevolod's death, the Kiev veche turned on Igor and offered the throne to Isiaslav, the son of Mstislav and grandson of Vladimir Monomakh. Isiaslav accepted the invitation, defeated Igor in a brief war, and in 1146 assumed the throne once occupied by both his father and grandfather. He was known as Isiaslav II.

Isiaslav reigned for eight tumultuous years. During most of that time, the grand prince was locked in combat with the prince of Suzdal, Yuri Dolgoruki, who was himself a pretender to the throne. Yuri was Vladimir Monomakh's youngest son and therefore Isiaslav's uncle. Both Isiaslav and Yuri recruited outside forces to support their claims. Ironically, both solicited help from the barbaric nomads who for generations had been enemies of Kiev. Yuri allied himself with the Cumans while Isiaslav employed the Pechenegs to aid in defending the city. Kiev changed hands several times as first Isiaslav and then Yuri gained the upper hand. Finally, in 1154, Isiaslav was slain and Yuri became the grand prince. His was a hollow victory, for Yuri, now 63 and a tired old man as a result of a lifetime of excesses, would be dead in three years' time.

The people's pent-up hatred for Yuri erupted in violence the moment the news of his death became public. Thousands of rioters stormed his palace, stealing what they could carry and destroying what they could not, and murdering many of Yuri's relatives and closest advisors.

After Yuri's death the Kiev veche moved to forestall the continued rule of their city by the northern line of the royal family. In 1157, the nobles called on Isiaslav's son, Mstislav II of Volhynia, to become grand prince even though he had no direct claim to the throne. Mstislav accepted and led a succession of short-term grand princes. Kiev fell into its darkest period as the armies of various princes fought violent battles in and around the city for the right to name the grand prince. The throne changed hands so many times that, even to this day, most of its numerous occupants remain anonymous. After Kiev was burned by various Russian armies, and after many of its people were massacred or driven into slavery, little of the city's former splendor and wealth remained, except for the coveted title of grand prince. Since its founding by Oleg as a center of political and commercial power, Kiev had withstood countless foreign invaders, only to finally fall victim to Russian princes who disdained the city itself and sought only the title of grand prince.

The struggle for the Kievan throne ceased and the end of Kiev as the center of Russian political power came in 1169, when Yuri's son, Andrey Bogolyubski, the 58-year-old prince of Suzdal and Rostov, stormed the city. Kiev was sacked and burned as if it were the capital of a foreign enemy. Never before had a Russian prince assaulted Kiev so viciously. Thousands of Kiev's remaining citizens were slaughtered, and thousands more were sold into slavery. Monasteries and churches were looted and burned; their priests were put to the sword.

The victorious Andrey proclaimed himself grand prince and declared the
northern city of Vladimir to be the new capital of Russia. As a final blow to
Kiev's prestige, Andrey installed his younger brother Gleb as prince of the
former capital. Kiev's influence vanished almost overnight, and the city quickly
slipped into oblivion as the empire's leading political center. It soon succumbed
to the steppe nomads: in 1203 the Cumans successfully attacked the former
capital and sacked what remained of it.

Moving the Russian capital north appears to historians to have been fully
justified because the population shifts at the time were northward, away from
the dangerous steppes and into the relative safety of the forests where many new
Russian towns were springing up. Entire regions were abandoned by rich and
poor alike as they sought a safer existence away from the open plains that were
vulnerable to attack by nomadic horsemen. The great migrations that began
before the fall of Kiev and continued for several decades divided the Russian
population into three distinct groups. Those who settled along the western
borders with Lithuania and Poland became known as the White Russians, those
who took up residence farther south were known as the Little Russians, and
those in the northwest were the Great Russians. Today, the descendants of the
White Russians live in Belarus, those of the Little Russians in Ukraine, and
those of the Great Russians around Moscow, the heart of modern Russia.

❖ ❖ ❖

When Andrey made the city of Vladimir his new center of power, he also
redefined the position of grand prince. The new settlements in the north
differed markedly from those in the south and from the older Russian cities of
the north, such as Novgorod. The new settlements were largely apolitical,
having been sponsored by the princes themselves. Citizens living in the southern regions had been encouraged to migrate north, away from the constant
threat of nomad raids and the violent civil wars, to populate the new towns.
The latter consisted mostly of farmers and related artisans, had no powerful
merchant class, and were more firmly under the control of their princes. Most
did not even have the traditional veche through which the wealthy of older
towns exerted political power, and their princes ruled with little or no trace of
the democratic practices found in the south. Andrey introduced this form of
absolutism and thereby changed how Russia would be ruled during the next
eight centuries.

Andrey regarded himself as an absolute monarch. He broke tradition by
discarding the long-standing advisory role that the elders of the princely guards

had formerly enjoyed and by refusing to consult with the boyars of his new realm. Ignoring all other influences, Andrey allied himself solely with the Orthodox clergy. Wanting to concentrate all power in his own hands, Andrey rejected the traditional sharing of authority with his brothers and went so far as to drive them out of his lands. Concentrating much of his energy on expanding and beautifying Vladimir, Andrey constructed many new churches and a cathedral to rival that of St. Sophia in Kiev, thereby earning the reputation of a great builder.

In 1174, Grand Prince Andrey's undisguised contempt for those in his service led to his murder by either the boyars, the members of his own body-guard, or a combination of both groups. For two days his naked body lay in the palace courtyard while mobs of city dwellers and peasants looted his residence. As the blood lust rose to a crescendo, several high officials were hunted down and killed; others fled the city in terror.

A bloody civil war ensued. After two years of fighting between Andrey's brothers and nephews, the war ended, and in 1176 Andrey's younger brother Vsevolod was awarded the title of grand prince. The civil war had also been a battle for supremacy between the city of Vladimir and the cities of Rostov and Suzdal. Vsevolod's victory confirmed Vladimir as the center of real power in Russia.

Vsevolod III, also called the "Big Nest" because of the legion of children he sired, followed his brother's blueprint for a strong, autocratic central govern-ment. He failed in several attempts to subdue Novgorod, which had become so independent and democratic that it referred to itself as a republic, but he fared better with the other principalities. One after another, the Russian princes swore allegiance to him. By the time he died, in 1212, Vsevolod III had exceeded Andrey's ambitions, having united most of northern and southern Russia under his personal rule.

As so often happened in the past, Vsevolod III's death triggered a new power struggle for the title of grand prince. Two of Vsevolod's sons, Konstantin and Yuri, contested the succession. Initially, Konstantin prevailed and assumed his father's throne, but Yuri never abandoned his quest. In 1218, Yuri murdered his brother and became grand prince of Vladimir, meaning of all the Russian principalities owing allegiance to the grand prince. Yuri II ruled much of Russia from Vladimir until 1238, when Mongol horsemen killed him. Throughout his reign, he would harbor a fanatic obsession to subjugate the Volga Bulgars who controlled the territory on his eastern borders. That obsession would cost Yuri his crown and ultimately his life.

CHAPTER 8

RUSSIAN PRINCES AS VASSALS OF THE KHAN

IN THE FIRST DECADE OF THE 13TH century, two widely divergent events had profound effects on Russia.

In April 1204, a heterogeneous army of Catholic crusaders, primarily Venetians, Frenchmen, and Germans, attacked and conquered Constantinople, compelling the emperor and the patriarch of the Orthodox Church to flee their capital for sanctuary in Asia Minor. The invaders revealed their inordinate hatred of the Greek Christians by wantonly slaughtering them and desecrating the beautiful city. Nuns were routinely raped and Greek clerics were murdered. Churches and cathedrals containing many valued works of art were destroyed. The crusaders' inhuman cruelty shocked the Greeks, who were convinced that even the heathen Turks would have been less barbaric had they taken the city. The disruption of the Byzantine church ended forever Greek dominance of the Russian church.

Shortly after Constantinople fell, a new supreme leader of the Mongol tribes was proclaimed in Mongolia, an obscure land thousands of miles to the east of Russia that had barely touched the Russian consciousness. Temuchin, better known as Genghis Khan, was the son of a chief from one of the most remote tribes in Asia. Orphaned at the age of 12, he was abandoned by everyone except his brothers until 1206, when he became the Mongol's leading khan. An untutored savage, Genghis Khan combined natural talent as a fearless leader and great military strategist and tactician with a dream of world conquest. His titles would include "Emperor of Mankind."

In 1215 a Mongol army commanded by Genghis Khan captured Peking, the capital of the Chinese Empire, and deposed the emperor. From there, Mongol warriors moved west and south, conquering new lands and expanding their empire. Wherever the Mongols went, defeated enemies were converted into allies and enlisted in the Mongol army, which quickly grew to several hundred thousand warriors.

About one year after the conquest of Peking, Genghis Khan sent three ambassadors to Bukhara to visit the court of Muhammad Ali Shah, the emperor

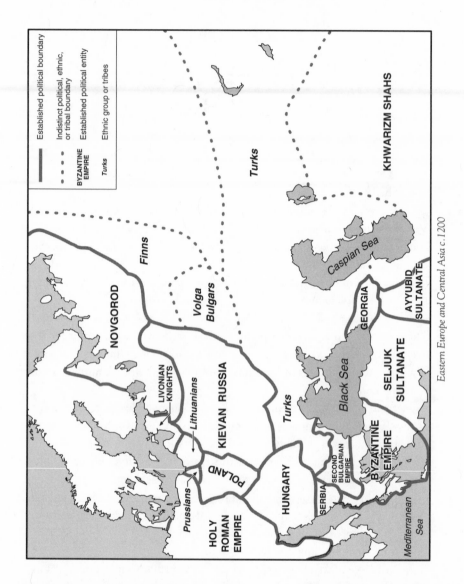

Eastern Europe and Central Asia c.1200

of Khwarizm, Transoxiana, and Khurasan, a vast empire stretching east from modern-day Iran on the Persian Gulf to the Indus River in northern India. Impressed with the Mongol's power and wealth, Muhammad entered into a trade agreement with them in 1218.

The pact was breached almost immediately. When the first Mongol caravan arrived with 500 camels loaded with gold, silver, sables, and other riches, one of Muhammad's governors accused the Mongol ambassador and the caravan merchants of being spies. Without even a perfunctory trial, the governor, Inalchuk Khwadir Khan of Ortar, massacred everyone in the caravan, including the ambassador and confiscated the camels and their precious burdens. Outraged by this act, the Mongols sent another ambassador to Muhammad. Escorted by only two Mongol warriors, the ambassador, Ibn Kafraj Boghra, demanded that Inalchuk Khwadir be punished for his crime. Muhammad, who could have settled the matter by arresting and trying the governor, foolishly murdered Ibn Kafraj Boghra and sent his head back to Genghis Khan with the two escorts, whose hair and beards Muhammad first burned from their bodies. A war was inevitable.

Following a brief, indecisive battle at the Fergana valley between 50,000 Khwarizmian cavalry under Muhammad's able son Jalal ad-Din, and 30,000 Mongols exhausted by their trek across the Tien Shan mountains, Genghis Khan marshaled soldiers from all corners of his empire and led a campaign that ended in 1221 with Muhammad's death and the destruction of his empire. Muhammad's former subjects were made subjects of the "Emperor of Mankind" and his soldiers were conscripted into the Mongol army.

Seeking better knowledge of the nations beyond the Caspian Sea that bordered on his newly acquired empire, Genghis Khan dispatched 20,000 horsemen on a two-year reconnaissance mission to determine the strength and predilections of his European neighbors. After a few scattered skirmishes, the Mongols, led by two of Genghis Khan's most popular and talented leaders, Jebe Noyan and Subedei Bahadur, entered Christian Georgia and clashed with a Georgian army of 70,000 on the Khuman plain. The Georgian troops were all but annihilated and the Mongols withdrew to regroup. In midwinter, when a second Georgian army was trapped in a mountain pass, the final obstacle to the Russian steppes was removed.

Crossing the Caucasus Mountains in midwinter, the Mongols defeated a massed army of Cumans, Volga Bulgars, Khazars, and Alans and entered the steppes. Confident of their own strength, the Mongols divided their force. Subedei rode southwest to the Sea of Azov, where he negotiated a treaty with merchants from Venice, and Jebe rode west to the banks of the Don River.

With most of his army destroyed or fleeing into Hungary and Byzantium, the Cuman khan, Kotian, pleaded with his former enemies, the Russian princes, for help against the invaders. Most of the Russians were pleased that the Cuman nomads who had regularly raided their towns and cities had been so badly beaten by this new and unknown army, but a few, including Mstislav the Bold—the prince of Galacia and the husband of a Cuman princess—understood what Kotian meant when he told the Russians that they would be the Mongols' next targets. A council of princes was called, at which the princes of Kiev, Kursk, and Chernigov, along with Grand Prince Yuri, heeded Mstislav the Bold's counsel and assembled a Russian army to reinforce the remnants of the Cuman army against the Mongol invaders.

Continuing on with the reconnaissance mission, Jebe and Subedei once again joined forces and camped along the Dnieper River. Hearing of the Russian call to arms, they sent ambassadors to the Russians to convince them that the Mongols meant them no harm and that they were returning to Mongolia. The ambassadors were killed and a Russian force led by Mstislav the Bold crossed the river and annihilated a Mongol rear guard. Emboldened by this minor victory, the Russian princes and their Cuman allies pursued the retreating Mongols. Unfortunately, no one prince was given overall command of the Russian troops, so each prince's force was left to operate independently. This lack of organization cost the Russians and the Cumans dearly.

For nine days the Russian and Cuman army tracked the retreating Mongols. The Russians were scattered across the steppes for miles because each prince insisted that his own army remain with him. In the valley of the Kalka River on May 31, 1223, the lead elements of the Russian force, primarily Galicians and Cumans lead by Mstislav the Bold, ran headlong into a Mongol ambush and a desperate battle began. Russian communications were so poor that as each prince arrived on the scene with his troops he was entirely unaware that a battle was under way. The totally disorganized Russians and Cumans were slaughtered by the Mongols and forced to take flight. More than 40,000 Russians, including six princes, died in the battle.

Thirty thousand Russian and Cuman soldiers fled more than 150 miles to the Dnieper River before the smaller Mongol force. The prince of Kiev employed his 10,000-man army as a rear guard to protect the fleeing Russians, but when he reached the Dnieper he found that his allies had crossed the river and burned their galleys to prevent the Mongols from using them. For three days the trapped Kievan army fought bravely against the Mongols, but after being tricked into thinking the enemy wanted to sue for peace, it was slaughtered.

Ordered by Genghis Khan to return to his camp, the Mongols withdrew from the steppes and rode east, leaving behind a badly beaten Russian army and a reputation for superb horsemanship and martial skills that soon spread throughout Europe. The Mongol's eastward march was interrupted by an attack by the Volga Bulgars. Jebe and Subedei swore that the Volga Bulgars would be made to pay for their ill-considered assault.

Partly out of fear and partly from bravado, the surviving Russian princes, and those who replaced the princes who had died, claimed that the Mongols had retreated to Asia out of fear. A few of the princes, as well as many churchmen, pleaded with Grand Prince Yuri II and the other princes to prepare to defend Russia and Christendom against these heathens who were sure to return. But the Mongols were quickly forgotten and the Russian princes returned to their accustomed disunity.

Genghis Khan died in August 1229, leaving as supreme khan his well-liked and warm-hearted son, Ogadai. The Mongol Empire—stretching east to the ocean, north to the great snowcapped mountains, south across fertile plains to India, and west to the steppes—was divided into sections, each ruled by a son or grandson who swore obedience to Ogadai. The western section, bordering on Russia, was divided between two grandsons, Orda and Batu. This border, considered by Mongol generals to be the weak link in the empire's defense, was the poorest territory controlled by the Mongols.

Batu was displeased because his share of the empire was Mongol in name only, and because it lacked the riches and resources of the other sections. But the western border offered the only opportunity left for real expansion, and Mongol planners looked longingly at their maps of Europe and dreamt of the great wealth that would be theirs once they conquered the nations of Europe.

At the urging of Subedei and Batu, Ogadai was persuaded to embark on a campaign in the west with Batu at its head. Early in 1236, Batu began to collect an immense army for the western invasion. Fifty thousand experienced Mongol warriors were joined by 20,000 war prisoners schooled in Mongol combat tactics, and supported by several corps of engineers from Persia and China. Batu's chief of staff was Subedei, who had brilliantly directed the reconnaissance campaigns against the Russians from 1221 to 1223. Subedei's superior talents as a leader of mobile forces were already legendary, and his fame would persist for centuries. Two of World War II's most respected strategists in mobile warfare, George S. Patton and Erwin Rommel, were ardent students of Subedei's methods.

Later in 1236, Batu and Subedei led their army northwest across the Ural Mountains, determined first to exact revenge on the Volga Bulgars who had attacked the retreating Mongols in 1223. The Bulgars called on Grand Prince Yuri II to help defend their territory. Yuri disregarded the fact that the Bulgars were the only bulwark between the Mongols and Russia; blinded by an innate hatred for the Bulgars, he ignored their pleas. Overwhelmed by the Mongol juggernaut, the entire Volga Bulgar population was annihilated.

The Mongols crossed into Russia in the winter of 1237, their sights set on the capital, Vladimir. Grand Prince Yuri II, learning that wives and children were traveling with the Mongol army, realized that this was not a simple raiding party of nomads but an army bent on conquest. However, nothing had changed in Russia since the disastrous defeat in the Kalka River valley in 1223. Princes remained preoccupied with their own internal quarrels and could not present a united front against the terrible onslaught of the Mongol invaders. Even if the princes had been united, it is doubtful that they could have stopped the invasion.

The Russian principality of Ryazan stood between Batu's advancing army and the city of Vladimir. Fearing the worst, Prince Yuri Ingvarevich of Ryazan sent envoys to Vladimir, begging the grand prince to provide troops to help defend his capital, Ryazan. He received no response.

The Mongols surrounded Ryazan and issued their usual demand for tribute. The heroic response was prophetic: "When there is none of us left, then all will be yours." Incensed, the Mongols stormed the town. On December 21, 1237, after five days of intense fighting in night and day shifts, the Mongols broke through Ryazan's defenses and slaughtered every living creature within its walls. One after another, Russian towns now fell to the Mongols, including the fortified cities of several princes. Resistance was viewed by the Mongols as treachery, and they gave no quarter. In those instances when a local prince submitted to Mongol demands, little if any harm came to his people, yet as stories of terrible slaughter preceded the Mongols, most cities offered stubborn resistance.

Moscow fell soon after Ryazan, and the main force of Batu's army raced directly to Vladimir. Grand Prince Yuri II left his sons in charge of the city's defense while he tried to conscript an army from the northern settlements to fight the invaders.

Shortly after the New Year, Vladimir was surrounded by the horsemen from the Asian plains. Despite strong resistance, the city fell to the Mongols and was subjected to merciless slaughter and pillage. When the Mongols discovered that the grand prince was not in Vladimir, but that almost his entire family had taken refuge in the cathedral, the building was burned to the ground, killing everyone inside. Learning the whereabouts of the grand prince, Subedei took a large force and sped north in pursuit. On March 4, 1238, the Mongols clashed with Yuri's army on the shores of the Sit River. The Russians were defeated and Yuri barely escaped with his life, only to be hunted down and killed within a week.

Meanwhile, Batu led his main Mongol force west toward Novgorod. However, fortune smiled on that most democratic of Russian cities when a benevolent spring thaw softened the marshes surrounding it for miles around, halting the Mongols' advance. The invaders had ridden with ease across the frozen rivers and marshes of northern Russia, but now the warming spring weather was turning the marshes into mud that their ponies found difficult to negotiate, curtailing the Mongols' ability to maneuver, which was fundamental to their success in battle.

Batu, again reunited with Subedei, elected to turn south toward the steppes and conquer what was left of the Cuman Empire. The Cumans were virtually defenseless before the mighty Mongol army. Thousands were slaughtered in battle, while thousands more, including their khan, Kotian, fled to Hungary and Byzantium. Those survivors who did not escape were conscripted into the Mongol army and trained to fight as Mongol warriors. The Cumans ceased to exist as a united people; the remnants of their population were scattered throughout central Europe and Asia Minor.

The Mongols settled along the coasts of the Black and Caspian seas for the summer, resting and preparing for the next year's campaign. During the next year and a half, Russian towns were systematically raided and subjected to Mongol domination. In 1239 the entire Mongol army moved out for the final conquest of Russia.

In the interim, there occurred an event that would alter for nearly 200 years the method for selecting the grand prince of Russia. The late Yuri II's brother, Yaroslav, approached Batu, asking for permission to assume the title of grand prince. Batu found Yaroslav sufficiently humble and agreed to the appointment, thereby setting a new precedent. Yaroslav had been prince of Novgorod, but he now assumed the name Yaroslav II, grand prince of Vladimir. He was the first Russian grand prince to be a vassal of the Mongol khan.

As a sign of his loyalty, Yaroslav sent his son Konstantin to the Mongol capital of Karakorum to pay respects to the great khan. When the election of a new supreme khan took place in 1246, Batu sent Yaroslav to Karakorum as his official representative to the coronation of the new khan. While there, Yaroslav was poisoned by the new khan's mother, who correctly considered Batu a rival for her son's throne. After Yaroslav's death, Batu appointed the former's eldest son, Andrey, grand prince. Andrey dutifully made the required pilgrimage to

Karakorum to pay homage to the supreme khan, but six years later the Mongols discovered that he was conspiring against them and he was forced to flee Russia.

In the winters of 1239 and 1240, Batu completed his conquest of the northwestern Russian territories and the southern principalities. Chernigov was sacked and burned in 1239, and Kiev was virtually eradicated in 1240 after putting up a brave but hopeless struggle. The once great city was reduced to little more than a thinly populated village. Six years later, a Catholic missionary, Joannes de Plano Carpini, traveled through Kiev on his way from Poland to preach the word of God to the Mongols. In his account of the trip, he described the road through Kievan territory as almost completely devoid of Kievans. Along the roadsides were the skulls and bones of countless people, all victims of the Mongols. In Kiev itself, he counted less than 200 homes for the pitiable remnant of a once proud population. The undoing of Kiev, begun by the Russian princes and the steppe nomads, had been completed by the Mongols.

From the collection of James P. Duffy

Grand Prince Alexander Nevsky

In 1241, with most of Russia under their control, the Mongols crossed into central Europe and attacked Hungary and Poland. In their wake they left in Russia a disjointed political structure almost identical with what they had found when they first arrived—an array of petty princes who were more concerned with family feuds than with preserving what remained of the Russian Empire. During this depressed period few princes distinguished themselves; most simply bowed to the authority of their Mongol overlords. But from the darkness that had descended over Russia one man rose to new heights—Alexander, the prince of Novgorod and son of Yaroslav II.

Temporarily exempt from Mongol control, Novgorod faced an old set of troubles. Situated in the northwest corner of Russia, Novgorod was an ideal target for various European powers ambitious to expand their holdings. One such threat came from the Swedes in 1240. Instigated by the pope, who wished to replace Orthodoxy in Russia with Catholicism, a Swedish army under Jarl Birger, who later would rule Sweden as regent, sailed up the Neva River with invasion plans. Accompanied by a small force comprised mostly of his personal bodyguard, Alexander attacked the Swedes on July 15 as they attempted to land. The small Novgorodian force sank several Swedish ships and drove the rest away. Coming at the time of the Mongol conquests, a Russian victory, however small, was reason for rejoicing. Novgorod celebrated the victory and the prince was henceforth known as Alexander Nevsky in recognition of the battle site. Soon after, Alexander quarreled with the city's veche. Tired of constantly fighting with the assembly, Alexander resigned as prince and left the city.

The following year, Novgorod's territory was invaded by the German Teutonic Knights, who were also looking to spread Catholicism. First they captured the city of Pskov on Lake Peipus, then they built a fort that effectively blocked the trade route to Novgorod. Desperate to be rid of the German menace, the citizens of Novgorod asked Alexander to return. He accepted their generous terms, overran the fort and drove the knights from Pskov. On April 5, 1242, the Teutonic Knights withdrew before Alexander's Novgorodian army and attempted to escape by crossing the frozen lake. There followed a spectacular battle fought on the ice. The knights employed their infamous "iron wedge" to split the Russian center, but Alexander quickly countered with a flank attack that sent the knights into full flight. Burdened by their heavy metal armor, many knights drowned when their horses crashed through the ice. During the next three years, Novgorod was pressured almost constantly by Lithuanian attempts at invasion, but each time Alexander successfully defended the principality.

The legends about Alexander Nevsky's courage and military leadership impressed the Mongols enormously, especially Batu. For his part, Alexander realized that the almost incessant warfare was undermining Novgorod's capacity to survive as an independent state. Backed by the city's leading citizens, he visited both Batu's court—by then called the Golden Horde and situated in Sarai on the lower Volga River—and the court of the great khan in Mongolia. By mutual consent, Novgorod was annexed to the Mongol Empire, and Alexander Nevsky initiated a policy of conciliation and cooperation with the Mongols that eventually saved Russia from the possibility of far greater devastation. Alexander's decision to submit Novgorod to Mongol rule had two beneficial effects. Not only would the principality escape a Mongol military invasion and the destruction and death it would entail, but the Mongols were now committed to help defend Novgorod against incursions by the Swedes, Finns, and Lithuanians.

Alexander's renown as a military hero, together with his cooperative attitude toward the Mongols, earned him Batu's respect. When Alexander's brother, Grand Prince Andrey, fled the country in 1252 after his army was destroyed by a Mongol force sent from Sarai, Batu chose Alexander to succeed him as grand prince of Vladimir. A good choice, Alexander was able to balance his loyalty to Russia (defending the interests of the northern populations against the Swedes and Lithuanians) with faithful service to the Mongol khan. This dual role earned Alexander the respect of the Russian upper classes but incurred the animosity of the peasants on whom Mongol taxes and tribute exacted a heavy toll.

The year following his appointment as grand prince, Alexander dispatched his son Basil to expel a Lithuanian army that had invaded Novgorod's territory. Three years later, Alexander led a combined Russian army in a successful campaign against Swedish invaders, and in 1262 his army withstood a German invasion. Although Mongol support may have played some small role in these victories, it was not until later in the century that Mongol and Russian troops actually fought side by side against their mutual enemies. Mongol formations in 1275 supported a successful Russian campaign against Lithuania, which had grown into a powerful state, and Russian regiments are reported to have participated in the Mongol conquest of southern China.

Perhaps recognizing the futility of a revolt against the powerful Mongols, Alexander discouraged opposition to the invaders. He went as far as mobilizing his troops against the citizens of Novgorod in 1257, when they revolted against the Mongol tax collectors and army conscriptors.

Early historians and chroniclers tended to focus on Alexander Nevsky's military exploits, and some even compared him with Alexander the Great. Although his military victories were important, they were for the most part temporary, since recurrent hostilities with the Swedes and Lithuanians persisted for centuries. The most important achievement of Alexander Nevsky as grand prince was his prevention of further destruction of the northern Russian principalities by the Mongols. Had he not submitted to the khan, and instead taken up arms against him, it is likely that revolts against the invaders would have triggered the massive retaliation for which the Mongols were noted.

An example of Alexander's favorable influence over the Mongols is his successful bid to save the population of Rostov from annihilation in 1263. Having revolted against Mongol tax collectors and driven them away, Rostov and other towns on the Volga River were targeted for punishment by the Mongol prince Berke. A Mongol army was on its way to exact retribution when Alexander intervened and convinced the Mongols to allow him to bring the wayward populations into line. It was Alexander's final service to Russia, for he died on the return trip from Sarai on November 15, 1263. His death, at age 43, was probably the result of exhaustion brought on by the stress of defending Russia from her enemies in the west and her conquerors from the east. When the metropolitan of the Orthodox Church announced Alexander's death to the people of Vladimir, he told them, "The sun of Russia has set."

Unless forced by opposition from the ruling classes, the Mongols took little interest in the administration of their Russian holdings. Most Russian princes found it easier to cooperate with their masters on important issues. In return the Mongols left the princes to rule their fiefdoms in relative peace and security, provided that taxes and tribute were paid on time. What opposition there was to the Mongol overlords came from the common people and centered more on economic than political issues. When the Mongols raised taxes, the wealthy and powerful Russian families simply passed on the new costs to their subjects, thereby creating among the poorer classes widespread resentment against both the princes and the Mongols. Such behavior frequently triggered small uprisings that were promptly put down by the princes and their troops. Generally, the Russian princes served as obedient vassals of the Mongols. Even Alexander Nevsky, the hero of many Novgorodian military campaigns, lost favor with the citizens of Novgorod because of his willing collaboration with the Mongols.

Russian history has embraced Alexander Nevsky as a great hero. He was esteemed by 20th century Soviets and glorified by the famous Soviet filmmaker Serge Eisenstein. Eventually he was canonized by the Orthodox Church.

When Alexander died, Batu, the khan of the Golden Horde, gave the hero's brother, Yaroslav of Tver, the title of grand prince of Vladimir. During Alexander's reign, Vladimir's influence over the other Russian principalities had begun to wane. This occurred partly because of resentment over Alexander's submissive posture toward the Mongols and the speed with which he put down anti-Mongol uprisings, but largely because of a realization that the true power in Russia had passed from the grand prince into the hands of a foreign invader.

The main impetus for Vladimir's ultimate decline, and for the disavowal of its resident prince as the grand prince of Russia, emanated from Novgorod, long a bastion of democracy and independence. As long as the prince of Vladimir could ensure security for Novgorod's vast commercial interests, the local leaders accepted his rule. However, a subtle change had occurred when Alexander came to be perceived as a vassal of the khan of the Golden Horde. Although he had remained a strong grand prince, and opposition to his rule had been generally limited to ineffectual grumbling, his death and the appointment of his brother Yaroslav as grand prince changed the situation dramatically.

During the first six years of Yaroslav's rule, Novgorod edged closer to declaring its independence from Vladimir. Yaroslav, anticipating the impending breakup and loss of Novgorod's tax base as well as fees collected on imports, began courting Novgorodian leaders and started to play a more active role in its political life. Complaining that the grand prince was interfering too much in the principality's internal affairs, the residents of Novgorod revolted against Vladimir in 1269. Recognizing the real seat of Russian power, Novgorod's leaders sent an emissary to the Golden Horde to voice their discontent. Ironically, the emissary who presented Novgorod's case against Grand Prince Yaroslav before the khan was Yaroslav's younger brother, Basil.

Having been supplied with virtually unlimited funds by wealthy Novgorod merchants, Basil distributed large monetary gifts to the khan's advisors, and perhaps even to the khan himself. As a result of this generous gift-giving, Batu sided with Novgorod in its dispute with the grand prince he himself had appointed. Although Yaroslav remained grand prince until his death in 1272, his influence was greatly diminished. Every prince and grand prince depended almost entirely on the support of the Golden Horde to enforce his authority, and Yaroslav's support was now sorely depleted.

The spectacle of Russian princes bribing the khan of the Golden Horde to settle their differences illustrates not only the absolute authority the Mongols enjoyed in the country but the depths to which Russia had sunk. Russia had slipped into a dark age from which it would not emerge for several generations. Isolated from the influences of European civilization, Russia turned in on itself. Principalities shrank, grew weaker, and were more prone to fratricidal and internal warfare as princely inheritances were divided and redivided among growing numbers of descendants. Much of the population had been slaughtered or badly abused. People were forced to work less productive lands farther north, missing the bountiful harvests of the Kievan period and to endure the burden of the Mongols' heavy taxes. In one sense, the Mongol conquest had drawn an impenetrable curtain between Russia and Europe, keeping the Russians from sharing in the benefits of European progress. In 1480, when Russia finally threw off the Mongol yoke, it found that it had fallen hopelessly behind the rest of Europe in the development of a "modern" culture.

❖ ❖ ❖

The Orthodox Church was virtually immune from the Mongol terror. As was their habit, the Mongols permitted religious orders to function unmolested. Religious leaders of all beliefs were welcomed by the Golden Horde. By royal charter, the Orthodox Church was exempt from taxation and received the khan's protection in return for the promise to pray for the khan and his family. It is ironic that the same period in which the Russian people suffered their worst oppression under the Mongol yoke was also the so-called Golden Age of the Orthodox Church. With Mongol approval, new monasteries were built and existing ones were expanded to such proportions that the monks could no longer till their own soil and had to hire peasants as laborers. The power and wealth of the Church rose to new heights while the majority of the people were driven into poverty, despair, and subjugation.

In 1272 the khan appointed Yaroslav's brother, Basil, to the rapidly weakening position of grand prince. During the next three decades, various princes who claimed a right to the throne vied with one another to win favor with the Mongols. The leading contestants in this spectacle were Alexander Nevsky's sons, Demetrius and Andrey. They not only challenged Basil, they also quarreled among themselves. Meanwhile, the Mongols played all sides, accepting gifts from each claimant and supplying troops to anyone who could afford to pay. From Basil's death in 1276 until 1304, the two brothers alternately held the title of grand prince, and in separate campaigns each led Russian armies in fending off invasions from Sweden, in 1293 and 1301.

While his older siblings warred over the title of grand prince, Alexander's youngest son, Daniel, was founding a dynasty that would endure longer than those of Kiev and Vladimir. Daniel was only 2 years old when his father died in 1263, but according to custom he was entitled to share in his father's legacy. Because he was the youngest son and had little clout, he was given the title of prince of Moscow, which was an insignificant small town that neither his brothers nor his uncles wanted. Because they considered his holdings unimportant, Daniel was left in peace for years while his uncles and brothers wrestled over the throne in Vladimir. Eventually, under Daniel's enlightened leadership, Moscow grew into a thriving, prosperous town, and the surrounding principality flourished as farmers migrated there to seek reprieve from the princely wars and a chance to till the land in peace. Moscow's merchants prospered and its bustling economy attracted traders from throughout Russia.

When Daniel died in 1303, his son Yuri succeeded him as prince of Moscow. Unlike his father, whose concerns were largely parochial, Yuri was interested in the wider scope of Russian political activity. He planned to expand his role and that of Moscow. The death of Grand Prince Andrey in 1304 afforded Yuri the opportunity to do so, but it also triggered a bloody feud over the throne.

Two men sought the title of grand prince in 1304. One was Yuri, the prince of Moscow, who, as Alexander Nevsky's grandson and only surviving direct descendant, claimed to be the sole rightful heir to Alexander's crown. The second, Michael, the prince of Tver, was a nephew of Alexander who based his claim on the fact that he was a member of the older generation. Michael argued that under established custom the older generation had first claim on the throne, preempting all challenges from succeeding generations. Both men traveled to Sarai to petition the khan for the appointment while their troops clashed in several battles that did little to alter the position of either camp concerning who should be grand prince. The dispute between Yuri and Michael would set the princely families of Moscow and Tver against each other for generations to come. The feud did not end until the last prince of Tver was killed during the reign of Ivan the Great toward the end of the 15th century.

In Sarai, the two Russian princes went about bribing as many Mongol officials as possible in their separate attempts to win the khan's favor. Michael, supported by the principalities of Vladimir and Novgorod, outspent Yuri and was given the Mongol charter to be grand prince. Disgruntled with the verdict,

Yuri immediately began plotting against Michael. Despite the fact that Novgorod had favored Michael, Yuri found many friends there. An ancient boundary dispute between Novgorod and Tver remained unresolved, and Yuri seized on this to win additional support. For several years a series of indecisive skirmishes were fought between the grand prince's army and Yuri's supporters, but the situation remained unchanged until 1312, when the khan of the Golden Horde died.

According to custom, Grand Prince Michael of Tver traveled to Sarai to pay homage to the new khan, Uzbek, and to have the charter appointing him grand prince renewed. Michael's appointment was renewed, but Uzbek persuaded him to stay in Sarai for an extended visit that ultimately lasted nearly a full year. Meanwhile, Yuri was gathering his forces and winning additional support.

The most influential of Yuri's new supporters was Peter, the metropolitan of the Russian Church. When Peter was first appointed by the patriarch of Constantinople and dispatched to Vladimir to assume his new post in 1310, Grand Prince Michael, who had proposed his own candidate to Constantinople, charged that Peter was unfit to be metropolitan. Cleared of the charge at a trial before an envoy of the patriarch, Peter had promptly taken up the cause of Michael's archrival, Yuri. The enormous power and wealth of the Church was now squarely behind Yuri's claim to the throne.

In Sarai, Michael complained to Uzbek about Yuri's conspiracies against him. The khan sent word to Novgorod, where Yuri had been appointed to the position of prince, that Yuri should come to Sarai to answer Michael's charges. Yuri arrived accompanied by several wealthy Novgorod merchants, each with a full money sack with which to buy influence at the Mongol court. The situation immediately turned against the serious and stoic Michael. The Mongols found Yuri to be a fun-loving man who hunted and feasted with his hosts. In fact, Yuri went further than any other Russian prince to nurture ties with the Mongols. He courted Uzbek's favorite sister, and when they wed, Uzbek, reluctant to have his sister appear in Novgorod married to simply another lowly prince, withdrew Michael's charter and appointed Yuri grand prince. Yuri returned home at the head of a Mongol army in 1318.

Conceding that his cause was lost, Michael relinquished all claims to the throne and returned to Tver, where he hoped to live out his days in peace. But Grand Prince Yuri, revealing a strong vengeful streak, attacked Tver without any provocation. Michael rallied his forces and surprisingly defeated Yuri's Mongols, capturing both the Mongol general and Yuri's wife. Although he is said to have treated his two important prisoners with great courtesy and care, Yuri's wife, the khan's sister, died while in Michael's custody.

When word of his sister's death reach the khan, it carried Yuri's charge that Michael had poisoned her. Uzbek summoned both princes to Sarai to hear the case against Michael. Once again, Yuri was welcomed as a companion and feted in the capital of the Golden Horde while Michael was treated like the outsider that he was. After a brief trial, Michael was found guilty and sentenced to death. He met a humiliating end, forced to walk for weeks behind a large Mongol hunting party in which Yuri rode as an equal. Choking from the dust of the thousands of horses and hundreds of wagons that preceded him, Michael, the former grand prince of Russia, trudged along carrying a large, heavy wooden frame that was bound to his head and wrists. Finally, after weeks of this punishment, he was pushed to the ground and trampled to death.

But matters rapidly worsened for the new grand prince as well. In return for his appointment to the crown, Yuri had pledged to Uzbek the timely payment of sharply increased tributes and taxes from the Russian principalities in his realm. Resentment against Yuri among the general population in northern Russia escalated as the Mongols' assessments multiplied. The grand prince was the chief tax collector for the Golden Horde, having responsibility for receiving the taxes and tributes from all other Russian princes. He was also the sole Russian ambassador to the khan. As such, he was the only Russian prince authorized to "know the Horde," which meant he had direct access to the khan and could appeal to him for military and political support. In practice, however, the khan's support usually proved to be unreliable, as when Uzbek abruptly withdrew his backing from Michael when Yuri wedded his sister. During this period, many Russians, nobles and commoners alike, viewed their grand prince more as a representative of the Mongol invaders than as the Russian monarch. This was especially true of Yuri, who not only married a Mongol but in many ways appeared to have become more Mongol than Russian.

Resentment against prohibitive taxes provoked military challenges to Yuri's title, as did the estrangement of Tver's princely family because of Michael's execution. Consequently, Novgorod was alternately defended when it was attacked by invaders and suppressed when it rebelled against higher taxes. Because of its remoteness from the Golden Horde, and because of the natural defenses afforded by its vast marshes, Novgorod was never subdued by the Mongols. Its citizens actually submitted to Mongol taxation voluntarily because Alexander Nevsky had persuaded them that acquiescence would prevent a full-scale Mongol invasion, with all the terror and bloodshed that entailed.

Hence, Novgorod's obligation to pay Mongol taxes and tribute was always tenuous and not infrequently resisted by force.

In Tver, Michael's son Dmitri, whose anger over his father's humiliation and murder earned him the sobriquet Dmitri of the Terrible Eyes, conspired continuously against the grand prince. Dmitri journeyed to Sarai to pay homage to Uzbek and to accept his charter as prince of Tver. While there, he filled the khan's head with stories about Yuri's injustices to his people and innuendos that the grand prince was withholding large sums of tax money from the Mongols. The suggestion that Yuri had embezzled tax money collected for the khan was the most significant, because the Mongols of the Golden Horde were no longer the fierce nomadic warriors who had swept in from Asia. They had acquired a new, opulent lifestyle that required vast sums of money to support. Sarai was no longer the small tent town that had sheltered the marauding Mongols between raids; instead, it had become a vast city housing thousands of citizens, and a vital center of commerce whose traders arrived from as far away as Venice. Money had replaced horses as the measure of Mongol status.

Uzbek had a reputation for vacillating and for being swayed by the last person to speak with him. Without hearing Yuri's defense against Dmitri's accusations, the khan not only gave Dmitri his charter as prince of Tver, he also named him grand prince. But Uzbek did not cancel Yuri's charter and in effect left Russia with two grand princes. Perhaps it was the Mongol leader's plan to goad the two into a war over the throne, after which the winner's loyalty to the Golden Horde would be unquestionable.

Although there may have been several small engagements, no significant military campaign developed between the two antagonists. Yuri decided to bide his time and win back Mongol support through diplomacy. Toward the end of 1324, Yuri journeyed to Sarai. It is unclear whether he was summoned by Uzbek or went of his own volition to seek an audience with the khan. In any event, Dmitri learned of Yuri's plans and attempted to prevent him from reaching Sarai. Yuri eluded Dmitri by taking a circuitous route that brought him to Sarai in early 1325. Furious over his failure to prevent Yuri from reaching his destination, Dmitri followed Yuri into Sarai. There, he confronted the rival grand prince, accused Yuri of murdering his father, and in a fit of rage thrust a dagger into Yuri's heart, killing him instantly.

The murder of a grand prince, even by another grand prince, demanded reprisal. Offended that Dmitri had dared to murder Yuri in the Mongol capital, Uzbek ordered Dmitri's arrest. Detained for a year, Dmitri finally met the same fate as his father under the hoofs of Mongol horses.

It was a vital Mongol interest that Russia have a strong grand prince to collect taxes and maintain order, so when Dmitri's younger brother Alexander arrived in Sarai in 1326 to claim the charter of prince of Tver, the khan also gave him the charter of grand prince. Alexander proved to be totally unsuited for either title. Within two years he had lost control of all the other Russian principalities and was even incapable of putting down an uprising against the Mongol tax collectors in his own capital. Unable to maintain control, Alexander fled into exile in Lithuania rather than face the wrath of the Mongols.

The Mongols required a grand prince who was strong enough to force the Russians to pay their assigned taxes and tribute, faithful in turning in to his masters the money he had collected, and loyal in performing the other duties and tasks assigned to him. They would find such a leader in Yuri's younger brother Ivan, who had succeeded him as prince of Moscow.

CHAPTER 9

THE RISE OF MOSCOW

IVAN I BECAME KNOWN TO HIS SUBJECTS as the "moneybag" because of his talent for amassing great wealth and using it to expand his territorial holdings; the prince also wore a sizable moneybag around his middle. According to legend, as he walked the streets of Moscow he would thrust his hands into the moneybag and distribute coins to the poor. Obviously, Ivan was extremely popular with the lower classes of his capital. His genius with money and his willingness to cooperate were precisely the qualities the Mongols sought in a vassal grand prince.

Ivan, who had been governing in Moscow since Yuri's death, quickly earned a reputation as an industrious, peaceful, and benevolent ruler. Peter, the metropolitan of the Russian Orthodox Church who had faced down false charges leveled against him by Grand Prince Michael, viewed Ivan as a close friend and advisor. Together they erected countless churches in Moscow and its territories, including the first brick church in Russia and the magnificent stone Cathedral of the Assumption. Ivan encircled his capital with a strong oak wall, forming a fortress called a kremlin. In creating this sanctuary, Ivan laid the groundwork that enabled Peter's successor, Theognostus, to move the seat of the Church from Vladimir to the well-protected Moscow in 1326. Thus, well before Moscow became the seat of political power in Russia, it was the center of the Orthodox Church, a far greater and more influential authority than the princely governments.

Ivan pursued with greater vigor his predecessor's policy of expanding Moscow's princely holdings. He loaned money to other princes, taking in return what amounted to mortgages on towns and villages within their realms. When the loans could not be repaid, the mortgages were called in and the territories were annexed as part of Moscow's princely domain. Through this strategy and similar ones, the tiny principality of Moscow gradually grew in size and importance.

With Novgorod and Tver in open rebellion against the Mongols, Uzbek, the supreme khan, summoned the prince of Moscow for help. Ivan had already petitioned the khan for the title of grand prince, so when the summons came from Sarai, he knew the charter of grand prince would be discussed. Ivan agreed to lead a Mongol army of 50,000 warriors against Tver in return for the title of grand prince. Perhaps Ivan wanted to convince the khan of his loyalty, or perhaps he simply wanted to inform the other Russian princes that he was firmly in charge. Whatever his motive, Ivan led the Mongols and his own Moscovite troops against Tver, devastating the entire principality and driving Prince Michael into exile in Lithuania, where his father, the former grand prince Alexander, had fled in 1328. As promised, Ivan was rewarded with the charter of grand prince. With Ivan's appointment, the center of political authority in Russia was transferred from Vladimir to Moscow.

Moscow was first mentioned in the ancient chronicles of 1147, when it was little more than an obscure rural settlement; yet in less than 200 years, it had become the de facto capital of Russia, home to both the grand prince and the metropolitan of the Orthodox Church. Among those churchmen who now journeyed to Moscow seeking ratification of Church appointments was the archbishop of Novgorod. The archbishop's visit was significant because Novgorod, a political adversary of Moscow, viewed the new grand prince as an upstart who threatened Novgorod's stature as Russia's leading commercial center.

Ivan I's reign would be no less militaristic than his predecessor's. Lithuania's Grand Duke Gedimin, who had come to the throne in 1316 and would rule until 1341, harbored imperialist ambitions that posed a serious threat to Russia. In contrast to the fratricide and familial betrayal of Russian politics, Lithuania's was positively tranquil. Gedimin's expanding Baltic empire was free of Mongol influence and did not depend on Mongol military support for its sovereignty. Soon, Lithuania was courting several Russian provinces and cities on Russia's western border. Because Lithuania shared with the western Russian princes a hatred for the Mongols and the other Russian princes who served them so obediently, it held sway over such important Russian towns and provinces as Tver, Chernigov, and Smolensk, and even over wealthy and independent-minded Novgorod and Pskov. The latter had grown in size and wealth to the point where it was no longer subordinate to Novgorod, although it remained a close ally.

Grand Duke Gedimin persuaded the former Russian grand prince, Alexander of Tver, to return from Lithuania to Russia, where he was welcomed by the leaders of Pskov and appointed prince in defiance of Ivan and the Mongols. In 1336, Alexander journeyed to Sarai for a promised audience with Uzbek. The khan forgave Alexander's earlier transgressions and returned to him the principality of Tver. His archenemy's reinstatement as prince of Tver unsettled

Ivan, who now made a trip to the Golden Horde and convinced Uzbek, probably with the payment of huge bribes, to reverse his decision. Uzbek then summoned Alexander to Sarai, where he was murdered by the khan's agents.

The threatened Lithuanian expansion, and especially Lithuania's détente with Novgorod, which constantly sought to extricate itself from Mongol domination and from under Ivan's reliable tax collections, underscored the Mongols' dependency on Moscow. They increased their support for Ivan, who, under their aegis, made minor princes with small holdings subservient to him in exchange for protection from the Mongols. Ivan thereby filled the purses of his Mongol overlords and of the Moscow boyars', as well as his own, from the taxes he collected. Russian historians commonly credit Ivan with achieving four decades of relative immunity from Mongol aggression.

Ivan cemented his personal ties with the Mongols by forbidding the other Russian princes from having direct contact with them. Because the Golden Horde was primarily interested in receiving Russian taxes, and because Ivan was an extremely efficient tax collector, Uzbek did not interfere. As long as Ivan collected the taxes and turned over the correct amount to the Golden Horde, the Mongols cared little who ruled the individual Russian principalities. It was through this double-edged strategy of isolating the other princes from Uzbek, and of controlling tax revenues, that Ivan built Moscow into Russia's new center of power. And it was by their own negligence that the Mongols encouraged Moscow's growing influence, which would eventually unite all of Russia and result in the destruction of the Golden Horde.

❖   ❖   ❖

The tensions between Novgorod and Moscow increased as Moscow became an increasingly successful commercial rival of Novgorod, due in part to Ivan's alliance with the Mongol khan. Clashes between the two principalities occurred periodically until 1335, when Novgorod finally capitulated and recognized the authority of Grand Prince Ivan. According to one ancient chronicle, when Ivan subsequently visited Novgorod he was hailed as the secular head of the Russian people. Although the title would not be recognized officially for another 200 years, Ivan I was the first Russian grand prince to call himself "czar," the ruler "of all Russia."

In many respects the nation that evolved from Moscow was more a product of the Mongol Empire than a legacy of Kievan Rus. From the Golden Horde Ivan and his successors learned methods of governing that were unheard of in Russia before the Mongol invasion. Among these methods were the universal taxation of all citizens, the periodic population census on which tax levies were based, the concept of universal service to the state, and, perhaps most important, the adoption of a system of land ownership in which the ruler was the principal landowner. Before the Mongols came to Russia, a Russian prince had been recognized as a ruler who also owned land on which people were paid to work. Under the Mongols, the princes, and ultimately the grand prince, became the owners of all the land. The principle of private property all but vanished under Mongol influence. Just as the Slav tribes had absorbed and Slavicized the customs and mores of earlier invaders, so too did the Russians absorb and make their own many of the governmental practices of the Mongols. Easily the most significant of these practices was the recognition of the head of state as the supreme autocratic ruler.

Ivan realized that earlier attempts to establish family dynasties had foundered on the question of succession. Even Yaroslav the Wise had erred in the manner in which he divided his realm among his heirs. In an effort to prevent a recurrence of previous failures, Ivan devised a system of rotation that would allow each of his sons to share in Moscow's wealth while his eldest son, Simeon, inherited the throne of grand prince. Simeon would also become the head of the family and thus responsible for the well-being of his mother, brothers, and sisters. Although each family member was given an inheritance of property within the Moscow principality, the right to dispose of that property was limited because the property was a component of the family's total holdings, which were the entire principality. According to Ivan's testament, should the principality be reduced in size, each family member's property would be reduced proportionately, so that each retained the same percentage of the total territory held by the family as a whole.

To ensure that his family's good relationship with the Mongols continued after his death, Ivan made all three of his sons—Simeon, Ivan, and Andrey—equal partners in collecting and paying the taxes that the Mongols had imposed. After their father's death, the three brothers would come to an agreement concerning their land holdings and official responsibilities that would further Ivan's goals of maintaining peace among his heirs and of continuing Moscow's dominance over the other Russian principalities. In their agreement, Prince Ivan and Prince Andrey swore to serve Grand Prince Simeon and to refuse granting asylum to any nobles who revolted against the grand prince. For his part, Simeon swore to abide by the apportionment of family wealth and holdings that had been set down in their father's testament.

When Ivan died in 1340 or 1341 (the date is in dispute), he was 50 years old. At about the same time, Uzbek, the most powerful of the khans of the Golden Horde, died, as did Gedimin. The deceased grand duke of Lithuania had annexed so much Russian territory that at the time of his death he ruled almost as many Russians as the grand prince "of all Russia."

Ivan's son Simeon the Proud, who would also call himself grand prince of all Russia, journeyed to the Golden Horde to have his inheritance confirmed by the khan. Because Simeon espoused his father's cooperative attitude, the new khan of the Golden Horde, Chanibek, gladly passed the charter to him. It was in the Mongols' best interest to have a single trusted Russian prince responsible for collecting taxes for them, instead of sending their own representatives into territories where Mongol tax collectors were regularly murdered by the oppressed Russians. During his reign as grand prince, Simeon traveled five times to Sarai to pay homage to the khan.

Simeon ruled at the pleasure of the khan for 12 years. He continued Ivan's policies, gradually expanding his territory and welcoming emigrants from other principalities and from the Mongol khanate that controlled most of what had originally been Kievan territory in southern Russia. Moscow's expanding population comprised mostly farmers who quickly accepted the grand prince's invitation to convert unused land into large tracts of tilled farmland that eventually produced abundant quantities of food. This migration, which was generally to the north and northeast, away from the Mongol raiders, usually included entire families who traveled together, sometimes, even the inhabitants of entire villages. As long as a man was free of debt, he could move his family wherever he wished.

The migrants would find land that suited them and rent it from the local prince. They would then build homes, usually small log structures, and allot each family a small plot of land on which to grow its own food. The bulk of the land was worked collectively, with each family assigned a section and an equivalent portion of the total rent. All decisions were made in meetings that everyone attended. Every man had a voice in how the village was run, and issues were usually resolved by unanimous consent. The meetings were chaired by an elder who was elected to serve as the headman. If the rent was paid on schedule, the princely landlords rarely interfered with the democratic management of the agricultural villages of northern Russia.

Foodstuffs, especially grain, were important to the grand prince because they were the only reliable weapon he had to keep the always rebellious and freedom-minded citizens of Novgorod in line. Novgorod had become enormously wealthy by assessing tariffs on goods passing through its ports, through the acumen of its own merchants as international traders, and through its huge fur industry. However, it lacked sufficient arable land to feed its own population, and thus was dependent on outsiders for the bulk of its grain. Because Novgorod's northern European neighbors and trading partners were themselves habitually short of grain, the principality had to rely on other Russian principalities to its south, in what is now known as central Russia, for its life-supporting grain. This dependency required that Novgorod maintain friendly relations with the rest of Russia, and at least a modicum of loyalty to the Russian grand prince. As the power of the grand prince in Moscow increased, so too did Novgorod's dependency on his goodwill. It was not a situation that cheered the hearts of the independent-minded citizens of Novgorod, many of whom participated in the election of their own officials and owed allegiance to no prince, but they had little choice if they were to avoid the hardship of food shortages.

Simeon relied primarily on his family's wealth to purchase, or acquire through the granting of mortgages, numerous villages and large tracts of land from the other princes. As the sole tax collector for the Mongols, he was able to siphon off a portion of the taxes he received from the other princes to fatten Moscow's treasury, thereby obtaining additional funds to finance his acquisitions. Moscow's wealth was further augmented by the lively traffic of merchants who sought the grand prince's protection for their business enterprises. Like his father, Simeon recognized that military confrontation with other Russian princes provided the Mongols an excuse to interfere in the country's internal affairs and put at risk the khan's support for Moscow. Instead, Simeon concentrated on the peaceful acquisition of territory and enjoyed a relatively tranquil reign. The exception was when he covertly encouraged disharmony within Tver's large princely family, which remained a source of potential opposition to Moscow.

Grand Prince Simeon continued the close relationship that Ivan had established with the metropolitan of the Orthodox Church. Just as Peter and Theognostus had been close advisors to Ivan, Alexis, the Moscow metropolitan during Simeon's reign and an enthusiastic advocate of a unified Russia, was an intimate of Simeon. This close relationship helped to sustain Moscow's predominance over all other Russian cities.

When he died in 1353, Simeon was only 36 years old. His death at such a young age is cloaked in mystery, but its cause was probably the plague that was devastating Europe during the 14th century. In his testament, Simeon had instructed his heirs to continue to rely on the advice of Metropolitan Alexis.

Simeon had died childless, leaving his possessions to his widow. With Russia not yet ready for a woman ruler, the title of grand prince passed to Simeon's brother, Ivan.

The new grand prince's demeanor earned him the sobriquet Ivan the Meek, although he is generally known as Ivan II. Confirmed in his position by the Mongol khan, Ivan II devoted much of his reign to consolidating the greatly expanded holdings he inherited from his brother. He contributed little in the way of expansion of Moscow's territory, but he did lessen the hostility between Moscow and the other principalities.

Ivan I had created for his youngest son, Andrey, a small principality southwest of Moscow called Serpukhov. When Andrey died in 1353, his estates went to his son Vladimir. Vladimir, as his father before him, remained loyal to the grand prince, effectively avoiding the historical conflict between brothers and uncles for the coveted title of grand prince.

While Simeon and Ivan II appeared to be loyal to their Mongol masters, meticulously accounting for the taxes and tribute demanded by the khan, they both covertly plotted to win Russia's independence from the Golden Horde. Agreeing with Simeon's firm conviction that Russia would regain its autonomy only when the princes recognized a strong central authority, Ivan II continued the consolidation of smaller principalities. It was, he claimed, only by obeying the grand prince and ending the fighting among themselves that Russians could "free themselves" from the control of the Mongols.

Perhaps the most important event of Ivan II's reign was one over which he had no control. The Mongol empire was experiencing the same sort of fratricide and civil war that had plagued the Russian principalities. In 1357, the Golden Horde was locked in a bloody conflict over who would be the khan and over the allocation of Mongol territories. The unrest would persist for 20 years, during which time nearly two dozen men would claim the right to sit on the throne of the khan. This internal turmoil diminished the power and prestige of the Golden Horde immeasurably. Although the Russian grand prince continued to pay taxes and tribute, the Mongols were gradually losing their hold on Russia.

When Ivan II died in 1359, he bequeathed to his sons the same division of responsibilities that had been established by his father. Although his eldest son, Dmitri, was only 9 years old at the time, Ivan II left him the Moscow sector that Ivan I had originally ceded to Simeon, thereby making the boy heir to the title of grand prince. Ivan II's youngest son, Ivan, received the original share that the late grand prince himself had inherited from his father. In Ivan II's testament, Vladimir, the son of Ivan I's youngest son Andrey, was reconfirmed as prince of Serpukhov. Until the new grand prince came of age, Metropolitan Alexis would act as regent for the boy and in effect be the actual ruler of Moscow. Alexis would pursue vigorously every opportunity to weld the Russian principalities into a unified nation.

Grand Prince Dmitri Donski

CHAPTER 10

DMITRI AND THE GREAT CRUSADE

DMITRI IVANOVICH OF MOSCOW, IVAN II'S ELDEST SON, governed for 30 years as grand prince and is revered as a true Russian hero. He inherited the throne as a young boy at a time when the Mongol invaders, who were the real rulers of Russia, were experiencing severe internal strife over leadership of the Golden Horde. It was a period of waning Mongol power, but also a time of increasing growth and power for another adversary, Lithuania. Eventually, Dmitri dealt with both of these antagonists; however, his first major crisis came from another Russian prince, his cousin Dmitri of Suzdal.

Even before the youthful Dmitri of Moscow could journey to Sarai to receive the charter of grand prince, Dmitri of Suzdal (located northeast of Moscow), who was a descendant of Grand Prince Vsevolod III and claimed a senior right to the title of grand prince, obtained in 1359 a charter from one of two competing khans of the Golden Horde. The Golden Horde was then locked in a chaotic domestic struggle for power between a host of claimants to the throne of Sarai. One early victor of these civil wars was Berdibek, who reputedly murdered 12 of his own brothers in his quest to be khan of the Golden Horde. The Mongols had sunk into the same quagmire of fratricide and treachery that the Russian princes had wallowed in for centuries.

Pressing his own claim to the title, Dmitri of Moscow in 1365 received a charter from the competing khan and hastily raised an army to march on Vladimir, where Dmitri of Suzdal had seated himself as grand prince. The prince of Suzdal's scheme to usurp the title of grand prince was doomed from the start. Princes, nobles, and wealthy merchants throughout Russia rallied to support Dmitri of Moscow. The rogue prince's own brother denounced his disloyalty to the son of Ivan II. Moscow's financial strength, its ability to satisfy the Mongol's demands, and the stability it had brought to Russian politics and commerce earned the young grand prince widespread support. Even many Suzdal nobles urged their prince to step down. Except for a handful of families who remained habitually hostile to the princes of Moscow, Dmitri of Suzdal enjoyed little support for his claim to be grand prince.

Leading a large military force, the boy grand prince rode into Vladimir with such strength that Dmitri of Suzdal quickly realized his cause was lost and renounced his claim to the throne in 1365. As an indication of the reconciliation between these rivals for the throne, Grand Prince Dmitri of Moscow later married a daughter of the prince of Suzdal. Metropolitan Alexis continued to be influential in Moscow's affairs. With his guidance, additional territories were brought directly under Moscow's control, usually through the proven method of outright purchase from impoverished princes. In 1367, undoubtedly preparing for the time when he would refuse to pay the Mongol tribute, Dmitri replaced Moscow's old wooden fortress walls with walls of stone, making the city virtually impregnable.

Novgorod and Tver continued to beleaguer the new grand prince as they had earlier ones. Michael of Tver, the son of Alexander of Tver, was determined to avenge his father's murder by the Mongols, who had acted at the instigation of Ivan I of Moscow. Also in 1367, Michael obtained a charter to the title of grand prince from one of the many successive khans of the Golden Horde. He then negotiated an agreement with his brother-in-law, Olgerd of Lithuania, who then invaded Moscow's territory and laid siege to the city in 1368. Dmitri's newly constructed stone walls kept the Lithuanian forces outside of the capital and the invaders were eventually driven off. Olgerd would make another abortive assault against Moscow in 1372, with even less success.

After Dmitri had stymied the first Lithuanian incursion, he assembled an army conscripted from several loyal principalities and retaliated against the rebellious Michael by attacking Tver and burning much of the city. Finally, in 1375, Michael and Dmitri reached a peaceful accord. Michael recognized Dmitri's "seniority" and his right to be grand prince, and pledged that Tver would sever its military alliances with both the Lithuanians and the Mongols. Olgerd's death two years later ignited an internal struggle for his throne, temporarily removing the Lithuanian threat to Moscow.

Dissenting Russian principalities continued to mount persistent but scattered resistance to Moscow's authority, notably Ryazan, whose Prince Oleg was driven from his capital by Dmitri's Muscovite army. In 1375, Dmitri replaced Oleg with a prince loyal to Moscow. He also replaced the princes of Galicia and Starodub, and forced the powerful prince of Rostov to submit to Moscow's authority. During his tenure, Dmitri expanded the authority of the grand prince to include more Russian principalities than ever before.

Dmitri's surprisingly successful Tver campaign, which he had waged with a coalition force, did not go unnoticed by Khan Mamai, the Golden Horde's powerful new leader, who recognized this development as a serious threat to the Mongol's continued jurisdiction over the Russians. The new ruler of the Golden Horde had reason to be concerned. In the past, the Mongols had relied on the conflicts between the princes of Russia to help maintain control over them; Dmitri's ability to build a coalition of Russian princes had the potential to change that. In addition to the peace treaty between Tver and Moscow, another, more significant pact had been signed by a number of Russian princes, including Michael of Tver, in which for the first time the princes swore to defend each other if any was attacked. The mutual defense treaty specifically named the Mongols as a potential aggressor, and promised support for the prince of Moscow should he decide to go to war against the Golden Horde. This milestone agreement marked a new, unified approach of the Russians in their dealings with the Mongol overlords.

Several Mongol princes tested the new alliance by attacking and sacking several Russian cities, including Nizhni Novgorod in the principality of Ryazan in 1375. Dmitri immediately responded, dispatching a Russian force that sacked and burned several Mongol villages. A series of retaliatory skirmishes and attacks escalated in intensity until Mamai decided he had to check the Russians' growing power or risk forfeiting the handsome tribute the Russians were paying. Mamai determined to break the Russian alliance and bring Moscow back into line. In 1378, he sent a great army into Ryazan with the intention of drawing the Russians into a large, open battle in which he anticipated destroying the Moscow-led coalition.

When Dmitri learned of the invasion, he quickly organized and led a Russian force into the small city of Ryazan. The two armies met in August 1378, near Ryazan on the Vozha River. The Mongols surveyed their opponents from the opposite shore, and, confident of victory, made the dangerous decision to cross the river to meet the Russians. Dmitri held his army in readiness, waiting until the Mongols reached shore before attacking in full fury. After three Russian assaults, the Mongol force finally broke and was soundly defeated. Mongol horsemen by the hundreds drowned trying to escape across the river or were stampeded into scattered flight. As the Mongols fled the battlefield, Dmitri triumphantly proclaimed to his troops, "Their time is past—God is now with us!"

The rout at Ryazan was a grievous loss for the Mongols. It was the first chink in the armor of invincibility that they had maintained during their dominance of the Russian principalities. Emboldened by his resounding victory, Grand Prince Dmitri decreased the amount of tribute he sent to Sarai. The Mongols' military debacle and lost tribute fostered a major confrontation between Mamai and Dmitri; the golden Horde had to reestablish its dominion over Moscow or lose control of all of Russia.

Mamai prepared for his revenge against Dmitri by first forming an alliance with Moscow's old enemy, Lithuania. The civil unrest in Lithuania had ended when Prince Yagailo ascended the throne and renewed the old expansionist ambitions against Russia in 1377. Dmitri responded by sending envoys through-out Russia, calling for a joint defense against the coming Mongol and Lithu-anian invasion. Many principalities sent troops to support the grand prince, but Tver, Novgorod, and Pskov reneged on their treaty obligations and withheld their support, probably believing it was unlikely that Dmitri could defeat a concentrated, Mongol-led army. Oleg, who had been reinstated as prince of Ryazan, again turned traitor and joined forces with the Mongols and the Lithuanians.

Dmitri made a pilgrimage to Sergius of Radonezh, a revered holy man, to seek his blessing and guidance for the coming battle. Sergius, who would later become St. Sergius, one of the Russian Orthodox Church's most beloved saints, encouraged the grand prince by telling him that it was his duty to protect Christians against the infidel Mongols: "With God's help you shall defeat them." Dmitri returned to Moscow and called for a holy crusade against the Mongols, using the power of the church to rally unprecedented support from the princes of Russia.

Mamai's campaign was built around a two-pronged pincer attack against the Russian army. He marched north with a force estimated at between 150,000 and 200,000 men, mainly Mongols from the Golden Horde and the Crimea, along with Turks, Armenians, and warriors from various other tribes that were obedient to the khan. Prince Yagailo advanced from the west with a large Lithuanian army. Between the two invading forces was Dmitri's army, which, according to some Russian chroniclers, numbered 200,000, but more likely included 70,000 to 80,000 men.

Grand Prince Dmitri led his army south in a maneuver designed to prevent the Mongol and Lithuanian armies from linking up and encircling him. He wanted to face each of these powerful forces individually, and not have to combat them at their peak strength. On September 6, 1380, the Russian army halted on the banks of the upper Don River. Dmitri's spies reported that Mamai had encamped near a large meadow not far from the opposite shore. Unsure of what to do, Dmitri called a war council to decide whether to wait for the Mongols to cross the river, as he had done in 1378, or ford the river and attack before the advancing Lithuanians arrived.

Several princes and military leaders feared having the river at their back in the event that their forces were overrun by the Mongols. The sight of drowning Mongols trying to flee across the Vozha River was still vivid in their memories. Dmitri favored crossing the river and attacking the Mongols while they were still encamped. The council was still in progress when a courier arrived from the Monastery of the Holy Trinity with a message from the holy man Sergius. "My Lord," the message began, "do not hesitate. March boldly on against the fierce enemy. Fear nothing, for God will help you." Thus inspired, the Russians crossed the Don and deployed themselves in positions where they were protected from encirclement on two sides by the river and one of its tributaries. Of course, that protection also served as a barrier to escape should the Mongols prove too difficult to beat.

The opposing armies were now separated by a great prairie-like plain known as the Kulikovo, or Field of Snipes. The flat, open terrain was intersected by numerous rock-bedded streams that made it difficult for the Mongol horsemen to maneuver. Dmitri picked the plain as the site for the battle. It was well chosen, for the terrain and the two rivers deprived the Mongols of their most effective tactic, circling around an enemy force and attacking it from all sides at once.

At six o'clock on the morning of September 8, 1380, the Mongol host appeared across the plain in full battle array. The Russian army, consisting mostly of infantry formations, drew up in a tight battle configuration that was organized into right, left, and center divisions. To the rear of the left division were the reserves. Concealed in a wooded area at the far left was a large cavalry detachment commanded by Prince Vladimir of Serpukhov, the loyal cousin of the grand prince.

When his forces were in place, Mamai, who directed the battle from a nearby hilltop, signaled for the first wave of Mongol horsemen to sweep down on the Russians, who broke the charge thanks to the strong resistance of the infantry formations. The morning quiet continued to be shattered by the sound of thousands of hooves, the clash of weapons, and the shrill, ear-piercing screams of successive waves of Mongol horsemen; still, the Russian infantrymen held their ground. After several hours of relentless pressure, the Russian center began to give way. The Mongols, sensing a weakness in the Russian line, concentrated their efforts at breaking through the middle. Finally they were successful, and the Russian infantry in the center formation fell back before the Mongol horsemen, whose frenzied mounts trampled dead and wounded Russians and Mongols alike. By then, however, both the Russians and the Mongols were exhibiting signs of exhaustion.

At precisely the right moment, when exhaustion weighed most heavily on them, the Mongol's apparent victory was snatched away when fresh cavalry troops led by Prince Vladimir burst from the woods and stormed the Mongol rear. The Russian infantry reserves were then brought up, and the right and left flanking divisions turned inward toward the center and attacked. The huge Mongol force found itself surrounded by Russians, most of whom had been held in reserve during the early fighting and were fresh for the battle.

Mamai watched in disbelief as the grassy fields of Kulikovo were turned to mud and the streams transformed into bright red rivers by the blood of thousands of men and horses. Incredibly, hundreds, and ultimately thousands of Mongols extracted themselves from the trap and escaped to the south. Realizing the battle was lost, the khan joined his troops and fled the carnage. His Lithuanian allies were still two day's march from Kulikovo when they learned of the Mongol defeat. Prince Yagailo turned around and went home without attempting any contact with either the Russians or the Mongols.

The Battle of Kulikovo was without doubt the bloodiest ever fought in Russia until that time. Approximately half the men who took part in the battle perished in the fighting. A large number of Russian princes and noblemen were lost that day, and it took the Russians nearly a week to bury their dead. Unlike his opposite number, Grand Prince Dmitri had taken an active role in the fighting, and when it was over he could not be found and was feared dead. After a frantic search, he was discovered under a pile of dead soldiers. Dmitri's armor was badly beaten, and he had received several severe wounds from which he would never completely recover.

As word of the great victory over the previously invincible Mongols spread throughout Russia, it was met with skepticism. When troops returned to confirm the rumors, there was widespread rejoicing as many Russians saw in the triumph the end of Mongol domination. Unfortunately, Kulikovo was a Pyrrhic victory. The Russian forces were too badly decimated to solidify their victory by tracking down the remnants of Mamai's army, or even the khan himself. A sizable number of the khan's forces thus were allowed to escape.

Dmitri returned to Moscow and was hailed as a hero. He was given the surname "Donski," after the Don River, the scene of his stunning victory. Vladimir of Serpukhov was thereafter known as Vladimir the Brave. Yet, although Kulikovo was a great victory, its effect proved to be short-lived. As soon as the Mongol yoke had seemed to lift, several of the Russian princes fell into their old ways, quarreling and fighting with one another. More ominously, the Mongols quickly began planning their revenge for the humiliation they had suffered at the hands of the prince of Moscow. The yoke could not be lifted so easily.

Mamai returned to Sarai and immediately began recruiting another army to invade Russia, but his defeat at Kulikovo spelled his own doom. Soon after he returned to his capital, a revolt ended with Mamai's departure, and the title of khan of the Golden Horde passed to Tokhtamych, a vassal of the great Turko-Mongol warrior Tamerlane (Timur the Lame). Strengthened by the patronage of Tamerlane, Tokhtamych rebuilt the army of the Golden Horde and determined to reestablish dominion over Russia and resume collecting taxes and tribute.

In 1382, the Golden Horde's new army swept through central Russia and attacked Moscow. Helpless against this new Mongol onslaught, and unable to defend his capital, Dmitri retreated northward and sought help from other princes in order to build a new army. Meanwhile, Moscow was surrounded and subjected to merciless assaults by the Mongols; the stone walls protected the city proper until a group of traitorous Russians threw open the gates. Mongols poured in, torching the city and slaughtering thousands of its citizens in a vengeful blood lust.

When the grand prince returned to his capital, he was shocked and saddened by the devastation he found. Weeping openly before the troops that had accompanied his return, Dmitri blamed himself for Moscow's destruction, saying that "our fathers" were happier never having defeated the Mongols. Because his victory over the Golden Horde had demanded retaliation, Moscow had been exposed to unthinkable barbarity.

Mongol control over Moscow was reestablished, and the payment of tribute and taxes to the khan was resumed. Although Dmitri's victory on the fields of Kulikovo had failed to end the Mongols' domination, it did diminish their influence on the Russians by shattering the aura of invincibility that the Mongols had previously enjoyed.

Resigned to his role as a vassal of the Golden Horde, Dmitri spent the remaining seven years of his reign consolidating his position as grand prince. He especially brought pressure to bear on the two most troublesome Russian principalities, Tver and Ryazan. He also worked diligently to rebuild Moscow's economy. In 1389, Dmitri Donski, the grand prince of Russia and hero of Kulikovo, died in his sleep at the age of 39. He was succeeded by his eldest son, Basil.

Basil I resumed the policy of expanding Moscow's holdings. During his reign, he annexed several principalities, most notably Nizhni Novgorod in 1392–1393, which gave Moscow its first foothold in the central Volga region. The growing influence and power of the Moscow grand prince was evident in the manner in which the Nizhni Novgorod boyars responded to Basil's imminent annexation of their principality. When the prince of Nizhni Novgorod made clear his determination to oppose the annexation, he could not rally his own nobles to his cause. Instead, they informed him that they proposed to recognize Basil's authority. The prince was forced to yield because he was powerless to oppose the grand prince without their backing. This would not be the last time that local nobles abandoned their prince in favor of the grand prince, and it presaged the gradual consolidation of the Russian principalities into one unified nation under the rule of the grand prince of Moscow.

❖ ❖ ❖

Basil proved to be a cautious, intelligent, and strong leader who inherited his father's determination to resist the Mongols. In 1395 a Mongol army, this time led by the widely feared Tamerlane, invaded Russia again. To meet this threat, Basil marched south with a large army conscripted from his principalities. The Russians camped along the banks of the Oka River and waited for their enemy. For reasons unrelated to the deployment of the Russian army, Tamerlane withdrew before reaching the Oka. Emboldened by what he and his advisors mistook for Mongol hesitancy to meet him in battle, Basil soon stopped paying the hated taxes.

Seeking to secure his eastern border, in 1400 Basil sent an army into the territory of the Volga Bulgars, laying to waste many of their towns, including their capital, Great Bulgar. Mindful that the Mongols remained a threat from the south and east, Grand Prince Basil sought a way to defuse the hostility that existed in the west between Moscow and Lithuania. One major step that he took was to merge the two ruling families by marrying Sophie, the daughter of Vitovt, the grand prince of Lithuania in 1391. Another was to settle the dispute over the location of the border separating Russia and Lithuania. The two grand princes met in 1408 and agreed to establish the border along the Ugra River, which was perilously close to Moscow.

Also in 1408, a Mongol army led by Edyzhei, the vizier of the Golden Horde, pretended to march to war with Lithuania when it suddenly veered north and, without warning, invaded Moscow's territory. The Mongols drove to the gates of the city, laying waste to the countryside as they went. Edyzhei besieged Moscow for a month until he was finally enticed to withdraw by the payment of a large sum and Basil's promise to resume paying the Golden Horde's taxes. Unknown to Basil, the vizier probably would have withdrawn without the bribe because he had just received word that a violent revolt had begun among the Golden Horde and that his troops were badly needed by the khan. In the end, Basil resigned himself to maintaining a policy of appeasement toward the Golden Horde, much as his father had done toward the end of his reign.

Around this time, a new breed of Russians began to appear. Mostly farmers, these Russians migrated back onto the vast steppes that their ancestors had fled generations before, to reclaim the rich productive land that seemed to stretch endlessly. The steppes were now ungoverned territory; Poland and the Golden Horde each claimed portions of it. Periodically, the Mongols would raid across the steppes, taking booty and slaves, but they did not stay to rule. Soon, the Russian farmers settled around tiny villages that were sprouting in isolated areas and organized themselves to drive away the Mongols and other bands of raiders. The Russians of the steppes became known as Cossacks, or "men of the free lance," meaning they owed allegiance to no ruler. The Cossacks fought off Mongol armies when they could; if the enemy force was too large, they harassed it, stealing horses and killing small groups of invaders who became separated from the main body. The Cossacks saw themselves as faithful followers of the Orthodox faith, defending Christianity againt the Asian infidels. Eventually, as the Cossacks grew in number, they became guardians of Russia's southern borders, and later, protectors of the Russian monarch.

When Basil I died in 1425, he bequeathed the title of grand prince and all his holdings to his 10-year-old son, who became Basil II. Because the boy was too young to govern, a regency was established under Metropolitan Photius, who proved to be a capable ruler. The stability that resulted from this peaceful transfer of power from father to son helped Basil II win the support of his father's boyars and subject princes. The only opposition to the young grand prince and to the regency came from young Basil's uncle, Prince Yuri of Galitch, and Yuri's family. The support of the Moscow military establishment and of Basil's grandfather, Grand Prince Vitovt of Lithuania, would help to ensure the boy's accession. Nevertheless, the succession of Basil II provoked a bitter feud, resulting in a bloody civil war that wracked the princely family. Basil II's reign was critical for the establishment of a family dynasty in Moscow, one that would ensure the unimpeded transfer of the throne of the grand prince from father to son.

Prince Yuri challenged Basil's right to rule, claiming that as the younger brother of the dead grand prince, he was the rightful heir. There was some validity to this claim: under the old system of dynastic succession, which had been used for centuries in the Kievan State, the title of grand princes had been passed from brother to brother, not from father to son. However, because recent grand princes had outlived their younger brothers, the succession had become patrimonial, from father to son. Basil I, who from his deathbed declared that his son, not his younger brother, should become grand prince, evidently had desired to formalize this new order of succession.

As was to be expected, Yuri went to the Golden Horde, in 1431, which itself had been greatly weakened by internal strife, and sought the khan's support for his claim. Young Basil's petition was presented to the khan by a Moscow boyar named Vsevolozhsky, who played to the khan's ego by conceding that Yuri's claim might be valid according to the antiquated custom, but reminded the mighty khan that he had the power to invalidate that ill-conceived practice. The khan agreed with Vsevolozhsky and gave the charter of grand prince to Basil II.

A furious Prince Yuri returned to Galitch, his principality, and mobilized a powerful force that attacked Moscow in 1433. After routing Basil's supporters, Yuri entered the city in triumph and, declared himself grand prince. However, Yuri found himself virtually without backing in the capital. There was hardly any support for him among the boyars, clergy, or citizens of Moscow, and Yuri soon recognized that he could not hold the throne for long under such conditions. In addition, boyars from throughout the territories ruled by Moscow were rallying to Basil's side, and a counterinvasion appeared imminent. Deferring to the country's mood, Yuri elected to step down and allowed Basil to return as grand prince.

No sooner had Yuri abdicated than his two sons, Basil the Squint-Eyed and Dmitri Shemiaka, persuaded him to change his mind. In 1434, Yuri again advanced on Moscow, but this time Basil's forces had secured their position, and Yuri met with a vigorous resistance. During the fighting, Yuri was killed. His death solidified Basil II's legitimate claim to the throne because even under the old system of succession the title of grand prince would now pass to the eldest son of the former grand prince. However, Yuri's sons continued their father's fight, determined to gain control of Moscow and claim the title for themselves.

The throne actually changed hands several times during the next few years as the bloody civil war raged. At one point in 1436, Basil the Squint-Eyed was taken prisoner by Basil II, who had him blinded, as was customary for hated adversaries. When Basil II was briefly imprisoned, Dmitri repaid his brother's mutilation by blinding the grand prince, who thereafter was known as Basil the Blind.

Eventually, Basil the Squint-Eyed was killed in battle, and his brother Dmitri was driven into exile in Novgorod, from where he conducted several ineffective forays into Moscow's territory. Dmitri met his end when one of Basil II's agents murdered him by poisoning his food in 1453.

The civil war with Yuri and his sons was only one of several important events that occurred during Basil II's 37-year reign. The Golden Horde, which had been greatly weakened by its own internal struggles for leadership, was breaking up into several separate kingdoms called khanates. One of these was the khanate of Kazan, established in 1437 by the Mongol leader Ulu-Mehmet after he was expelled from the Golden Horde following an unsuccessful coup. In 1445, Ulu-Mehmet invaded Moscow's territory in an attempt to persuade the grand prince to pledge loyalty to him and, more importantly, to convince him to pay the Mongol tribute to Kazan instead of to the Golden Horde. Basil, determined not to be drawn into the Mongols' affairs, called his army together and marched against the invaders. During the fighting, the blind grand prince fell into Mongol hands and was held as a prisoner. Ulu-Mehmet, hoping to cultivate Moscow as an ally against his Mongol opponents, had no desire to offend the grand prince's followers, and consequently Basil was treated well during his imprisonment. The grand prince was ransomed for a large sum and brought with him to Moscow a number of Mongol princes whom he had taken into his service.

Among the Mongols who joined Basil was Prince Kasim, a descendant of Genghis Khan. Basil rewarded Kasim's loyalty by giving him a town on the Oka River around which he could establish a Mongol khanate, Kasimov, that became a vassal state of Moscow.

The power pendulum that had long swung in the Mongols' direction was beginning to drift back toward the Russians. When Moscow was ruled by Prince Daniel, the youngest son of Alexander Nevsky and founder of the Moscow dynasty, the principality had occupied approximately 500 square miles. By the time Grand Prince Basil II died in 1462, Moscow governed an area larger than 15,000 square miles. The empire of the Golden Horde was toppled by the same kind of turmoil that had crippled Russia's growth during the preceding centuries: internal battles over who would inherit the throne. With a Mongol khanate established in Kazan on the Volga River, and another in the Crimea, the Mongols were no longer a unified force to be feared. Some Mongol armies began swearing allegiance to European monarchs, including the grand princes of Moscow and Lithuania, and fought against other Mongol armies from the various khanates. In 1452, Basil II ceased paying taxes and tributes to any Mongol authority. Moscow was finally independent of the Mongol overlords.

❖ ❖ ❖

Also during Basil's reign, the Orthodox Church claimed its independence from Constantinople. Byzantium, under siege from the powerful Turks, sought the help of the Catholic pope. Struggling for survival, the Orthodox leaders attended a meeting with Catholic Church leaders—the Council of Florence—in 1439. In return for the promise of armed intervention from the Catholic European kingdoms, the Greek Orthodox churchmen signed an agreement recognizing the supremacy of the pope. One of those at the meeting was the Russian metropolitan, Isidore, who by birth was a Greek. Isolated from the political and religious life of Constantinople, however, most Russians failed to appreciate the plight of the Greeks, who sought to save their Church from destruction at the hands of Islamic Turks from the Ottoman Empire. When Isidore returned to Moscow and offered a prayer for the pope, Basil had him arrested and imprisoned in a monastery. In 1443, a council of Russian churchmen elected Archbishop Iona of Ryazan metropolitan and voted to condemn the Council of Florence agreement.

By the time the Turks conquered Constantinople in 1453 and converted the revered Church of St. Sophia into a Muslim mosque, the Russian Orthodox Church had become totally independent of the Greek Orthodox Church. The separation of the two Churches and the fall of Constantinople, although contributing to Russia's freedom from foreign influences, also helped perpetuate its isolation from more advanced European neighbors.

❖ ❖ ❖

In 1456, Basil dealt a blow to Novgorod's independence. Citing the fact that Dmitri Shemiaka had been given sanctuary there after he and his brother failed to wrest the throne from Basil, the grand prince launched a campaign against Novgorod. The campaign ended with an agreement giving the grand prince unprecedented powers over what until then had been an independent state. Of greatest importance, the Novgorod veche was prohibited from issuing official documents without the grand prince's approval and signature. Novgorod was also required to deny entry into its territory to any prince who was hostile to Basil. This pact marked a major step toward Novgorod's ultimate incorporation into the realm of Moscow, which was finally accomplished by Basil II's son, Ivan.

Despite the civil war he had fought against his uncle, Prince Yuri, and Yuri's sons, Basil II strengthened the Moscow dynasty. His grandfather, Grand Prince Dmitri Donski, had ruled for 21 years; his father, Grand Prince Basil I, for 41 years; and he himself ruled for 37 years. This unparalleled continuity of a single family's rule over a Russian principality, not to mention the family's possession of the coveted title of grand prince, was unique in Russian history and a harbinger of future dynasties. It also spelled the end of the old system whereby the crown passed to the grand prince's brothers before his sons, a system that had provoked so much bloodshed and destruction in the past. From Basil II's time onward, the eldest son, if there was one, would inherit his father's crown, usually without a challenge. When Basil died in 1462, the title of grand prince passed to his eldest son, Ivan.

Part Four

SOVEREIGNS OF ALL THE RUSSIANS

Czar Ivan III "the Great"

CHAPTER 11

THE TRIUMPHS OF IVAN THE GREAT

OF THE THREE RUSSIAN MONARCHS WHO HAVE been anointed with the appellation "the Great"—Ivan, Peter, and Catherine—perhaps the least known to Westerners is the first, Ivan the Great, the eldest son of Basil II.

According to legend, an old monk named Michael Klopsky approached the bishop of Novgorod in 1440 to tell him there was great joy in Moscow because a son had been born to Grand Prince Basil. He predicted that the infant prince would become a famous ruler who would conquer many princes, and that Novgorod would fall to him, never to rise again.

Ivan was 22 years old when he inherited the title of grand prince. To preclude a dispute with Ivan's four younger brothers, Basil II had Ivan named cosovereign before his own death. When Basil died, Ivan became Ivan III. By the time of Ivan's own passing, his contribution to uniting the Russian principalities had earned him the sobriquet "gatherer of the Russian lands." Year after year during his 43-year reign, he devoted his energies to purchasing, conquering, or otherwise acquiring principalities, cities, and towns, which were incorporated into Moscow's territory.

The republic of Novgorod, Ivan's largest and most important acquisition, was chafing under the terms of the agreement that Basil II had forced on it. The leading Novgorod boyars were determined to test the new grand prince's resolve. To help free themselves from the grip of the grand prince of Moscow, they looked west, to Roman Catholic Lithuania and Poland, for support.

The Republic of Novgorod the Great, as it was known, had become a far-flung capitalist empire ruled by a clique of powerful, wealthy boyars and merchants with extensive commercial interests. Its capital was home to numerous foreign mercantile organizations that gave the city a distinctly European air not found in the other large cities of Russia. The boyar's control over the political and commercial life of the republic subordinated the common people who had been the backbone of Novgorod's independence. The erosion of personal liberties among the general population bred an intense dislike of the wealthy class and led to a gradual decline in the people's willingness to compromise their own lives and welfare to preserve the republic. Novgorod's free institutions, such as the veche, had come under the total control of the wealthy, and a majority of the citizens considered annexation by Moscow preferable to the indignities imposed on them by their own nobles. Moscow's agents were aware of the attitude of much of Novgorod's populace, and took every opportunity to support groups favoring annexation to Moscow, including funneling funds to them. Consequently, Novgorod was divided between the general population, which was supported by some boyars and clergy who sought relief from the oppression of the wealthy, and the moguls and high-ranking clergy, who obviously profited from the continued independence of the republic. The relationship of the two camps reached a critical juncture in 1471, when the Novgorod boyars negotiated mutual defense treaties with Lithuania and Poland that were clearly aimed against Moscow. The boyars then made the highly inflammatory gesture of demanding the return of territory that had been ceded to Basil II in 1456.

An enraged Ivan led an army north into Novgorod territory, surrounded the capital, and laid siege to it. The Novgorod boyars at first had difficulty raising an army sufficiently powerful to have any hope of victory, but they finally succeeded and sent it out to battle the grand prince. When the two forces met on the banks of the Shelonya River, the Novgorodians performed poorly. Rejecting the thought of fighting other Russians while awaiting help from Lithuanians and Poles, many Novgorodians were reluctant combatants. The archbishop of Novgorod's personal regiment flatly refused to fight against the grand prince. As a result of the mass defection of most of its defensive force, Novgorod quickly fell to Ivan.

The Novgorod nobles, including the archbishop, visited Ivan's camp and prostrated themselves before the grand prince. Ivan demanded a pledge of loyalty to him as their lord, and to his son as the future grand prince. The Novgorodians quickly acceded. They were then assessed a large reparation for the cost of Moscow's campaign against them, forced to abrogate the treaties with Poland and Lithuania, and made to relinquish several large tracts of land to the grand prince. Finally, they were forced to agree that the archbishop of Novgorod would thereafter be appointed by the metropolitan of Moscow. It was a severe humiliation for the boyars and the clergy, but they had no option other than to agree to Ivan's demands.

Most of Novgorod's citizens applauded Ivan's treatment of their aristocracy. To help ensure their continued support, Ivan channeled even more money into Novgorod's pro-Moscow factions to strengthen their position against the pro-Lithuanian and pro-Polish boyars. Secure in his assessment that a majority of the population was loyal to him, Ivan returned to Novgorod four years later with only a small ceremonial escort. He was greeted by massive crowds chanting his name, and was treated with the respect that was due him as their lord. The climate was right to end the opposition that he knew still existed among the wealthy families, and Ivan seized the opportunity to convene a royal court of justice. He had brought before him a group of leading boyars who were his most outspoken antagonists. Ivan quickly committed several to imprisonment and ordered others taken to Moscow for trial. He returned to Moscow immediately after the court had finished its business. The removal of the boyars to Moscow for trial provoked renewed animosity among the Novgorod nobles, which is precisely what Ivan had wished to accomplish by his unusual action. Resentment boiled over among the pro-Polish and pro-Lithuanian factions as boyars insisted that a citizen of Novgorod could only be judged in Novgorod. "Novgorod is its own judge!" was their angry cry.

Envoys from Moscow and Novgorod shuttled between the two cities, seeking a compromise, but for long months the balance favored neither side. During one meeting between Ivan and ambassadors from Novgorod, the Novgorodians addressed Ivan as "sovereign" instead of as the customary "lord." This subtle but important difference spoke volumes, especially to Ivan. As the lord of Novgorod, Ivan was considered the leading noble of the principality, with far-reaching but limited powers. As sovereign, however, he would be the supreme ruler, with absolute power. The distinction was significant for the future of Novgorod and Russia, and Ivan grasped it immediately, asking, "Does Novgorod recognize me as its sovereign?" The question threw Novgorod's representatives into a quandary. Recognizing Ivan as sovereign would mean the end of Novgorod's independence, something the boyars would surely oppose. If they recognized him as their sovereign, Ivan explained, they would come under the protection of the grand prince of all the Russians. In return, he would demand a concession that Novgorod had never granted to any previous grand prince: the Yaroslav Palace, in the center of the city, must serve as the residence for his appointed governor. Past governors and princes sent to Novgorod from Kiev and Vladimir had always been required to live in a fortress on the outskirts of the city; they had never been permitted to live within the city proper. This policy, strictly enforced since the earliest days of Novgorod's independence, had helped to keep the governor or prince as an outsider with limited direct contact with the general population. Shocked by the grand prince's demand, the delegates told Ivan they could not respond without first consulting the veche, and then they returned to Novgorod.

While Ivan waited in Moscow for an answer, Novgorod was thrown into turmoil. Heated debates among the members of the veche culminated in physical brawls as pro– and anti–grand-prince factions rioted in the streets. Finally, when a decision was reached, it was a stunning blow to Ivan, who had expected the veche to bow to his demands. The Novgorod veche told Ivan: "We pay homage to you as our lord but not as our sovereign. We cannot let your governors live in the Yaroslav Palace." Compounding the affront to the grand prince, the veche declared that his governors would not be permitted to "interfere in our affairs." A furious Ivan immediately declared war on Novgorod and dispatched couriers to his vassal princes and servitors, directing them to prepare for battle.

In November 1478, Ivan the Great again besieged Novgorod, his forces ringing the city and choking off its food supply. In less than two weeks, and without the occurrence of any major military engagement between the opponents, a delegation of several boyars and the archbishop of Novgorod approached the grand prince and sued for peace. With the Novgorodian people fighting amongst themselves about whether to support the grand prince or the veche, and with food stores exhausted, the boyars had recognized that their cause was lost. The final blow had come when the grand prince of Lithuania had disdained their appeals for military assistance.

Despite their unenviable position, the Novgorodian delegation made a bold attempt to mollify Ivan without yielding entirely to his direct rule. They offered to pay him a sizable annual tribute if he would grant them a degree of autonomy. Essentially, they wanted to retain their own court system and to receive Ivan's assurance that he would not require Novgorod's citizens to serve him outside the borders of the republic. Scowling at the prostrated boyars, Ivan told them he would rule Novgorod the way he ruled Moscow. In other words, he would be the absolute ruler of the republic, which would no longer exist after he annexed it to his domain. Outlining his demands for ending the siege, Ivan told the archbishop that the bell that announced meetings of the veche, the so-called voice of Novgorod, must be removed, and that Novgorod would no longer elect its own governor.

Ivan's demands spelled the end of Novgorod's independence, a condition that the delegates clearly understood. They asked for, and received, time to present Ivan's terms to the veche before responding. For eight days the veche argued about what could be done. Finally, as December came to an end, Novgorod surrendered. The Yaroslav Palace was prepared for Novgorod's new sovereign, and the bell that had called members to the meetings of the veche was removed from the palace tower.

As he had done before, Ivan convened a court of justice where the boyars who had opposed him were tried. A number of them were executed, while others, along with their entire families, were exiled to distant parts of Ivan's realm. When he returned to Moscow, Ivan took with him the famous bell that had symbolized Novgorod's independence.

The end of the Novgorodian republic was a major event in the creation of a unified Russia, and certainly a milestone in Ivan the Great's reign. Novgorod's demise and annexation to Ivan's Moscow foretold the fate that awaited the remaining independent principalities and republics of Russia. One by one, other settlements, cities, and even entire principalities were annexed by Moscow. Among the most important of these were Yaroslavl in 1463, Dimitrov in 1472, and Rostov in 1474. In all, Moscow tripled in size during Ivan's 43-year tenure. This was accomplished by Ivan's expert use of diplomacy, his judicious use of military power, and his employment of the proven methods of purchasing lesser principalities or granting mortgages to impoverished princes who invariably failed to repay their debts and thus lost their inheritances.

Ivan made a grievous error in his treatment of Novgorod, at least from an economic standpoint, because he failed to grasp the importance of having a thriving commercial center on the Baltic coast. The 8,000 or more leading Novgorod families that he exiled were replaced by wealthy Moscow merchants whose traditionally closed or preferential business practices brought ruin to Novgorod's capitalist economy. In 1495, Ivan aggravated this blunder by driving from Novgorod the numerous German merchants who were part of the Hanseatic League, a confederation of merchants that controlled most of the trade in the Baltic Sea region. Eventually, Novgorod, once the commercial jewel of Russia, lost its old trading partners and became just another provincial backwater.

❖ ❖ ❖

The year 1472 would prove to be an important one for Ivan as well as for the Russian people. Ivan's wife, Maria of Tver, had died in 1467, their union having produced only one son, Ivan Ivanovich. But the grand prince wanted more male offspring to ensure that one of them would survive to inherit his title. It now was time for Ivan to remarry. For his new bride, he chose a woman who would bring to their marriage not only beauty and intelligence, but the prestige of the Byzantine Orthodox Church and the Byzantine Empire—Zoe Palae-ologus, the niece of Constantine XI, the last emperor of Byzantium. Constantine had died defending the walls of Constantinople during the Ottoman Turk's final, and victorious, assault on the city on May 29, 1453. Since then, with many other refugees from Constantinople, Zoe had been living in Rome under the aegis of Pope Paul II and later Pope Sixtus IV. Constantinople remained occupied by the Muslims, and the Greek Orthodox Church was still subject to the whims of the Ottoman sultan. The Roman Catholic Church hierarchy had seen an opportunity to renew its campaign for unification with the Orthodox Churches that it had begun at the Council of Florence, while simultaneously cultivating a potential ally in the war against the Turks. The Roman Church therefore had proposed a marriage between the Russian grand prince and the

Byzantine princess. Ivan had accepted the proposal, but for completely different reasons.

Princess Zoe's arduous trek to Moscow carefully circumvented the danger posed by Ottoman incursions into central Europe. Her entourage, which included the high-ranking Roman Catholic cardinal Antonio, proceeded north from Rome to Lübeck, a German port on the Baltic. There, she boarded a ship that took her to Reval in what is now Estonia, where she was met by a bodyguard of Teutonic Knights who accompanied her to the shores of Lake Peipus. On the final leg of her journey, a contingent of Russian boyars escorted her via Pskov and Novgorod to Moscow. To the princess, born and raised amid the splendor of Constantinople and Rome, the barren landscape and wooden homes and churches of the Russian settlements must have been depressing, to say the least.

As the Princess's party approached each village and town enroute to the Russian capital, Cardinal Antonio unwrapped a large wooden Latin cross and carried it into the village ahead of the princess's entourage. When the cardinal prepared to do the same thing upon entering Moscow, the metropolitan objected and threatened to leave the city if Ivan permitted it, even if only as a gesture of respect for the cardinal. As a result, Ivan denied permission and Antonio put away his cross before entering the gates of Moscow. Following ceremonial presentations and receptions, the princess's Catholic escorts were hustled off to Rome. Zoe, who adopted the name Sophia, married Ivan in a grand wedding that rivaled the pomp of Constantinople in its heyday.

The marriage had consequences that were the opposite of what the Roman Church leaders had hoped for. The Russian people viewed the union of their grand prince with a Byzantine princess as a confirmation that their Church was the successor to the Greek Orthodox Church, and that their ruler, Ivan, was the protector of the true faith. From the Roman Church's perspective, the Greek Orthodox Church, which at the time of its declining influence had become increasingly more agreeable to reunification, was now replaced by a more strongly antipapal Russian Orthodox Church. Ivan also had no inclination to join a united front against the Ottomans; his focus remained on the unification of Russia. Sophia would ultimately have a profound influence on Ivan, bringing about a change in the status of the grand prince that would affect Russia for four and a half centuries.

❖ ❖ ❖

Ivan continued to annex territory, absorbing lesser principalities, towns, and villages so swiftly that his bureaucratic establishment had difficulty keeping abreast. Ivan saw himself as the sovereign ruler of all Russians, including those living in territories controlled by Lithuania and Poland. That view inevitably led to confrontations. Ivan's wife, Sophia, longed for the grand, imperial Constantinople lifestyle in which she had been raised. At her urging, Ivan adopted the double-headed eagle of Byzantium as Russia's coat of arms: one head looked east, the other west (that is, one looked forward, the other backward). Under Sophie's influence, Ivan also instituted Byzantine ceremonial practices in his own court, including the solemn church-based coronation. He began signing documents with the title "czar," a Slavic version of the Roman "caesar," and declared himself the "sovereign of all Russia." But Ivan recognized that he would not be taken seriously as a sovereign as long as he might be forced to prostrate himself before a Mongol khan. Although Moscow no longer paid an annual tribute to the Golden Horde, it still sent periodic "gifts" of large sums of money. Sophia's censure of this practice fueled Ivan's determination to rid himself of the Mongols. She reportedly told him that she and her father had given up all their worldly possessions when they fled Constantinople rather than live under the yoke of the Muslim Turks. She chided Ivan that she did not want to continue living as a Tartar slave.

Sophia's admonition went to the heart of Ivan's vision of the grand prince's status as the supreme autocratic ruler of all the territories that were part of the old Kievan Empire, including the provinces now controlled by the king of Poland. Ivan saw himself as the heir to the throne of the Eastern Roman Empire, and as such he subscribed to the concept that Moscow was the "third Rome," destined to succeed Rome and Constantinople as the emerging capital of the Christian world. With much of Russia now united under one ruler, the moment to throw off the Mongol yoke had come. Ivan took the first step toward his goal by refusing to send any more "gifts" to the khan of the Golden Horde.

Khan Akhmad responded by sending his envoys to Moscow in 1475 and summoning Ivan to present himself at Sarai. Suspecting the Mongol leader of treachery, and convinced that he would be ransomed for back taxes, Ivan refused to travel to Sarai. Instead, he sent Akhmad a small selection of gifts. But gifts were not what Akhmad needed; he required funds to keep his tenuous holdings together. Three years later, the khan sent a second delegation to deliver to Ivan a letter demanding immediate payment of all back taxes and tribute.

Ivan III was notorious for his volatile temper. When the Mongol emissaries presented the khan's letter, he scanned it, tore it to shreds, and flung the pieces in their faces. Seething over what he perceived as an intolerable insult,

Ivan seized the portrait of Akhmad that the khan had sent with the envoys so that Ivan could prostrate himself before it; Ivan hurled it to the floor and stomped on it. The Mongol envoys recoiled in horror at this offense. Ivan then ordered the khan's entire delegation to be put to death except for one member, whom he sent back to Sarai with a message for the khan. Ivan threatened the khan with the same treatment that he had given to the khan's portrait if he troubled Ivan again.

The Golden Horde, drained by years of internal dissension, and diminished by the emergence of rival hordes—especially the Crimean Horde, which maintained close ties to Moscow—was in no position to challenge Ivan the Great's united Russian army single-handedly. Therefore, Khan Akhmad turned to Moscow's traditional foe, Lithuania, for help. In 1480, Akhmad signed a covenant with Casimir IV, the king of the consolidated Polish-Lithuanian kingdom, to invade Moscow and restore Mongol dominance over the grand prince. The agreement called for the Mongols to invade Russia from the south while Lithuania attacked from the west.

In late September 1480, Akhmad's Golden Horde army crossed into Moscow territory. When Ivan learned of the incursion, he quickly mustered a large force that he personally led against the invaders. Guarding against a possible Lithuanian attack from his rear, Ivan prevailed on Mengli-Geray, the khan of the Crimean Horde, to attack Poland and keep the Lithuanian-Polish army occupied at home.

Just as a century earlier on the banks of the Don, a great Mongol army and a powerful, united Russian army led by a Moscow grand prince clashed on the banks of the Ugra River. Akhmad's army reached the river before the Russians, but he chose not to cross it for fear of fighting a battle with the river at his back, which would sever any avenue of retreat. When the Russians arrived, they deployed on the opposite bank and waited. For weeks, both sides did little other than hurl occasional insults and arrows across the river. By late October, the river had started to freeze, beginning its metamorphosis from an obstacle to a natural bridge leading to the enemy's camp. When the river had frozen sufficiently solid to permit the Mongol cavalry to cross, Ivan, never a brave warrior, attempted to flee, but was forced by his son and other military commanders to remain with his troops. Fearing an all-out cavalry assault, the Russians quickly withdrew to a more defensible position in the hills to his rear.

Akhmad observed the withdrawal with amused contempt, but wary that it might be a tactic designed to draw his army into a trap, he remained where he was. While the Mongols were watching the Russian withdrawal, a messenger from Sarai brought news that the capital was under attack by a combined force of Moscow Russians and Crimean Horde Tartars. Fearing his capital might fall, Akhmad immediately retreated from the field on November 19 and hurried back to Sarai. But the attack on his capital was essentially a ruse to lure him away from Russian territory. Akhmad was killed in a coup soon after his return to Sarai, and in 1500 the Crimean Horde, assisted by reinforcements from Moscow, overran the Golden Horde's capital city. Akhmad's successor died in the fighting, and the Golden Horde ceased to exist.

Akhmad's withdrawal from the Ugra River had presaged the end of the Mongols' oppression of Russia. Their cruel, bloody dominance which had begun with the inhuman slaughter of tens of thousands of Russians and had persisted for more than two and a half centuries, ended ingloriously without so much as a minor skirmish.

No longer obliged to pay homage to a foreign ruler, Ivan the Great assumed the title of autocrat and began signing documents with the title "czar of all the Russias." Ivan's next major acquisition in his "gathering of the Russian lands" was Moscow's longtime nemesis, Tver, which was ruled by Prince Michael, the senior member of the only family to seriously rival the princes of Moscow.

In 1483, Michael signed a treaty with Casimir IV, who was simultaneously grand duke of Lithuania and king of Poland. Angered whenever Russian princes entered into outside alliances against other Russians, Ivan dispatched an army to Tver to punish Michael. Before Ivan's forces could strike against Tver, Michael recanted and declared that he was a loyal "younger brother" of the grand prince. Two years later, the recalcitrant Michael attempted to reinstate his agreement with Casimir, but Ivan's agents intercepted his messages to the king of Poland. A Muscovite army quickly marched on Tver, but again Michael quit the field without a battle, this time escaping to the sanctuary of Lithuania. Tver's towns and municipalities submitted before Moscow's forces could attack, swearing allegiance to the grand prince. Michael's death a short time later in Lithuania, probably at the hands of Ivan's agents, ended a family feud that had begun in 1304.

When Casimir IV died in 1492, Lithuania divorced itself from Poland, and Casimir's eldest son, John Albert, became the Polish king. At the same time, the Lithuanian nobility elected John Albert's younger brother, Alexander, grand duke of Lithuania. In 1494, Ivan exploited the dissolution of this once powerful union. He pressured Grand Duke Alexander into accepting a treaty that ceded to Moscow a collection of small principalities along the

Russian-Lithuanian border whose princes had previously pledged their services to Ivan in exchange for his protection. Actually, Alexander simply was formalizing what was already a fait accompli. He further agreed to recognize Ivan as the "sovereign of all Russia." Alexander's marriage to Ivan's daughter, Yelena, cemented what appeared to be amicable relations between the two rival nations.

Cordial relations between Russia and Lithuania were short-lived, however, as a growing number of principalities along the border switched their allegiance from Lithuania to Russia. Alexander reproached his father-in-law about this but received little satisfaction. By 1500, Ivan and Alexander were confronting each other across a bitterly disputed border. The dispute erupted into open warfare when Yelena complained to Ivan that her husband was mistreating her. Ivan again called on the khan of the Crimean Horde for assistance, while Grand Duke Alexander allied himself with the Livonian Knights. The decisive battle of the campaign was waged along the banks of the Vedrosha River. The Russians ended the battle by capturing the Lithuanian military commander and routing his army. In 1503, Lithuania agreed to reinstate the treaty of 1494, and Russian-Lithuanian relations reverted to the previous precarious peace.

Consistent with his reputation as the "gatherer of the Russian lands," Ivan could not rest until all the territory originally controlled by Kiev and the previous Russian grand princes was returned to the fold. He expanded his objectives to include any lands occupied by Orthodox Christians who were governed by Catholic or Muslim rulers; this placed him again in direct conflict with Poland and, of course, Lithuania, the two Catholic countries that ruled Kiev, Galicia, Smolensk, and Polotsk. Ivan categorized his relations with Lithuania and Poland succinctly, saying that peace with them was "nothing but the drawing of a breath for the gathering of new strength."

❖ ❖ ❖

Ivan the Great was a cruel, cold-blooded autocrat who nevertheless frequently exhibited a cowardly streak. His timorous behavior when Akhmad, the khan of the Golden Horde, invaded Russia in 1480 is a classic example. At first, Ivan attempted to flee Moscow before the Mongols arrived, but was then forced to lead his troops to the Ugra River when he was humiliated by the leading boyars and the bishop of Rostov, who accused him of being a runaway. When it first appeared that Akhmad would cross the frozen river, Ivan bolted for Moscow but was forced to return by his son. Fortunately for Ivan, the Mongols withdrew without giving battle.

Ivan's true claim to greatness lay in his vision of a great and independent Russia united under one ruler, and in his contribution to achieving that vision. He was the first ruler of a free, independent and unified Russia, and he personally must be credited with completing the unification of that nation. His father and grandfathers established the foundations for unification, but Ivan was the one who achieved it.

Influenced by Sophia, his second wife, Ivan also made many changes that altered the old Russia. The grand prince was now a czar, the autocratic ruler of all Russia, and under his guidance a government bureaucracy capable of running the vast new empire evolved. A considerable measure of power within that government rested with the council of boyars, the *boyarskaya duma*. Consisting for the most part of nobles who had formerly ruled their own principalities but were now subjects of Czar Ivan, the duma was a forum for the political expression of men who once had held ultimate authority in their own right. Although not a formally constituted branch of government, the duma enjoyed relatively broad powers, probably because Ivan recognized its value as a release for the pent-up resentment of some of the princes. Toward the end of Ivan's reign, official documents were prefaced with this statement: "The czar has decreed and the boyars have decided. . . ." But the boyars' imprimatur was merely a formality. Clearly, the operative wording was "The czar has decreed."

Taxes were now levied only by the czar, and the princes were paid for their services and loyalty through a system that Ivan himself had devised. They received both land and money as a form of salary, usually more land than money because the czar, who now owned all the land in Russia except for the considerable property held by the Orthodox Church, had much more land than cash at his disposal.

Ivan's practice of granting land in return for military service soon created a new class of citizens, a kind of landed gentry called servitors. Ivan distributed lands confiscated from the Mongols, Lithuanians, Poles, and Novgorod nobles to tens of thousands of these servitors, men not of princely blood who promised in return to be ready at a moment's notice, mounted, fully armed and provisioned for combat when the czar called. The servitors who received larger grants maintained strictly enforced quotas of armed warriors who were pledged to serve the czar. Through this system, Ivan could speedily muster a powerful, self-supporting army without draining his treasury.

Sophia's Byzantine heritage, together with the beginning of the Italian Renaissance, had an enormous impact on Moscow. Encouraged by her husband, she imported Italian craftsmen and artisans to give the Russian capital a much needed face-lift. The city's drabness was soon transformed into sparkling grace and beauty. The remaining wooded walls that had protected Moscow from attack were replaced with stone walls. New homes for the czar and the wealthier nobles were built of stone and brick; many of these homes had the beautiful arches, towers, and balconies that were typical of Italian architecture. Ivan began inviting artisans and craftsmen from other European countries to work and teach in Russia, hoping to foster a renaissance of traditional Rus skills that had fallen into disuse during the Mongol oppression, when the great majority of the people had devoted all of their energies to simply surviving.

Russia experienced other significant changes during Ivan's rule. In 1497, the czar introduced a unified code of laws. Foremost among the targets of his reforms was the serious problem of judicial corruption. Too often the laws had been circumvented by the wealthy, who were able to avoid lawful punishment by bribing dishonest judges. The new code established a network of assessors who supervised the work of judges and reviewed their decisions.

Also during Ivan III's reign, a serious schism that would have a lasting effect on Russia developed in the Orthodox Church. The Orthodox clergy split into two violently opposed camps. A reform group, led by an ascetic monk named Nil Sorsky and called the "non-possessors," insisted that the Church, and especially the monks who founded and populated a great many settlements throughout Russia, should own no worldly goods, including land. This position was a radical departure from the long-standing practice of monasteries owning large tracts of land. In 1503, the Church was estimated to own as much as one-third of all the land in Russia. These Church lands were cultivated by peasants who paid a portion of their yield as rent. The non-possessors held that monks should take a vow of poverty and live among the people. Sorsky also demanded that the Church and the state be separate entities, implying that the czar should not be regarded as the head of the Orthodox faith. This was an even more radical demand because the Russian Orthodox Church had taken from Byzantium the doctrine that the nation's ruler was also the leader and guardian of the faith. If the non-possessors prevailed, the czar's status as absolute ruler would be seriously undermined.

The opposing group of clergy, called the "possessors," was led by the powerful and wealthy abbot of Volokolamsk, Joseph of Volok. His faction supported a powerful and wealthy Church allied closely with the monarch. His followers believed that in return for the czar's protection, the Church owed the czar total ecclesiastic support and obedience. The two factions also differed widely over the treatment of heretics and nonbelievers. Sorsky, who disavowed ritualistic Church ceremonies, objected to the severe discipline, including the death sentence, meted out to heretics, while Joseph, a strong disciplinarian, was outspoken in his call for harsh punishment of nonbelievers and the death penalty for heretics.

When the dispute between the two factions reached a climax at a Church council in 1503, Ivan was caught in a dilemma. He sorely wished to confiscate monastery lands, which he needed in order to acquire more servitors to buttress his power as czar, much as he had when Novgorod fell. But the non-possessors' demand for separation of Church and state threatened his role as autocrat. At first he encouraged Sorsky, but when finally forced to choose, Ivan had no alternative except to come down on the side of the possessors. The state and the Church were joined by too many common interests, and Ivan was a prisoner of that relationship.

At roughly the same time, another group, called the "Judaizers," challenged the basic teachings of the Church. Founded by a Jew named Zechariah who lived in Novgorod, the Judaizers refused to worship the Virgin Mary and the saints, and recognized Jesus as simply a prophet, not the Messiah. They accepted the Old Testament but rejected the New Testament as heretical. The case against the Judaizers was presented to a Church synod in 1504. Joseph of Volok, representing the conservative elements in the church, won a powerful condemnation of the Judaizers. Although Ivan sympathized with the Judaizers' position that all Church property should revert to the state, as with the non-possessors, he was forced to defer to the demands of the Church hierarchy and suppressed the movement, sometimes with brutality. A large number of its leaders were burned at the stake to the cheers of thousands of spectators urged on by clergymen.

Also during Ivan's reign, three legends calculated to support the credo that Moscow was the third Rome and the center of the true faith circulated. The first held that the apostle St. Andrew personally had brought Christianity to Russia, thus confirming the Orthodox faith's direct link to Christ and his teachings. The Second was the wholly fictitious account of the Moscow grand prince's lineal descent from the Roman emperor Caesar Augustus through an alleged bastard son named Prus. The third legend, and in many ways the most significant, helped to establish the Russian Orthodox Church as the successor to the Greek Church and as the bearer of the true faith, with the grand prince as the guardian of that faith. According to this myth, which was often repeated by the leading clergymen of the time, Grand Prince Vladimir Monomakh's grandfather, the Byzantine emperor Monomachus, had invited Vladimir to be coruler of Byzantium and, by extension, coruler of the Orthodox Church. The emperor allegedly sent Vladimir a crown, scepter, and other royal paraphernalia as a sign of his coregency. No matter how often this legend was repeated, it was impossible to explain away the glaring discrepancy that Vladimir had become grand prince of Kiev in 1113 while Emperor Monomachus had died in 1054. Obviously, the two rulers could not have met, and it is ludicrous to suggest that the Greek aristocracy or the Greek clergy would have tolerated such an absurd arrangement in any case, for at the time many in the higher classes of Byzantine society had regarded the Russians as barbarians.

Toward the end of Ivan III's reign, the question of choosing his successor loomed large. He had married twice, the first time to Maria of Tver, who bore him a son, Ivan, who died in 1490. But the younger Ivan had married Helen of Moldavia, and that union had produced a son, Ivan III's grandson, Dmitri. Helen aligned herself and her son with boyars who resisted the changes Ivan had brought about with the help of his Byzantine second wife, Sophia. Ivan and Sophia had had a son, Basil, around whom were gathered nobles who supported the czar's new policies. Ivan struggled with the choice of his grandson Dmitri or his son Basil as his successor as czar of Russia.

In 1498, following a quarrel with Sophia, Ivan proclaimed his 15-year-old grandson his heir. The boy was crowned as grand prince in an elaborate ceremony. But by the start of the new century, Helen, who had been an ardent supporter of Nil Sorsky and the non-possessors, had lost favor with her father-in-law. In 1502, Ivan deposed Dmitri as grand prince and replaced him with the 23-year-old Basil. Basil's coronation incited a group of disgruntled boyars to plan a palace coup, but when word of the plan reached Ivan, he quickly ordered the plotters arrested. Several boyars were executed as an example to other would-be conspirators, and the rest were sent into exile. This was the first in a long series of aggressions against the boyar class by the czars.

Ivan the Great established in Russia two strong traditions that survived into the 20th century. The first was the supposition that the czar ruled by divine right. Ivan articulated this doctrine in his reply to an offer from Frederick III, the Holy Roman emperor, to recognize Ivan as a king. It was a most generous offer because the emperors of the Holy Roman Empire were loathe to recognize kings who might someday turn against them. Ivan wrote in his reply: "We by the grace of God have been Sovereigns over our land from the beginning. . . . We have our ordination from God . . . and we pray God that God grant us and our children forever to be as we are Sovereigns over our land, and as we have not heretofore wished ordination from anyone, so now we do not wish it."

The second tradition grew largely from Sophia's Byzantine heritage. Urged by his wife, Ivan borrowed from Byzantium many regal ceremonial rituals that helped to isolate the czar from everyone except his closest advisors. Previous grand princes had remained close to the people, but as the high ceremonial rituals were assimilated into his daily activities the Russian ruler became increasingly aloof from the population and from all but the most elite members of the boyar and servitor classes as well.

In October 1505, Ivan the Great died quietly in his bed. It is said that his passing went unmourned because by then he had alienated his second wife and his heir, and had left behind many enemies who had fallen victim to his drive to unite Russia.

CHAPTER 12

MOSCOW AS THE SEAT OF ALL POWER

IVAN THE GREAT'S TESTAMENT PARTITIONED HIS REALM among his male heirs but broke with the traditional method of succession, thereby temporarily suspending the chaotic power struggles of the past. Although Ivan bequeathed territory to each of his five sons, he named Basil grand prince with supreme political power. Basil III's principality was larger than those of his four brothers combined, and included the key cities of Moscow, Tver, Novgorod, Pskov, and Vladimir. Ivan's will also directed that if any of the sibling princes subordinate to Basil died without a male heir, their principalities would revert to the grand prince.

Even in death, Ivan had an impact on the continuing effort to unify Russia. While preparing his testament, he had his sons sign an accord allocating to the grand prince many powers formerly vested in individual princes. Among the prerogatives ceded to Basil under the agreement were the right to coin money, and jurisdiction over serious criminal cases. With these and similar innovative reforms, Ivan established the principle of a strong central government with a hereditary ruler and a single seat of power in Moscow.

Basil III pursued his father's objective of unifying all the Russian people by dealing harshly with any prince, including his brothers, who was suspected of plotting against him or challenging his central authority. In this sense, his reign was a direct extension of his father's. In 1511, Basil's brother Simeon, the prince of Kaluga, was accused of conspiring to break with Moscow and ally himself with Moscow's perennial foe, Lithuania. Confronted with the accusation, Simeon faced sure death, but he was saved only when Church officials and family members beseeched Basil for clemency. Little is known of Basil's relationship with his younger brothers, however, chronicles confirm that he had secret agents watch them for signs of challenge to his authority.

Basil ruthlessly enforced another of his father's reforms, the one that had abolished the "right of departure," the centuries-old custom that had permitted princes to abdicate their allegiance to the grand prince and, in effect, join forces with Lithuania. Although the princes remained free to leave Lithuanian service and join Moscow, the reverse now constituted treason and was punishable by death. This fate was narrowly avoided by the prince of Ryazan, who disavowed his allegiance to Moscow and was preparing to defect to the Lithuanian camp. Basil's agents arrested him. Facing certain death, the prince managed to escape and flee to Lithuania, but he lost his principality, which Basil immediately integrated with Moscow. Ryazan was a significant acquisition.

Next, Basil moved against Pskov in 1510 in his drive to further Russian unification. Although nominally part of his domain, Pskov had retained a considerable measure of independence since breaking away from Novgorod in 1348, and its citizens still guarded that status jealously. Yet 50 years after gaining autonomy, Pskov's leaders had recognized that their small principality could not survive indefinitely as an independent state, and they had sought protection in an alliance with Moscow. The arrangement had been largely informal until Basil II had forced Pskov to acknowledge the grand prince of Moscow's authority to appoint its ruling prince, thereby replacing a form of popular elections for the post. The Pskov electorate retained only the rights to vote their prince out of office or to veto the grand prince's choice. Ivan the Great had pressured Pskov into relinquishing the veto power, but the veche had refused his demand to discontinue its regular meetings. These meetings had become a source of continual annoyance to the grand prince because they often turned into violent confrontations between the veche and Moscow's appointee.

Following one such confrontation in 1510, Basil III sent troops into Pskov to remove the city's bell, which was used to call the veche's members to meetings. Future meetings of the veche were banned, and Moscow took over the administration of all government offices, effectively terminating local government in Pskov. After Pskov lost its independence, other principalities rapidly submitted to Moscow, some voluntarily, others through force, as Basil III pursued his father's objectives of annexing all territory in which Russians lived and regaining lands formerly ruled by Russian grand princes. Three times during 1513 and 1514, Basil fought Lithuania for Smolensk, a vital trade center at the headwaters of the Dnieper River that Moscow greatly coveted. In the third attempt, he succeeded in wresting control of Smolensk from the Lithuanians and incorporating it into his personal domain.

Flushed with success, Basil increased the pressure that Ivan had brought on the autonomy of the Russian nobility. Princes were stripped of their sovereignty and of the hereditary rights to their principalities. Those who resisted came in for harsh treatment. Several were imprisoned while others were executed following charges of treason. The rest were forced to accept new roles as vassals of the grand prince, forfeiting the special privileges they had considered their birthright. Grand Prince Basil III quickly earned the reputation of a ruler who did not tolerate disobedience. In many ways he was more brutal and autocratic than his father. Before Basil's reign ended, all the independent or semiautonomous Russian principalities had ceased to exist. Either the princes had voluntarily submitted to Moscow's rule or Basil had confiscated their lands. Unhappy boyars longed for a return to the days of Basil's father, Ivan III, whom they viewed as having been at least sympathetic to their problems.

No law curtailing the rights of the nobility was ever introduced by Ivan or Basil, yet through artful subtlety they reduced the nobles, many of whom had once been sovereign princes of important domains, to rival sycophants who quarreled over such petty matters as who sat in a more favorable chair at the grand prince's banquet table or which military chiefs of which family outranked those of other families.

While the boyars squabbled over such trifles, both Ivan the Great and his son Basil gradually shaped the framework of absolutism that became the government in Russia. Both father and son supported a system of hereditary claims to government posts that was so complicated, it frequently provoked bitter conflicts among the noble families. This system further diverted their attention from the grand prince's resolute usurpation of power and authority. Under the system, called the *mestnichestvo*, no boyar could be compelled to perform official duties at a level beneath those performed by any member of his family, and none could be forced to accept a government post below any grade held by a member of a lower-ranking family.

By a clever political ploy, Basil also diluted the boyars' strength and crippled their capacity to mount a united resistance to his encroachment on their authority. Basil brought into Moscow's select clique the boyars of former sovereign princes; these boyars now owed their positions not to hereditary rights but to the grand prince himself, effectively stacking the deck in his favor.

Basil III believed he had an opportunity to annex the coveted Church lands to his own domain. An unresolved problem from the time of Ivan the Great, the dispute between the disciples of Nil Sorsky, the "non-possessors," and the Orthodox Church hierarchy, represented by Joseph of Volok, had spilled over into Basil's reign. Ostensibly, the issues had been settled at the 1503 Church council when Sorsky's views were soundly rejected. However, the basic differences remained. The "non-possessors" held that the churches and monasteries should not own land, and that the grand prince, as the secular leader of the country, had the authority to intervene in Church matters.

Following Sorsky's death at age 65 in 1508, his mantle passed to a monk named Vassian the Cross-Eyed. Vassian was the former Prince Patrikeev and a cousin of Basil III whom the latter had coerced into the monastic life after Patrikeev was found guilty of treason, probably for supporting the Judaizers. Nevertheless, as Sorsky's successor, Vassian's views favored Basil's stake in the debate, which continued to seethe beneath the surface. Basil, sensing an opportunity to capitalize on this clash of religious ideologies, brought a Greek named Maxim to Moscow in 1518, purportedly to translate Greek Orthodox writings into Slavonic. It was an odd choice because Maxim knew nothing of the language of the Slavs. Maxim translated the books from Greek into Latin, and then his assistants translated the Latin into Slavonic. Maxim was also a singularly curious choice from another standpoint. For several years he had lived in Rome, where he became a devoted disciple of Girolamo Savonarola, a fanatical monk who for a time had ruled Florence as a priest-king, and who had supported the invasion of Italy by King Charles VIII of France. A fiery opponent of papal wealth and secular authority, Savonarola was excommunicated by Pope Alexander VI and burned at the stake in a Florentine square after the French had been driven out of Italy.

The parallels in the doctrines espoused by Savonarola and Nil Sorsky led inevitably to a close bond between Maxim and Vassian. This alliance has led some historians to speculate that Basil's true purpose in bringing Maxim to Moscow was to have the two radicals rekindle the old controversy, thereby creating a pretext for Basil to strip the monasteries of their land. He could then use that land as payment to the nobles who had been conscripted for service in the grand prince's army. If Basil's bringing Maxim to Moscow was part of a strategy to seize Church land, it failed.

Daniel, the metropolitan of Moscow who succeeded Joseph of Volok, denounced the alliance between Maxim and Vassian as a threat to religious order. At Daniel's direction, and with Basil's tacit approval following Daniel's support of the czar's divorce, Maxim was arrested in 1525 and charged with a variety of crimes against the Church, including heresy and black magic. Tried before an ecclesiastical court of Orthodox bishops that was presided over by Metropolitan Daniel, Maxim was declared guilty, excommunicated, and imprisoned in the monastery at Volokolamsk. Released in 1551, he died soon thereafter. Six years after Maxim's trial, Vassian was convicted of heresy by a Church tribunal. Also imprisoned in the monastery at Volokolamsk, Vassian never emerged alive. Both he and Maxim left a body of writings, but their imprisonment signaled the end of the non-possessors' movement.

As for the grand prince, the Church's vast land holdings remained for the most part beyond his reach. Late in his reign, he issued a decree prohibiting the monasteries from acquiring additional lands without royal approval, but it proved difficult to enforce. Meanwhile, the monasteries grew wealthy from the

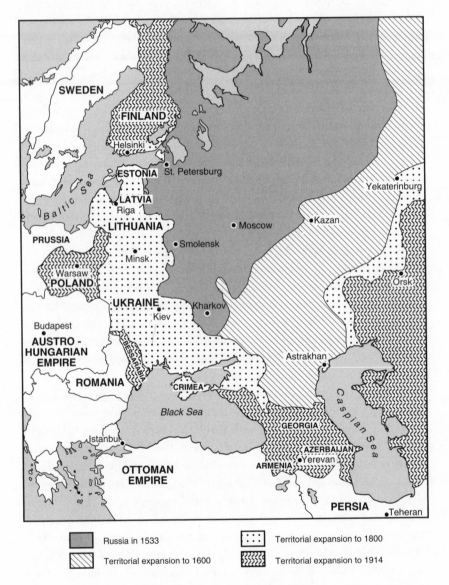

Russian Expansion in Europe (1533–1914)

production of the peasants who tilled Church land. Some nobles, whose estates were at risk of being confiscated by the central government, gave their land to the monasteries in return for life tenancies. Along with the land came the peasants, who were only slightly better off than indentured servants. According to rumors at the time, Basil was not above occasionally funneling monastic funds into his own treasury.

❖ ❖ ❖

Like his predecessors, Basil III was plagued by the continued presence of Mongol kingdoms and nomadic bands along Moscow's southern and eastern borders. Although the age of the Golden Horde had passed, the Crimean Mongols and those in Kazan still represented a constant threat to Moscow. Resentful of the grand prince's increasing power, they periodically exerted pressure on Moscow. Sporadic fighting between Mongol and Russian forces continued, with neither side gaining an edge, until 1521, when a Mongol army from Crimea reached the gates of Moscow. The Mongols naively withdrew after exacting a promise that the grand prince would resume paying tribute to their khan. The tribute was never paid, and the truce was short-lived. Other roving Mongol bands regularly marauded Russian towns and cities, but they owed allegiance to no particular khan and were little more than bandits. Basil's recourse was to reinforce the Russian settlements along the southern and eastern frontiers.

Throughout his reign, Basil kept his father's expansionist goals firmly in sight. He instigated an ill-fated coup of sorts on his western frontier, along the border with Russia's powerful long-time rival, the Lithuanian-Polish kingdom. His unlikely allies in this endeavor were the Knights of the Teutonic Order, with whom Russians had clashed for decades. In 1517, the knights formed an alliance with Basil against Sigismund I, the king of Lithuania and Poland, hoping to recover territory lost years earlier to the Lithuanians and Poles. The alliance collapsed when a Polish army routed the knights, who thereafter fell into a swift decline and eventual obscurity.

Under Basil's tenure, Russia continued its transit out of isolation from the rest of Europe that Ivan had begun. In 1482, Ivan had established diplomatic relations with Hungary; the first Hungarian ambassador to the court of the grand prince arrived in Moscow 23 years later. In 1493, Ivan had signed with Denmark a mutual protection pact against aggression by Sweden, another old Russian enemy. Six years later, Emperor Maximilian I of the Holy Roman Empire had sent an ambassador to Moscow. Western Europe was beginning to recognize that beyond Lithuania-Poland's eastern border lay an emerging, if still somewhat primitive, colossus.

Three years after inheriting his father's throne, in 1508, Basil negotiated a 60-year armistice with Sweden, bringing relative stability to Russia's northwestern frontier. The accord led to a resumption of relations with the Hanseatic League, the consortium of merchants controlling trade in the Baltic region that Ivan the Great had driven from Novgorod. During these armistice years, Russian trade missions periodically plied the routes between Moscow and Rome, but permanent commercial ties could not be firmly established because the pope wanted Russia to accept Catholicism and join the crusades against the Turks, whereas Moscow was seeking alliances against the Catholic kingdom of Poland. Basil's efforts to persuade the Turks to join in an alliance against the Crimean Mongols also came to nothing.

Basil missed a rare opportunity to form an alliance with another young, expanding empire in 1532 when Babar, the Mogul emperor of India, sent a mission to Moscow in search of an "amicable and brotherly" association with the grand prince. Unable to verify whether Babar was a legitimate sovereign or an adjutant owing his allegiance to another, Basil turned down the offer. In fact, Babar, a descendant of Genghis Khan, had impeccable credentials, but the Russian knew nothing of India and so lost the opportunity to acquire a potentially powerful ally.

Venturing farther west politically than any of his predecessors, Basil sent an official communiqué to Paris in 1518 in a failed attempt to enlist France's participation in an alliance against Poland. The French did not even send a reply.

If Ivan the Great was the architect of a unified Russian state under one ruler, his son, Basil III, must be credited with building on his father's principle of autocratic rule and extending that rule to the far reaches of the Russian lands. Although the title "czar" was used infrequently by Ivan, Basil applied it often to himself and passed it on to his son. The title is well-deserved, for Basil III continued his father's labors as the "gatherer of the Russian lands." Between 1462, when Ivan the Great ascended the Moscow throne, until the death of his son in 1533, the territory ruled by the grand prince increased almost sevenfold, from 430,000 to 2,800,000 square kilometers.

All Russian lands fell into one of three groups. One group included the land owned by monasteries and churches; another group included the land owned by those who served the grand prince—the boyars and the military and civilian leaders who were paid for their services in land; the third group included all the other Russian land, which was owned by the grand prince. Peasants were generally free to move about but could not own land unless it was given to them by the grand prince. In effect, however, the grand prince—who could take back the land he had given, and if he really wanted to, could also confiscate Church holdings—personally owned all of Russia's land.

Basil III would rule until he died of an infection of unknown origin on December 3, 1533, at the then venerable age of 54. His first marriage, to Solomonya Saburov, had been childless. Needing a male heir to preserve the fledgling dynasty, Basil divorced Solomonya in 1525, over the objections of the boyars and a number of Church leaders. Although the divorce violated canon law, Metropolitan Daniel sanctioned it, telling Basil that he (Daniel) himself would bear the sin, if there was one. A grateful Basil then abandoned all thought of supporting the non-possessors and backed Daniel completely. The metropolitan seized the opportunity to quash the movement by arresting Maxim, the Greek translator, and the monk Vassian, the non-possessors' leading proponents.

Daniel's consent to Basil's divorce, in exchange for official license to prosecute his campaign against the non-possessors, was the first in a series of concessions that Church leaders made to the czar. By century's end, these concessions had transformed the Church from, to use a Greek concept, an entity in "harmony" with the state, into a servant of the state answerable not only to the grand prince but to government bureaucrats as well. The Orthodox Church, in order to survive its enemies and preserve its wealth, sacrificed its autonomy to the secular ruler of Russia.

Within months of his divorce, Basil remarried. His second wife was the beautiful Helen Glinsky, a niece of Prince Mikhail Glinsky, a Lithuanian lord who had entered Basil's service before the wars over Smolensk. Helen produced two sons; the first-born, and heir to the throne, was named Ivan, after his grandfather. The second son was Georgi. Just 3 years old when his father died, Ivan was destined to be the dominant figure in the history of 16th-century Russia.

Czar Ivan IV "the Terrible"

CHAPTER 13

IVAN IV: FROM ENLIGHTENMENT TO TERROR

T HE MANY LEGENDS AND FOLKTALES ABOUT BASIL III's first son, who was crowned Ivan IV in early childhood, have been so distorted and embellished through centuries of retelling that it is difficult to separate truth from fiction. It is known, however, that when the 3-year-old boy inherited his father's throne he was thrust into a world of incomprehensible terror and privation. Ivan suffered a humiliating childhood that firmly molded the fearsome characteristics for which he would become known forever as Ivan the Terrible. A complicated tyrant, Ivan's effect on Russia and her people would be profound.

Shortly after Basil's death, Ivan IV was crowned grand prince in Moscow's Cathedral of the Assumption. Couriers announced to the roughly 12 million inhabitants of the far-flung empire that a new grand prince reigned in Moscow, but it would be more than a decade before the child-prince would rule in his own right. Ivan, along with his infant brother Georgi, was quickly shunted aside and his royal authority was ignored as the boyars fought to rule in his stead.

Basil III's greatest concern had been to safeguard his family's succession to the throne against just such would-be usurpers. From his deathbed, he had created the Regency Council of trusted boyars to govern on behalf of his young son until Ivan was 15, the legal age of manhood. Basil's worst fears had not been unfounded. His own younger brother, Prince Yuri, was the first to challenge Ivan's right to the throne. Even as Basil lay dying, Yuri had begun assembling a group of boyars who would support his claim to the Moscow throne. His efforts were destined to fail, however, because few nobles believed he had any real chance against the boyars and princes who were loyal to Basil's wishes. Yuri's abortive conspiracy led to his arrest by the Regency Council and to his imprisonment in a dungeon, where he was left to starve.

Ivan's mother, Helen, made her own bid for control of the Regency Council, and it, too, met with opposition, although of a less violent sort. Helen claimed that as the mother of the new grand prince she was entitled to rule as regent during his minority, citing as a precedent for her claim the regency of Olga, who had ruled for 10 years in the middle of the 10th century during the minority of her son Sviatoslav. Helen's uncle, Prince Mikhail Glinsky, whom Basil had appointed to head the Regency Council, quietly denied her claim, telling her to step aside so he could ensure her son's eventual accession. Although Helen lacked Olga's qualities of leadership and boldness, she would rapidly mature politically and emerge as an altogether different woman.

Refusing to accept the rejection of her claim, Helen conspired against the Council. She aligned herself with an opposing group of boyars led by Prince Ivan Obolensky, a powerful Duma leader and a courageous soldier whose family had been closely linked to the grand princes of Moscow for several generations. As "master of the horse" to Basil III, Obolensky had been the grand prince's close confidant, despite the widely held belief that he was Helen's lover both during and after Basil's tenure.

Because Glinsky was considered a foreigner by many Russian nobles—he was a Lithuanian prince who had changed sides just before the Smolensk wars—he had great difficulty implementing the decisions of the Regency Council. A struggle for supremacy between the Council and Obolensky's Duma stymied Glinsky's efforts to carry out Basil's will. This battle for control of the Russian government ended in August 1534, when the Duma ordered Glinsky to be seized on charges of usurping the crown. The unfortunate prince was blinded and thrown into a prison where he, too, died of starvation. With Obolensky now in effective control of the Regency Council as well as the Duma, Helen's claim was upheld and she was installed as regent. Her first official act was to replace the Council members with men of her own choosing.

Under Obolensky's guidance, Helen's four-year rule was distinguished by military and diplomatic successes. Basil's stunning victory over the Lithuanians and his capture of Smolensk in 1514 had sorely injured the pride of the king of Lithuania and Poland, Sigismund I. A tall, powerfully built soldier, Sigismund had come to the throne of the combined kingdoms in 1506 at the age of 39. Although he was prevented from raising a strong standing army by a nobility that feared the king's power, Sigismund repaired Lithuania-Poland's military fortunes. He crushed the mighty Teutonic Knights in 1517 and incorporated Danzig into the Polish kingdom, giving the Poles a vital seaport on the Baltic. In 1525, he defeated a Prussian army and forced the duke of Prussia to swear allegiance to him.

Still smarting from his humiliating defeat by the Russians and from the loss of Smolensk, Sigismund carefully monitored the political turmoil in Moscow that had been fueled by the power struggle between the Glinsky-led Regency Council and the Obolensky-controlled Duma. Losing Smolensk to Russia had not only bruised Sigismund's ego but, more importantly, it had also left Russian troops less than 250 miles from the Lithuanian capital of Vilna. During the especially tumultuous Moscow summer of 1534, Sigismund took advantage of the infighting within Russia's leadership and successfully attacked three Russian cities, Bryansk, Starodub, and Chernigov. The Lithuanian forces met little resistance, at least in part because of a breakdown in command resulting from Glinsky's arrest and the arrest and exile of many of his supporters.

The Lithuanian attacks were the first test for Helen as regent. With Obolensky's guiding hand clearly evident, Russia launched a fierce counterattack at the end of October 1534 and drove deep into Lithuania, halting some 35 miles from Vilna. For the next 15 months the battle seesawed, with towns and settlements sometimes changing hands several times, before the Russians gradually gained the upper hand.

By the end of February 1536, Sigismund recognized the futility of continuing the war. With Russian troops firmly rooted inside Lithuania, he called for negotiations to end hostilities. Moscow, flushed by a series of stunning victories against her old enemy, might have been less inclined to negotiate had it not been for a new threat from another direction. While Russian troops were occupied with Lithuania, a well-planned series of attacks by Mongol forces breached Russia's eastern and southern frontiers. But the Mongols were soon repulsed, and the Lithuanians and Russians attempted to open the peace negotiations.

A stubborn animosity born of centuries of hatred spilled from both sides as they argued first about where the negotiations would take place (the Russians finally prevailed and the meetings were opened in Moscow), then over which side had started the war. After months of stalemate, a Russian ultimatum forced the Lithuanians to submit a declaration of their proposed terms. Moscow's delegation listened to the Lithuanian demands and then stormed out of the meeting in anger.

When the adversaries finally returned to the negotiating table, the Russians demanded, as a condition for resuming the talks, that the Lithuanians recognize Smolensk as a permanent part of Russia. The Lithuanians responded that King Sigismund would accept the condition if the Russians compensated him for Smolensk with one of their cities. Novgorod and Pskov were among the candidates suggested for exchange. But the partys' hatred for one another was too deeply inbred for either side to bend; the talks were hopelessly deadlocked. Finally, a five-year armistice was reached, but the deep-seated causes of the conflict remained. The shaky armistice commenced on March 25, 1537.

Helen fared better in other international negotiations. Russia had enjoyed peaceful relations with Sweden since 1508, when the countries signed a 60-year armistice. Now Russia sought Sweden's assistance in dealing with the recurring threat from the Lithuanians and Poles. In a shrewd diplomatic coup, Helen negotiated with Sweden's king, Gustavus I, a new agreement that opened free trade between the two countries and guaranteed Swedish neutrality in any future wars between Russia and Lithuania-Poland.

In domestic matters, Helen introduced a controversial but much needed currency reform that helped to stabilize Russia's chaotic economy. She replaced the system of clipped coinage (whereby cizitens were issued money that could be cut up as needed) with a new one of silver coins on which was depicted a mounted knight holding a spear called a *kope*. The coin became known as the kopeck. Helen also moved Russia significantly closer to realizing her husband's goal of a holy Orthodox empire. She built numerous magnificent churches and monasteries throughout the country so that all the faithful would have a place in which to worship.

Not unlike Moscow's earlier rulers, Helen was quick to eliminate her enemies, real or imagined. Among these was Basil III's youngest and last surviving brother, Prince Andrew of Staritsa. Andrew had been distant from the political arena until the dying Basil named him to the Regency Council. When Helen became regent, she removed Andrew from the Council and he returned to his estates in Staritsa.

Although historians are divided about what started the sequence of events that led to Andrew's murder by Helen's troops, most agree that the prince was a quiet, peaceful man who enjoyed a simple lifestyle on his estates with his wife Evfrosina and his newborn son, Vladimir. Some say Andrew provoked Helen by asking for permission to expand his land holdings. Others suspect that the more likely reason for Andrew's murder was that the regent learned that rebellious boyars who viewed her as a Lithuanian usurper and feared her willingness to torture and murder with little provocation were conspiring to overturn the regency and install Andrew as grand prince. Although recent grand princes had inherited the throne through the fledgling system of passing the crown from father to son, many Russians still favored the traditional practice of passing the crown to the late grand prince's siblings, which held open the possibility of reversing the existing system and allowing Andrew to inherit his brother's throne. Russia needed a strong grand prince, these Russians said, not a child whose foreign-born mother ruled in his place. For whichever reason, or possibly for a combination of both, Helen marked Andrew for death.

Early in 1537, Helen invited Andrew to Moscow, ostensibly to discuss a renewed threat from the Mongol khanate of Kazan. Suspecting a trap, Andrew declined to be drawn away from the protection of his own forces in Staritsa. Pleading illness, he claimed he was too weak to travel.

Andrew's refusal to meet with Helen strengthened her conviction that he posed a serious threat to her power. A court physician whom she sent to Staritsa reported that the prince was in good health. Andrew's fate was decided when Helen's agents in Staritsa reported that a large number of supporters were gathering at Andrew's court for some unknown reason. Enraged, Helen dispatched three columns of Moscow troops to capture the reluctant prince and bring him to Moscow. As the lead column neared Staritsa, Andrew bolted for

Lithuania with an armed escort. Before he reached the border, a second column of Moscow troops intercepted his small force, and he turned north toward Novgorod, possibly hoping to find allies among the perpetually disgruntled boyars of that former republic. Some Novgorod forces joined Andrew, but the city as a whole was intimidated by the imminent arrival of the three Moscow columns led by Helen's lover and confidant, Prince Obolensky, and turned the prince away.

In late May, Andrew's force was surrounded by the much larger and better equipped army from Moscow. Andrew decided to accept an offer of clemency for himself and his followers from Obolensky in exchange for surrendering peacefully. In Moscow, Helen nullified the clemency agreement and had Andrew imprisoned. After he was killed a few months later, his wife and son were forced to forfeit their princely inheritance. The other men who had accepted Obolensky's clemency offer were also betrayed: all were tortured and executed.

Andrew's murder was the event that provoked the other disgruntled boyars to act. He had been, after all, the son of a grand prince as well as a widely popular member of the royal family. Many boyars, especially those who were excluded from Helen's loyal clique, had finally wearied of her cruelty and arrogant behavior toward them. On April 3, 1538, Helen died suddenly, after complaining of severe stomach pains; she was almost surely the victim of a poison that had been introduced into her food by an agent of the boyars. The following week, the Duma had Obolensky arrested; he was thrust in a tiny cell and literally beaten to death by his jailers.

Since his father's death, Basil III's son, Ivan, had remained isolated, ignored by everyone except his much-beloved nurse, Agrafena, who was Obolensky's sister. Ivan had been oblivious to the events that brought down his mother's regency until a few days after Obolensky's arrest, when soldiers arrived at the palace and took Agrafena away. Although she escaped her brother's fate, her head was shaved and she was banished to a convent at Kargopol, a town in the far northern reaches of Novgorod province.

Not yet 8 years old, Ivan was by most accounts an intelligent, sensitive boy who was also a voracious reader. His father's early death, the isolation of the last five years, his mother's indifference toward him and her subsequent murder, and the loss of his cherished nurse doubtlessly traumatized the child who was destined to rule Russia. Except for his deaf-mute brother Georgi, who was Ivan's only playmate, and his maternal grandmother Anna, who was allowed limited visiting privileges with the boys, Ivan had been deprived of "loving care." It had been a tragic, frightening time for the young prince. As one biographer of Ivan put it, before the child-prince became Ivan the Terrible, he was Ivan the Terrified. Ivan's brutal behavior later in his life is testimony to his never having forgotten nor forgiven the childhood indignities he had suffered.

Ivan's circumstances worsened before they improved. The boyars responsible for his mother's death wanted her forgotten, not made into a martyr, so ignoring the little grand prince's feelings, they quickly buried her without public mourning or ceremony.

Without Helen and Obolensky, the Regency Council was powerless, and therefore the Duma took over the reins of government. Unhappily for Russia, and especially for the young grand prince, the Duma was sharply divided between two warring factions representing two rival clans, the Shuiskys and the Belskys.

The Shuiskys, descendants of Alexander Nevsky, belonged to the senior line of the house of Rurik, which made them pretenders to the throne. The Belskys were originally from Lithuania, but the clan's founder was a niece of Ivan the Great, which, in their reasoning, gave them a claim to the throne that was at least equal to that of the Shuiskys. Neither clan had any real interest in deposing Ivan and actually occupying the throne. Their primary interest was in controlling the government and treasury in order to advance their own selfish interests without regard for the grand prince or the nation.

Ivan's loneliness deepened without Agrafena to look after him, and the boyars alternately neglected or abused him. Left to fend for himself, and with no one concerned about his health or well-being, he became a virtual ragged beggar in his own palace. The boyars only showed interest in him on those rare occasions when his presence was required at a ceremony, such as the arrival of a foreign diplomat who wished to present his credentials to the monarch. In these instances, Ivan was cleaned up, his rags were exchanged for ceremonial robes, and he was placed on the throne, deceiving the visitors into believing that Russia's monarchy was stable. After the ceremonies, Ivan would be stripped of the robes and hustled back to his quarters to be forgotten again.

The rivalry between the Shuiskys and the Belskys escalated into a bloody feud. Armed men roamed the palace, seeking out enemies and frequently bursting into Ivan's quarters, where they shoved the grand prince aside, over-turned the furniture, and ransacked the closets. These men took whatever they wanted, including Ivan's personal possessions, as if he did not exist.

Living in near poverty, Ivan witnessed the worst kinds of cruelties that man can inflict on his fellow man. Murders, beatings, and verbal and physical abuse became commonplace in the palace. Unable to strike out at his tormentors, Ivan took out his terrible frustrations on defenseless animals, which he subjected to the horrific tortures he fantasized inflicting on the men who terrorized him. It was in this environment, as the distraught boy grew into adolescence with no moral direction, that the character of Ivan the Terrible was molded.

As the balance of power tilted toward the Shuiskys, who were by far the more ruthless, the Belskys, joined by several churchmen, nobles, and government officials who remained loyal to the boy, drew closer to Ivan. The chief loyalist was Basil III's former state secretary, Fyodor Mishurin, whom Ivan began to look upon as a protector. On February 2, 1539, Prince Basil Shuisky, the head of the clan, led a raid on the palace, rounding up a number of Belskys and others among Ivan's supporters. Most were exiled or imprisoned. Mishurin received special treatment, probably because he was close to Ivan, or possibly because he was a commoner who had opposed the Shuiskys. In any event, Mishurin was skinned alive and left on public view in a Moscow square. Once again, an intimate of Ivan's had been taken from him forcibly.

During the next few years, the situation in Moscow deteriorated so badly that almost all semblance of order disappeared. The streets became unsafe as gangs of escaped slaves and criminals roamed at will while the members of the government thought only of fighting each other. Only once during this period did the government act in concert. In 1541, when the Crimean Mongols invaded Russia, the boyars put their differences aside and joined forces to repel the invaders. But once the enemy had been driven off, the boyars fell back into their old ways.

By the beginning of 1542, Prince Andrew Shuisky, reputed to be a cruel and corrupt person, had firm control of the government. In March of that year, Shuisky replaced the metropolitan of the Moscow Church, a vociferous supporter of Ivan, with the archbishop of Novgorod, Macarius. A "Christ-like" gentleman, the 60-year-old Macarius was selected for the post because he was popular with all segments of society, and Shuisky hoped that through him he could win converts to his side. The appointment proved ruinous for the Shuiskys and for the rule of the boyars, however, because Macarius was determined to restore the monarchy and ensure Ivan's rightful place on the throne.

Macarius became part of the grand prince's inner council and one of his confidants. Ivan's 15th birthday, when he would reach legal age, was still more than a year away, but the grand prince began preparing to assume control of the government and planning how to deal with the men who had abused him for so long, especially Andrew Shuisky, for whom Ivan harbored a special hatred.

On September 9, 1543, an incident took place that convinced Ivan he could wait no longer. The grand prince was meeting with two of his closest supporters, Metropolitan Macarius and Fyodor Vorontsov, in a palace dining room when Prince Andrew and a group of his supporters burst into the room and attempted to drag Vorontsov off to be murdered. Macarius and the grand prince interceded and a scuffle ensued, during which the metropolitan's robes were trampled and torn. Furious, Ivan decided that he would accept no more insults from the hated usurper.

Three months later, on December 29, Ivan surprised the boyars by calling them to a meeting. He reproached them for their neglect of him and the nation, and upbraided them for their misconduct, telling them he would punish their leader as an example. At a signal from Ivan, a heavily armed group of the grand prince's huntsmen seized Prince Andrew Shuisky and dragged him off. Outside, before a large crowd of Moscow citizens, the screaming prince was thrown into an enclosure with a pack of starved hunting dogs who immediately fell on Shuisky and devoured him.

Ivan's life changed dramatically on that day. The boyars conceded that their rule had ended and that the boy whom they had abused and manipulated was now a man-child to whom they owed allegiance and absolute obedience. For his part, Ivan's complex personality would develop, Janus-faced, in opposite directions. In one of his identities, he was a mean-spirited youth who threw dogs and cats from the Kremlin walls to watch them suffer, and who roamed the Moscow streets with a gang of young ruffians, beating people indiscriminately. In his other identity, Ivan continued to devour books at an incredible pace, learned to be a musician, wrote extensively, and became an excellent horseman. Each of Ivan's multiple-personalities would influence how he ruled in the coming years.

Everything Ivan read—including church history and religious texts, histories of Russia, of the Golden Horde and of Rome, and the lives of the saints—was internalized: Events in the lives of great leaders were compared to those in his own life, and references to the power and authority of monarchs became a part of his own thinking. In this way, his belief in the absolute power of the monarch was formed and sustained.

In mid-December 1546, Ivan convened a special session of the Duma. He announced to the assembled nobles that during the coming year he would marry and be crowned in an extravagant ceremony. Unlike his father and grandfather, both of whom had married foreign royalty, Ivan would wed a Russian girl. He also emphasized that his would be a double coronation, as grand prince of Moscow and as czar of all Russia. Ivan also promised to fulfill the Orthodox Church's destiny by making Moscow the third Rome.

The coronation came first. On Sunday, January 16, 1547, in Moscow's sumptuous Cathedral of the Assumption, Ivan was crowned czar and autocrat of "all the Russias." The glittering ceremony, a careful balance of religious solemnity and royal pomp, had been planned in every detail by Ivan himself. Ivan and Metropolitan Macarius occupied two thrones on a raised, red-carpeted platform that had been specially constructed for the occasion in the center of the cathedral. Standing before the thrones was a table that held the crown and coronation garments that legend claimed had been given to Grand Prince Vladimir Monomakh by the Byzantine emperor Constantine Monomachus. Ivan put on the royal robes and Macarius placed the crown on the youthful prince's head, declaring him czar "according to our ancient customs."

In his lengthy oration, the metropolitan declared that God had chosen Ivan to be czar. He called on God to bless Ivan and counseled the grand prince to be a wise leader. The assembly, composed largely of bishops and other churchmen, sang a recessional as the new czar walked from the cathedral to appear before the thousands of subjects crowding the cathedral square. As Ivan passed through the throng on his way to the Cathedral of the Archangel Michael to pay respect to his ancestors buried there, his brother Georgi poured gold coins over the czar's head and on the ground before him, a custom borrowed from early Byzantine coronation rituals and symbolizing that the wealth of the empire was Ivan's to dispose of as he saw fit. The entire coronation ceremony was calculated to impress all Russians—whether churchmen, nobles, or peasants—with the power and majesty of their ruler, to demonstrate that the grand prince of Moscow was indeed the czar of all the Russians. For his ceremony, Ivan had drawn heavily from the elaborate coronation services for the Byzantine emperors at Constantinople, reinforcing the conviction that Moscow had supplanted Constantinople, which was once hailed as the second Rome.

Ivan chose his wife with the same methodical and meticulous care he had taken in preparing for his coronation. For several months prior to the coronation, eligible young princesses and daughters of noblemen had been presented to the teenage grand prince for his inspection. Ivan was instantly smitten by the beauty and charm of Anastasia Romanovna-Zakharyina-Yuryeva, whose family had faithfully served a succession of grand princes. Interestingly, a grandson of one of Anastasia's brothers would be crowned czar nearly two centuries later, beginning the reign of the house of Romanov that would last until 1917. Anastasia's family was popular with the lower classes, but many boyars resented the marriage because she was not from a titled family. These boyars also were frustrated by Ivan's failure to choose his wife from one of their own daughters, which would have given them some direct influence on the czar.

Ivan and Anastasia were married on February 3, 1547. For their wedding trip, the couple made a pilgrimage to the Monastery of the Holy Trinity, traveling the entire 40 miles on foot despite the freezing temperatures. By all accounts, Anastasia had a quieting effect on Ivan, who still harbored a powerful hatred for the boyars who had persecuted him during his childhood and, he suspected, were now plotting against him regularly.

❖ ❖ ❖

During the early period of Ivan's reign, the administrative functions of the government were handled by two brothers of Ivan's mother, Prince Yuri Glinsky and Prince Mikhail Glinsky. The Glinsky family, too, had endured every form of outrage from the boyars following the collapse of the Regency Council, including murder and torture. The Glinsky brothers used their offices to exact revenge on the boyar Duma. Ivan trusted his uncles to run the government in a manner that protected his interests, and he either was unaware of the Glinskys' behavior or looked the other way. In any event, their abuse of not only the boyars but other citizens as well soon began to draw strong protests from the people of Moscow.

In the spring and early summer of 1547, a series of fires ravaged sections of the capital city, which had been built almost entirely of wood. On June 3, the great bronze bell in the Ivan the Great Tower in the Kremlin fell when the belfry caught fire. Rumors, probably started by anti-Glinsky boyars, that the Glinskys were responsible for the fires spread quickly, and on several occasions mobs of angry citizens rose to riot and loot.

The worst fire began in the afternoon of June 21, when the grand Church of the Holy Cross was consumed by flames. Fanned by sudden winds, the inferno leaped out of control and quickly gutted the central parts of the city, killing 2,000 people and leaving thousands more homeless. To the superstitious population, the collapse of the Ivan the Great Bell, the fiery destruction of several churches and cathedrals, and the sacrifice of so many lives was too great a calamity to attribute to chance or accident. Either God was chastising them, or some evil force was at work. The rumormongers soon unmasked as the evil forces the Glinsky brothers and their mother, whom the crowds dubbed "Anna the witch."

Rioting broke out on a large scale, forcing Ivan to invest the city with loyal troops. Later in June, the boyars' demands for an investigation into the cause of the fires brought renewed calls for the Glinskys to be put to death. When Prince Yuri Glinsky tried to pacify a mob gathered in the square outside the Cathedral of the Assumption, he was dragged from the church and murdered. Prince Mikhail Glinsky and his mother—Ivan's maternal grandmother, Anna—retreated to the safety of their respective estates. When the mob threatened the czar's life if he did not surrender the Glinskys, Ivan turned his troops on it. The rioters quickly dispersed and the city fell quiet under his threat of further military action.

As Ivan toured the ruined city he began to understand what had driven the people to such rebellious actions. The poverty created by the fires was devastating: thousands of people were not only homeless but also bereft of most of their belongings, possessing nothing more than the clothes they were wearing when they had escaped the flames. Ivan was saddened by what he saw. The fearful scenes had a profound effect on him, and therefore on all of Russia.

Ivan realized that he could no longer delegate the administrative responsibilities of government to others, that he alone must rule Russia. He would have to alter his lifestyle and assume the responsibilities of governing the country or risk new threats from the same boyars who had incited the mobs that had actually sought his life.

Ivan began this new era of governance by making an emotional speech to a large crowd in Red Square, calling for a unity of effort in rebuilding the city. The czar urged Muscovites to put aside the injustices of the past and to trust him to watch over his people. He promised important social reforms that would benefit everyone, and he promptly began a program to rebuild Moscow's burned-out central sections.

To advise him on a wide variety of matters, Ivan created the Chosen Council, a panel of trusted advisors also known as the Council of the Elect. The most important member of the Council was Metropolitan Macarius, who remained Ivan's closest advisor and a strong disciple of autocracy. Another prominent member was an archpriest from Novgorod named Silvester, who had authored an important work titled *Domostroi*, or "Home Management," which was a how-to manual that offered guidance on everything from diet to discipline. For instance, it included this advice for fathers of girls: "make her afraid of you, and you will preserve her from bodily impurity"; and this for fathers of sons: "beat him frequently, and you will rejoice over him afterwards."

A third important member of the Council was Alexis Adashev, who had originally come to the court as a playmate of Ivan's and was later appointed chamberlain to the grand prince. Most of the remaining members of the Council were boyars judged by Ivan to be loyal and honest. The most prominent of these was Prince Andrew Kurbski.

In full control of his government at last, and with a council of trusted advisors for guidance, Ivan launched a program of reforms that shook the foundations of the Russian state. In 1549, he convened a broad-based assembly of delegates from around the country to discuss with them his plans for reform. In this remarkably democratic manner, Ivan solicited recommendations for reforms directly from the people, bypassing the self-serving boyars of the Duma. The following year, he announced a reformed code of laws and a new system for dispensing justice. Criminal acts now were clearly defined, and punishments were prescribed for each; judges, who were appointed by Moscow, would share their benches with representatives elected by local populations, in an effort to curb the practice of corrupt judges selling justice to those who could afford it. The new code replaced long-standing customs that had operated to the advantage of local princes and noblemen. Now magistrates would, at least in theory, enforce the laws equally, without discrimination against persons of low station.

Next, Ivan extended the reforms to local governments. As with most of his reforms, Ivan aimed these at the boyar class, hoping to erode its influence. Until now, local governments had been run by governors who were nominally appointed by the grand prince but in practice answered to the Duma. Ivan's new law replaced most of the governors with local leaders elected by the people. In those cases where, for whatever reason, it was impractical to remove the Moscow-appointed governor, the local population could elect all other members of their government, including special assessors who would monitor the governor's conduct in office. Ivan hoped that these measures would reduce the corruption that had riddled the previous system of appointed governors and that had brought constant complaints from outraged citizens. As for the central Moscow government, it was to become more professional through a division of labor and responsibilities. The Foreign Office was established, as was the Bureau of Criminal Affairs, the Land Office, and the Office of Military Affairs. Under Ivan's firm hand, the government of Russia was quickly becoming a modern, stable one.

Ivan's reforms uprooted other established ways of doing things. Even before his coronation, Ivan had recognized that the practice of raising armies from among the nobility and the landed gentry to fight a specific campaign no longer met Russia's needs. The nation required a small standing army of well-trained professionals who could serve as the nucleus of a larger army that would be conscripted as needed. As a first step, he created an elite force of 3,000 men called the Streltsi, or musketeers, to be the heart of the new army. A formal militia system was also established, and men were assigned to regiments where they were trained in such basics as artillery and engineering. Ivan wanted to extinguish the lingering threat from the remaining Mongol khanates to the south, and he also harbored ambitions to expand his empire by conquest. To achieve these objectives, he needed a modern, professional army, not one haphazardly thrown together on brief notice.

Moscow's grand princes had long coveted the Church's extensive land holdings, and Ivan was no exception. The Church owned roughly one-third of the arable land in Russia, and many monasteries looked more like wealthy estates than like houses of contemplation and prayer. Most were surrounded by monastery-owned villages that housed the peasants who, in the employ of the monks, worked the land. The old tradition of monks living in isolated monasteries and working the soil was all but lost, replaced by wealthy monasteries in which the monks acted as overseers of the peasant laborers. However, Ivan was not so naive as to expect that he could confiscate land from monasteries and churches over the strong opposition of his close friend and advisor, Metropolitan Macarius. In 1551, Ivan struck a compromise with the metropolitan, allowing the Church to keep its land but prohibiting it from acquiring additional land without the czar's permission. A Church council ratified Ivan's decree on Church land. Macarius, acting as an instrument of reform, took advantage of the council meeting to formalize and regulate the affairs of the Church. Strict rules of conduct were imposed on the clergy, which Ivan insisted should be more conscientious, moral, and devout.

❖ ❖ ❖

Ivan's military reforms had come none too soon. Along the southern and southeastern borders of his realm, three khanates, the last remnants of the Golden Horde, continued to beleaguer his subjects. The populations of these khanates were no longer purely Mongol, but an amalgam of the original Mongol invaders and the Turkic tribes, known as Tartars, that were native to the regions. The populations of the three khanates—Kazan,

Crimea, and Astrakhan—still functioned much as their Mongol ancestors had, raiding and looting Russian settlements and carrying off peasants to be sold into slavery. Although the Mongol forces were still primarily horsemen mounted on small ponies, they had been introduced to more modern techniques of warfare, such as artillery.

By 1551, the Tartar raids posed a serious threat to Russian border settlements. Ivan now took the offensive, launching a well-planned attack against the khanate of Kazan. His victory over the Kazan Tartars won Russia a vast region along the Volga River. A newly constructed fortress solidified Russia's foothold in the khanate of Kazan itself.

The campaign was renewed in June 1552, when Ivan personally led an army of 100,000 troops down the Volga toward the fortified city of Kazan, the capital of the khanate. Recognizing the futility of facing this large force with its garrison of 30,000 defenders, Kazan called on its sister Tartar state, the khanate of Crimea, for help. The Crimean Tartars, reinforced by well-trained Turkish troops, marched north toward Moscow, hoping to relieve the pressure on Kazan. At Tula, on the road to Moscow, the Tartar and Turkish column was turned back by that city's militia. With the Crimean force in full retreat, Ivan besieged Kazan in late August and waited for its surrender. He had come equipped with more than 150 heavy artillery pieces and a group of German military engineers who were experienced in reducing large fortifications. With these superior modern capabilities in place, Ivan knew that Kazan could not wait for other Tartars to organize a force of sufficient size to relieve the city. One Tartar force did attempt to relieve Kazan, but it was easily repelled.

The khan of Kazan, Prince Yadigar, mounted a skillful defense that held off the invaders for nearly two months, but in the absence of outside support, Kazan was doomed. Russian artillery pounded Prince Yadigar's walls for weeks, but the city, built atop a tall hill, withstood the barrage. Finally, on Sunday, October 11, Ivan's German engineers successfully mined the fortifications. Powder charges placed at two strategic locations at the base of the wall blew out holes large enough to allow thousands of Russian infantry to pour into the city. Hand-to-hand fighting continued for days as the Russians, repelled at first, regrouped and counterattacked, successfully capturing large sections of the city. Thousands of Russian prisoners were freed and joined in the fighting. When the city finally fell, and most of the Tartars had been slaughtered or driven into the nearby woods by Russian cavalry, Ivan staged a triumphant entry into Kazan and claimed it as part of his empire. Within days of the victory, Ivan learned that Anastasia had borne him a male heir. The jubilant czar rushed back to

Moscow with the main body of his army in tow, leaving a small garrison to occupy Kazan.

Two years later, in 1554, a second Tartar stronghold, Astrakhan, capitulated to another Russian army. Ivan appointed his own candidate as khan to rule Astrakhan as an autonomous state. When in 1556 the czar discovered that the new khan was secretly plotting with the khan of Crimea, he retook control of the region; he also abolished the Astrakhan khanate and incorporated its territory into Russia as a province.

Ivan's victories over Kazan and Astrakhan extended the Russian nation to the Caspian Sea in the south and to the Ural Mountains in the east, annexing nearly 1,000,000 square kilometers to Ivan's realm. The remaining Tartar khanate, Crimea, was a vassal state of the powerful Ottoman Empire. Fearing that the Ottoman sultan would react violently to a Russian invasion of Crimea, Ivan left that conquest to a future czar. Meanwhile, two further attempts by the Crimean Tartars to invade Russia, in 1557 and 1558, were turned back by Ivan's force.

In the midst of these wars, during the first week of March 1553, Ivan had fallen ill with a high fever, probably caused by pneumonia, which gave every sign of ending his life. Like his father before him, Ivan dictated a deathbed testament naming his infant son Dmitri heir to the throne. He demanded that the princes and boyars swear an oath of allegiance to the child, but most were unwilling. The reasons for their reticence were numerous. Some did not want to encourage another prolonged regency, others feared that Anastasia's low-born family would control the regency to the detriment of the boyars, and still others, looking hungrily on the anticipated end of the dynasty, championed their own candidates for czar. Although Ivan's startling recovery ended all uncertainty, he never forgave the treachery of those around him when they thought he was dying.

The two principal defectors among Ivan's closest advisors, Silvester and Alexis Adashev, had both lobbied vigorously against the son of Ivan inheriting the throne; they had put forward their own candidate for czar, Prince Vladimir Staritski, whose father had died in prison, put there on the order of Ivan's mother, the regent Helen. Although Silvester and Adashev retained their posts, Ivan no longer sought their counsel or listened to their advice. The infant Dmitri was destined never to occupy the throne of Russia. A few months after Ivan's recovery, the baby drowned when a nurse accidently dropped him into a river while the royal couple was visiting a monastery to give thanks to God for Ivan's restored health.

After Ivan's resounding victory over Kazan, his troops began calling him Ivan Grozny, which has been taken to mean "the terrible" or "the dread," but is more accurately translated as "the awesome." Looking to further expand his empire, Ivan targeted Livonia, a small, Baltic-coast nation ruled by descendants of the Teutonic Knights who called themselves Knights of the Sword but were commonly known as the Livonian Knights. Livonia was a prize that Ivan dearly coveted, an outlet to the Baltic Sea. On another foreign front, Ivan was attempting to cultivate allies in western Europe. Following the chance arrival at Archangel several years before of an English merchant ship that was looking for a route to Cathay, Ivan, seeking a commercial and military alliance, dispatched Russia's first ambassador to London in 1556.

After much diplomatic maneuvering between the Livonian Knights and the Swedes, the Lithuanians, and the Poles, each of which had its own designs on Livonia and had incited a civil war there, the grand master of the Knights, Wilhelm von Furstenberg, was forced to sign an agreement in September 1557 making Livonia a protectorate of the kingdom of Poland-Lithuania. The pact violated an earlier treaty that the Knights had signed with Russia. This violation, combined with the continued efforts of Livonian merchants to control Russian trade through the Baltic, gave Ivan the excuse he needed to go to war.

The first phase of the war began in January 1558, when Ivan's army of Russian and Tartar troops breached the Livonian border at three places. According to one of the expedition's military leaders, Prince Andrew Kurbski, who later defected to the Lithuanians because of Ivan's abuse of the boyars, the Russian army crossed into Livonia along a 40-mile front. Several cities were bypassed by the Russians in their haste to reach the Baltic seaport of Narva, the primary objective of their invasion. In May, Narva was secured and the Russians promptly set about expanding its harbor to welcome large trading ships from Europe. With the Livonian Knights' monopoly on trade between Russia and western Europe broken, merchants from as far away as Holland and France rushed to Narva to negotiate trade agreements with the Russians.

Meanwhile, the Russians pursued the war, advancing south and west of Narva with virtual impunity. By summer's end, 1559, Russia controlled most of Livonia. By prior agreement, the Lithuanians were required to assist Livonia if it was invaded, and so by the end of the year Lithuanian troops occupied sections of Livonia, frustrating Ivan's plans for the total conquest of the country. The situation became even more precarious for the Russians when Lithuania, Denmark, and Sweden decided to divide Livonia among themselves, forcing Ivan to be at war with all three of these powers at once.

When an unrelated dispute between Sweden and Denmark distracted those two nations, Ivan attacked Lithuania, seizing Polotsk and several other important cities. In 1563, the grand duke of Lithuania, Sigismund II, who was also the king of the dual monarchies of Poland and Lithuania, sued for peace and conceded Polotsk to Russia.

While this first phase of the war over Livonia was progressing, a tragedy of enormous consequence for all of Russia took place in Moscow. Ivan's much loved wife Anastasia—the czar's young and beautiful "little heifer"—succumbed to a lingering illness in the summer of 1560. Although he had no actual evidence against them, Ivan raged against the boyars, whom he suspected of having poisoned Anastasia. In 1554, Anastasia had given birth to another son, Ivan, who replaced the tragically lost Dmitri as heir to the throne. Of Anastasia's six children—Anna, Maria, Dmitri, Ivan, Evdokia, and Fedor, who was born in 1557—only two, Ivan and Fedor, survived to their second birthday.

Silvester and Adashev were among those whom Ivan blamed for Anastasia's death. Ivan had distrusted his former close advisors ever since they had refused to recognize the infant Dmitri as heir to the throne at the time that Ivan appeared to be dying. Silvester, who was an Orthodox priest, was now exiled to a remote monastery, and Adashev was sent to fight in the Livonian War, where he died under mysterious circumstances. The two were treated less harshly than the boyars, on whom Ivan exacted retribution in a wave of torture executions. Ivan later justified his actions when he wrote that if the boyars "had not taken from me my young one [Anastasia], there would have been no sacrifice of blood."

The years before Anastasia died had been a time of enlightenment for Russia. Ivan pursued relations with England, opened the port of Archangel to British merchant ships, and started trading directly with western Europe, despite strong opposition from Sweden, Denmark, and Lithuania, which together controlled the Baltic Sea. He brought to Moscow a wide variety of artisans to teach his people the new trades that were essential for success in the modern world (coopering, shipbuilding, and typography, among others), and he employed numerous foreign teachers of various academic subjects. He instituted sweeping reforms in the Church and the army, as well as in the way the country was governed. He ended forever the threat from the Tartar descendants of the Mongols, expanded Russia's territories, and was moderately successful in curbing the boyars. Events would soon demonstrate that he was also extremely popular with the Russian people.

Ivan had become very distraught after Anastasia's death. Angry and depressed, and with his old cruelty resurfacing, Ivan raged against his enemies, real and imagined. To some observers he appeared unbalanced. Shortly before Christmas in 1564, Ivan suddenly packed his belongings and treasure and, with what remained of his family, secretly left Moscow to take up residence at Alexandrovskaya Sloboda, a fortified hunting lodge 60 miles northeast of the capital. The citizens of Moscow, regardless of their class, were shocked and mystified by the czar's departure from the capital. Everyone waited to see what he would do next. The suspense ended a month later when two letters arrived from the czar. The first, addressed to the metropolitan, condemned the boyars and the clergy for treasonous acts against the throne, and announced Ivan's intention to abdicate. The second letter, which was to be read to the citizens of Moscow, included Ivan's assurance that he did not blame the people for his present unhappiness.

Moscow was thrown into chaos. The populace, fearing a return of the bloodshed that had prevailed during Ivan's childhood, railed against the nobles and beseeched Ivan not to abdicate. The boyars, however, faced a dilemma. On one hand, they feared the people, who were demonstrating on the streets daily in increasing numbers, calling for Ivan's return. On the other hand, the absence of the czar meant that the boyars could once again exert their influence on government affairs, but they feared that Ivan might be testing them to see who would take advantage of his absence. Recalling the fate of those who had refused his "dying wish" for his infant son's legacy, the boyars, too, reluctantly favored Ivan's return. A delegation consisting mostly of boyars went to Alexandrovskaya Sloboda to beg his return. Ivan at first refused, but after a month of negotiations he agreed to come back on two conditions. First, he demanded absolute power to punish anyone he deemed disloyal—including by exile or execution—and to dispose of their estates as he wished. Ivan's second demand was for authority to establish a second, private state within Russia that would be absolutely loyal to him. Trusted boyars would govern the larger part of the nation in his name, but Ivan alone would rule the section of the country deemed to be his private domain. The boyars agreed and Ivan returned to Moscow in triumph.

Was Ivan's threatened abdication a ruse? No one outside his closest circle of advisors knew for sure, and none of the advisors ever revealed the truth. It is likely that Ivan used his threat, with its implications for internal strife and even civil war, as a weapon against the boyars' stubborn resistance to his campaign to strip the nobility of its traditional powers and hereditary rights. With this daring step, Ivan solidified his position as absolute ruler of Russia. Whereas previously he had been a Caesar in name only, now Russians of all stations acknowledged him to be a true czar.

The instrument of Ivan's new rule was the Oprichnina, meaning "apart" and derived from "widow's portion," that land given to the wife of a prince after his death. The Oprichnina became a separate police state within Russia. The Oprichniki, as its members were called, were hand-picked by Ivan and swore to him a personal oath of allegiance that permitted neither God nor man to come between them and their czar. Most Oprichniki were from the lower classes and many were criminals and thugs who had no compunction about killing anyone Ivan disliked or about confiscating estates for their own use; they could be tried only by their own courts and were in fact above the law. Not all the Oprichniki were criminal types, Ivan having included several loyal boyars in their ranks. Among the boyar members were two of particular prominence: Boris Godunov, whose sister had married Ivan's youngest son Fedor; and Nikita Romanov, the late Anastasia's brother. Other members were drawn from the landed gentry; these had acquired their properties as payment for military service to the czar and owed him their personal loyalty. In all, there were some 6,000 Oprichniki. The mere sight of the Oprichniki instilled fear: they dressed in black, the traditional color of death, and rode black horses, from whose saddle hung two emblems—those of a broom and a dog's head. The broom signified the rider's mission to sweep Russia clean of Ivan's enemies; the dog's head symbolized that he was watchful for the czar.

Eventually, nearly half the land in Russia was removed from the jurisdiction of the regular government, usually through confiscation, and made part of the Oprichnina, the czar's private domain. The Oprichnina's territory was not one continuous section of the country, but numerous parcels that included countryside, portions of towns, even individual streets in Moscow and the other cities. Some of these parcels were given to Oprichniki thugs, usually to the most ruthless of them, in return for their service to the czar. The Oprichnina lay almost entirely within the original borders of old Muscovy; it stretched far to the north, leaving the lands along the western, southern, and eastern borders, which were constantly threatened by outlaw bands and foreign invaders, to the central government to rule and defend. Ivan's goal in creating the Oprichnina was to reduce the influence of the princely families, especially those with hereditary rights that challenged his claim to absolute dictatorship. In this he succeeded. But because he did not smash the boyars' hold on the Duma, the real seat of government, he failed to remove the boyars from power.

The cruelty that symbolized the second part of Ivan's reign is clearly visible in the way he administered both the Oprichnina and the country. It also raises the question of whether the czar had become insane, perhaps as a result of his grief over Anastasia's death. The atrocities ascribed to Ivan and his Oprichniki became legend. It is to this period that the appellation "the Terrible" is incorrectly attributed. In 1570, on the basis of unproven accusations of treason, Ivan attacked Novgorod with a hand-picked force. He sacked and burned the province, and decimated the city of Novgorod so thoroughly that it never recovered. Observers reported that so many bodies clogged the Volkhov River, which bisects the city, that it overflowed its banks. Ivan and several Oprichnina leaders also formed a pseudomonastic order and regularly performed sacrilegious masses that were followed by extended orgies of sex and torture. Clergymen came in for special treatment by Ivan, who ceaselessly suspected the Church of treason. Often the Oprichniki would burst into a church during mass and either abduct the priest or murder him in front of the congregation. Not even the highest Church officials were safe, as Moscow's Metropolitan Philip learned after he called for the czar to disband the Oprichnina. Without warning, Philip was dragged from his church and thrown into a dungeon from which he never emerged.

Some of Ivan's strangest behavior occurred in 1575, when he again threatened to abdicate the throne while retaining control of the Oprichnina. This time he appointed a successor, a Tartar general who had converted to the Orthodox faith and taken the name Simeon. The Tartar was placed on the Moscow throne and Ivan retired to a country estate. Ivan made regular visits to the capital to pay homage to the new czar, referring to himself as "Ivan of Moscow," a simple prince. This charade lasted for a year and shook the foundations of the empire as everyone pondered Ivan's motives. While many historians have speculated about the reason for Ivan's bizarre actions, no one really knows what was behind them.

The czar's most heinous crime took place on November 19, 1581. Ivan, whose temper was by then habitually out of control, was arguing with his son and heir, the 27-year-old Ivan, about the clothes the younger man's wife was wearing. The czar thought her wardrobe was immodest, and the younger Ivan made the mistake of challenging his father's opinion. In a sudden fit of rage, Ivan raised his iron-tipped staff and struck his son a mortal blow to the head. The prince lay in a coma for several days before succumbing to his wound.

Even in foreign affairs, events turned against Ivan. Previous successes quickly became failures. The Swedes, Poles, and Lithuanians drove the Russian army out of Livonia and very nearly conquered Russian territory before an armistice was signed. Relations with England soured. Ivan, furious that Queen Elizabeth I had refused his request for asylum should he need it (a strange request from an autocratic ruler whose throne was in no real danger), at first banned British merchants from trading with Russia, then allowed them to resume trading but levied such high tariffs on them that the trade all but vanished.

On March 18, 1584, Ivan the Terrible died suddenly as he was preparing to play a game of chess. Although 54 at the time, Ivan appeared much older. The years of abuse had left his body so badly broken that, in his last years, he had to be carried on a litter, even when moving about in his own palace. According to the instructions he had prepared before his death, Ivan's head was shaved, he was dressed in the robes of a monk, rechristened "Jonah," and buried in Moscow's Cathedral of St. Michael the Archangel next to the body of the son he had murdered.

Ivan left behind a joyless Russia. Hardly a family of noble birth had not been touched by his murders, and some had been completely eliminated. The countryside had been devastated by the breakup of the old great estates; that action had scattered the peasants and greatly reduced the amount of cultivated land. Countless acres of arable land had been abandoned during the terror of the Oprichnina, and the forests had begun reclaiming land that had been cleared decades and even centuries earlier. On the throne of Moscow Ivan left a weak, simpleminded son, Fedor, whom Ivan himself had said was unfit to rule. This was the legacy of Ivan the Terrible.

CHAPTER 14

THE END OF THE LINE OF RURIK AND THE TIME OF TROUBLES

ON JUNE 10, 1584, FEDOR I WAS crowned czar of all the Russias. Although his slain older brother Ivan had had a strong personality and had been eminently qualified to rule the vast Russian Empire, Fedor, 27 when crowned, was believed to be a weakling who lacked the intelligence to rule; by his own father's reckoning, Fedor was ill-equipped to be czar. But the very qualities that distinguished him from his father—his calm and peaceful demeanor and deep devotion to the Orthodox Church—served him and Russia well. Fedor brought 14 years of peace to his greatly troubled country. He was the salve that Russia needed to heal the deep scars inflicted by Ivan the Terrible's Oprichnina.

In appearance, Fedor was virtually the opposite of his father, except for the prominent Greek nose that both had inherited from Ivan III's Byzantine wife. Where Ivan was tall and sturdy, with stern, penetrating eyes, Fedor was small and had short arms and virtually no neck. His stooped shamble was caused by runty legs that were too weak to properly support his body. His eyes had a glazed look, and his face wore a permanent guileless smile that was variously ascribed to religious ecstasy or simple-mindedness, depending on the observer's point of view. Fedor appeared far better suited to a monastic life of prayer and meditation in a solitary cell than to wielding power at the center of a great and ostentatious court. Because of his devoutness, Fedor's subjects began calling him the "Sanctified Czar."

Ivan the Terrible, anticipating his own death, had tried to smooth the path for his "humbly gifted" son by creating a five-member advisory council to help him rule. The two most influential council members were Fedor's uncle, Nikita Romanov, and Boris Godunov. The remaining three members, Prince Bogdan Bielsky, Prince Ivan Shuisky, and Prince Ivan Mstislavsky, were highly regarded boyars. Nikita Romanov died only months after Czar Ivan, leaving Boris Godunov as Fedor's principal advisor. The 33-year-old Godunov had long been one of Ivan the Terrible's favorites, and he had strengthened that relationship when his sister Irina married Fedor, and when he himself married the daughter of the Oprichniki commander Maliuta Skuratof, Ivan's notorious and feared henchman. Because Fedor was unfit to rule and not interested in doing so, Boris became a surrogate czar. As a consequence, Fedor's reign is often referred to as the first reign of Boris Godunov.

Clever and ambitious, the handsome Boris Godunov had been at Ivan's side when the czar died, and he had pledged his faithfulness to Ivan's slow-witted son. Now he quickly demonstrated his loyalty to the dynasty and his competence to serve its monarch. Recognizing the potential danger of a revolt by the old-line aristocracy, a boyar class that had suffered greatly under Ivan's rule, Boris immediately called on the captains of the Kremlin guard to keep their powder dry, their matches lighted, and the gates secured. As word spread of Ivan's death, Godunov, in his role as lord protector, sealed the czar's treasury, stationed additional troops at key border points, and circled Moscow with 12,000 additional gunners. An English official who was in the capital at the time described Boris's swift, decisive action as "a thing worth beholding."

Trusting that his government was secure in Boris Godunov's capable hands, Fedor busied himself by visiting monasteries and churches throughout his realm; he delighted himself by ringing the bells that called the faithful to mass. For his part, Godunov repaid Fedor's trust, serving him faithfully to the end of the czar's life. Acting for the czar, Boris presided over the Council of Boyars and managed Fedor's personal interests and those of Russia, both in domestic and in foreign affairs.

The Russian court that Fedor inherited was more powerful and wealthy than any that had come before. The power lay in the unification of Russian lands that had been achieved by his father, grandfather, and great grandfather, while much of the new wealth had come from recent conquests. Silks, spices, incense, and jewels had flowed into Moscow from Kazan and Astrakhan, and sable and black-fox furs were arriving from distant Siberia, which had recently been invaded by a small private army of Russian freebooters. But Fedor would not pass any of this power and wealth to an heir.

By the time Fedor gained the throne, his marriage to Irina had not produced a son, and it appeared unlikely to do so. Everyone recognized that if Fedor died without a male heir, the long-ruling dynasty begun by Rurik would come to an end. The opportunity to gain control of the throne and start a new dynasty intrigued the boyars. Although none had a direct legitimate claim, at least two potential candidates had impressive lineages. The claims of both candidates would require twisting the line of succession beyond recognition, however, and whoever succeeded Fedor would be creating a new precedent.

Boris Godunov himself had aspirations to be czar in his own right. Actually, Boris was far removed from the line of succession. He was not from the aristocratic families, several of which could trace their ancestry back to one of the early grand princes of Kiev or Moscow, but was the descendant of a Mongol chief who had converted to the Orthodox faith and had entered the service of Moscow during the reign of Ivan I. His lack of royal ancestry was not an insurmountable obstacle to the throne, but it meant that he would have to eliminate many potential rivals.

Boris proceeded to investigate closely each conceivable rival, searching for a weakness in that person's claim to the throne. The only direct descendant of the late czar was Dmitri, the 3-year-old son of Ivan the Terrible and Maria Nagaia. Ivan had married six women after Anastasia's death; Maria Nagaia, the daughter of a favored foreign-service official, whom he married in 1580, was the last. The marriage produced the boy Dmitri, but because Orthodox canon recognized a man's right to no more than three wives, Dmitri was deemed to be illegitimate and therefore not a legal heir. In any event, the boy was too young to be czar, and few people of influence in Russia wanted another disastrous regency, especially for a child who was not a legitimate heir. In 1584, Boris managed to banish Dmitri, his mother, and her influential family to Uglitch, a town 200 miles from the capital. There the former czarina Maria lived in regal splendor befitting the widow of a czar, even holding a court of her own. Czar Fedor wept when Dmitri was sent away, because he genuinely loved his half-brother and realized that Dmitri, illegitimate or not, was the only hope for the continuation of the dynasty. Boris and Irina, who were both devoted to the gentle czar, convinced Fedor that Dmitri could fall under the influence of the boyars, who would use the boy to try to topple him.

Other rivals for the throne could come only from the aristocratic boyars. Like other powerful boyars such as the Romanovs, Godunov was not of noble birth but was a "new man," one who had risen to prominence by serving Ivan the Terrible. Ivan had enriched them and made them boyars to counter his old enemies among the aristocrats. The gulf between the old-line boyars and Ivan's "new men" was deep. Among those boyar families with ancient lineage were the Shuiskys, Golitsins, Kurakins, and Vorotunskys. These families had resented Ivan's appointment of lower-born men to their ranks. They especially disliked Boris and were jealous of his close connection to the royal family and of the power Czar Fedor had invested in him.

The first serious attempt to dislodge Godunov from his privileged position was made by members of the Shuisky family. Although their earlier treachery during Helen's regency had culminated in young Ivan IV's having Prince Andrew Shuisky fed to dogs, that did not dampen the clan's ardor to conspire for the crown. The Shuiskys now began a subtle, covert campaign to undermine Boris. They fabricated a rumor that his fellow council member, Prince Bielsky, had poisoned Ivan and was plotting a similar fate for Fedor as part of an elaborate scheme to capture the throne for Boris.

The citizens of Moscow, who revered their peaceful czar, raged against Bielsky, demanding that he be handed over to them. Incited by Shuisky agents, thousands of armed men besieged the Kremlin and actually held the palace for three days. Godunov knew that he was the Shuiskys' real target, and while he had no special liking for Bielsky, he convinced Fedor that the mob outside the walls were wrong and that Bielsky was innocent and should be removed from Moscow for his own safety. Fedor agreed, and Bielsky was escorted under protective guard to Nizhni Novgorod. Satisfied that their czar was now out of danger, the mob dispersed. The Shuiskys were too powerful to be brought down, but Boris managed to have several leaders of the mob arrested and thrown into dungeons.

Persisting in their efforts to drive a wedge between Fedor and Boris, the Shuiskys contrived with Metropolitan Dionys, an opponent of Godunov, to pressure the czar into divorcing Irina because their marriage had produced no heir. They planned to encourage him to marry a daughter of one of the old-line boyar families. Boris learned of the plot and managed to drive Dionys from office. Tired of the Shuiskys' conspiracies, he then acted without the czar's support and had Prince Ivan Shuisky and other senior members of the family exiled or murdered.

By the end of 1587, Boris Godunov was the only remaining member of the advisory council that Ivan had appointed for Fedor. Grateful for Godunov's faithful services, Fedor appointed him "master of the horse," a post of greater importance than the title might indicate. Boris was, in effect, regent of Russia. He was viewed by many, including representatives of England's Queen Elizabeth I, as "Lord Protector of Russia."

❖ ❖ ❖

In December of the previous year, 1586, the elected king of Poland, Stephen Bathory, had died suddenly. (It was Bathory who, in 1577, had reversed Ivan the Terrible's victories over Poland by retaking Polotsk, the city that Sigismund II had ceded to Russia in 1563.) Poland was now locked in a bitter internal dispute over who would succeed to the throne. Boris Godunov thought to take advantage of that conflict and acquire the Catholic crown of Poland for Fedor. But the Polish electors refused to seriously consider an Orthodox monarch as king of Poland, and the crown was given to a Swedish prince who took the name Sigismund III.

Boris had greater luck in extending the empire to the east. In 1581, a force of 1,000 Cossack freebooters had invaded Siberia and ousted Kuchum, the Mongol khan of Siberia. The expedition had been sanctioned by Ivan the Terrible and financed by the Stroganovs, Russia's wealthiest merchant family. The Cossacks, led by a legendary bandit named Yermak, had driven the khan from his capital at Sibir and established Russian dominance over the vast area and its numerous local tribes. By the summer of 1585, with Fedor installed as czar, Yermak's grip on Siberia, always tenuous at best, weakened considerably as promised reinforcements failed to arrive and his supplies became exhausted. Lured into a trap by Kuchum, Yermak and most of his men were killed. The surviving Cossacks withdrew to the west, across the Urals, leaving the khan in control of Siberia. The following year, Boris Godunov sent a strong Russian army into Siberia and recaptured the territory for the czar. Unlike Yermak's pillaging forces, the Russians were determined to stay. Boris directed them to fortify two trading centers, Tobolsk and Tyumen, which became the gateways for the vast riches of Siberia that would flow into the czar's treasury in Moscow.

❖ ❖ ❖

Since 1453, when Constantinople had fallen to the Turks, the Russian Orthodox Church had been virtually cut off from its Eastern Orthodox origins. However, the Russian metropolitans had remained subject to the patriarch in Constantinople, who lived under the control of the Muslim Ottoman sultan. Boris saw an opportunity to sever the Church's ties to Constantinople when, in 1588, Patriarch Jeremy visited Moscow in search of financial assistance for his impoverished patriarchate. Boris pleaded with Jeremy not to return to Constantinople, but the patriarch refused. Boris then used bribes, threats, and deceptions to coerce Jeremy into creating a special Moscow patriarchate whose leader would be designated by the czar. To avoid the appearance that Boris had handpicked the new patriarch, the names of three prominent churchmen were submitted to Fedor, who made his selection with gentle prompting from Boris and Irina. On January 26, 1589, in a solemn ceremony at the Cathedral of the Assumption, Job of Rostov, the metropolitan of Moscow and a close ally of Boris Godunov, was consecrated as Russia's first patriarch. For the first time in its history, the Russian Orthodox Church was independent of the Church hierarchy in Constantinople. It was a great coup for Boris Godunov.

Czar Fedor gave Boris full authority to act on behalf of the crown in foreign matters, and Boris quickly began efforts to recover from Sweden the Russian towns along the Gulf of Finland that had been lost during the second part of Ivan the Terrible's reign. When the Swedes refused to give up the towns, Boris mobilized a formidable Russian army and coaxed Fedor into leading the troops into a war against Sweden. The war, which lasted from 1590 until 1595, eventually ended with the Swedes suing for peace and agreeing to withdraw from the towns.

On May 15, 1591, there occurred a startling event that tainted Fedor's reign even though he personally had no part in the event. The former czarina Maria and her son Dmitri, with no designs on the throne, had been living peacefully in exile in Uglitch, but on that day Moscow was stunned by reports that the boy had been murdered. Boris Godunov was immediately accused by his enemies of orchestrating the murder because he wanted to succeed Fedor to the throne, and Dmitri had posed a potential obstacle to that ambition. Versions of how young Dmitri died, and of who killed him, abounded. According to one rumor, the youth's throat had been slit and his murderers, in turn, had been killed by the enraged citizens of Uglitch. Maria's brothers and uncles, who despised Boris for having exiled them, had accused Godunov's agents of the crime and had provoked the townspeople into hanging the agents and dismembering their bodies. A Godunov spokesman said the boy had been playing with a knife and had fallen on the blade during an epileptic seizure.

Boris sent a commission of inquiry to Uglitch to investigate the young prince's death, and surprised everyone when he appointed Basil Shuisky of the ruthless Shuisky family to head the inquest. The commission committed two glaring errors that would haunt Russia. First, it failed to positively identify the victim's body as that of Prince Dmitri. Then, it buried the boy in a rural cemetery at Uglitch, instead of taking him to Moscow for a royal funeral and interment alongside Ivan the Terrible and Ivan's other children.

After hearing testimony, the commission ruled that Dmitri's death was an accident. But many people, including the leading boyars, were unconvinced and secretly believed that Boris had arranged Dmitri's murder. Whether the boy's death was an accident or a murder has never been resolved, and for centuries historians have debated what actually transpired on May 15, 1591. Czar Fedor, greatly saddened by his half-brother's death, appears to have accepted the commission's finding and never questioned whether Boris was involved.

The controversy surrounding Dmitri's death was quickly overshadowed by far more serious concerns that same year. A major fire gutted large portions of Moscow, and in late June came word that 150,000 Tartar horsemen were riding night and day toward Moscow. The terrified populace began burying its valuables, and those who could prepared to leave the capital. The khan of the Crimean Tartars was making what would be the final Tartar attempt to capture Moscow, destroying Russian towns and settlements along his route. Because most of the Russian army was engaged in fighting the Swedes, the capital was virtually defenseless against the approaching horde.

Although he lacked both military training and experience, Boris took command of Moscow's small garrison and enlisted every citizen in preparing the city's defense. Trenches were dug along the city's perimeter, and the earth was used to build ramparts. Barricades were hastily constructed to impede the Tartar horsemen, and monasteries were converted into fortresses from which the defenders could fire in relative safety. The czar, apparently oblivious to the approaching danger, remained inside the Kremlin.

At dawn on July 4, 1591, the first group of Tartar horsemen attacked Moscow's defenses in what was probably little more than a skirmish intended to intimidate the Russians. These initial attackers were easily repulsed when Boris called out some of the troops he was holding in reserve inside the city. For some unfathomable reason, the khan then failed to throw the full force of his army against the city, but instead committed his troops piecemeal, enabling the Russians to maintain a successful defense. Although the Tartars far outnumbered the Muscovites, they still fought with bows and arrows and swords, which were no match for the cannons and matchlock rifles of the Russians. The day ended disastrously for the Tartars as thousands of their dead and dying covered the ground before the city's ramparts.

To discourage a night attack, many Russian batteries continued a sporadic firing through the night. When the khan asked several Russian prisoners why that was being done, they told him it was to signal that the main Russian army had returned from the war with Sweden. The khan believed the lie and, fearing encirclement, immediately began to withdraw his troops. The following morning, when Godunov and his military commander, Prince Fedor Mstislavsky, saw what was happening, they pursued the Tartars with virtually the entire Moscow garrison, turning the Tartar withdrawal into a full retreat and finally a complete rout. Had the khan known the true strength of Godunov's small force, and that by giving chase it had left the city undefended, he would have easily annihilated his pursuers and taken Moscow. However, the Russians' boldness won the day, and what might have been a serious tactical blunder became a resounding victory as the khan retreated headlong into Crimea. Boris, who only days before had been reviled as Dmitri's suspected murderer, was now hailed by the people of Moscow as a savior.

❖ ❖ ❖

Rurik's dynasty ended quietly on January 8, 1598, when Czar Fedor I, the son of Ivan the Terrible and the great-grandson of Ivan the Great, died peacefully in his bed after a brief illness. Once again, in Moscow rumors were rife that the czar had been poisoned, but there was no evidence to support such speculation and no clear motive for murder.

Fedor had left no instructions for naming a successor, and he had no male heirs who could claim the throne. Several aristocratic families were direct descendants of Rurik and could lay claims to the crown, but none wanted to risk a confrontation with the powerful Boris Godunov. The crown went, as Boris and Patriarch Job knew it would, to Fedor's wife, Boris's sister Irina. Irina had collapsed when her beloved husband died. Blaming herself for not having given Fedor a son to inherit the throne, Irina from her room sent word that she was renouncing all earthly possessions and stations and entering a convent. Boris rushed to her side and convinced her that she must accept the crown for the good of Russia. In a daze, she agreed, and Boris announced to the gathered boyars that they must swear an oath to serve the czarina. The patriarch concurred and offered his prayers for the dead czar and his successor. Each boyar in turned kneeled before Job, kissed his cross, and swore allegiance to Irina. Thus began the period of political turbulence around the throne of Russia that is known as the Time of Troubles.

Devastated by Fedor's death and by her failure to produce an heir, Irina believed that she alone was responsible for the end of a glorious dynasty that had ruled Russia since 862. In Fedor's last years, she had grown closer to the Church because of her desire to bring forth a son. A daughter, Theodosia, had been born in 1592 but died within a few months. After Fedor's death, Irina continued to seek refuge in her faith during her time of grief. Despite her brother's pleading, she changed her mind and refused to accept the crown, leaving Moscow to live in the Novodevichi Monastery, where she became Sister Alexandra and found peace in prayful solitude. Boris made one last effort to persuade her to accept the crown, but she refused.

The historical record is unclear about Boris's motives in trying to convince Irina to ascend the throne. It is no secret that he coveted the crown, hoping to found a new dynasty, but he was aware of the risks. Whether he was sincere in wanting his sister to become Russia's first female monarch, or whether it was a ploy to buy time in which to organize his own campaign against the boyars, is uncertain. Boris surely realized that the boyars, especially those of old aristocratic families, would never willingly accept the descendant of a Tartar as their czar. Through his sister's reign, or even a regency, he could have remained the de facto ruler, possessing everything but the title.

Following Irina's abdication, large crowds gathered in Moscow's Red Square, where they grieved for their beloved czar and beseeched Irina to succeed him. Several prominent boyars tried to sway the crowd with a proposal that either the Duma (the popularly elected representatives) or the Council of Boyars govern the country, but the people did not want a recurrence of the turmoil of Ivan the Terrible's boyhood, when the boyars had openly fought one another for control. Then, prompted either by Boris's agents or by the recollection of his great victory over the Tartars at Moscow's very gates, the crowd cried, "Let Boris be czar!"

When Patriarch Job and a delegation of bishops and boyars approached Boris with the people's proposal, he at first rejected it. Knowing that he needed to establish a claim to the throne that could withstand the challenges of the boyars, Boris told the patriarch that he would accept the proposal if a Zemsky Sobor, or national assembly, elected him czar. The faithful Job called for the Zemsky Sobor, which consisted of local elected officials from throughout the country, to meet in Moscow. Many Zemsky Sobor delegates were from the landed gentry and had closer ties to the "new men" of Moscow, such as Boris Godunov, than to the several aristocratic princes who also sought the crown and were armed with more legitimate hereditary claims.

The boyars made an abortive attempt to resolve the issue before the Zemsky Sobor convened. Acknowledging that Boris was too powerful to defeat outright, they offered to make him czar if he would accept a limited monarchy similar to Poland's. Realizing that he would become little more than a figurehead if he accepted this offer, Boris refused.

On February 17, 1598, the Zemsky Sobor met under the chairmanship of Patriarch Job and, to no one's surprise, elected Boris Godunov czar of Russia, thereby officially sanctioning what many have called his second reign. Boris delayed accepting the crown until August and used the intervening months to solidify support from the army and the gentry. He also prepared himself for the possibility that a serious challenge would surface from among the disgruntled boyars.

During his own reign, Boris Godunov continued the enlightened, if occasionally cruel, administration that he had overseen as Fedor's surrogate czar during the previous 14 years. At the new czar's urging, bright young men were sent abroad, many to England, to be educated and to acquire the customs of sophisticated and cultured countries. Following an exceptionally poor harvest, the czar opened the government's warehouses and distributed grain to the needy. He instituted judicial reforms aimed at treating all men as equals before the law, and reversed an earlier law that had denied peasants the right to move from one estate to another. Although his reign was characterized by good works, Boris feared that the boyars would lift themselves from their lethargy and disarray and organize against him. Seeing enemies and potential enemies everywhere, Boris maintained an extensive and costly network of spies and informers. There was hardly a boyar household that did not have a servant in the czar's employ.

In reality, most boyar families posed no real threat to Boris. They constantly fought among themselves and were, for the most part, unpopular with the people. Moreover, their wealth and influence had been greatly diminished by Ivan the Terrible's Oprichnina. The family Boris feared most was the Romanovs. Although neither they nor Boris could claim the throne through bloodlines, a Romanov had been the wife of one czar, Ivan the Terrible, and the mother of another, Fedor I. These facts gave the Romanov family a claim that was marginally stronger than Boris's, which was based on his association with the late Czar Fedor I.

Because of their strong ties to Ivan, the Romanovs had survived the Oprichnina terror better than most noble families. Boris respected and feared the Romanovs' power. In June 1601, acting on a dubious accusation that the Romanovs were plotting to poison him, Czar Boris confiscated their estates and exiled them to widely dispersed locations, including Siberia's endless wastelands, which would become the favored place where Russian rulers sent their opponents during the next three and one-half centuries. Boris banished Fedor, the eldest of the Romanov clan and a nephew of Czarina Anastasia, to an isolated monastery in the far northern forest region of Archangel. Fedor Romanov was forced to become a monk and given the name Philaret; his wife was compelled to enter a convent; and their son, Michael, was exiled to the Monastery of St. Cyril in Byelozero, in what would later be a part of Russia.

That same year, weeks of torrential summer rains caused major floods that swept away livestock and destroyed crops ripening in the fields. When an early freeze prevented new plantings and killed seeds already in the ground, Russia suffered its worst famine in memory. By the tens of thousands, peasants abandoned the landowners' estates and migrated south, where the promise of fertile lands taken from the Tartars by Ivan the Terrible offered hope. Many joined the growing communities of the Cossacks who roamed the steppes, fished the rivers, and raided for a living. The migration became so large that the estate owners, especially the landed gentry who owned their estates and service to the czar, had insufficient workers to till their land. The flight of the peasants forced the czar and the Duma to enact a law making the desertions a crime with serious punishment, thus beginning the transformation of free Russian peasants into serfs who were tied to land owned by others.

Unable to deliver on his promise to feed the people of Moscow, where reports of cannibalism were common and more than 100,000 starved to death, Czar Boris Godunov, whose popularity with the people of the capital had helped him win the throne, quickly fell into disfavor. The habitually superstitious Russians saw the rains, the early frost, and the peasants' flight as God's punishment for something that Boris had done, perhaps for his treatment of Czarina Alexandra's family, or even for the murder of young Dmitri, the half-brother of the late Czar Fedor.

❖ ❖ ❖

Practically from the day on which Dmitri died in 1591, there were rumors that the youth who was buried in the cemetery at Uglitch was not Dmitri. According to the gossip, Prince Dmitri had been saved from the killer's blade and spirited away to safety. In 1602, these rumors became widespread, and a starving, desperate populace became increasingly convinced that Ivan the Terrible's illegitimate heir still lived and would be their salvation. Boris's extensive network of spies and informers kept him abreast of the people's mood, and he genuinely tried to find evidence that the boy had survived, even torturing members of several boyar families who, it was said, had given Dmitri shelter during the intervening years. He uncovered no proof and managed only to turn more people against him as word of his efforts spread.

In 1604, a young man professing to be the czarevitch Dmitri came to Moscow's attention. The early life of this youth, who would later be called the False Dmitri, is as shrouded in mystery as his claim to the throne of Russia. Ostensibly, he had been living in the home of Fedor Romanov and was forced

Czar Dmitri "the False"

to flee when his master was taken into custody and exiled. Conflicting accounts have him living as a monk, riding with a band of Cossacks on the steppes, and working in the kitchens of a Russian nobleman in the Ukraine. Wherever his earlier travels took him, he ended up in Poland in the employ of a Polish prince, Adam Wisniowiecki, the owner of vast estates along the Polish-Russian border. In the fall of 1603, when the prince slapped him during a confrontation, he castigated Wisniowiecki by saying that the prince would not treat him that way if he knew that he was Crown Prince Dmitri, the son of the late Czar Ivan of Russia. When the incredulous prince challenged his claim, Dmitri, as he is called because his real name is not known, produced a jewel-encrusted cross that he said had been used at his baptism.

Although it is unclear whether or not Prince Wisniowiecki actually believed Dmitri's account of his narrow escape from Boris Godunov's assassins, the Polish nobleman saw an opportunity to attack the hated Russian ruler in Moscow. In March 1604, Wisniowiecki presented Dmitri to Poland's King Sigismund III, who also welcomed the chance to strike a blow at Russia. The king concurred with the young man's claim of being the czarevitch Dmitri, heir to his father's dynasty.

Word that the heir was alive and living in Poland under the protection of the Polish king spread rapidly throughout Russia. Boris sealed the western frontier and ordered that anyone attempting to cross without authority be arrested. Ignoring the czar's ultimatum that Prince Wisniowiecki hand over Dmitri or face reprisals, the Poles moved the pretender farther into Poland, prompting a Russian army raid that destroyed the Prince's estates. Meanwhile, Dmitri renounced Orthodoxy and embraced Roman Catholicism there by increasing his support in Poland, especially among the Jesuits, several of whom had joined his entourage. His convenient conversion to Catholicism was kept secret in order to avoid estranging the Orthodox Russians whose support he would need in any bid for the Moscow crown.

At this time, Russia's southern and southeastern regions were ripe for revolution. Many of the inhabitants were former peasants who had fled the large estates in central Russia during the famine, and either had joined the growing Cossack communities or were largely sympathetic to them. The Cossacks were fiercely proud of their independence and answered to no authority, especially the central government in Moscow. To a Cossack, freedom was everything. Russian armies were regularly sent south to put down the Cossacks' lawlessness and bring them under Moscow's rule as taxpaying citizens. An incident in the spring of 1604 showed how powerful the Cossacks had become. When the czar's brother and chief of police, Simeon Godunov, led a military force into the Volga region to put down a revolt, his column was attacked by Cossacks. Simeon barely escaped capture and was forced to flee north with only a handful of his troops, the remainder having been killed, captured, or scattered by the attackers. The Cossack chieftain, or "hetman," returned several prisoners to Moscow with a message for the czar: the Cossacks would soon be coming to Moscow at the head of an army supporting "Czar Dmitri."

In this climate, the False Dmitri found fertile ground to mobilize an army in support of his claim to the throne. With secret backing from the Poles and the Catholic Church, which saw an opportunity to divorce Russia from its Orthodoxy, Dmitri began his military campaign against Boris by crossing from

Poland into Russia in September 1604. The czar launched a propaganda campaign against Dmitri, charging that he was not only an imposter but a tool of the Polish nobles. Prince Basil Shuisky, who had presided over the inquiry into Dmitri's death, corroborated Boris's statement that Dmitri definitely had died in 1591, and that the man claiming to be Dmitri unquestionably was an imposter. Patriarch Job, whose position depended on Boris's remaining on the throne, renounced Dmitri as a usurper in league with the Catholics. But the effect of these attacks on Dmitri was the opposite of what was intended, as mobs daily packed the streets around the Kremlin, devouring every piece of information or misinformation about the resurrected heir.

Boris was unsure of what to do about Dmitri, in part because he was unsure whether the man was actually whom he claimed to be or an imposter. Matters became more complicated when the czar's agents gathered information indicating that there were actually two pretenders, one possibly being the real Dmitri and the other an imposter, or both false claimants to the throne. The Kremlin wrestled with the problem of how to stop the Dmitri who had won unofficial support from the Polish king, including a large grant of money to finance his cause.

Hoping to establish at last whether the boy buried in Uglitch was really Dmitri, Boris had the former czarina Maria, Dmitri's mother, secretly brought to Moscow, where he questioned her. After her son's funeral, on Boris's orders she had been sent to a convent, where she was given the name Sister Martha. Now she reportedly told the czar, whom she obviously hated because she was convinced he had killed her son and had exiled her to a spartan life of confinement, that her son had been secretly taken from Uglitch before the assassins could reach him. The revelation left Boris no less confused than before because he did not know whether to believe her. Boris had hoped that she would testify that her son was dead, thereby ending both the controversy and Dmitri's threat to his reign. Sister Martha was quickly returned to her convent.

Even the exhumation of the body buried at Uglitch failed to settle the question that all Russia was asking: Was the boy in the grave Dmitri Ivanovich, the heir to the throne? Compounding his mental anguish, Boris was suffering from physical pain. His right foot was constantly wrapped in bandages because of severe gout, and he no longer had the appearance of a strong and confident man. The trials that he and Russia had endured during his reign, and the unexpected appearance of a claimant to the throne who called himself the son of Ivan the Terrible, had aged Boris beyond his 52 years.

Dmitri's movement gathered momentum as Cossack bands and others joined his growing army of followers. He quickly took control of several towns along the route to Moscow, beginning at the border, but was halted on November 11, 1604, at Novgorod Seversk. The fortified town's garrison, under the command of Peter Basmanov, fought off first an artillery barrage, then an attack by Polish lancers, and finally three attempts to set the thick oak and mud walls surrounding the town afire. As his army was besieging Novgorod Seversk, Dmitri received an almost continual flow of officials from other towns in the area that had voted to join his cause. The newly born hatred for the once popular Boris Godunov had broken the back of resistance to Dmitri's forces in the Russian countryside, and Dmitri reaped the benefits.

Fearing for his realm, Boris sent 50,000 well-equipped troops commanded by Prince Fedor Mstislavsky, a hero of Moscow's epic stand against the Crimean Tartars, to relieve Novgorod Seversk. By the third week of December, the relief force was deployed less than 10 miles from Novgorod Seversk. Unable to pull his infantry from around the city because the garrison was making frequent sallies outside the walls to attack the besiegers, Dmitri sent a force of Cossacks and Polish lancers against Mstislavsky. In a surprise attack the mounted force galloped into the Russian camp and dispersed the relief troops, many of whom either secretly supported Dmitri or were unwilling to fight against a possible son of Ivan the Terrible and heir to the throne.

Dmitri's quick victory over the army from Moscow created more problems than it solved for the pretender. The relief army had little in the way of booty with which to satisfy the large contingent of Cossacks among Dmitri's forces, and it carried no treasury with which to pay the Polish lancers who had begun demanding their salaries. Unable to satisfy either group of mercenaries, Dmitri soon found that his army was melting away. By the second week of January 1605, he had less than 1,500 men with which to continue his siege of Novgorod Seversk. Fortunately for Dmitri, Basmanov, still in command of the town, had no idea that his assailant's forces had dwindled to so low a level. Had he known the state of Dmitri's army, he surely would have launched a massive counterattack that undoubtedly would have destroyed Dmitri, ending his threat to Boris's reign.

Word of the widespread defections from Dmitri's army did reach Moscow, however, elating Boris, who had gone into depression when his own relief force had been scattered. Anxious to finish off Dmitri, Boris sent Prince Basil Shuisky with about 30,000 reinforcements to help Mstislavsky regroup his army and attack Dmitri. Meanwhile, Dmitri was bolstered by the arrival from the southern reaches of the Dnieper River of roughly 12,000 Zaporozhian Cossack cavalry, who claimed they would fight for him without pay. Abandoning his siege of Novgorod Seversk, Dmitri moved his rejuvenated army 12 miles to the northeast, to Putivl, a town that had already accepted him as the heir apparent.

The reorganized Moscow relief force, under the combined leadership of Mstislavsky and Shuisky, attacked Dmitri's army on January 20, 1605, and routed it: nearly half of the Cossacks were killed by heavy artillery and sustained firing from more than 10,000 musketeers. With Dmitri driven farther to the west, Mstislavsky and Shuisky squandered their resources by invading towns that had gone over to the pretender, and killing and torturing thousands of officials, instead of pursuing the remaining enemy force and decimating it.

A final victory for the czar's forces appeared imminent when, on April 13, 1605, Boris Godunov suddenly died. The cause of his death was unknown, but again poison was widely suspected. The throne of Russia now passed to Boris's 16-year-old son, Fedor. Reputed to be highly intelligent and well-liked, Fedor Godunov was crowned Fedor II, and his mother, Marya, was named regent. Once more, intrigue and deception prevailed in Moscow. Although some boyars willingly swore allegiance to Fedor and Marya, without Boris to protect them many others considered it safer to hedge their bets and found ways to delay taking their oaths. One of those who did not swear allegiance to the new czar was Peter Basmanov, the defender of Novgorod Seversk, whom Czar Fedor II named to direct the campaign against Dmitri.

Fedor Godunov and his mother were to hold the reins of power in Moscow for only a few weeks. Basmanov apparently had had second thoughts about Dmitri's true identity. He initially had labeled him a common criminal, often referring to him as "the thief." Then, to the surprise of both camps, on May 17, 1605, Basmanov told his soldiers that he believed Dmitri was indeed Ivan's son and the rightful heir to the throne. Joined by the overwhelming majority of his troops, Basmanov threw his strength behind the faltering Dmitri, giving the pretender the impetus he needed to march on Moscow.

Meanwhile, efforts continued in many quarters to learn the truth about the pretender. Dmitri's real identity still remains clouded, although most historians agree that he was not Ivan the Terrible's son. There is a strong, although unproven, conviction that he was actually Gregory Otrepiev, the son of a minor official in a rural village, who became a monk after failing in every other occupation. Otrepiev resided in a monastery in or near Moscow during 1601 and 1602, but he incurred the displeasure of both Church and state authorities when he began telling other monks that he expected someday to be czar. Learning of his imminent arrest, Otrepiev fled Moscow for the south. He lived among the Cossacks for a while, evidently convincing many of them that he was Czarevitch Dmitri Ivanovich, before moving on to Poland. If Gregory Otrepiev actually was the pretender, he was either a consummate actor, or he came to believe his own fantasy about being Ivan's son. Although most of the Poles and the Russian boyars supported him because they saw in him a way to depose Boris Godunov, many others did believe his story. Dmitri the Pretender conducted himself in the manner expected of a czar, with great dignity and intelligence. In battle he was brave, and in sophisticated company he was charming and convincing. Dmitri has been described as homely, with wild red hair that resisted all efforts to keep it from standing on end. His large nose and a substantial wart occupied most of his face, and one of his arms was longer than the other, a deformity that also afflicted the real Dmitri.

Dmitri's forces grew daily, swollen with defectors from the Russian army, as he advanced toward the capital. Inside Moscow, mobs of his supporters swarmed through the streets, attacking those who earlier had favored Boris. In Red Square, the mob placed Prince Basil Shuisky on a platform and called on him to tell the truth about what had happened to Dmitri Ivanovich in 1591. Realizing that he faced certain death if he repeated his original story—that he had personally seen the young Dmitri placed in his grave—Basil recanted. He told the mob that Boris had ordered the czarevitch killed, but that his agents had mistakenly murdered a priest's son who had been sacrificed to save the heir to the throne. It would not be the last time that Basil Shuisky changed his story.

The mob then rushed the Kremlin guards and quickly overwhelmed them. Czar Fedor, his sister, Xenia, and his mother, Regent Marya, were carried off. The Godunovs were held under house arrest at the family home in the city.

On June 10, a group of thugs operating on orders from two princes who represented Dmitri's camp killed both Czar Fedor II and his mother. Fedor's sister, Xenia, said to be a beautiful virgin, was carried off, her fate unknown, although it was rumored at the time that she was banished to a convent. At the end of the month, Dmitri rode triumphantly into Moscow, where he was greeted by cheering crowds and ringing church bells. One of his first acts was to return the czarevitch Dmitri's mother, Sister Martha, to Moscow. The two met privately for several minutes. What transpired between them can only be surmised, but after the meeting Sister Martha declared that Dmitri was indeed her son and the son of Ivan the Terrible. She was given an apartment in the Kremlin, where she lived in the luxury befitting the wife of one czar and the mother of another.

Dmitri was crowned on July 30, 1605, in a grand ceremony inside the Kremlin's Cathedral of the Assumption. He immediately had Boris Godunov's confidants executed or exiled, and called back to Moscow the surviving boyars that the late czar had exiled. Among the first to return was Father Philaret, the former Fedor Romanov, who elected to remain in the Church and accepted Dmitri's appointment as metropolitan of Moscow. Philaret was reunited with his wife and his son Michael, both of whom had been exiled by Boris. Patriarch Job, a creation of Boris Godunov, was stripped of his credentials and driven into exile in a remote monastery.

At first Dmitri retained his popularity, although many Muscovites wondered why a Jesuit priest had participated in his Orthodox coronation ceremony. Soon people in the capital began to speak out against the many Catholic priests and Polish nobles who surrounded the new czar. The Poles, who behaved as if Moscow was an occupied city, despised the Russians, who returned the sentiment. In addition, the people of Moscow heard disturbing rumors that Czar Dmitri planned to marry a Polish Catholic woman, which would constitute heresy in the eyes of Orthodox Russians. The more conservative elements of Moscow society were also critical of the new czar's lifestyle. Foregoing the devout religious observances of previous czars, Dmitri ignored revered traditional customs, including attending mass, and was often seen walking about the city, dressed in Polish clothing. Many people resented that the czar acted like a common man, albeit a wealthy one. Through the centuries, Russians had always felt secure with authoritarian rulers who exhibited the strength to lead the nation and protect it against foreigner invaders or usurpers.

Dmitri's harmonious relationship with the Poles began to sour when, despite the insistence of the Jesuits who had accompanied him throughout his campaign, he gave no sign of beginning the promised conversion of Russia from Orthodoxy to Catholicism. Either he never intended to fulfill his promise, or he realized that to do so would make him a heretic in the eyes of Russians and cost him the throne and probably his life. He did temporarily placate the Poles and the Catholic clergy by announcing his intention to unite Christian Europe under his leadership and drive the Ottoman Turks from Europe; however, it was an empty gesture, as everyone recognized immediately.

Just as his predecessor had hoped to found a new dynasty, so Dmitri understood that he would have to marry and father a son in order to leave an heir. An heir would confirm his legitimacy as czar in the eyes of the people (who viewed such a child as a divine mandate) and help him rebuff the boyars, who, having used him to depose Boris, no longer needed him and had begun plotting against him. In his 10-month reign, which was distinguished by his poor judgment, Dmitri's choice of a bride was his most critical blunder. Instead of making a practical, political selection from among the many attractive daughters of the loyal boyar families, he allowed his emotions to dictate his choice.

While living in Poland, Dmitri had met and fallen in love with Marina Miniszech, the daughter of a minor Polish nobleman who was one of his earliest supporters. Their love had survived their long separation as Dmitri led his armies against Czar Boris, and in November 1605, Dmitri, through an emissary, petitioned King Sigismund III for permission to marry Marina. The king of Poland was happy to approve the marriage, which he believed would cement relations with the czar. Sigismund also anticipated that the devout Marina would influence Dmitri to keep his promise to convert Russia to Catholicism.

In late November, a Catholic marriage ceremony was conducted in Cracow, with a proxy standing in for the absent czar. Present at the ceremony were King Sigismund III, a representative from the Vatican, Sweden's Princess Anne, and Dmitri's personal envoy. Cardinal Maciejowsky, the archbishop of Cracow, performed the ceremony. After several months, delay, Marina joined her husband in Moscow in May 1606.

Marina's arrival in Russia's capital on May 2 stunned the Muscovites. She was accompanied by her father and an impressive retinue that included many Catholic clergymen and Polish nobles. Six days later she and Dmitri were married again, this time in an Orthodox ceremony conducted in the presence of numerous Catholics and without the bride's converting to Orthodoxy. That same day she was crowned czarina. Several days of wild celebrations followed, with the hated Poles taking a more active part than the Russian nobles. Moscow's citizens resented everything that had occurred. They were chagrined that the czar's wife was a Catholic who had no intention of converting. Shocked by the drunken behavior of the Polish wedding guests, who roamed the streets singing Polish songs, and outraged by reports that Dmitri intended to build a Catholic church inside the Kremlin, Muscovites were primed for a revolt against the czar.

The disgruntled crowds that gathered daily outside the Kremlin to protest these indignities were skillfully manipulated by the boyars, especially by agents of Basil Shuisky, for whom Dmitri had outlived his usefulness. Eventually incited to anarchy, the crowds became a screaming mob that attacked Poles and Catholic priests. Some of the latter took to wearing fake beards to disguise themselves as Orthodox clergy.

Czar Dmitri's marriage to a Catholic, together with the general Russian hatred for Poles, resulted in violence on Saturday, May 20, when armed men employed by the boyars led rioters into the Kremlin and then into the czar's quarters. Peter Basmanov, the turncoat hero of Novgorod Seversk, tried to protect Dmitri but was cut down, and his body was thrown from a window. The mob had been told that the Poles were plotting to kill Dmitri and take over the country, so most of the rioters thought they were acting to save the czar, not to kill him. But those in the vanguard had their orders and knew precisely what their mission was. Dmitri tried to escape by leaping from a window; he broke a leg in the fall and was shot dead by someone working for the boyars. Meanwhile, most of the rioters had forgotten why they had broken into the Kremlin and turned instead to looting. The bodies of Dmitri and Basmanov were hung in Red Square for all to see, and Basil Shuisky again changed his story, now assuring the people that the true Dmitri had died in Uglitch in 1591. The False Dmitri's body was dismembered and burned. The ashes were fired toward Poland from several cannons because many people believed Dmitri was a sorcerer who possessed the power to bring the separated parts of his body back together again and rise from the dead. Overnight, rumors sprung up among the common people, alleging that this was exactly what had happened with the scattered ashes; if Dmitri could rise from the dead once, who was to say that he could not do so again?

Most of the Poles who remained in Moscow were experienced soldiers, and they fought off the gangs that attacked their homes. Czarina Marina went into hiding, protected by an armed guard of Polish hussars who had been sent by her father. In a few days, Moscow quieted down as its citizens returned to their regular schedules and looters counted their booty.

Basil Shuisky had engineered Czar Dmitri's murder to gain the throne for himself, but a hastily convened Zemsky Sobor never actually elected him czar. Instead, prodded by Shuisky's agents, a mob in Red Square demanded his immediate appointment. The Council of Boyars reluctantly agreed after Basil promised that he would share power with it. He also promised that any boyar accused of a crime would be tried by a jury of his peers before being punished. These were empty promises made by a man lusting for power, a fact not lost on the council members, many of whom were descendants of Rurik and therefore qualified to claim the throne. However, Basil Shuisky had organized and controlled the events that brought down the False Dmitri, and he was obviously prepared to use his power over the mobs against the disorganized boyars who might oppose him. On May 27, 1606, Basil Shuisky was crowned czar, choosing the title Basil IV to indicate his own ancestral ties to the earlier rulers of Russia.

The new czar inherited a hopelessly chaotic Russia. In the countryside, bands of Cossacks raided towns and looted almost at will. Several minor princes revolted against Moscow's rule, and Czar Basil IV had great difficulty mounting sufficient forces to put them down. Several more false claimants to the throne appeared among groups with revolutionary leanings. The Ural Cossacks rose in revolt behind a man claiming to be Czar Fedor's son. Fedor never had a son, but he did father a daughter named Theodosia, who died within a few months of her birth. The pretender, who called himself Peter, said that his mother, Czarina Irina, had feared that Boris Godunov would kill him in order to keep his own path to the throne open; hence, Irina had claimed she had given birth to a girl. The czarina then had her son taken quietly from Moscow and substituted as her own an infant girl who had been born to a servant. The Ural Cossacks' revolt was quickly quashed. So was another, led by a soldier who had been imprisoned by the Turks for several years before he could organize a rabble army of escaped slaves, peasants, deserters, and Cossacks.

Realizing that his own position was severely threatened by the spate of pretenders who saw profit in claiming they were the young Prince Dmitri, Basil IV had the body that had been buried in Uglitch disinterred. In a solemn procession led by Basil himself, the casket was carried through Moscow's streets to the burial crypt reserved for czars and their families in the Cathedral of the Assumption. To convince the populace that here, at last, was the real Dmitri, Basil's agents circulated stories that several miracles had occurred near the site where the body was originally buried. These stories were intended to prove to the superstitious and devout people that the body was that of the true Dmitri, and that Dmitri had actually died in 1591, for only by dying could Dmitri perform miracles.

❖ ❖ ❖

The frequent turnover of czars—from Boris Godunov to Fedor II to the False Dmitri to Basil IV, four in all in less than two years—eroded the people's confidence in the stability of the Moscow government and widened the gap between the boyars and the rest of the population. People began to view themselves less as Russians and more as belonging to a social class. They resented the boyars for conspiring to kill at least two czars, Fedor II and the False Dmitri, and for installing one of their own on the throne. The Russian people thought of the czar as their protector against the greed of the boyars. If the nobles placed the crown on the head of one of their number, as they did, there would be no one to stand between the boyars and the defenseless people. Muscovites began deriding Basil as the "boyar czar."

Basil Shuisky was czar in name, but he did not enjoy the absolute power held by his predecessors. His authority had been compromised by the concessions he made to the Council of Boyars in exchange for its approval of his accession. The numerous revolts taking place around the country also restricted the size of his realm as one province after another fell, even temporarily, under the control of some rebel leader. Most of Basil's time on the throne was spent trying to hold on to it.

In June 1607, a man claiming to be both the czarevitch Dmitri and the late czar Dmitri (the False Dmitri) presented a serious challenge to Basil's reign. Little credibility would have been given to the imposter had it not been for the support his claim received from the former czarina Marina, the False Dmitri's Polish wife, who swore he was her husband and that he had managed to escape Basil Shuisky's assassins. Calling himself Prince Dmitri, this man of obscure background gathered about him a large and diverse army that included Cossacks; Russian, Polish, and Lithuanian soldiers of fortune; angry peasants; escaped slaves; and disgruntled minor nobles who had suffered financial losses at the hands of the boyars.

In the spring of 1608, Prince Dmitri led his army of at least 30,000 men south toward Moscow. Along the way, around Volkhov, he defeated an army commanded by the czar's brother, Dmitri Shuisky, who then fled back to Moscow. In mid-summer, Prince Dmitri's forces reached Tushino, a few miles from Moscow, where he built a fortified camp, declared himself czar of Russia, and established a court and bureaucracy to rival the Moscow administration. Neither Dmitri nor Basil IV was able to unseat the other, and military activities between the two capitals settled down to routine skirmishes. Czar Dmitri acted as if Czar Basil did not exist. He collected taxes in the areas his forces controlled, issued land grants and titles, and judged and punished criminals. Every dissatisfied citizen and malcontent who harbored a grudge against Czar Basil flocked to Czar Dmitri's realm in Tushino. Among these was Metropolitan Philaret, the former Fedor Romanov, who had been freed from exile by the False Dmitri. Philaret had himself appointed patriarch of Tushino, filling an important position in the pretender's court because a patriarch of the Church was supposed to advise the czar on religious matters.

Numerous towns and cities recognized Prince Dmitri as czar, and his authority expanded to include large portions of the country. His military forces gradually gained control of all the roads leading to Moscow, effectively block-ading the city. The blockade was only partially effective as a brisk correspon-dence between the two capitals was maintained by families that regularly switched sides or that had members in both camps: with the battle over who was the true czar at a stalemate, many prominent households were hedging their bets by supporting both czars. Prince Dmitri reinforced his claim to the throne by bringing Sister Martha, the young Dmitri's mother, to Tushino; there, she publicly avowed that Prince Dmitri, who in no way resembled her son, was actually the real Dmitri and Ivan the Terrible's rightful heir. These were curious times, made even more curious by the extreme lengths to which ambitious leaders and their follows went in order to gain their objectives. No one really believed that Prince Dmitri was the former czar Dmitri, yet the former czarina Marina insisted that he was her husband and she lived with him as his wife. No one really believed that Prince Dmitri was the reincarnation of the czarevitch Dmitri, who had died in 1591, yet his mother, the former czarina Maria, insisted that he was her son. Even more astonishing was the widespread support he was able to assemble for his self-proclaimed regime, although that may have been more a reflection of popular disaffection with Basil than a demonstration of genuine support for Dmitri.

The blockade of Moscow continued through the end of 1608 and into the new year. Inside the Kremlin, Czar Basil was hoping to receive assistance from the larger Russian cities, most of which remained noncommittal and were waiting to see which czar would prevail. To balance the help that King Sigismund III of Poland was channeling to Prince Dmitri, Czar Basil sent his nephew, Prince Michael Skopin-Shuisky, to Sweden to obtain aid. In February 1609, the able and intelligent young prince negotiated an agreement with Sweden's King Charles IX. Russia abandoned its claim to Livonia and ceded a small stretch of territory along the Russian-Swedish border; in return, it received a detachment of 5,000 seasoned troops under General Jakob De la Gardie to help Czar Basil break Prince Dmitri's stranglehold on Moscow.

Swedish participation in Russia's civil war brought a declaration of war against Moscow from Poland's King Sigismund III. In September 1609, a Polish army invaded Russian territory and laid siege to Smolensk.

Throughout most of 1610, Prince Skopin-Shuisky led De la Gardie's Swedish cavalry south, recapturing towns and important roads from Prince Dmitri's forces, and destroying several bands of Cossacks and other brigands who had been plundering cities and towns loyal to Moscow. At the same time, an army of Russians was clearing the eastern provinces of Prince Dmitri's supporters and gradually making its way to the capital. This volunteer army had been raised and equipped by the merchants of the northern cities of Vologda, Kholmogory, and Ustyug, who had been conducting a lively and profitable trade with British ships in the White Sea. The merchants required a stable government in Russia in order to continue in business, and they considered Prince Dmitri, whom many referred to as the "Brigand of Tushino," as little better than a thief. On March 12, 1610, the two armies—Prince Skopin-Shuisky's Swedish cavalry and the northern volunteers—converged on Moscow and lifted the siege.

Meanwhile, the well-fortified and garrisoned city of Smolensk refused to yield to the Polish invaders. Sigismund ordered the Polish troops in Tushino to buttress his army outside Smolensk. Aside from the Cossacks, who for the most part were good fighters but at heart were brigands in search of loot, the Polish troopers were Prince Dmitri's most dependable soldiers, and he could not afford to lose the men, who nevertheless obeyed their king's command and deserted Tushino to join in the siege of Smolensk.

Confronted with the desertion of his Polish troops and the collapse of the Moscow blockade, Prince Dmitri abandoned Tushino and fled southwest to Kaluga, where he attempted to raise another army among that city's lower classes but with only modest success. Czar Basil sent a relief force under his brother, Prince Dmitri Shuisky, to lift the siege of Smolensk, but on June 24 the Poles routed it completely. Smolensk remained under siege.

Prince Dmitri's Russian supporters in Tushino knew what would happen if they fell into Basil's hands and decided to throw in their lot with the Poles. They sent a deputation to King Sigismund, proposing that his 15-year-old son, Ladislaus, become czar of Russia. In return, they asked that Poland recognize the prerogatives of the Orthodox Church and the rights of Russian nobles. Sigismund agreed and sent his top military aide, General Stanislas Zholkievski, to Moscow with a sizable army. Prince Dmitri, who continued to claim that he was the rightful occupant of the Russian throne, was also marching on the capital with the new army he had raised in Kaluga.

In early July, both armies reached Moscow, where they maintained an uneasy peace. Not wanting a confrontation with the large Polish force, General De la Gardie withdrew his Swedish contingent from Moscow and repaired to Novgorod, which he occupied as if it were a Swedish vassal state. Inside Moscow, partisans of Dmitri and the Poles campaigned to win support for their side from the city's population, and Czar Basil's situation grew more precarious. Rioting soon broke out in the streets as the claimants' supporters battled with each other. On July 17, an armed mob assembled in Red Square and demanded that Basil step aside or face bloodshed inside the Kremlin. Wearied by the bitter fighting and turmoil, Basil relinquished the throne. He was seized by a group of boyars and forced to take the vows of a monk.

The potentially hostile forces surrounding the city prevented the convening of the national assembly, so the Duma decided to appoint a regent to rule until a new czar could be selected. The appointment went to the president of the Duma, Prince Fedor Mstislavsky, who was now an old man too weak to rule. Ignoring Prince Dmitri and disregarding the agreement with the Poles that proposed Ladislaus as new czar, Patriarch Hermogen urged the Duma to select a Russian of royal blood as czar. The Duma instead ignored the patriarch. Observing that Prince Dmitri's followers were little more than a collection of looters and thieves who would lay waste to the city, the boyars elected to renew their earlier choice, king Sigismund's son. Deputies were sent to the Polish camp to urge General Zholkievski to drive Dmitri's army away so the city's gates could be opened to him. The general agreed, and on September 20 the Polish army entered Moscow.

The boyars swore allegiance to Ladislaus as the czar-designate. They sent a deputation to King Sigismund, who was camped outside Smolensk with his main army, to ratify the agreements made earlier with the boyars from Tushino. With his army now in control of Moscow, Sigismund no longer needed to mask his true intentions. He told the Moscow representatives, who included Hermogen's rival, Patriarch Philaret, that he himself proposed to rule Russia as king, and under no circumstances would he permit his son Ladislaus to convert to Orthodoxy, a condition the Russians had insisted on but which he had never actually approved. Remembering what had happened when the False Dmitri married a Catholic woman, the boyars knew that the Russian people would never accept a Catholic czar and would tolerate even less a Polish king occupying the Moscow throne. Sigismund ignored their pleas and sent several of them, including Philaret, to Poland as hostages.

When the news of Sigismund's demand reached Moscow, the boyars and the entire city became despondent. General Zholkievski, unhappy with his king's decision, retired from the military and returned to Poland. He was replaced by General Alexander Gosiewski, who disregarded the Duma and set up a military dictatorship to rule Moscow. One of his first acts was to make it illegal for Russians inside the city to bear arms. Polish troops gathered all the arms they could find, leaving the population virtually helpless in the face of the well-equipped Polish soldiers.

Without a czar the Russian nation faced extinction. The Poles occupied the capital and most of western Russia, and the Swedes held Novgorod and almost all of northwestern Russia. Suddenly, the pretender, Prince Dmitri, became a viable option for restoring Russian self-rule. By December 1610, Prince Dmitri, who had returned to Kaluga after the Poles had driven his army away from Moscow, was experiencing a resurgence of popularity. But on the 21st of that month, he was murdered by one of his own men in a personal dispute, and the last Russian claimant to the throne was gone. In the absence of a Russian candidate, even the Swedish government made a bid for the throne, advancing its own Prince Philip as a potential czar. The Swedes seriously considered establishing Novgorod as the new capital of Russia and crowning Philip czar, but nothing came of the plan. In Moscow, the boyars were forced to accept a compromise: Ladislaus would be czar, and Sigismund III of Poland was to be regent until the new czar arrived in the city.

Though Russia was now without a political leader, Patriarch Hermogen proved to be a strong voice on behalf of his country. Assuming the mantle of national leader, the patriarch called on the Russians to rise and drive out the foreign invaders. He was soon arrested by the Polish military government and thrown into jail, where he died after prolonged torture. Before he died, however, the Poles forced Hermogen to address a large audience in Red Square; he was instructed to urge the people not to resist Sigismund's government. Instead, the courageous clergyman used the opportunity to tell the throng that God would bless those who rose up to save the sovereignty of Moscow, and would curse those who were traitors to Russia. That was the last time Hermogen was seen alive. In January 1612, the patriarch died in his prison cell at the hands of his captors.

The united Russia of the three Ivans and the two Basils was now divided into three sections. One, centered around Moscow and the territory west of the capital, reaching to the Polish border, was ruled at least nominally by the king of Poland, Sigismund III. His army of occupation daily registered the contempt of the Russian population under its control. In the northwest, centered around the city of Novgorod, the Swedes held sway, although their hold on the rural population was less than they would have liked. The remainder of Russia had no ruler or government of any kind. Without a central government, this southern and eastern portion of the country faced the real possibility of regressing to the time when Russia was not a nation at all, but a series of principalities ruled by local princes and boyars. This situation was intolerable for the more conservative elements of Russian society, especially the Church and the merchant class, for whom a united and stable country was vital. This period of domestic instability and foreign domination has become known as the "National Phase" of the Time of Troubles. It ended with the eventual expulsion of the Poles and the Swedes, and with the founding of an entirely new dynasty that would rule Russia into the 20th century.

❖ ❖ ❖

Patriarch Hermogen's death had left the Russian Orthodox Church without a central figure who could hold it together, but that void was soon filled by Abbot Dionysus and the monks of the well-fortified Monastery of the Holy Trinity, located 40 miles north of Moscow. The monastery had been founded by one of the most revered saints in the Russian Church, St. Sergius, which gave it a special place in the hearts of the devout. Abbot Dionysus and the other monks living there were deeply pious and, more importantly, devotedly nationalistic. Their unbridled resistance to Polish occupation had caused Sigismund to send a Polish detachment there with orders to arrest the monks and occupy the abbey, but the invaders had failed and instead laid a siege that lasted several months. From his enforced confinement, Abbot Dionysus secretly sent inspirational messages to churches throughout the country, calling on the Russian people to unite against the foreigners and bring about the salvation of Russia.

In October 1611, one of the abbot's letters was read to a congregation attending mass in the cathedral in the town of Nizhni Novgorod on the Volga River. Located east of Moscow, the town was beyond the control of either the Poles or the Swedes. In the congregation was a butcher named Kozma Minin, who had grown wealthy as a cattle dealer and had once been elected mayor. Motivated by both the abbot's predicament and his call to save Russia and Orthodoxy from the foreign invaders, Minin publicly pledged all his possessions to the cause and convinced many of his fellow merchants to follow his lead. With the donated funds and the help of his friend, Prince Dmitri Pozharsky, a former Russian general who had been wounded while fighting against the Poles, Minin raised an army bent on liberating Russia. Minin, who acted as quartermaster, arranged to clothe, arm, and feed the new volunteer army, and Prince Pozharsky accepted appointment as its commander. Together, they built the army from the many peasants and small landowners who converged on Nizhni Novgorod from throughout Russia. As word of the army's formation spread, thousands of volunteers flowed daily into the town.

Minin and Pozharsky decided to pacify the countryside northeast of Moscow before marching on the capital. The area had been overrun by Cossacks and other criminal bands that were freely raiding cities and settlements, and it presented a potential danger to the new army's supply lines. Toward the end of March 1612, Prince Pozharsky led his army of probably no more than 100,000 men northwest along the Volga to Yaroslav. Along the route, the prince routed a number of brigand and Cossack bands. Once Pozharsky was in Yaroslav, his forces continued to clear the countryside of Cossacks and even of some Swedish troops who had been sent to occupy the city. Minin and Pozharsky now convened a national assembly to give their cause a nationalist cast. The delegates, who came from as many cities and districts as possible, formed a government-in-exile to rival the Polish-dominated government in Moscow. Pozharsky favored electing a czar to lead his army against the Poles in Moscow, but his plan was shelved when word reached Yaroslav that a large Polish army was hurrying toward Moscow to reinforce the capital's garrison. In August, Pozharsky led his army out of Yaroslav toward Moscow.

King Sigismund had ordered a reserve force commanded by General Jan Chodkiewicz to drive off an undisciplined Cossack army that had besieged the capital for several months; the Polish garrison had been forced to seek safety behind the Kremlin walls, where it faced certain starvation if the siege continued. The Cossacks were strong enough to maintain the siege with the active cooperation of the local population, but lacked the forces to achieve victory over the Moscow garrison or the approaching relief army. With ambitions of placing one of their own on the throne, the Cossacks sent an assassin to Yaroslav to murder Prince Pozharsky, who himself was emerging as a serious contender for the throne. The plot failed and Pozharsky continued to Moscow with his mighty army. The siege, already crippled by dissension between Cossack chieftains, soon collapsed.

Pozharsky's arrival outside Moscow with the new national army had caused the Cossacks to split into two distinct camps. One was led by Hetman Zarutsky, who had married the False Dmitri's Polish widow, Marina Miniszech, probably to enhance his own chances for acquiring the throne. Zarutsky soon withdrew from Moscow and rode off to pursue more attainable objectives in Astrakhan. The remaining Cossacks were loyal to Prince Dmitri Trubetskoy, who petitioned Pozharsky to join forces with him. The offer was rejected by the government-in-exile, which had accompanied the army, because it feared and mistrusted the Cossacks more than the Poles.

As the Polish relief column approached with food and supplies for their besieged countrymen inside the Kremlin, Pozharsky sent a detachment led by Minin to stop it. Although the battle went badly for the Russians, and Pozharsky was obliged to send reinforcements, the Cossacks sat by passively, taking no part in the action. At a critical moment, when it appeared the Russians would succumb, Abraham Palitsyn, a monk traveling with Pozharsky, exhorted the Cossack horsemen to prevent the foreign Catholic invader from destroying their Russian Orthodox brothers. The Cossacks responded to his plea and joined the Russian army, driving the Poles westward.

The Pozharsky-led siege of Polish-occupied Moscow continued and intensified. The Russians and the Cossacks realized that neither could succeed without the other, and when they learned that King Sigismund himself was planning to lead the main Polish army to relieve Moscow, they united behind a common cause.

Although there remained much mutual mistrust and dislike in both camps, the united Russian-Cossack force proved powerful enough to win the war. On October 22, 1612, the Cossacks took Kitagorod, a Polish stronghold near the Kremlin, and the Kremlin itself fell a few days later when the Polish garrison, reduced to cannibalism and seeing no hope of relief, surrendered. With the capital in their hands, Pozharsky and the Cossack Prince Trubetskoy organized a large force and sent it west. In December, it crushed King Sigismund's advancing Polish army, and Sigismund fled back to Poland.

The victorious Russians quickly set about restoring order in Moscow. They began a rebuilding program because much of the city had been burned down by the Poles during the Cossack siege. Delegates were summoned from throughout the country to attend a Zemsky Sobor that would select a new czar. By mid-January 1613, Russians of all classes—including nobles, the landed gentry who had supported Prince Pozharsky, Cossacks who had supported Prince Trubetskoy, the clergy, and even the peasants—had gathered in Moscow to form the first truly representative body in Russian's history.

Before the national assembly convened, a three-day feast was declared to celebrate the demise of the foreign usurpers, to cleanse Russia of foreign influences, and to purge those attending the assembly of the sins of the Time of Troubles.

Part Five

THE HOUSE OF ROMANOV

Czar Michael I

CHAPTER 15

MICHAEL ROMANOV AND THE NEW DYNASTY

W HEN THE ZEMSKY SOBOR, NUMBERING BETWEEN 500 and 700 members, began its sessions in January 1613, the first order of business was to establish minimum conditions that a claimant to the Russian throne must satisfy before he could be seriously considered for election as czar. The first condition, imposed despite scattered opposition, was that the candidate be a Russian. This requirement eliminated Prince Ladislaus of Poland, Prince Philip of Sweden, and another foreigner sponsored by the Hapsburgs of Austria from consideration. It also eliminated several Tartar princes who coveted the throne.

In addition, the Zemsky Sobor decided that a candidate must be unencumbered by past alliances with the factions that had battled for control of the throne during the Time of Troubles. This provision eliminated many reputable aspirants from noble families who had a genuine historical claim to the throne but who had participated in the recent military confrontations over who would be czar. Each of the two victorious armies offered its own candidate. The Cossacks nominated a young boy named Dmitri—Marina Miniszech's son by her second husband, Prince Dmitri—but the assembly swiftly rejected him. The army of national liberation put up its commander, Prince Pozharsky, but he withdrew himself from consideration. Several more candidates were advanced, including a boyar who remained imprisoned in Poland, but many delegates thought it ludicrous to elect a czar who was already a prisoner of a foreign power.

After some behind-the-scenes caucusing between the Cossacks and the landed gentry, who were well-represented in the army of national liberation, a new candidate whom both powerful factions could support emerged. Precisely which group nominated 16-year-old Michael Fedorovich Romanov is unclear.

Michael Romanov was too young to have been tainted by the struggles for the throne during the Time of Troubles. His father was the former Fedor Romanov, whom Czar Boris Godunov had forced to take religious vows and had given the name Philaret. Later, Prince Dmitri, the second False Dmitri, had appointed Philaret patriarch of Tushino, which pleased the Cossacks who had supported the Second False Dmitri's claim to the throne. Patriarch Philaret had also become a patriotic hero when King Sigismund III of Poland imprisoned him. Michael Romanov's election was virtually assured when a leader of the powerful Don Cossacks called him the "natural born czar." Moreover, the Romanovs actually had a tenuous connection to the crown through Michael's aunt Anastasia, Ivan the Terrible's popular and beloved first wife; this thin thread was enough to satisfy those among the landed gentry, the boyars, and the clergy who insisted on some measure of continuity with past czars.

In a forerunner of modern political polls, the national assembly sent representatives around the country to quietly take the pulse of the populace. They reported that Michael Romanov was an overwhelming choice with the people, ending any residual opposition to his selection. On February 21, 1613, the first Sunday of Lent on the Orthodox calendar, Michael Romanov was unanimously elected czar. The assembly announced Michael's appointment to a cheering throng in Red Square.

On March 13, a delegation from the national assembly arrived at the convent near Kostroma where Michael was staying with his mother, Sister Martha, who had taken that name after Czar Boris Godunov forced her to take the veil. Mother and son had been held hostage inside the Kremlin during the Polish occupation, but had fled to the relative safety of the convent when the Poles capitulated. Given the fate of the six previous czars, neither Sister Martha nor Michael were enthusiastic about his election. Sister Martha told the delegates that her son was too young to be czar and that she was unwilling to trust his safekeeping to a Russian population that had betrayed a half-dozen czars to whom it had pledged its loyalty. Besides, she reproached them, there was no empire left, the crown's treasures had been stolen, and there was no money with which to pay the army, so why should her son want to become czar? The delegates responded that all the towns "have come to an agreement and will be faithful." Beseeching her for approval, they pleaded that "we have all been punished" for the foolishness of the past.

In the end, there was no refusing the crown of Russia, not after the national assembly had voted unanimously for Michael and the crowds in Moscow had chanted his name. On July 11, 1613, his 17th birthday, Michael Fedorovich Romanov was crowned Michael I, czar of all of Russia.

The Empire of Russia, as it was now called, was in a worse state than what Sister Martha had described to the Zemsky Sobor's delegates. The decade of the Time of Troubles had left much of the country devastated. The populations of entire towns had vanished, whether from starvation, war, or simple flight from both. Land that for generations had produced bountiful crops to feed the millions of Russians now lay fallow, rapidly succumbing to encroaching forests. The agricultural capacity of the empire had shrunk to dangerous levels. The lands owned by the Monastery of the Holy Trinity, where the monks had held out so gallantly against the Polish siege, were a microcosm of the entire country. During the Time of Troubles, the monastery's productive crop land was reduced to one-fourth of what it had been a decade earlier. Censuses taken after Michael Romanov's accession designated nearly half the settlements in the central portion of the country as "formerly a village," and vast tracts of once cultivated fields as "waste land." Although no reliable figures exist, the population is estimated to have plummeted during the Time of Troubles from 14 million people to 9 million. Sister Martha's assessment of the devastation was frighteningly understated.

In addition, certain events that took place during the Time of Troubles were to have a far-reaching impact on Russia and on the stability of the throne.

During the upheavals, for example, the lower classes, especially the numerous peasants who had joined the campaigns of different claimants and usurpers, had learned a powerful lesson that they would not forget for 300 years, namely that the mob could unseat one czar and replace him with another.

❖ ❖ ❖

Michael I, who ruled Russia from 1613 to 1645, was a delicate youth who suffered from a painful foot ailment. His selection as czar was as much a surprise to him as it was to many who knew him. Although his mother's protestations to the national assembly delegates might have been a facade, Michael's personal reluctance to accept the title was probably genuine. To help him rule a nation that was at war with both Poland and Sweden and facing the prospect of renewed famine, with a countryside infested with outlaw bands often numbering as many as a thousand with a threatened revolt in Astrakhan by the Cossack leader Zarutsky, and with a virtually nonexistent treasury, Michael asked the Zemsky Sobor to remain in session in Moscow. In addition to the national assembly, Michael relied heavily on the boyar-dominated Duma for advice and help. Soon the young czar, whose father remained in a Polish prison and whose mother had returned to her duties as a nun following the coronation, was surrounded with self-serving bureaucrats who used their positions to enrich themselves and their families.

Michael was neither a competent nor a full-time czar. Lacking a formal education, he had spent most of his young life in an exile enforced by Boris Godunov, or in the austere conditions of Polish-controlled Moscow under Cossack siege. He was easily diverted by many playthings, including a collection of clocks with which he filled his rooms. But guided by leaders of the national assembly, he took effective action against Russia's enemies, including the Rebel Cossack hetman Zarutsky. With the relentless Marina, his current wife and former wife of the False Dmitri, goading him on, Zarutsky staged a full-scale revolt in Astrakhan, where he hoped to establish an independent state along the lower Volga River. He had sought help from the shah of Persia, but his request went unanswered. In the summer of 1614, Michael sent an army down the Volga to destroy the rebellion. After several clashes, Zarutsky's forces scattered and the hetman and Marina were captured and taken to Moscow. Zarutsky and Marina's son by Prince Dmitri were executed, and Marina was thrown into prison, where she either died of natural causes or was killed. Other Cossacks, Polish freebooters, and Russian brigands who roamed the countryside were offered amnesty if they joined the Russian army to fight against the Swedes, who still controlled Novgorod and most of the northwest; those who refused were hunted down and killed. This approach helped establish internal order and resolved one of the regime's three major problems. Although the countryside was not totally pacified, the campaigns against the rebels and brigands ushered in a period of relative calm.

Two other major problems remained: the near bankruptcy of the country, and the continued occupation of Russian territory by both the Poles and the Swedes.

The liberation of Novgorod was the first of these problems to be resolved, although not to Russia's complete satisfaction. Continuous fighting along the border between Russia and occupied Novgorod had become increasingly costly for King Gustavus II Adolphus of Sweden. In 1617, he appealed for an end to the fighting, and Sweden and Russia signed the Treaty of Stolbovo. The treaty mandated the withdrawal of the Swedish forces from Novgorod and all surrounding territory, but left them a narrow stretch of land bordering on the Gulf of Finland. This effectively closed the ports of Narva and Koporye, the gateways to the Baltic, to Russian commerce, leaving Archangel, on the White Sea in the far north, as Russia's only port for trade with western Europe.

Michael was especially anxious to settle the war with Poland because he wanted to free his father from prison. His opportunity came in September 1618, when Prince Ladislaus, who had never recanted his own claim to the Russian throne, led an army to the gates of Moscow. The Polish invasion was stopped outside the capital and a stalemate ensued. The Poles knew that time would work against them. They were a long way from their own territory, and additional Russian forces were racing to relieve the city. The Poles now faced the possibility of being surrounded and annihilated by an enemy that was certain to show no mercy. When negotiations opened between the antagonists, the Poles were stunned to learn that the main Russian condition for peace was freedom for the czar's father; they were not asked to return any Russian territory, not even Smolensk, nor was Ladislaus requested to drop his claim to the throne. The Armistice of Deulino, signed in December 1618, obtained Philaret's release from prison, along with that of other important Russians held in Poland, but ceded a large portion of Russian territory along the Polish and Lithuanian borders to Poland.

Michael's treaties with Poland and Sweden were not brilliant diplomatic coups, but they brought peace at a time when it was essential for Russia's survival.

In 1619, Philaret returned to Moscow and became patriarch of the Russian Orthodox Church, a post that had been vacant since the Poles murdered Patriarch Hermogen in 1612. Philaret's dutiful son then took the unprecedented step of naming him co-czar with the title of "great sovereign," which until then had been reserved for the czar alone.

Until his death in 1633, Philaret would be the sole master of Russia. Czar Michael stayed in the background, allowing his father to rule in his name. With no religious training, Philaret was ill-prepared to be head of the Church, but his court experience, energy, and ambition made him a suitable de facto ruler of Russia. In addition to reforming the government's financial operations to help rebuild the treasury, and instituting religious reforms, Philaret, hoping to insure the continuation of the new Romanov dynasty, found Michael a bride. (The couple had one son, Alexis, who would eventually follow his father to the throne.)

Continued Polish occupation of Russian territory, especially of Smolensk, was unacceptable to most Russians. In 1621, Poland was at war with Sweden to its north, and with the Ottoman Turks to the south. Thinking he could capitalize on Poland's predicament and revise the unpalatable clauses of the Armistice of Deulino that had won him his freedom, Philaret obtained the approval of the national assembly for a declaration of war against Poland. The Russia military remained too feeble to wage a full-scale war, but with Poland occupied with powerful adversaries on two sides, the recovery of Smolensk seemed possible. The effort came to nothing, however, after the Poles defeated the Turks near Khotin, freeing troops to protect Poland's Russian holdings.

After King Sigismund III died in 1632, Philaret tried again to retake Smolensk. A 32,000-man Russian force besieged the occupied city for eight months, until the new king of Poland, Ladislaus IV, still claiming the throne of Russia, arrived with a relief army and crushed the Russians. This humiliating defeat was aggravated by Ladislaus's harsh demands. Czar Michael I was forced to give up all Russian claims to Livonia, Estonia, and Courland, and to pay Poland a tribute of 20,000 rubles. Michael's only consolation was Ladislaus's concession to stop referring to himself as czar of Russia.

❖ ❖ ❖

When Philaret returned from his Polish prison in 1619, he found his son, Czar Michael, deeply influenced by the manipulative Saltykov family. An extremely corrupt clan, the Saltykovs, who were related to Michael's mother, had successfully isolated the czar from other influences and had used their privileges at court to enrich themselves. Philaret promptly exiled them to Siberia in his capacity as co-czar. When Philaret died in 1633, Michael brought the Saltykovs back from their Siberian exile and reinstated them to their former prominence as court advisors.

Most peasants continued to work on land owned by the Church, the boyars, the landed gentry, or the government. They were required to pay rent, in the form of money or crops, for the land they farmed. Although technically free, the peasants were usually indebted to the landowners and therefore unable to move. During his reign, Czar Boris Godunov had forbade large estate owners to kidnap peasants from small estates, usually those of the landed gentry who had received their land from the czar in return for their pledge to fight in his wars. Kidnapping or buying peasants from small estates had become a common practice among wealthier nobles because of the endemic labor shortage. Boris also had set a limit of five years on the time during which a landowner could recover a peasant who had escaped from his obligations.

Following the Time of Troubles, during which the population was reduced or scattered to the far reaches of the empire and even beyond, the labor shortage worsened and the landowners pressured Czar Michael to extend the time limit for recovering fugitive peasants. In 1634, Michael issued a decree extending to 10 years the time in which a landowner could reclaim a fugitive peasant. In 1642, Michael extended the time limit to 15 years, effectively extinguishing any suggestion that the peasants were free and firmly establishing a feudal society in rural Russia. Freedom to work the land and to move from one place to another now became a forbidden dream for millions of Russians. Michael's decree established serfdom, which would fuel Russia's economy and foment most of Russia's internal disorders during the next three centuries.

In 1642, Michael was given the opportunity to extend his empire southward to the Black Sea and to acquire for Russia a badly needed warm-water port, one open to trade all year long. Early in 1637, the powerful Don Cossacks, joined by the Zaporozhian Cossacks, had attacked the Turkish fort at Azov, which guarded the Don River's access to the Black Sea. The Cossacks had long raided Turkish settlements in the lower Don Valley, but the attack on Azov was no simple raid. This time they were determined to capture the fort and drive out the Turks.

The Cossacks took Azov and slaughtered the entire Muslim population. Shortly after establishing themselves in their new capital, the Cossacks were attacked by a large Turkish army believed to number around 240,000 men. The Turks launched at least two dozen assaults against the fort, but each was driven off by the 10,000 tenacious Cossack defenders. But unable to hold off the persistent Turks indefinitely, the Cossacks offered Azov to Czar Michael. It was a grand prize for Russia, if it could be held against the Turks. Not only was the Cossack offer an opportunity to expand the empire, it also held the promise of increased trade with Europe. Michael convened the national assembly, which no longer sat in regular session, and put the question of Azov to the delegates.

Although some factions within the assembly favored joining the fight, most representatives argued against accepting the Cossack offer; to accept it would mean a prolonged and costly war with Turkey, an undertaking that the impoverished Russian treasury could not afford. Michael therefore instructed the Cossacks to abandon Azov, which they did reluctantly. He also sent a letter of apology to Sultan Ibrahim I of Turkey, in which he called the Cossacks unruly brigands.

❖ ❖ ❖

In July 1645, Czar Michael I died, leaving his throne to his 16-year-old son Alexis, whose appointment was confirmed by the national assembly. Alexis Romanov would be called the "Quiet One" by many of his countrymen; he would occupy much of his time with the daily rituals of the Church and the state. His reign would be plagued by frequent local uprisings brought on by the universal enslavement of the peasants in the feudal system known as serfdom, established by his father.

Before Michael died, he had named a boyar, Boris Morozov, to be his son's guardian. Not unlike many favorite confidants of czars past and future, Morozov proved to be a disastrous choice. Greedy and calculating, he used every imaginable scheme to extort wealth and power from his youthful ward. When Czar Alexis chose a wife, Morozov married the future czarina's sister, thereby strengthening his bond with the young czar. After Alexis married Maria Miloslavsky, Morozov moved his in-laws' entire family into the czar's inner circle, further depleting Alexis's already strained treasury.

Alexis was fascinated with Western culture. He and his family attended the concerts of orchestras from western Europe. He dressed his children in clothing from Germany and introduced many innovations to Russia, from brass bands and gilded coaches to Western art and architecture. His interest in Western culture led him to encourage a broad liberal education for his children, and he established progressive schools that taught Latin, Greek, and astronomy. But Alexis himself remained a product of his traditional Russian education: he was an extremely religious man who could argue the finer points of Orthodox theology with the most learned clergymen.

Alexis also had a keen appreciation for the crown's vital interest in preventing the further erosion of peasant labor on the estates of his wealthy supporters. In 1646, he signed a law abolishing the time limit for a landowner to recapture a fugitive peasant. From then onward, peasants were no longer free—any peasant who deserted his landowner's estate would forever be liable to arrest and return.

The status of the Russian peasant, now called a serf, was the equivalent of slavery. Under the law, once a landowner registered his serfs' names, his serfs were forever bound to the land, no matter who became its owner and no matter how the serfs were treated. Serfdom became hereditary: all the offspring of a registered serf were bound to the land their father was tied to. The law no longer made a distinction between serfs and free peasants, a fact that induced many serfs to flee to the fringes of the empire, where they were welcomed by Cossacks bands. Laws prohibiting the sale of serfs were routinely ignored as individuals and entire families were bought and sold in the same manner as slaves. The Russian peasants became the property of the landowners—a class that included the Russian Orthodox Church, which still retained vast holdings—and the state itself. This enslavement of most of the population by a privileged minority not only caused unrest throughout the nation, it corrupted Russia's very core by making its society dependent on a system in which abuse and suffering were routine.

Alexis I's rein was plagued by peasant uprisings. Some, like the peasant revolt of 1648, were the direct result of policies instigated by the czar's advisors, who sought to enrich themselves at the people's expense. For example, one of Boris Morozov's henchmen, Nazarios Chistoi, whom Morozov had made secretary of state, imposed a fourfold increase in the tax for salt, a commodity that was vital for the preparation and storage of fish taken from the Volga. Unable to salt their catches, Volga fishermen lost thousands of tons of fish and were driven into financial ruin. A state monopoly on the sale of tobacco, which was believed by many to be forbidden by God and had been outlawed earlier (smoking had been punishable by death), incited segments of the population to riot.

The first major disorder occurred in Moscow in May 1648. An angry crowd approached the czar and his party, who were returning from a pilgrimage, and respectfully asked that he remove the advisors who were behind the oppressive policies. Alexis told the crowd that he would consider its petitions, but several officials in his entourage, fearing that the crowd would convince the czar to oust them, began whipping the people to drive them away. The crowd responded by attacking its tormentors, who were the very men it had come to denounce, stoning several of them to death. The person who struck down the hated Chistoi shouted "Traitor, that's for salt."

After the initial bloodshed, the crowd became a mob and ran wild through the streets of Moscow, sacking the homes of wealthy state officials, including Morozov's. One group actually found its way into the Kremlin, but was driven out by the czar's bodyguards, a detachment of foreign troops. It took a personal appeal from Czar Alexis the following day, in which he thanked the people for bringing the iniquities to his attention and promised to remove the offenders, to restore calm to the city. But the rioting spread beyond Moscow—government officials and foreigners alike were violently attacked, and prisons in at least a half-dozen cities were stormed. Only an amnesty signed by Alexis finally restored peace.

One important consequence of these riots was the creation of a new code of laws, the first in almost 100 years. The Code of 1649, as it was called, systematized a wide variety of existing laws and regulations. The new code, which would last 200 years, had 25 chapters covering every imaginable offense. In principle, the code professed to treat all citizens alike, but because only peasants could be flogged for committing any of the 141 offenses that carried that penalty—a punishment that often proved fatal—in practice the new code was much harsher on them.

Rioting again broke out in Moscow in 1662, this time over the devaluation of the silver coins then in use, and their replacement by copper coins. Once again, the czar's advisors had selfishly manipulated a government action intended to benefit the people. The devaluation, which Alexis intended to relieve the financial strain on the government, was used by many advisers with control over imports to raise prices on imported goods. The resulting inflation made what little money the people held even less valuable, and completely wiped out any savings. The country, which never fully recovered from the financial devastation of the Time of Troubles, was now thrown into deeper economic chaos. Had Alexis been less like his father and more like the czars of the late 15th and early 16th centuries, he might have exerted more control over his advisors and taken effective action against them, thereby saving himself and Russia much anguish. But, like Michael I, Alexis was easily manipulated by those around him.

❖ ❖ ❖

During Alexis's reign, Moscow reclaimed the Ukraine, the cradle of the Russian nation, which had been held for years by Poland. It was not because of any initiative on the czar's part that this was accomplished; the Ukraine was thrust up on him by the Cossacks.

In 1647, a Cossack chief named Bogdan Khmyelnitsky, who had been employed by the Polish government, was insulted by a Polish nobleman. Unable to gain redress from the Polish government, Khmyelnitsky fled the Ukraine for the Crimea, where he enlisted the assistance of the khan of the Crimean Tartars. Khmyelnitsky returned to the Ukraine with a Tartar army supplemented by numerous Cossack bands, which had joined his campaign to drive the Poles out of the Ukraine and make it an independent state.

The following year, the joint Cossack and Tartar force defeated the Polish army in two decisive battles, encouraging the Ukrainians to revolt. Khmyelnitsky was elected hetman of the Zaporozhian Cossacks and led them in several more victorious campaigns against the Poles. But the Tartars proved to be unfaithful allies: the new king of Poland, John II Kasimir, bribed the Tartar khan to desert Khmyelnitsky just before a critical battle near Zborovo, in eastern Galicia in 1649. The two-day battle proved indecisive, except that the Polish king realized he had underestimated his adversary's true strength and decided to negotiate mutually agreeable terms. This was welcome news to the Cossacks, who feared that the Polish army might crush them without their Tartar allies. The agreement recognized Khmyelnitsky as hetman of all the Cossacks, and raised the number of legally registered Cossacks to 40,000. Raising the quota had been a continuing aim of Cossack leaders because any Cossacks who were not registered were considered to be escaped serfs by both Russia and Poland, where the feudal system had also been adopted. The treaty also required that the Poles cease all attempts to unite the Orthodox Church with the Catholic Church, and that Catholics be free to travel throughout Cossack lands. Within a few months, however, fighting broke out again, and the Cossacks, facing overwhelming Polish forces, were forced in 1650 to accept a new treaty that was less favorable than the earlier one. The number of Cossacks who could be registered was reduced to 20,000. Of course, the Cossacks who could not be registered refused to return to serfdom, and the hetman lost their support.

Khmyelnitsky soon realized the futility of trying to free the Ukraine from Polish control without Russia's help. In the summer of 1653, he appealed to Czar Alexis for assistance, pledging in return the allegiance of the people of Little Russia, which was what the Russians called Ukraine. The Russians attempted to mediate between the Cossacks and the Poles, but the Polish government considered the matter an internal one and viewed Russian intervention with disfavor.

On October 1, 1653, Czar Alexis put the question of annexing Little Russia before the members of the national assembly. None could deny that annexation would entail a costly war with Poland that Russia could not afford, but most felt that the Ukraine was both Orthodox and Russian and so should be reunited with the rest of Russia. The assembly voted unanimously to support the Cossacks. On January 8, 1654, the Rada, or council of the Cossack army, met. Khmyelnitsky told the assembled warriors that they could not stand alone against the powers around them and would have to decide where they would place their loyalty. The options were the king of Poland, who was hated by most Cossacks because of past Polish subjugation and because he was a Catholic; the sultan of Turkey, who was rejected because he was seen as an even worse infidel, a Muslim; or the czar of Russia, who, like the Cossacks, was Orthodox and related by blood to their own Russian ancestors. The vote in favor of the czar was unanimous.

The treaty between Czar Alexis and the Cossacks that led to the Ukraine becoming part of the Russian Empire established the number of free or "registered" Cossacks at 60,000, although this number was always far exceeded, without objection from Moscow. The Cossacks were allowed a large measure of autonomy, including diplomatic relations with other countries except Poland and Turkey. By this treaty, Czar Alexis expanded his empire southeast to the Dnieper River, which became the border between Russia and Poland. In the inevitable war with Poland that followed, Moscow won control of Smolensk and Kiev, two important acquisitions that raised Alexis's stature considerably.

Certain events during Alexis's reign led some Russians to call the czar the Antichrist. In 1652, the able metropolitan of Novgorod, Nikon, was appointed patriarch of Russia. Nikon soon became a close advisor of the czar, who often left him in charge of the government during his frequent absences for military campaigns. Alexis treated the patriarch with the same respect that Michael I had showed his father, even calling Nikon "Great Sovereign." Alexis referred to the patriarch as his "intimate friend." Two years after Nikon became patriarch, he called a Church assembly to correct the numerous errors that had crept into the Russian translations of the religious texts used in Orthodox services throughout the country. Some clergymen saw the changes, most of which were very minor, as perversions of Orthodoxy and resisted them. An imposing figure, the patriarch was a man of short temper and little diplomacy. Nikon's intransigence, and the ignorance of his opponents, led to a schism known as the Raskol. The dissidents, called Roskolniki, continued to follow the old texts and later became known as the Old Believers. At first Alexis supported Nikon, and the Old Believers started rumors that Alexis was not really the czar but the Antichrist, sent to punish Russia for her sins. In 1658, the soft-spoken czar and his strident patriarch fell out when the latter tried to revive a medieval precept that the Church should have authority over the czar and the state. Neither Alexis nor the Council of Boyars could tolerate that idea, and Patriarch Nikon was eventually defrocked; he ended his days in self-imposed exile at a remote monastery.

Czar Alexis neared the end of his reign as a widower with eight children, two boys and six girls. Because the boys were rather sickly, Alexis feared for the succession after his death. He found a second wife, the strikingly beautiful Natalia Naryshkin. She was actually younger than several of the czar's own daughters, all of whom were strong-willed individuals, especially the oldest, Sophia, who might have inherited her father's crown if it had been legal for a woman to do so. Natalia gave Alexis three more children, two girls and a son, Peter, who was born in the summer of 1672.

September 1, 1674, was New Year's Day on the Orthodox calendar. Czar Alexis took this occasion to bypass the worrisome process of choosing his successor, which required the approval of the Duma and an election in the national assembly. Sidestepping the issue of whether an elected czar could pass his crown to his son without the approval of the electors, Alexis presented his heir, Fedor, to a crowd of Muscovites assembled in Red Square. The joyous celebration was attended by the high clergy, members of the Duma, and representatives of foreign governments who lived in the capital. The approving cheers of the people in Red Square was the only ratification Alexis needed to successfully declare Fedor his designated successor.

By this inspired act, Czar Alexis transformed the system by which he and his father had been elected czar. Once he had openly and forcefully presented his oldest son as his heir, no vote was required. No one dared oppose him, and quite likely no one of consequence actually disputed his selection. When Alexis died at age 47 in 1676, his 14-year-old son became Fedor III, czar of Russia, Little Russia, and White Russia (Byelorussia, located southwest of Moscow), which had also been acquired from the Poles in the last war.

Fedor III was the product of a dramatically different education than the ones his father and grandfather had received. Unlike them, he had received, at Alexis's insistence, a European-style education. Fluent in the formal Slavonic that was used at the court and in the Church, Fedor also spoke Latin and Polish, wrote poetry extensively, and tried his hand at prose. He was also a prolific letter writer, and a large volume of his writings have survived.

Fedor suffered from an unidentified ailment that confined him to his bed or couch most of the time. His illness forced him to leave the administrative functions of the court to two close advisors, Ivan Yazykov and Alexis Likhachev. Fedor's brother Ivan was simple-minded and partially blind. The two boys got along well, and both adored their little half-brother Peter, who was four when their father died. But Peter and his mother were not adored—not even welcomed—by Fedor's sisters, especially Sophia. Consequently, Natalia and her son lived in a villa near Preobrazhenskoe, the late Czar Alexis's favorite retreat, several miles outside the capital. Leading members of the Naryshkin family had been exiled far from Moscow by Alexis's first wife, Maria Miloslavsky, whose family now controlled the government.

Fedor's ill health and confinement made him a somewhat mysterious figure. We do know that despite the disapproval of the more pious churchmen who constantly hovered around the czar, he favored European ways, at one time even suggesting that Russians should comport themselves more "according to the new European manner." These same clergymen strived to stifle what they called the "Latin culture," which they equated with Catholicism, but Fedor liked the ideas he found in the Latin books he had sent to him from Kiev, where Western influence was far greater than in Moscow.

We also know that the czar was concerned about the education of his little half-brother and godson, Peter. On at least one occasion, Fedor remarked to his stepmother, Peter's mother, Natalia, "Your Imperial Majesty, it is high time that our godson were instructed." A semi-invalid, Fedor surrounded himself with bright young men who were also educated in Western thought. The little that is known of him and his enlightened contemporaries suggests that had he been in better health and survived beyond his 20th year, Fedor III might have been one of Russia's great reforming czars, as his half-brother would be in the next century.

Through Prince Basil Golitsin, a personal confidant, Fedor III put in place the beginnings of a massive military reform program that emphasized Westernizing the command and unit structure of the army. In 1681, Fedor signed the Treaty of Bakhchisarai with Turkey, after the Ottomans had defeated Poland in a war and won control of the Ukraine west of the Dnieper River. The treaty restored the old borders of the Russian Ukraine to their previous location, with Moscow controlling the east bank of the river.

In another important reform, Czar Fedor abolished the cumbersome mestnichestvo system of precedence for government and military appointments, which were determined by family status. In a solemn palace ceremony, the register books that meticulously listed the ranking of every noble and servitor family since the third quarter of the 15th century were burned. Appointments to high government and military posts were no longer restricted to privileged candidates, but could be awarded on the basis of ability and experience. This reform was supportive of Fedor's military reorganization program.

On April 27, 1682, at the age of 20, Czar Fedor III died without leaving an heir.

CHAPTER 16

THE CONSOLIDATION OF THE EMPIRE: PETER THE GREAT TO PETER III

WHEN FEDOR III DIED WITHOUT A DIRECT heir, intrigue and violence predictably ensued. The clear choice to succeed Fedor would have been his 16-year-old brother Ivan, if it had not been for his mental and physical infirmities. Had a woman been eligible to inherit the throne, Fedor's 25-year-old sister Sophia would have been crowned, but women could qualify only for the role of regent. Next in line after Ivan was his half-brother, Peter. Because

Map of "Moscovy" c.1690

From the collection of James P. Duffy

❖ 187 ❖

of Peter's above-average height, which would eventually reach close to seven feet, and his mature comportment, he appeared much older than his 10 years.

Determined to avoid a bloody conflict between the families of the former czar Alexis's two wives, the Miloslavsky and Naryshkin clans, Patriarch Joachim met secretly with leading boyars to solicit their support for Peter. Russia, he told them, needed a strong, healthy czar who could remain on the throne for an extended reign, not another incapacitated monarch who was not expected to live long. The validity of the patriarch's argument, and the boyars' distrust of the Miloslavskys, decided the issue: most agreed to support Peter, although a few boyars favored Ivan.

When the boyars gathered inside the Kremlin palace for their final farewell to Fedor III, as was the custom, the patriarch asked the assembly, "Which of the two princes shall be czar?" In this informal vote, those favoring Peter far outnumbered Ivan's supporters, but a Miloslavsky partisan insisted that the choice should be left to the people. He undoubtedly was referring to a Zemsky Sobor. The calling of a national assembly would give the Miloslavskys more time to win supporters. Joachim, still determined to avoid a violent clash between the opposing families, and wary of the several weeks' delay before an assembly could be convened, agreed to let the people decide and quickly stepped to a balcony overlooking Red Square. The patriarch's agents had primed the crowd that had gathered to pay final respects to Czar Fedor, and when Joachim called out to them, "Which of the two czarevitches do you want to rule over you?", the overwhelming response of the "people" was for Peter. The Miloslavsky supporters watched helplessly as the issue was settled. Peter Alexievich Romanov was to be the next czar of Russia.

❖   ❖   ❖

The dead czar was eulogized and laid to rest in the Cathedral of the Archangel Michael. During the service, Fedor's sister, the czarevna or imperial princess Sophia, entered the cathedral escorted by a group of monks. It was an astonishing breach of protocol, since only a widow or czarina was allowed to attend a czar's funeral service. Natalia, who was present with her son, Peter, left the service before it ended in order to avoid a direct confrontation with Sophia.

Immediately following Fedor's entombment, Sophia, who anticipated exile for her relatives and the enforced life of a nun for herself if Peter was permitted to take the throne, began plotting against the Naryshkins. She intimated to the crowds gathered for the funeral that her poor brother Fedor had been poisoned by those with ambitions for the throne, meaning of course the Naryshkins. Along with her uncle, Ivan Miloslavsky, she found allies among the regiments of the Streltsi, a sort of praetorian guard that was assigned to protect the Kremlin. Many Streltsi had grown rich by engaging in commercial enterprises, which they often pursued more intently than their military duties. They had come to think of themselves as having special privileges that a czar had to recognize if he was to rule. During the tenure of both Alexis and Fedor, the Miloslavsky family had cultivated close ties with Streltsi officers, and it was to them that they went with whispers that the Naryshkins planned to kill Ivan, Fedor's brother and rightful heir to the throne, and to disband the guard regiments.

It did not matter that none of this was true; the Streltsi welcomed the excuse to exert their influence. The Streltsi revolted on the morning of May 15, when Miloslavsky propagandists appeared in the Streltsi districts and proclaimed that the Narshykins had murdered Czarevitch Ivan and several leading boyars. The agents cried out that the daughters of Alexis, the czarevnas, would be slain next. The aroused troops swiftly formed into regiments and, with banners flying, marched on the Kremlin, calling for the murderers' blood.

The palace residents were shocked when thousands of shouting Streltsi suddenly appeared in Cathedral Square inside the Kremlin walls, demanding the traitors who had killed Ivan. To their surprise, Czarina Natalia appeared at the top of the Palace's Red Stair with the new czar, Peter, in one hand, and the czarevitch Ivan in the other. The troops listened quietly as she assured them that no one had been killed by traitors, that Peter and Ivan stood before them, and that they had been duped.

Several Streltsi cautiously ascended the stairs and approached the youths. Peter stood erect and showed no fear before these well-armed men, but Ivan was terrified. Asked if he was really the czarevitch, Ivan stammered that he was. Satisfied, the men returned to the square and told their comrades what the boy had said. Then a man greatly respected by many Streltsi, Artamon Matveev, a former Streltsi commander who had recently returned from six years of exile imposed by the Miloslavskys, joined Natalia and the two boys. He reminded the Streltsi of their long history of loyal service to the czars since the time of Ivan the Terrible, and of how they should not stain that reputation by further disobedience. Many soldiers remembered Matveev's impartial leadership with admiration and heeded his advice to return home.

The revolt might have ended there except for the foolishness of a Streltsi colonel named Prince Michael Dolgoruky, who was universally hated by the guard. Thinking the revolt was over, Dolgoruky stepped to the head of the stairs and in the foulest language threatened severe punishment to any soldier who did not immediately leave the square. That triggered a violent backlash. Firing muskets and with raised pikes, the soldiers stormed the palace. Dolgoruky and Matveev were seized, flung from the balcony, and landed on the pikes of those below. Before the czar, the czarevitch, and the czarina, the two were then hacked to pieces by a hundred swords.

Three days of terror and bloodshed began as thousands of Streltsi swarmed through the palace searching for "traitors," meaning any boyars they happened to find. Special targets of their search were Natalia's brother Ivan Narshykin, who was accused of plotting to murder the czarevitch Ivan, and a Dutch doctor named Van Gaden, who was said to have poisoned Czar Fedor. On the third day, Ivan Naryshkin surrendered himself to save the remainder of his family, and Doctor Van Gaden was caught. The two were dragged from the Kremlin into Red Square, where the dismembered bodies of earlier victims were piled. Naryshkin's and Van Gaden's hands and feet were severed, and their torsos mutilated and hacked into small pieces, which were ground into the blood-soaked mud of the square. Satisfied, the Streltsi returned to the Kremlin, swore their allegiance to the royal family, and then went to their homes.

Peter Romanov would never forget the traumatic, morbid experience of seeing his relatives and supporters slaughtered by the mob. He would forever associate the Kremlin with the blood lust that occurred there.

At the instigation of Sophia and the mighty Miloslavsky family, the Streltsi were rewarded for their achievement: each man received a lump-sum payment that was raised by auctioning their victims' property and melting down the czar's gold and silver dinnerware. A triumphal column celebrating the Streltsi's deed was erected in Red Square, and their designation was changed to the more impressive-sounding Palace Guard. The rebellious soldiers returned once more to the Kremlin and demanded of the frightened boyars and churchmen that Alexis's two sons be made co-czars, with Sophia serving as regent until they came of age. If their demands were not met, the Streltsi made it clear, they would return and resume the slaughter.

On May 26, 1682, Ivan Romanov and Peter Romanov were crowned co-czars of Russia, with Ivan becoming the senior or first czar because he was older. In the same ceremony, Sophia Romanov was declared regent. Czar Peter and his mother returned to the villa at Preobrazhenskoe, and those Naryshkins who had survived the Streltsi revolt were either sent into exile or forced to take religious vows. Peter was allowed to enter Moscow only for state occasions that required the presence of both czars.

From a series of letters that Sophia wrote, it appears that she was deeply in love with Prince Basil Golitsin, a man who had served both Czar Alexis and Czar Fedor and was a champion of the latter's Westernizing reforms. Homely, overweight, with unsightly patches of hair sprouting on her face, Sophia was hardly a beauty. But she was an ambitious woman of outstanding intelligence, and undoubtedly she realized she had little chance of winning Golitsin unless she could offer him something of real value. Some historians have suggested that she meant to keep the throne for herself and share it with the prince if he married her. Meanwhile, she was able to draw Golitsin close to herself by appointing him minister of foreign affairs, thus making him a senior advisor.

Sophia's regency began on shaky ground, partly because of her machinations against Peter and the Naryshkins. One of the conspirators who had helped to provoke the Streltsi revolt was Prince Ivan Khovansky, whom Czar Alexis had removed as governor of Pskov because of his incompetence. Sophia repaid Khovansky for his part in the revolt by giving him command of the newly redesignated Palace Guard. The traitorous Khovansky immediately began plotting to seize the throne for himself, by using the Palace Guard, which numbered some 22,000 men and was the sole substantial armed force in the capital. His opportunity came quickly, in 1689, with the revival of the Raskolniki revolt against the Church and the state (the Raskoniki were the clergymen and laymen who had opposed Patriarch Nikon's revisions of Church practices and liturgy, the so-called Old Believers).

Many of Khovansky's troops were sympathetic to the Old Believers' cause and supported their wish for a return to the old texts and customs. During the first week of July, a debate about the changes that Sophia's father, Czar Alexis, had condoned began inside the Kremlin. Patriarch Joachim argued that the changes were needed and correct. The Old Believers demanded a return to the old ways and even suggested to Sophia, who continued to support the patriarch, that she might be better off if she retired to live in a convent.

Khovansky acknowledged that he was in complete sympathy with the Old Believers and began planning for another Streltsi attack on the palace. Sophia's informers in the Palace Guard told her of the plan, and, pretending to make a religious pilgrimage, she moved her court from Moscow to the nearby, well-fortified Monastery of the Holy Trinity. From there she sent out a call for regular army troops and members of the gentry. Once she was protected by a substantial force, the regent invited Khovansky and his two sons to a celebration in the nearby town of Vosdvizhenskoe. The prince sensed the danger in the summons but had little choice other than to obey.

On September 17, Khovansky arrived with both of his sons. The prince and his eldest son were arrested and promptly executed by soldiers of the regular army, but his younger son managed to escape and returned to Moscow, where he rallied the Palace Guard which immediately rose in revolt and occupied the Kremlin. Threatened with a siege by Sophia's regular army troops, against whom it was no match, the Palace Guard soon abandoned the Kremlin and threw down its arms. Several of its leaders were executed while others were sent into exile. The Streltsi monument in Red Square was torn down, and the regiments that had joined the revolt were stripped of their privileges and placed under the tight control of one of Sophia's trusted lieutenants. Future Palace Regiments were selected based on their direct loyalty to the monarch.

Sophia's regency was marked by mixed results. In 1686, she signed a treaty with Poland's King John III Sobieski, who three years earlier had driven the Turks from the gates of Vienna. It was supposed to result in "perpetual peace" between the two rival nations. Three years later, she concluded Russia's first treaty with China, thereby establishing the empire's first recognized border with that Asian country. But her foreign policies also had their setbacks. In 1687 and again in 1689, Prince Golitsin led two campaigns against the Tartar khan of the Crimea. Both times he commanded an army of more than 100,000 men, and both times he met disaster. The first campaign bogged down in the remote and uninhabited steppes, where a huge wildfire destroyed the grasslands and killed thousands of Russian horses. The second campaign ended in a battle against the Turks that cost 20,000 Russian lives, with another 15,000 Russians taken prisoner. These disasters ultimately brought down Sophia's regency.

Although Sophia's reign as regent of Russia was not distinguished by any great or lasting accomplishments, its very occurrence is notable. At the time, women in Russia, even women of royal birth, were little more than chattel. The wives and daughters of czars spent most of their time in seclusion, received little if any education, and had no influence at all on affairs of state. Sophia was an anomaly. With no real support other than the occasional and brief backing of the Streltsi (who quickly turned on her), she nonetheless managed, through sheer willpower and personal courage, to rule the nation for seven years when in fact she had no legitimate claim to the throne. Although Sophia eventually suffered the fate she feared most—life in a convent—she set a precedent that allowed four women to exercise their lawful claims to the Russian throne and serve as legitimate sovereigns during the next century. She also demonstrated that a woman could be as bloodthirsty as a man in the pursuit and retention of absolute power.

❖ ❖ ❖

Peter I, later known as Peter the Great, spent his early years as czar residing in the villa near Preobrazhenskoe with his mother and a few other close relatives, including his sister, Natalia. Peter's mother, Czarina Natalia, was a woman of the old Muscovy school despite the fact that she had been raised in the home of her guardian, Artamon Matveev, a highly intelligent man with a deep interest in the culture of western Europe. Peter's sister Natalia, with whom he remained close, shared his enthusiasm for Western ideas and customs.

During Sophia's regency, Peter busied himself with pastimes that might interest any youth with an abiding curiosity. He was especially fascinated by mechanical things, habitually dismantling gifts to see what made them work, and expertly reassembling them. He was good with his hands and devoted endless hours to woodworking and carpentry. Although Sophia was always suspicious about those around the young czar who might be plotting against her, she worried little about Peter himself because he always seemed too preoccupied with other activities to conspire against her.

Peter's villa was not far from Moscow's German Suburb, where foreigners of all nationalities were required to live. The young co-czar spent countless hours in the German Suburb, working with and learning from a wide variety of craftsmen, many of whom produced works that Russians had never seen before. Despite his title, co-Czar Peter was a veritable apprentice to many of these men, who appreciated the youth's interest in them and their work. Unlike previous heirs to the throne, Peter was not raised in the stifling atmosphere of the Kremlin, with its rigid routines, but instead lived a relatively free existence and chose his own friends. Those friends were frequently the foreign adventurers who had come to Russia to seek their fortunes, and the foreign artisans who practiced their trades and crafts among the less-advanced Russians. This was the continuing education of the future czar, whose formal instruction had been cut short when his half-brother and godfather, Czar Fedor III, died. What Peter learned thereafter he learned from his playmates—whether they were common-ers from the nearby village or young aristocrats from princely families—and from the foreigners who befriended him.

By the time he turned 11, in June 1683, Peter had developed a keen interest in military matters. Instead of having to play with wooden guns and swords, co-czar Peter could have the genuine instruments of war sent to him from military supply warehouses. From the sons of the large staff employed in and around the villa, and from the noble families who remained close to the Naryshkins, Peter recruited a small force that he called the Preobrazhenskii, after the nearby village. When the Preobrazhenskii reached regimental size—about 300 boys—he formed a second regiment, which he named the Semenovskii, after another local village. Each regiment was structured to resemble an actual regiment in the Russian army, with infantry, cavalry, and artillery companies. The juvenile soldiers, who lived in barracks, drew soldiers' pay, and stood guard duty, were outfitted with swords, muskets, and even cannons requisitioned from the Moscow armory. Their uniforms were specially designed under Peter's direction, and the youths trained in exactly the same manner as the real army, which they would eventually become. Sophia and her counselors were amused by Peter's activities and provided him with everything he wanted for his "toy soldiers." But the noble families who opposed the regent saw a deeper significance in what Peter was doing and sent their sons to Preobrazhenskoe to join him.

Lacking the ability to properly train his boy soldiers, Peter enlisted several foreigners with military experience to drill and instruct them in the basics of military discipline and the art of war. The co-czar himself enlisted in his army, first as a drummer, then as a cannoneer. His fascination with artillery led some of his companions to call him Bombardier Peter, a nickname he evidently enjoyed. He drilled for long hours on the parade ground and carried a full pack on the marches demanded by the German and Dutch instructors. He was in every way a simple soldier, as were his comrades, many of whom would remain his closest associates throughout his life. It was a very democratic army, with boyar sons marching and living alongside the sons of artisans, gamekeepers, and even serfs. Rank was attained not by birth but by merit.

Peter probably never intended to use the regiments against the regent, but in time they would become the nucleus of Russia's first modern army and serve as the Imperial Guard until the fall of the dynasty in 1917. The regimental "war games" were as authentic as the practice maneuvers of any full-blown army, even more so because Peter's soldiers often used real cannon balls and live shot in their muskets. Occasionally, some of the boy soldiers were wounded, or even killed, during their practice campaigns.

By the time he was 13, Peter had tired of field exercises and longed to train his regiments in the defense and storming of fortifications. That year his troops constructed a wooden and earthen fort along the banks of the nearby Yauza River, where they fought many sham battles. He gradually expanded the fort into a complex of buildings with its own garrison and court, and called it Pressburg.

Three years later, Peter was given a sextant by a boyar who had bought it in Paris. No one in Russia had ever seen such an instrument, and Peter had difficulty finding someone who knew how to use it. Not even the foreign soldiers that he hired to train and lead his regiments, most of whom had never been at sea, could help.

Peter finally found in the German Suburb an old Dutch merchant named Franz Timmerman who could use the mysterious device. Timmerman startled Peter by using the sextant to quickly and accurately calculate the distance to a specified house; a servant paced off the distance and reported that Timmerman was correct. The co-czar implored the old gray-haired man to teach him to use this wonderful tool. Timmerman explained that Peter would first need to acquire at least a rudimentary knowledge of arithmetic and geometry, and Peter readily agreed. In a short time Peter became proficient with the sextant, and Timmerman, who had traveled throughout much of the world and had much to tell the inquisitive youth about the wonders beyond Russia's borders, became his constant companion. Peter called Timmerman "mein friendt."

Peter was with Timmerman one day in June 1688, rummaging through some storage buildings on the former estate of Nikita Romanov, when he came across a sailing sloop that Timmerman guessed was of British origin. Timmerman said it was much better than the boats that plied Russia's lakes and rivers. "Why is it better?" Peter asked. The co-czar was familiar with the bulky flat-bottom boats used in Russia, and intrigued by the British vessel's deep, rounded hull and pointed bow. "Because it can sail into the wind and against the wind," Timmerman explained. Peter was of course anxious to try this, but the Dutchman pointed to the rotting timbers and said it would have to be repaired before it could be floated. A Dutch shipwright named Karsten Brandt, who was working as a carpenter in the German Suburb, was called in and Peter watched him replace the rotted timbers and tar the hull. Brandt launched the boat in the nearby river and demonstrated how to tack with the wind. Peter was enthralled and quickly joined Brandt in the boat. Taking the tiller, the co-czar quickly learned how to maneuver the boat. That day Peter acquired the lifelong obsession with ships and sailing that eventually led to his building the first two fleets in Russia's history. (The origins of the boat, which Peter called "the grandfather of the Russian navy" and which today remains on display in the Russian Navy Museum in St. Petersburg, has never been determined. Some believe it was a gift from Queen Elizabeth I to Ivan the Terrible, who had no use for the craft and stored it on his wife's family estate.)

The year 1689 was a pivotal one in Peter's life. His mother, concerned about the future of the dynasty, chose a wife for her son, who was married on February 6. The unfortunate bride, Eudoxia Lopukhin, came from an aristocratic family but, as was typical of most contemporary Russian women, had little education and even less interest in the affairs of the world around her. She was the worst possible choice for a young man with Peter's curiosities and energy. Their marriage was a farce: Eudoxia lived in the villa with her mother-in-law, who soon tired of her presence, while Peter was constantly away with his friends in the German Suburb, among the beautiful young women who flaunted their Western customs and dress.

Sixteen eighty-nine was also the year in which relations between Peter and the regent Sophia reached a climax. Golitsin's disastrous second campaign against the Crimean Tartars had undermined Sophia's position. Even among the Streltsi there were rumblings about her administration. The pressures to which she was subjected led her to suspect that Peter's mother and her family were plotting to depose her. Matters came to a head during a religious ceremony in Moscow. In one of Peter's rare appearances in the capital, he told Sophia she could not walk with him and Ivan as an equal, but must follow behind. Peter also reviled her for paying Golitsin and his generals after their debacle. Enraged, Sophia, who in spite of having taken a new lover was still devoted to Golitsin, moved to eliminate Peter and keep the throne for herself.

Sophia had begun calling herself "autocrat," although she was little more than a temporary caretaker until Peter and Ivan reached manhood, at which time she would be required to step down. Of course she sought to avoid this future, trying several times during her reign to have herself or one of her brothers formally crowned.

On the night of August 17, 1689, several regiments of the Palace Guard moved inside the Kremlin compound, ostensibly to escort the regent on a pilgrimage to a nearby monastery the following morning. They had also been brought inside the compound to protect Sophia from a rumored assault by Peter's "toy soldier" regiments. But the Naryshkin family's spies interpreted the move as preparation for an attack on the villa at Preobrazhenskoe and sent two loyal Guards officers to alert Peter. Arriving well after midnight, the officers roused Peter from his sleep. Told he must leave immediately because the Palace Guard regiments were on their way, Peter, recalling the horrors of the Streltsi revolt of 1682, jumped from his window and rode off while still in his nightshirt. A short time later, several of his officers caught up to him with his clothes, and the party rode all night for the safety of the Monastery of the Holy Trinity. His mother and wife soon followed, accompanied by Peter's regiments of former boy soldiers who had since matured into a formidable force.

Ironically, Peter's troops were commanded by his close friend Prince Boris Golitsin, a cousin of the regent's favorite. Within hours they were joined by a detachment of approximately 1,000 Palace Guardsmen loyal to Peter. During the next few days, regular army units flocked to Peter's side and camped around the monastery. Soon the best fighting units in the Russian army, regiments trained in the Western military tradition and led by Western officers, joined the co-czar's camp. Their commander was Peter's close friend, the Scotsman Patrick Gordon, whom Peter fondly called Patrick Ivanovich.

Sophia soon perceived that her position was untenable. In desperation, she sent the patriarch to the Monastery of the Holy Trinity to arrange a truce, but he immediately crossed over to Peter's side. Meanwhile, Sophia's support from the former Streltsi units in the Kremlin and around the city gradually dissolved. They had pledged their loyalty to the two czars and to the regent, but in the final analysis Czar Peter, even if he was only the "second czar," had a stronger claim on their loyalty than the regent. It had also become obvious that Peter was going to win as additional forces joined him at the monastery, and no one wanted to be on the losing side because that could mean death as a traitor.

Finally, Sophia capitulated and resigned as regent. A few of her closest advisors were executed, but most, including Basil Golitsin, were exiled to Siberia. Sophia went to live in a convent near Moscow, and Peter implored Ivan, his half-brother and co-czar, to rebuff anyone who tried to interfere in his affairs or dictate policy. Ivan, who was married and had two daughters, had no interest in ruling Russia and was pleased just to be left alone. His poor health and his reluctance to act as a ruler probably safeguarded him from any number of potential assassins in both camps.

Peter was too restless to take up the reins of government just yet. Instead, with co-Czar Ivan's approval, he appointed his mother regent. It was a poor choice. Although Czarina Natalia was devoted to her son, she proved to be a terrible administrator. In addition, she was of the old, reactionary Muscovite tradition and reversed many of Sophia's more progressive policies, including the training of Russian troops by Western officers, who were all dismissed. The Westernization begun under the two previous czars and continued by Sophia was abruptly halted, and Moscow slipped back into the xenophobia of its past.

Peter resumed his vagabond lifestyle during Natalia's regency. He was the first czar to go to Archangel on the White Sea in the far north, and there he saw an ocean for the first time. He met with the captains of British and Dutch sailing ships and learned techniques of seamanship from them. Impressed with their vessels, he placed an order for a frigate to be built in Holland. He also built his own boat and learned to sail with a small flotilla on a lake near Archangel.

Even after the deaths of his mother in 1694, and of his brother the co-czar Ivan in 1695, Peter did not immediately return to the capital to take charge of the government. Instead, he left Moscow in the care of incompetent family members and corrupt supporters who depleted the treasury and did him great disservice. While this was occurring, Peter was leading an army against the Turks at Azov, the fortress that the Cossacks had occupied briefly in 1642 and had offered to his grandfather, Czar Michael. This time, Peter was determined to capture the fort and permanently occupy it with a Russian garrison to ensure his country's access to the southern sea route to Europe.

Czar Peter I "the Great"

From the collection of James P. Duffy

❖ ❖ ❖

The campaign against Azov seemed like a great adventure to the 23-year-old czar when his advisers suggested it to him. The Turks, with whom Russia was technically if not actively at war, were preventing Russia from using the Don River to reach the Black Sea, which would provide a year-round route for trade with western Europe and, perhaps more importantly, would provide the Russian navy, still only a dream in Peter's head, access to the world's oceans. The Don ran south from its headwaters in central Russia, passed beneath the walls of the Azov fortress and into the Sea of Azov, then into the Black Sea, from which the Mediterranean could be reached. The Turks were also the sponsors of the khan of the Crimean Tartars, who seemed forever to be at war with Russia. Some of the keener minds in Moscow hoped that a defeat for the Turks at Azov would convince them to withdraw their support of the khan, there by making him more amenable to Russian terms or even vulnerable to an invasion. The Tartars were regularly raiding Russian towns in the south, kidnapping thousands of Peter's subjects to be sold in the Ottoman Empire's slave markets. And there was also pressure from Poland, Russia's ally in the long-standing war with the Turks; the Polish king complained that Moscow was doing nothing while the Poles remained in the field.

Peter had little interest in the political aspects of the campaign, but he saw in it the opportunity to test the small fleet of warships that the carpenters in the German Suburb had built for him. He himself had worked with a hammer and a saw alongside his foreign friends, watching the fleet take shape.

The plan to attack Azov appears to have been suggested to Peter by one of his closest companions, a brilliant Swiss adventurer named François Lefort. Although he never held an official position at Peter's court, either at Preobrazhenskoe or later in Moscow, Lefort was, until his untimely death at age 43 in 1699, Peter's closest friend and intimate. One of many foreign officers in the Russian army, Lefort was Peter's party giver and the ringleader of a group called the Jolly Company. The czar had built a special brick palace for Lefort and secretly provided him with the money to maintain an almost constant stream of parties, the occasions for much drinking and debauchery; many Muscovites were shocked when they learned that Peter maintained his own quarters at Lefort's. Lefort saw greatness in Peter and urged him to use his military power for conquest and to establish closer relations with western Europe. Capturing Azov would help Peter do both. Lefort constantly urged his friend to embark on exploits that would bring glory to the czar and to Russia.

Before beginning the campaign against Azov, Peter choreographed one final, spectacular, war game. In the fall of 1694, along the banks of the Moscow River, two Russian armies clashed under the czar's direction and critical eye. The war game had a cast of more than 30,000 men on horse and on foot dragging cannons. Peter had prepared a book outlining the entire plan for the campaign, including the locations of supply trains and troop encampments. Defending a fort along the river was an army that included Peter's "boy soldiers," who were now actually young men, plus regiments of the regular army and some local militia. The attacking force was an army made up mostly of regiments from the Palace Guard, plus a large cavalry detachment.

Although no live shot or shells were used, the cannon, carbines, and muskets contained gunpowder in order to simulate actual battle conditions. Peter was dismayed when the attacking force assaulted the fort after the defenders had taken part in a large banquet that featured much drinking, and emerged victorious, for this tactic ran counter to the advice in the Western books he had studied on siege warfare. The next day, the czar made the victorious attackers return all prisoners and start again. With both sides now following Peter's instructions, the attackers took three weeks to capture the fort a second time. It had all been done by the book, and Peter was satisfied with the results.

The 1695 campaign against the Turks included two Russian armies. The first army, which would attack Azov, included 31,000 men in three divisions that had been assembled from the Palace Guard, Peter's own regiments, and artillery and cavalry units trained by European officers. The divisions were led by François Lefort, Patrick Gordon, and Boris Golitsin. Peter took the rank of bombardier sergeant and commanded a company of artillery. The army's overall strategy was formulated by the three divisional commanders and the czar in joint meetings; otherwise, each division acted independently. The army left Moscow in the spring and traveled mostly by boat, first down the Volga, then the Don. At Tsaritsyn, the army's equipment and supplies had to be portaged over land from river to river, an experience that years later prompted Peter to begin construction of a canal connecting the Volga and the Don.

The second Russian army included 120,000 men and was commanded by the able boyar Boris Sheremetev. Supplemented by a large detachment of Cossacks, it crossed the steppes and attacked a series of Turkish forts along the southern reaches of the Dnieper River, which empties directly into the Black Sea.

The campaign to drive the Turks from Azov failed. Peter played a dual role in the campaign: he was supreme commander at the counsel meetings and a bombardier in battle. The Russians blockaded Azov by land but were unable to stem the flow of supplies and reinforcements that poured into the city's port from Turkey. Even the land siege was less than total, with Tartar cavalry regularly breaking through the Russians' lines in both directions and constantly harassing the Russians in their own camps. The Russian supply lines were stretched so thinly that the Tartar horsemen regularly made off with the supplies. The territory around Azov was sparse and unable to sustain the Russian troops. Peter watched as failure upon failure befell his army. Finally, as winter neared, Peter conceded defeat and withdrew with what remained of his army. Even the retreat, in which the troops were harassed by Tartar cavalry and plagued by heavy rains, proved to be a disaster as the army slowly crawled back to Moscow. A foreign diplomat traveling with the army reported that "the whole steppe for five hundred miles" was littered with dead men and horses "half-eaten by the wolves." Sheremetev, meanwhile, had added to Peter's humiliation with a series of stunning successes along the Dnieper, taking most of the Turkish forts before he, too, withdrew in anticipation of the cold weather.

The anti-Western cliques in Moscow were quick to blame the defeat of Peter's army on the foreign officers and their Western methods, citing Sheremetev's victorious army, which had no foreign officers, as proof. Peter ignored their arguments and planned a new campaign against Azov. From the crucible of defeat at Azov, a new Peter emerged. He may have been defeated, but he did not lose heart nor sight of his objective. No longer was he the boy-czar playing at war; he had become, through this humiliation, a man. The Russian historian S. M. Solovyev has described Peter as having "been matured by the defeat, and he showed remarkable activity in remedying the disaster."

The long hours spent watching Turkish ships unload supplies and troops almost unhindered during his siege convinced Peter that Azov would never be taken unless he controlled the harbor around it. In the first campaign, his small fleet had been little more than an annoyance to the Turkish navy. To remedy this, he ordered monasteries and boyar estates to finance shipbuilding enterprises and, where possible, to build ships themselves. At Voronezh on the Don, he established a great shipbuilding project, recruiting soldiers and serfs for the manual labor and bringing in foreign shipwrights and carpenters to direct the work. Once the frigate he had ordered from Holland arrived in Archangel, in 1695, Peter had it cut into sections and brought overland to Voronezh for the workmen to copy. Throughout the country, ships and boats of all sizes were constructed, then cut into manageable sections and transported to Voronezh for reassembling. An estimated 30,000 men worked at the makeshift ship-yards at Voronezh, building the czar's fleet. As ships were finished men were trained to operate them by the Dutch and Swiss sailors hired by Peter. The czar seemed to be everywhere, hammering alongside serfs, hauling sections of ships with startled soldiers, and instructing landlubber Russians in sea-manship. It was a stupendous undertaking that by May 1696 had produced a fleet of some 30 ships.

The siege of Azov resumed during the first week of June with the new fleet and some 80,000 troops, 25,000 of them from various Cossack communi-ties. Czar Peter changed his posting from bombardier sergeant to skipper of one of the ships, and made Lefort, who had army but not naval experience, the admiral in command of the fleet. Overall command of the army was given to Alexis Shein, a boyar with little military experience but a reputation for honesty and good judgement. Shein was ably assisted by Patrick Gordon, who had more experience in warfare than any other man in Peter's forces.

Working in coordination with the Cossack horsemen, the new Russian fleet sealed off the fort's port on the Sea of Azov to supplies and reinforcements. The siege was almost 100-percent effective. When the fort repeatedly withstood Peter's cannon barrages, he put 15,000 troops to work building a large earthen mound from which to scale the walls. On July 27, a band of about 2,000 Cossacks, tired from shoveling earth, galloped up the mound and stormed the city. The first wave was driven back by the Turks, but the Russian infantry, emboldened by the second reckless Cossack charge, followed their comrades up the mound and into the city. With the enemy now inside the walls, Azov's defenders quickly capitulated. The terms of surrender allowed the Turkish army to leave the fortress peacefully and sail for home aboard Turkish ships that were allowed into the harbor by the fledgling Russian navy.

On October 10, Peter's triumphant army returned to Moscow and a tumultuous welcoming parade. Each returning dignitary rode in a gilded car-riage, except the czar. The bewildered crowds watched Admiral Lefort, General Shein, Patrick Gordon, and others ride past, but not the czar; finally, thanks to his great height, he was spotted walking on foot at the rear of the procession among the captains who had commanded the ships of his fleet. Moscow was aghast to see the czar parading with common seamen and wearing a German-style naval uniform and a jaunty three-cornered hat with a long white feather.

Soon after his return to the capital, Peter, jubilant over the performance of his small fleet, began enlarging the navy. He ordered the temporary shipyards at Voronezh expanded and given permanent installations. He had thousands of peasants and their families uprooted from their land and sent to the coast of the Sea of Azov to establish colonies near the mouth of the Don. Several former Streltsi regiments, to their great dissatisfaction, were posted to garrison duty in Azov. Monasteries, boyars, and towns were assessed funds for the czar's ambitious shipbuilding program, which envisioned not merely ships capable of blockading nearby ports, but great sea-going vessels capable of navigating the world's oceans. Hundreds of experts were imported from Europe to help with the construction of the new Russian fleet, which would be based on the Sea of Azov near the mouth of the Don. Fifty carefully selected young Russian men were sent to England, Holland, and Italy to study shipbuilding and navigation. A new era in Russian history began with this first effort at turning Russia into a world-class sea power.

❖ ❖ ❖

With news of Russia's great victory over the Turks spreading rapidly through Europe, François Lefort convinced Peter to visit western Europe and capitalize on his triumph at Azov. Peter was preparing for the trip when a revolt broke out among the former Streltsi. The men resented being stationed at Azov, far from their profitable commercial enterprises in Moscow. Several regiments marched toward the capital to join those still stationed in the city, where, it is alleged, they intended to replace Peter with Sophia. Locked in a convent not as a nun but as a prisoner living in luxury, she probably knew nothing of the Streltsi's plans. The revolt was speedily put down and the conspirators, including several boyars who were also Old Believers, were tortured and executed in the vilest manner reminiscent of Ivan the Terrible.

In 1697, Peter embarked on a journey that would be recalled as one of the highlights of his reign. The consequences of this journey would forever change Russia from a backward semi-Oriental empire existing in a shadowy isolation, into an important participant in the affairs of Europe. On March 10, a party of 250 Russians, led by Lefort, left Moscow and traveled west on a multipurpose mission. One of the Russians' goals was to make new friends in the West and to win support for a renewal of the European war against Turkey. Renewal of the war was important to Peter because his new fleet would remain locked in the Sea of Azov unless the Turks could be driven out of Kerch, which controlled the strait between the Sea of Azov and the Black Sea. Peter also wanted to learn everything possible about Western development, especially modern shipbuilding and navigation. He was determined to create a formidable navy for Russia.

One of the servants traveling in the Great Embassy, as the czar's party became known, was a simple sailor named "Peter Mikhailov." Although Czar Peter's disguise fooled almost no one, it being nearly impossible for someone who towered almost a foot above everyone else to travel incognito, it permitted Peter's hosts to play along with the "game," as they called it, and allowed him to avoid the crushing boredom of official ceremonies.

Peter and his party traveled through Swedish-held Livonia, where a series of minor mishaps left him with a great dislike of the place, then through the Duchy of Courland, where they were warmly received by Duke Casimir, and then to Brandenburg, where the czar met the elector and future first king of Prussia, Friedrich III. In Prussia, a colonel of artillery taught Peter the most effective way of firing a cannon. In Hanover, he was entertained by the electress Sophia, who found him to be a man of "great qualities and unlimited natural intelligence." She regretted that he had not received a better education. Arriving in Holland in early August 1697, well ahead of his slower-moving embassy, Peter went to Zaandam, the home port of many of the Dutch carpenters and shipwrights living in Moscow's German Suburb. He quietly took up residence in a small wooden house rented for him by Herrit Kist, a blacksmith who had worked for Peter in Moscow, but the czar of Russia had to leave within a few weeks when people learned who he was and began following him around. He probably gave away his identity when he began visiting the families of men who were working for him in Russia.

Next, Peter went to Amsterdam, where he spent nearly five months working as a carpenter in the shipyards of the Dutch East India Company. Officials of the company arranged for Peter to live in a house within the walled yards so he would not be bothered by the crowds. Each day he went to work with a crew building a 100-foot frigate that the company, for obvious reasons, had decided to name *The Apostles Peter and Paul*. Peter usually ate his meals, especially lunch, with his fellow laborers, who called him carpenter Peter even though they knew who he really was.

Peter was the consummate student. He visited factories, mills, museums, workshops where sails and rope were manufactured, laboratories, and botanical gardens. He had several private meetings with William of Orange, who was both stadholder of the United Netherlands and King William III of England, and about whom the czar had heard so much from the Dutch merchants and craftsmen in Moscow's German Suburb. His efforts to enlist William in a war against Turkey came to nothing.

When *The Apostles Peter and Paul* was completed, Peter helped launch it, and to his great surprise the ship was given to him as a gift in the name of the people of Amsterdam. In an uncharacteristic display of emotion, he hugged the official who presented him the ship and immediately changed its name to *Amsterdam.*

After working for months alongside the Dutch carpenters, Peter realized that they built their ships by rote and understood little about the theory of naval architecture. For the latter, he knew he would have to go to England. William III provided a British warship to take Peter and a handful of his party to England while the remainder stayed in Holland either to pursue negotiations with the Dutch government or to continue their education in sail-making and navigation. While in England, Peter recruited several engineers and shipwrights as well as other professionals. On April 27, 1698, Peter returned to Holland. Three weeks later, he moved on to Vienna, where he hoped to enlist the Hapsburg emperor in his war with Turkey.

Arriving in Vienna on June 16, Peter encountered a stifling bureaucracy rivaling that of Moscow. Meetings with the emperor, whose official title was "His Most Catholic Majesty Leopold I, Emperor of the Holy Roman Empire, Archduke of Austria, King of Bohemia, and King of Hungry," proved fruitless. The emperor, concerned about the plans of his rival, Louis XIV of France, had accepted an offer of a negotiated peace from the Ottoman sultan, whose army he had defeated at Zenta the previous September. The most Peter could get from Emperor Leopold was a promise that he would not sign a treaty without the czar's knowledge of the terms. The Austrian foreign minister secretly advised Peter to seize Kerch before the peace talks started, because the Turks would never give it up at the negotiating table. (Kerch was a settlement that dominated the strait that connects the Sea of Azov with the Black Sea. Control of Kerch would give Peter access to the Black Sea.)

Disappointed that his diplomacy had failed and that he could find no allies for his war against the Turks, Peter prepared to continue his travels. Next on the itinerary was Venice, where the czar hoped to learn more about building and navigating the oared galleys he was constructing at Voronezh for trafficking Russia's many rivers. Before he left Vienna, however, a message arrived from Moscow telling him that the former Streltsi regiments in Azov had once again revolted and were marching on the capital. The communiqué had been sent a month earlier, and Peter had no idea whether troops loyal to him had stopped the rebels, or whether at that very moment the Kremlin was occupied by the Streltsi, with Sophia back on the throne. The next day, July 19, Peter rushed from Vienna on horseback, taking Lefort and a few others with him. Part of the embassy had already left for Venice, and those members still in Vienna prepared to return to Moscow.

Peter's party rode night and day, stopping only for meals and to change horses. At Cracow, he met a messenger who was on his way to Vienna with a letter for the czar, relating that Shein and Gordon had met the Streltsi rebels on the road to Moscow and, with a large force of loyal troops, had defeated them. The revolt was over. Nearly 200 former Streltsi had died in the fighting or were executed soon after, and approximately 2,000 were in prison. Peter was relieved by the news. He decided to stay in Poland for a short time and visit the new king, Augustus II, who was also the elector of Saxony and who owed his new throne in part to the support Peter had given to his candidacy.

The Streltsi revolt had not been a serious threat to Peter's rule. In the spring of 1697, after long months of backbreaking work rebuilding the fortifications at Azov, four Streltsi regiments had been ordered to the Polish border in case the selection of a new Polish king rekindled the smoldering animosity between the two countries. The troops had hoped to return to their families in Moscow and resented the extended duty. Several Streltsi envoys had gone to Moscow to petition the czar to permit the troops to visit their families and look after their commercial affairs in the capital. The envoys had returned with the starling news that the czar had left the country more than a year earlier, that a group of boyars was running the government, and that Peter's whereabouts were unknown. The latter was only partially true because court officials were in regular communication with Peter during his entire trip. In fact, Peter was actually showing more interest in the day-to-day operations of the government during his journey than he had before he left.

Rumors had spread quickly among the angry troops: the czar was reported being held prisoner in Sweden or having abandoned the Orthodox faith in favor of some German Protestant sect. Grasping the apparent opportunity to return home and resume their privileged positions under a new ruler selected by them, the Streltsi had revolted and four regiments had advanced on Moscow in mid-June. Once they had crossed the Moscow River and were within sight of the city, the regiments were confronted by troops from the Moscow garrison. Then, several detachments of foreign troops had appeared behind the Streltsi with 25 cannons. The leaders of the revolt had handed General Alexis Shein and his everpresent adjutant, General Patrick Gordon, a list of their complaints and demands. After these had been rejected the Streltsi attacked, but the rebels were so hopelessly outnumbered and outgunned that the battle lasted just a few minutes. The regiments were disarmed and were being held for Peter's return, when their punishment would be decided. A few leading rebel officers and instigators had already been executed or placed in chains.

Meanwhile, in Poland, Peter and Augustus were getting along famously. They exchanged uniforms and weapons, and more importantly they concluded an alliance for a war against their mutual enemy, Sweden. The Poles wanted to drive the Swedes out of Poland's northern territory, and Peter wanted to regain the Baltic coast that Michael I had relinquished in return for Sweden's withdrawal from Novgorod. After personally witnessing the tremendous wealth of a small country like Holland, which had been built almost entirely on a thriving seaborne commerce, Peter was more determined than ever to build both a naval and a commercial fleet. Ports on the Baltic Sea were as important, perhaps more so, for achieving this goal as access to the Black Sea, because the Turks at Constantinople still blocked Russia's access to the Mediterranean and its southern European ports.

Peter returned to Moscow on September 5, 1698, determined to propel Russia into the modern world and to punish the Streltsi for their revolt. One of his first acts was to personally cut off the long beards worn by the nobles of his court. The shocked men stood in terrified silence as Peter, a barber's razor from Holland in his hand, shaved off the beards that Orthodox teaching decreed be worn. To many Muscovites, this was an appallingly sacrilegious act, one that also stunned the entire nation as word spread through Moscow and then the rest of the country. Although the devout believed the long, bushy beard was God's gift to men, Peter saw it as it was viewed in the West, as signifying that Russia was a backward, semi-Oriental nation lacking the refinements of Western civilization.

Peter also issued a new regulation requiring every man to shave, except those in the clergy and the peasants. Any man seeking favors from the czar had better not appear before him with a beard. Strong objections from the Church eventually brought a revision in the regulation: any man desiring to keep his beard could do so provided he bought a beard license. The license required that he wear a bronze medallion picturing a beard as evidence that the tax had been paid. Any man without a medallion who was found wearing a beard was shaved on the spot. Later decrees, or ukases, required the wearing of Western-style clothing and outlawed the traditional long coats and high boots of ancient Muscovy. Russian women, who had dressed in clothing resembling the religious habits worn by nuns, now appeared in and around Moscow wearing dresses and shoes imported from western European capitals. On its face at least, Moscow was beginning to look more Western and less Oriental.

Peter did not treat the Streltsi rebels lightly. Under torture when first arrested, the rebels had admitted their crimes but had obstinately refused to implicate anyone in Moscow. Peter wrongly suspected Sophia and her family had been behind the affair; he remembered that they had had his uncle hacked to pieces, and he believed they were still capable of overturning him and returning Sophia to the throne. There followed a frightful period of torture interrogations and daily executions, yet the Streltsi remained stubbornly silent on Sophia's alleged role in their revolt. Peter himself wielded the axe that decapitated several of the leaders. Bodies were strung up outside the former regent's convent window, and her brother's corpse was dug up and exposed. Peter personally questioned Sophia but could uncover no evidence that she had been involved in the revolt. Unable to do her any real bodily harm for fear it might provoke more rebellions, Peter forced Sophia to take the vows of a nun; she was locked away in the convent, never to appear in public again.

Peter also took the opportunity to send his wife, whom he detested but until now had tolerated, to a convent at distant Suzdal, where her head was shaved and she was forced to take religious vows. Their 8-year-old son, Alexis, who rarely saw his father, was placed with Peter's sister Natalia and given a German tutor. With Eudoxia gone, Peter spent more time with his mistress, Anna Mons, the daughter of a German Suburb wine merchant. Now he shamelessly appeared in public with the German woman on his arm.

Other changes were rapidly taking place throughout the country. While abroad, Peter had hired nearly 1,000 engineers, technicians, mathematicians, and other specialists. These men arrived in Russia and quickly set about building ships, digging canals, training Russian sailors, and performing myriad other duties previously unknown in Russia. Although many of the changes, such as the outlawing of beards and the Westernization of dress, were symbolic, they had a disturbing effect on a population devoted to the old ways that had been institutionalized through the Orthodox Church.

Soon the Old Believers were fomenting rumors that Peter was an imposter, perhaps even the Antichrist, and that the true czar was either dead or a prisoner in a heretical western European country. Among the pious, blindly devoted masses, almost everything Peter did gave a ring of truth to these rumors. They saw Peter's edict banning beards as a blasphemous act that confirmed the rumors, as did Peter's obvious disdain for the sacred traditional Orthodox

religious ceremonies in which his predecessors had participated. In the eyes of
the people, Peter himself provided the final proof. On December 15, 1699, the
czar changed the New Year from the traditional September 1 to January 1 to
coincide with the change of year in the rest of Europe. He also decreed that the
years should be counted from the birth of Christ and not from the world's
creation, which until then had been the benchmark. (Until Peter's edict,
Russians had designated the current year as 7207, not 1699.) These actions
ignited among the people great animosity toward the czar, as did his taking up
the habit of smoking a pipe, which had been long forbidden in Russia. To make
matters worse, word had leaked out that Peter had attended Protestant religious
services in Holland and a Catholic mass in Vienna, where he also had a private
meeting with Cardinal Kollonitz, the Catholic primate of Hungary. If Peter was
indeed the true czar, then had these heretical foreign churchmen turned him
away from Orthodoxy? The question was on the lips of millions of his countrymen.

Aside from the czar's foreign advisors, who generally practiced heretical
religions, Peter had among his associates many Russians. However, because
most of the latter who held high places at court wanted to see Russia Western-
ized, they, too, were viewed as heretics. If Peter was to succeed in taking his vast
country into the modern world, much of the population would have to be
dragged along, resisting his every attempt at progress. He was prepared to do
just that, no matter who opposed him.

❖ ❖ ❖

Although a warm-water port for war and merchant ships remained his
dream, Peter knew he could not gain access to the Black Sea without a powerful
ally to help him defeat the Turks. In the absence of such an ally, the czar turned
his attention away from the Black Sea in the south and toward the Baltic Sea
in the north. He began prolonged negotiations with the Ottoman Turks, hoping
to end Russia's decades-old war and secure his southern frontier. An agreement
was finally reached in July 1700. Peter did not gain access to the Black Sea for
his 18 frigates anchored in the Sea of Azov, nor for the merchant fleet being
built at Voronezh, but he did win a permanent ambassadorship at the sultan's
court, putting Russia officially on an equal footing with the established European powers. That recognition was important to Peter's future plans.

❖ ❖ ❖

In 1699, Peter suffered several traumatic personal losses. In March, François Lefort, the ardent friend and close advisor who had encouraged Peter to launch the campaigns that captured Azov, and who had suggested the Great Embassy, which introduced the czar to new horizons for Russia, died. Lefort succumbed to the effects of years of heavy drinking and debauchery when he fell ill with a fever following a drinking bout conducted on an outdoor patio in the freezing Moscow winter. Lefort's death devastated the czar. In his grief, Peter upbraided the boyars, whom he forced to attend the funeral, accusing them of secretly rejoicing in his friend's death, a charge that was likely accurate. In November, Peter's other close friend, Patrick Gordon, who had helped the youthful czar organize his personal regiments and was the genius behind the successful campaign against the Turks at Azov, died. Peter felt Gordon's loss dearly, both personally and professionally, as he prepared to build a new Russian army.

Having already accomplished much in a short time, Peter now wanted to build a large, well-trained standing army along the lines of those in western Europe. He decided to make his boyhood regiments the nucleus of the new Russian army. They had been bloodied in the two Azov campaigns, and although they performed poorly in the first, they proved to be better units than the vaunted Streltsi during the successful second campaign.

During the winter of 1699–1700, Peter recruited and took an active part in training a 32,000-man army for his planned Baltic operations. It would be supported by thousands of Tartar and Cossack cavalry. By Russian standards it was an unusual army, not only because of its Western-style uniforms and training, but also because the sons of peasants and nobles stood side by side as equals, and because promotions were based on ability, not on the accident of birth.

On August 20, 1700, 11 days after the peace settlement with the Turks had removed any threat from the south, Czar Peter I declared war on Sweden. At the turn of the century, the Kingdom of Sweden was a formidable foe. A series of strong and intelligent rulers had built a vast, wealthy empire that encompassed not only Sweden but also Finland, Livonia, Estonia, the formerly Russian coast of the Gulf of Finland called Ingria, and portions of the formerly German Baltic coast. Three years earlier, the 15-year-old Charles XII had inherited the throne, and Peter had sensed that conditions were favorable for challenging the untried youth. In January 1700, Augustus II of Poland had declared war on Sweden, and Denmark had done the same shortly thereafter. When Russia entered the fray, it became known as the Great Northern War.

The young King Charles, whose first three years on the throne had been dissipated in exuberant youthful pursuits, quickly redeemed himself by successfully attacking Denmark and forcing the Danes to withdraw from the war on the very day Russia entered it. At the end of November, Charles's army crossed the Baltic, dispatched a Russian force four times its size, and then laid siege to the fortified town of Narva. The 40,000 Russians stationed in the area had been taken by surprise; after nearly one-quarter of them had been killed or taken prisoner, the remnants retreated across their own border. They left behind all their artillery pieces and supply wagons, as well as a dozen general officers among the prisoners.

Despite his army's intensive training, Peter's foreign-born officers had little faith in their Russian troops. The only units that had performed well during the initial battle were the czar's two personal regiments, now called the Imperial Guards, and one other infantry regiment. Peter, who until the night before the final Swedish assault had been present throughout the siege, had gone to Novgorod to speed up the departure of reinforcements for Narva. He could not have expected the Swedes, many of whom he knew had been traveling for several days and were probably exhausted, to attack so soon. This was not an unreasonable assumption, but his departure was interpreted by the victors as cowardice, and a Swedish medal struck to commemorate the victory showed the czar in full flight.

Battle casualties had reduced the attacking Swedish force to less than 9,000 effectives, and many of them were drunk on the alcohol they had confiscated from the Russian camps. Fearing that the Russians might discover his true strength and vulnerability to a counterattack, King Charles released most of the Russian prisoners and goaded them into stampeding their retreating comrades. Instead of pursuing the Russians, whom he no longer considered a viable threat, Charles XII turned his attention to the Poles. During the next six years the young king would wage war against Poland, until September 1706, when Augustus II abdicated the Polish throne to return to Saxony and a pro-Swedish Pole named Stanislaus Leszcynski was made king of Poland by Polish nobles under pressure from Charles. Nearly a year and a half later, in January 1708, Charles would lead his army against the only powerful foe he had left, Russia.

❖ ❖ ❖

The humiliating defeat at Narva had depressed Peter so much that he might have accepted any terms the Swedish king offered, but the czar's depression had quickly given way to renewed determination: He would build a new and more powerful army and conquer the Swedes for all time. No one escaped the czar's new conscription program. Although thousands of men volunteered for the new army, and every volunteer was accepted, tens of thousands more were conscripted. Symbolic of Peter's drive to rebuild the Russian army was his order to strip the churches and monasteries of their bells, which were melted down for use in manufacturing cannons. More than 200,000 men were enlisted in the army between 1700 and 1709.

During these years, as Peter rebuilt his army he also had to deal with a series of revolts. Some, like the one in Astrakhan in 1705, were in opposition to the mass conscriptions. Others, like the Don Cossack uprising two years later, were the result of constant agitation by the Old Believers, who were determined to stop the czar's reforms. The new army performed well in dealing with these rebellions, putting them down with such brutal force that other disgruntled subjects were deterred from rebelling.

The new army was a vast improvement over the one defeated at Narva. Training placed more emphasis on battle strategy and made better use of modern weapons, especially the 30,000 flintlock muskets with bayonets that Peter had purchased from England. Many of these had been distributed to small enterprises around the country to be copied, and soon Russia was producing thousands and then tens of thousands of its own flintlocks. Assuming his customary subordinate role, Peter appointed Boris Sheremetev commander in chief of the army. Sheremetev had routed the Turks and Tartars along the Dnieper River during Peter's failed first campaign against Azov. Twenty years older than his czar, Sheremetev was a supporter of Peter's Westernizing reforms; he had toured Europe for nearly two years, meeting with popes and emperors, and had been made a Knight of St. John while in Malta. He was also the best general Russia had at the time.

The war with Sweden was renewed in January 1708, when Charles XII crossed the Vistula River in Poland with an army of almost 50,000 men and headed for Moscow. With a long record of impressive victories, Sweden's army was feared throughout central Europe and Russia. Had Charles remained on course for the Russian capital instead of turning south, there is every reason to believe he might have taken Moscow. However, he committed the same blunder that Napoleon and Hitler would repeat centuries later, allowing himself to be drawn into the heartland of this vast country, where his troops would suffer from a lack of food and other supplies.

❖ ❖ ❖

The intervening years had not been totally without conflict between Sweden and Russia. Small battles and skirmishes were routine, and Russia won more than her share of them. In January and again in July 1702, Sheremetev soundly defeated a Swedish army defending Livonia, and except for a few isolated forts, the entire province fell into Russian hands. The Russians took thousands of prisoners and incarcerated thousands more civilian sympathizers. One of the latter was a 17-year-old girl named Martha Skavronskaya, whom Sheremetev took into his household as a serving girl. Overjoyed with these successes, the czar promoted Sheremetev to field marshal and awarded him the Order of St. Andrew, which was created by Peter after England's Order of the Garter.

In June and September of the same year, the fledgling Russian navy—little more than a collection of small galleys because Peter had no way to transfer his ocean-going ships from the Sea of Azov to the Baltic—attacked the Swedish fleet in Lake Ladoga, Europe's largest lake. The Swedes were forced to abandon the lake to the Russians.

The following spring, 1703, Peter himself led a successful attack on a Swedish town five miles down the Neva River from the point where the river, which flows from Lake Ladoga, empties into the Gulf of Finland. The Russians captured several Swedish warships that had been sent to defend the town, and the czar himself was among the troops who boarded the ships under enemy fire. For this feat Peter and his troop commander, General Alexander Menshikov, were later awarded the Order of St. Andrew. Menshikov, who had accompanied Peter to western Europe as his personal orderly, knew almost as much about ship carpentry as the czar. A six-footer, Menshikov was well above the average height of most Russians, yet he was dwarfed by Peter. He quickly became the czar's favorite and enjoyed a degree of intimacy with Peter that no one, including Lefort, ever had before. Menshikov, who embodied the enlightened Russia that Peter was striving to create, was the only man who Peter said could "speak for the czar."

Peter was exhilarated. His rejuvenated army and his new navy had each won an important victory. With control of the coast and access to the Gulf of Finland, Peter now had an outlet to the Baltic Sea. Although Russian ships could not yet transit this mostly ice-free route, Peter knew he had taken a giant first step toward that goal. With year-round access to Baltic ports, Russia could trade with western Europe on a large scale.

One day in 1703, Peter Romanov, czar of all the Russias, stood at the Gulf of Finland. On the barren marshlands, hundreds of miles from any Russian

From the collection of James P. Duffy

Czar Peter I "the Great"

settlement, he gazed out at the Gulf and imagined a long line of commercial
sailing vessels unloading cargoes and taking on goods, just as he had seen on
the Thames in London and at the Amsterdam docks. Here, Peter would end
Russia's exclusion from the community of trading nations and lead his country
into the world of international commerce. According to the most popular of
several legends, Peter was standing on Hare Island in the middle of the Neva
River when he knelt down and cut two strips of sod from the earth. Intersecting
them to form a cross, he ordered that the fort of St. Peter and St. Paul be built
on that spot. The date was May 16, 1703. The fortress, supported by wooden
pilings sunk into the mud and with canals for streets, would grow into a town,
then into a city. The city would be named St. Petersburg, after the czar's patron
saint. During World War I, its name would be de-Germanized to Petrograd,

then changed to Leningrad after the Bolshevik Revolution of 1917, and then revert to St. Petersburg by popular vote in 1991.

Tens of thousands of conscripts were sent to the desolate marshlands on which Peter's "paradise" would be built. Cossacks, Tartars, soldiers, peasants—even entire towns—were moved there to engage in the massive construction project. No one was exempt, and thousands would die from exposure, exhaustion, or disease exacerbated by chronic food shortages and inadequate housing. The czar constantly would require replacements for the multitudes who found their last resting place in the bleak terrain around the new city.

❖   ❖   ❖

While Peter's fortress city was being built, the protracted war with Sweden continued to its climax in 1708. When King Charles XII's invading army started toward Moscow, he expected it would be joined by reinforcements coming from Livonia. Czar Peter personally led the Russian army that intercepted the 12,000-man Swedish reinforcement column near Lesnaya and destroyed it. Peter also captured a large supply train intended for Charles's army, which elsewhere was making halting progress behind the Russians who were retreating before Moscow. The Russians' scorched-earth tactics were leaving no crops for Charles's soldiers and no fodder for their horses.

To Peter's bewilderment, Charles abruptly altered his course and turned south. The Swedish king had decided to head for the Ukraine, where the Cossack hetman, Ivan Mazepa, had promised to support the invasion with a great Cossack revolt. The strategy failed. Mazepa delivered only a few thousand Cossacks to Charles's campaign; the rest remained loyal to Moscow partly because of the proximity of Menshikov's powerful Russian army, which had mercilessly crushed an earlier Cossack revolt. Charles found himself deep in the Russian steppe with his supply lines virtually nonexistent and his expected ally unable to produce the promised troops. The once invincible Swedish army soon began to suffer from hunger and disease amid a population that was indifferent at best, and hostile at worst.

Charles XII, unaware of Peter's smashing victory at Lesnaya, confidently awaited the arrival of the 12,000 reinforcements and the badly needed supplies. He learned the ominous truth in early October while camped near the fortified Russian town of Mglin. Instead of the 12,000 fresh troops and enough supplies to restore his debilitated army's vitality, less than half that number of bedraggled, hungry troops arrived without supplies or cannons. Their arrival did nothing to improve the Swedish position; in fact, it made the situation worse by adding thousands more starving men to the beleaguered camp.

Desperate for a safe winter refuge, Charles elected to go farther south into the Ukraine and winter at Baturin, the capital of the Ukrainian Cossacks on whom he still counted for support. His left, or eastern, flank was vulnerable to the main Russian army, which Sheremetev and Peter had marched south, while to Charles's right, Menshikov was leading a force of crack Russian cavalry. The Swedish army, along with Mazepa's rebellious Cossacks, made a frantic dash cross country for the protection of the fortress at Baturin, to no avail.

On November 3, in a bold stroke, Menshikov's cavalry, reinforced by mounted infantry and artillery sent by Peter, captured Baturin before Charles could reach it. Lacking sufficient troops to hold the city against the Swedes, Menshikov slaughtered its inhabitants, estimated at between 7,000 and 9,000 people, and burned it to the ground. When Charles and Mazepa arrived with their starving army, Baturin no longer existed. The czar, furious at Mazepa's betrayal, had him removed as hetman and excommunicated from the Orthodox Church. Peter then had his own candidate, Ivan Soropadsky, elected hetman of the Ukrainian Cossacks.

Seeking to win allies against Sweden from among the nations of western Europe, Peter sent his envoy, Andrei Matviev, to Amsterdam and London. The czar wanted to gather support for his claim to the coast of the Gulf of Finland, including clear title to his new city of St. Petersburg. Matviev's mission failed. The Dutch and British both vetoed the Russian proposal. In his desperation, Peter had asked England's Duke of Marlborough to use his influence with Queen Anne; he offered the duke an enormous financial bribe and his choice of one of three Russian principalities as his personal domain—Kiev, Vladimir, or Siberia. The duke had been tempted, but he declined.

The Swedes, cut off from reinforcements and supplies, barely survived the severe winter on the open steppes. By the summer of 1709, the Swedish king's once invincible army had been reduced to a specter of its former self. In June, the ill-clad, ill-fed Swedes, desperately short of ammunition, confronted the Russian army. Peter arrived at the front early in the month, and instead of assuming his usual subordinate role, he took command of all Russian forces facing the Swedes. In mid-June, the armies faced each other across the Vorskla River near the town of Poltava. The Swedes now suffered a serious blow to their morale when King Charles was badly wounded in the left foot while inspecting his troops within musket range of an advance party of Russians. Charles ignored the wound and concluded his inspection, but hours later his boot had to be cut from his infected foot and he was ravaged with fever.

On June 21, the Russians crossed the river and entrenched themselves north of the Swedish lines. The following day Charles, who was still suffering the effects of fever and had to be carried in a litter, learned that reinforcements he had expected from Poland would not be coming. In addition, the Ottoman sultan had denied the khan of the Crimean Tartars permission to give Charles aid. Charles had an effective force of 25,000 men in 24 infantry battalions and 17 cavalry regiments, but the numbers are deceiving. The cold winter and constant skirmishing with the Russians had left most of these Swedish formations badly undermanned. The Russian army's strength was nearly 100,000 men.

The great final battle began in the predawn hours of Monday, June 28, 1709, when Swedish infantry advanced against a series of earthen redoubts that the Russians had constructed during the night. At sunrise, a ferocious cavalry battle was underway, with more than 20,000 horsemen taking part. The Russian cavalry withdrew at Peter's direction even though Menshikov's forces had the upper hand. Wary of the Swedish army's reputation for battlefield surprise, Peter feared his cavalry might be encircled and destroyed. Despite Peter's overcautious decision, his army achieved a bloody victory by nightfall, capturing thousands of Swedes and their Cossack allies. Among the prisoners was the Swedish army commander, Field Marshal Carl Gustav Rehnskjold. King Charles, invalided by his wound, escaped to the Ottoman border with his Cossack ally Mazepa. When Charles crossed the Bug River into Turkish territory, he had with him only a small portion of his army's treasury and less than 600 troops. Mazepa died within a month. King Charles remained in Turkey as a virtual hostage of the sultan; he was unable to return to Sweden until 1715.

❖ ❖ ❖

Peter was concerned about other matters besides war during the first decade of the 18 century.

In the fall of 1703, he met a 19-year-old Lithuanian girl who was a member of Alexander Menshikov's household, Martha Skavronskaya, the very same Lithuanian prisoner who had been captured in Livonia in 1702 and who had become one of Field Marshal Sheremetev's domestic servants. During her time with Sheremetev, she converted from Catholicism to Orthodoxy and had adopted the name Catherine. Evidently taken with the comely servant, Menshikov had induced the old field marshal to release her to his household. Later,

Catherine's rivals would accuse her of having been the mistress of both Shere-metev and Menshikov, but there is no evidence to support that allegation.

Catherine did become the czar's mistress, however, beginning in the fall of 1703. In 1707, Peter married her but kept the relationship secret out of fear that the public would criticize his marriage to an illiterate foreign peasant girl. During her years with Peter, Catherine had 12 children, but only two survived past infancy. Displaying innate intelligence, compassion, and a total commit-ment to Peter, Catherine became his closest confidant.

Meanwhile, King Charles's detention by the Ottoman sultan had left Sweden without a strong monarch. Old alliances against Sweden were revived as Denmark invaded its southern provinces and Augustus II crossed into Poland from Saxony to regain the Polish throne. Peter sent Menshikov's cavalry to Poland to aid Augustus, his "faithful ally." The czar sent Field Marshal Shere-metev and his army to Riga with instructions to drive the Swedes back across the Baltic.

In 1710, Russian armies conquered Estonia and Livonia, and captured the coastal fortresses of Riga, Dünamünde, Pernau, and Reval. That same year, Peter arranged for his niece, the late co-Czar Ivan's daughter Anna, to marry the duke of Courland, who governed a semi-autonomous part of Poland. Soon after, Peter's army invaded Finland, then a possession of Sweden, and seized the coastal towns of Keksgolm and Vyborg. Toward the end of the year, Peter sent a scathing message to Ahmed III, the sultan of the Ottoman Empire, demanding that he expel Charles. The sultan had been urged by various sources—including Charles XII, the khan of the Crimean Tartars, his French allies, and even his own mother—to challenge Russia. Peter's victory against the Swedes had temporarily stilled these voices, but his caustic, arrogant demand tilted the sultan toward their view.

In November, Sultan Ahmed III declared war on Russia. Finally freed of the restraints put on him by the treaty of 1700 between Russia and the Ottoman Empire, the Crimean khan, Devlet Gerey, led his Tartar horsemen into Russia in January 1711, to loot and to capture prisoners to sell in the slave markets. The raid was also calculated to divert Peter's attention from the menacing Turkish posture on the Danube, but the Tartar invasion collapsed when the Cossacks, under Peter's hand-picked hetman, Soropadsky, drove it back across the steppes.

Intoxicated with his victory over Charles, Peter, who had begun to think of himself as the protector of the Christians living under Ottoman rule, used the opportunity of Turkey's declaration of war to invade the Balkans. He incorrectly assumed that the Christian populations of Moldavia and Wallachia would rise up against their Muslim rulers and join his campaign. Although the Moldavians did support the Russians, Wallachia's powerful and wealthy Prince Brancovo remained loyal to the sultan.

In March 1711, as Peter was preparing to leave Moscow for the Balkans, he informed his sister Natalia and his half-brother Ivan's widow and two daughters that Catherine was his wife. He told them that if he died in the coming campaign they must acknowledge her as his widow and the lawful czarina. This was of vital importance to Catherine, who was joining the czar on the campaign, because it began the process whereby her status would one day be officially recognized. However, it seems that the former peasant girl was satisfied with her position and never pressured Peter to publicly acknowledge her as his wife, although he repeatedly told her he planned to do so.

Peter's army merged with Sheremetev's, which had come from the Baltic region, at Jassy, the Moldavian capital, in early June 1711. The combined Russian army numbered 40,000 men but was not ready for battle. After only a few small skirmishes, Peter found himself backed up along the Pruth River and surrounded by more than 200,000 Ottoman Turks. Facing almost certain annihilation, Peter extricated his army by accepting a Turkish proposal that he return Azov to them and dismantle the Russian fortress there.

A dejected Peter returned to Moscow with Catherine. In February 1712, he married her a second time, now publicly and with the pomp and solemnity appropriate to the marriage of a czar. The Lithuanian peasant girl was crowned empress of Russia. Peter had begun referring to himself, especially among foreigners, as emperor, a title he apparently favored over czar, which connoted a long association with Asia. Peter wanted his empire to be a part of Europe, not of the East.

Having lost most of his earlier gains in the far south, Peter concentrated on the war against Sweden and on tightening his control of the Baltic coast. He brought most of Finland under Russian control as a result of the invasion of 1713, and the following year Rear Admiral Peter Romanov led his navy on a successful strike against the Swedish fleet in the Baltic. Surrounded by enemies, Sweden finally came to terms with Russia and her allies—Denmark, Poland, Saxony, Prussia, and Hanover—in 1721. The Treaty of Nystadt gave Russia permanent possession of Livonia, Estonia, and, most importantly, Ingermanland, where the czar was building St. Petersburg. Russia also retained a portion of Finland.

❖ ❖ ❖

While Peter was engaged in the war with Sweden, his son, Czarevitch Alexis, was speaking out against his reforms. Brought up under the influence of Orthodox priests, Alexis disdained the many changes his father had brought to Russia. Peter feared that after his death Alexis would reverse his policies and undo many of his progressive innovations. Catherine's only two surviving children by Peter were girls and therefore could not inherit his crown. Determined to resolve the issue, Peter pressed Alexis to either decide in favor of his programs or disclaim them. Alexis's response to his father's pressures was to flee Russia in November 1716, and to go into hiding under the protection of the Austrian emperor. Alexis hid in an alpine castle for nearly a year, until Peter's agent, Peter Tolstoy, discovered his whereabouts and eventually coaxed him to return.

Linked to innumerable conspiracies against Peter, both real and manufactured, the 27-year-old heir to the Russian throne was tortured before he died in the Peter and Paul Fortress in St. Petersburg on June 26, 1718. Forty lashes of the knout had been administered to him as he awaited death under a penalty handed down by a court for his "designs of rebellion." Not the simple whip intended for routine discipline, the heavy leather knout was a diabolical tool that inflicted such terrible wounds that few victims survived more than 40 blows.

The remainder of Peter's reign was consumed with the further development of St. Petersburg, the continued expansion of the Baltic Fleet, and plans to invade Asia. A brief war with Persia won Russia access to the Caspian Sea, and long-neglected negotiations with China were reopened. Through the Baltic conquests, Peter had achieved his goal of opening a "window on Europe," and European customs now made a great impact on the younger "new men" who emulated their czar. In many ways, Peter was a frenetic visionary who tried to accomplish more for his country than any one man could hope to do, even with the awesome authority of a czar.

❖ ❖ ❖

Peter the Great died in the predawn hours of January 28, 1725. The cause of death was probably a combination of the apoplectic seizures to which he was susceptible, and the effects of his prolonged submersion in the icy Neva River while assisting in the rescue of a capsized boatload of soldiers the previous November. Peter's periodic seizures would quake his entire body. Catherine, ever the faithful companion, was the only person capable of bringing peace to the czar during these fits of convulsion; she would force him to lie next to her and rest his head on her lap while she gently stroked his head. Often this would bring him not only peace but sleep, and she would remain there, with his head on her lap, for hours, until he awoke, refreshed and at peace.

Peter died leaving the question of succession unresolved. In his last hours, the czar had tried to name his successor in a written statement. He got no further than "Give everything to . . ." before his strength failed. He then summoned his 17-year-old daughter Anne, who could read and write, to help him record his wishes. Unfortunately, Peter died before Anne reached his bedside.

When he died in 1725 at the age of 52, Peter left an emerging nation ready to join the modern society of western Europe. Several hundred Russian factories were producing high-quality goods for the rich markets of Holland and England. Peter had also established a well-trained standing army of more then 200,000 battle-tested men, and a formidable navy of 48 warships and nearly 1,000 smaller craft that had humbled the once mighty Swedish fleet. His widespread accomplishments were recognized by the national assembly, which posthumously bestowed on him the grandiose titles "Father of the Country," "Emperor," and "the Great."

There were two leading candidates for Peter's crown, each with powerful sponsors. Peter's wife Catherine had the backing of the late czar's inti-mates—men like Menshikov, usually of common birth, who had risen high in Peter's world through their ability and who stood to lose everything if the boyars regained control of the government. A second candidate, Peter's 9-year-old grandson Peter, Alexis's son, was proposed by many of the boyars and the clergy who hoped through him to reverse Peter the Great's Westernizing policies.

While the czar lay dying, a council of boyars and leading government officials, most of whom supported the boy, had met to preempt the national assembly by selecting the new monarch. However, when the council learned that the palace in which it was meeting was surrounded by the Imperial Guards regiments, who were fiercely loyal to Peter the Great and Catherine and whose support Menshikov had solicited for Catherine, the matter was quickly settled. The council declared Catherine "autocrat, with all the prerogatives of her late consort." The chubby, uneducated Lithuanian peasant girl and former war prisoner became Catherine I, empress of Russia, the empire's first female monarch.

Peter the Great's passing spawned a period in which Russia would be ruled primarily by women. For the most part, these monarchs proved to be too weak, too young, or too ignorant of Russia to contribute much to Peter's programs for growth. From the day Peter died until Catherine the Great assumed the throne in 1762, the crown would pass in quick succession from one claimant to another. Peter himself was responsible for this situation; he executed his son Alexis, the only direct male heir, and died without leaving a will. In 1722, Peter had decreed that the monarch had the sole right to name his successor, but he failed to provide a mechanism for electing a new czar if the incumbent died without making his selection known, as Peter himself did.

With Peter's death, foreign influence over the throne increased, another result of his policies. As part of his Westernizing strategy, Peter had arranged marriages between his family and non-Russian nobles. Anne, his eldest daughter by Catherine, had married the duke of Holstein; Peter's two nieces, Anna and Catherine, the daughters of the late co-czar Ivan V, were married to German dukes as well: Anna to the duke of Courland, and Catherine to the duke of Mecklenburg. Peter had tried but failed to marry his youngest daughter, Elizabeth, to King Louis XV of France. These international marriages allowed petty German nobles to vie for the crown of a vast empire to which they had no real ties, and ultimately diluted the line of Russian rulers with foreign blood. Peter the Great was the last "pure" Russian monarch.

Catherine I would rule until her own untimely death on May 7, 1727. Although she lacked a formal education, the empress was hardly a fool. She understood that it was the army, especially the Imperial Guard regiments, that had won her the crown. After vowing to continue Peter's policies, Catherine excused the soldiers from their physical labors on Peter's numerous building projects throughout the nation. Army pay, which was habitually late, began arriving on time, and fresh uniforms were supplied when needed. Already closely linked to the soldiers in her massive army because she had so often accompanied Peter on his military campaigns, Catherine regularly appeared before her troops at military reviews and parades.

Although devoted to Peter's memory and determined to continue his reforms, Catherine lacked the administrative ability to rule the vast and mighty empire he had left behind. She had a quick mind and faultless tact with people of any rank, but she had been Peter's helpmate, not his co-ruler, and the affairs of state were beyond her capacities.

Peter the Great had respected Menshikov's opinions and had frequently asked for his advice, but the final decision had always been the czar's. Menshikov had never had more power or influence than the czar had permitted. With Peter gone, Menshikov now became the most powerful person in the empire, even more powerful than the empress, who allowed him free rein to do as he wished. While Catherine spent most her time cultivating close relations with the army, or expending huge sums of money on clothes and jewelry ordered from the best houses in Paris, Menshikov created a virtual dictatorship. Audaciously flaunting his power before the boyars, Menshikov soon made a host of enemies, including even some of the officials who had supported Catherine over Alexis's young son, Peter.

Less than a year into Catherine's reign, the more powerful nobles and many of the "new men" who had emerged under Peter the Great's patronage began muttering about a coup that would depose Menshikov and allow the council of nobles to select a new monarch. Rumors also circulated that the army of the Ukraine, under Prince Michael Golitsin, a member of an old aristocratic family, was threatening to revolt and remove Catherine in favor of Peter. The empress appeared to be unaware of these threats, but Menshikov was not. Acutely alert to his own vulnerability should Catherine be toppled, he tried without success to pair his young daughter in marriage with Peter and thereby assure himself a role as regent if Catherine was forced off the throne.

Peter Tolstoy's survival was also tied to Catherine's. Tolstoy was one of the few nobles that Peter the Great had embraced; he had represented the czar at Constantinople at the start of the war that ended with the disaster at the Pruth River. He had also served Peter well by locating Alexis in his Austrian hideaway and persuading him to return to Russia with assurances of amnesty, knowing in advance that Peter would undoubtedly condemn the heir to die. The last thing Tolstoy wanted was for Alexis's son Peter to come to the throne. The boy could be expected to deal harshly with anyone who he felt was culpable in his father's murder.

Peter Tolstoy could see that events would inevitably lead to Catherine's removal, and possibly to the execution of Menshikov and himself. In late 1725, he resolved to curtail Menshikov's avarice and avoid a coup d'état. His solution was to create a governing body that would "lighten the heavy burden" on the empress and help keep Menshikov in check. He arranged a series of meetings between Menshikov and the leading members of the old aristocratic families. Tolstoy included in these meetings Charles Frederick, the duke of Holstein, who had married Princess Anne, Peter's and Catherine's daughter. The duke disliked Menshikov and harbored ambitions to gain the Russian throne for himself or his wife. Numerous roadblocks prevented the duke from achieving this goal, not the least of which was that when Anna had married a foreigner, she had been required to renounce any claim she might have to the throne, whether for herself or her heirs.

Out of these meetings a new central organ was created to run the affairs of the Russian Empire—the Supreme Privy Council. The six original council members were Alexander Menshikov, Peter Tolstoy, Admiral Fedor Apraxin, Count Gavric Golovkin, Baron Andrew Ostermann, and Count Dmitri Golitsin. Catherine approved the council but added Frederick of Holstein to its membership before investing the full authority of her government in the new body. Menshikov remained in charge, since most of the council members were either in his debt or intimidated by him.

Catherine's single major accomplishment—a one-third reduction in taxes—was done at the urging of Menshikov and the Supreme Privy Council. The exodus of Russian peasants to the southern and western frontiers had not only continued unabated, but had actually accelerated under Peter the Great's oppressive taxes. Large tracts of arable land had reverted to wild growth as the peasants who tilled the soil fled to escape the heavy taxes and the abuse of the tax collectors. Official estimates based on periodic government censuses revealed that between 1719 and 1727 nearly a quarter of a million peasants left the fields for the southern steppes. Their departure deprived the government of taxes and depleted the army's pool of conscripts as many joined brigand bands that roamed the steppes, robbing travelers and raiding settlements.

Menshikov satisfied the empress that the excessive tax burden on the peasants was both intolerable and counterproductive. Russia was threatened with the loss of almost its entire peasant class, which would result not only in widespread famine but also in a substantial reduction of the government's tax revenues. Appealing to Catherine's fondness for the army, he explained that "the peasants and the army are like soul and body; without the one you cannot have the other." The empress understood that without a vast peasant population to supply the recruits who made up the bulk of her army, she would have no army to defend her throne. In January 1727, she signed a decree reducing by one-third the soul tax that Peter the Great had levied on the male members of each household to pay for his military reforms. Catherine also forgave the back taxes owed by peasants, who probably would never have been able to pay them anyway, and lowered by one-third the number of peasants conscripted into the army.

Catherine I succeeded where Peter the Great had failed when she named her successor before she died. Catherine could have chosen either of her two daughters, Elizabeth or Anne; such a choice would have continued the dynastic line within her family and firmly established the precedent of a woman occupying the throne. Instead, she chose Peter, Peter the Great's grandson by his first marriage and the son of the disgraced Alexis. She provided no public explanation for this unusual choice.

On May 6, 1727, after several months of illness, Catherine I died from the lingering effects of a chill she had contracted in January while participating in the annual Blessing of the Waters of the Neva. She had stood for hours in frigid weather, reviewing long columns of parading troops, and fallen ill immediately after.

❖   ❖   ❖

In a convoluted scheme to remain in control, the resilient, crafty Menshikov had prevailed on Catherine while she was ill to choose as her successor the 11-year-old Peter, who was crowned Peter II. Menshikov had also obtained Catherine's approval of his arranging the betrothal of his 16-year-old daughter Maria to the young prince and future emperor, but the boy shunned both father and daughter and nothing came of the proposal. After Catherine's death, and before Peter II was able to assert his authority as czar, Menshikov still held control. He exiled his estranged former friend, Peter Tolstoy, and pressured Charles Frederick, the duke of Holstein, into leaving Russia with his wife, Catherine's daughter, Anne, and returning to his own capital of Kiel. The following year, in 1728, Anne died shortly after giving birth to a boy, Carl Peter, named after his grandfather, Peter the Great. The boy would eventually became Peter III.

Peter II was a handsome youth who, like his grandfather, was tall for his age. The new emperor cared little for governmental affairs, instead preferring to spend almost all of his time riding and hunting with his sister, Natalia, and his aunt, Catherine's 18-year-old daughter Elizabeth. He left the government in the hands of Prince Menshikov, who was now more powerful and feared than ever before. He enemies called him "the most haughty Goliath."

Preoccupied with the affairs of state, Menshikov ignored the young czar and failed to notice the growing danger in the person of Peter's new companion, Prince Ivan Dolgoruky. Dolgoruky, the scion of an old aristocratic family that had earlier produced several Russian grand princes, was the son of Prince Alexis Dolgoruky, a longtime adversary of Menshikov. Ivan baited the neophyte ruler, telling him that the regent was behaving as if the czar did not exist, and urging him to defy the overbearing Menshikov. Peter was reluctant to challenge Menshikov because he, too, feared the regent's influence over the Imperial Guards. Had Menshikov been aware of Ivan's treachery, he surely would have eliminated him.

Peter II's opportunity came in July 1727, barely two months after Catherine's death. While Menshikov was bedridden with a debilitating illness, Peter seized the reins of government. By the time Menshikov's health had recovered, Peter had stripped him of all offices and ordered the former regent and his family, including his daughter, the hapless Maria, into exile at their estate near the former Cossack capital of Baturin in the Ukraine. The following April, Prince Menshikov, once the most powerful man in Russia, was deprived of the great wealth he had accumulated while in government service and exiled to Siberia, where, accompanied by Maria, he lived out his days chopping wood to heat his meager cabin. Menshikov died in November 1729, all but forgotten by those who had deposed him. Maria died a short time later.

Meanwhile, Prince Alexis Dolgoruky deftly maneuvered to gain favor with Peter by arranging to have his daughter, Catherine, betrothed to the boy czar. Peter II moved his court from St. Petersburg (Russia's capital since Peter the Great established it there in 1712) to Moscow, which again became the cultural and political capital of Russia. The move was motivated by Peter's hatred of St. Petersburg, and was intended as a slap at his grandfather, Peter I. The czar appointed Alexis Dolgoruky, the latter's brother Prince Basil Dolgoruky, and a member of another old boyar family, Prince Dmitri Golitsin, members of the Privy Council, but the Dolgorukys' plans for his daughter were frustrated when Peter II died of smallpox on January 11, 1730, before he could marry her. Because Peter II died without a direct descendant and without having named his successor, the throne of Russia once more became an open prize to be claimed by the strongest challenger.

Immediately following Peter II's death, the Supreme Privy Council, now dominated by members of old boyar families, met to name the new monarch. The Dolgoruky family claimed the throne for the late emperor's fiancée, the 17-year-old Catherine Dolgoruky, who was said to be pregnant with Peter's child, but Prince Golitsin's opposition was too great to overcome. Golitsin had spent years studying the liberal constitutional monarchies of western Europe, and he had resolved to modernize both the method of choosing the Russian monarch and the administration of the monarchy. He wanted to limit the autocratic power of future czars to that exercised by the kings and queens of England. Golitsin also opposed another prominent candidate, the late Empress Catherine's daughter Elizabeth. Empress Catherine had provided in her will that if Peter II died childless, her daughters should inherit the throne. Golitsin opposed Elizabeth because he considered her too superficial and fun-loving to be taken seriously, and also because she had been born before her mother and her father, Peter the Great, were married.

The Privy Council finally settled on a candidate that a majority of its members could support—Anna, the daughter of Ivan V, Peter the Great's half-brother and co-czar, and the recent widow of the duke of Courland. The council offered Anna the throne, provided that she accept numerous restrictions on her authority as empress. Anxious to escape the German aristocrats who were vying for her favors as duchess of Courland, Anna quickly signed the agreement sent to her by the council. The agreement required that Anna not remarry and not attempt to name her successor. It also restricted her freedom to make war or peace without the council's approval, and stripped her of the rights to levy new taxes and to make military appointments above the rank of colonel. The council retained control of her fiscal privileges and forbade her to confiscate a nobleman's property or to chastise him without a trial. On its surface, the agreement appeared to be a step toward a constitutional monarchy, but it was actually a cunning stratagem to transfer power from the monarch to the eight members of the Privy Council.

While Anna was en route to Moscow for her coronation, details of the agreement spread among the landed gentry, whose members included most of the officers and men of the Imperial Guard. Anxious to prevent the old boyar families on the Privy Council from regaining their former power, the Guards regiments assembled before the Moscow palace where the council was meeting, to protest the agreement. Arriving at the Moscow suburbs, Anna learned of the Guard's opposition to the agreement she had so hastily signed. She waited to see the outcome of the Guards' protest. But recognizing the possibilities implicit in the Imperial Guards' objections to the council's thinly veiled ruse, she appointed herself a colonel of the Preobrazhenkii regiment of the Guards and invited the officers to dine and drink with her.

On February 25, 1730, Anna entered Moscow with the full backing of the Imperial Guards, and, challenging the Privy Council's presumption to restrict her authority, she shredded the agreement. During the next several years, Anna would either execute, exile, or imprison each member of the Privy Council. The council itself would be disbanded.

Anna of Courland was 37-years-old when she became the second empress of Russia at the end of April 1730. For nearly 20 years she had lived in Courland, acquiring the customs and habits of her late husband's German citizens, and was thoroughly German in speech and thought. A year after her coronation,

Anna moved the royal court back to St. Petersburg, which had developed into the most cosmopolitan, Europeanized city in her realm.

Anna's reign, which lasted until her death in 1740, was a nightmare of cruel and arrogant abuse of the Russian people. Anna brought a large following of Germans with her, including one notorious lover, Ernst-Johann Biron. Each of these Germans exhibited undisguised disdain for Russia and all things Russian. Russian nobles found themselves excluded from her predominantly German court, which was one of extreme extravagances as the empress made up for her years of privation in her impoverished Duchy of Courland. The cost of maintaining Anna's court was five times that for Peter the Great's, who himself was no piker. She dealt harshly with dissenters, exiling on average 2,000 people to Siberia each year. She also honed Peter the Great's secret police organization into a feared arm of her government, rooting out anyone who spoke against the empress or her German-dominated court.

Like Peter the Great, Anna had a fondness for persons with unusual deformities: she populated her palace with dwarfs, giants, hunchbacks, and fools. She also filled the courtyards and gardens with all sorts of animals, which she delighted in shooting from her windows. Anna made no effort to improve her stout, masculine appearance and coarse manners, which hardly gave her a regal bearing. Yet since being widowed after only a few months of marriage, she had attracted a long list of lovers.

Cognizant of the Imperial Guard's capability to depose as well as to protect her, Anna decided to strengthen her position by forming two new Guards regiments, the Izmailovsky and the Horse Guards. Placed under the command of one of Anna's closest advisors from Courland, Count Carl Gustavus Löwenwolde, the officers for these regiments were drawn from the noble families of northern Germany and the Baltic principalities and duchies.

Although he held no official title in Russia, Ernst-Johann Biron was a power behind the throne. Anna had him named a prince of the Holy Roman Empire, a rather empty title since the empire existed solely on paper, but more importantly, she pressured the Courland Diet to elect him duke of Courland. Because of Biron's influence on the empress, whose bed he shared regularly, Russian historians have called the period of Anna's reign the Bironovshchina, or "Age of Biron." Ignoring his duties in Courland, Biron remained in St. Petersburg, close to the throne of real power. He was instrumental in convincing the empress that the crown must be kept on Ivan V's side of the family and not be permitted to revert to Peter the Great's descendants. Ivan V's only other child, Catherine, who had married the duke of Mecklenberg, had one daughter, also named Anna, who had recently married the prince of Brunswick and took the title Princess Anne of Brunswick-Bevern-Lunenburg. If the empress were to die suddenly, the throne, if it was to be kept in Ivan V's family, would have to pass to another German noblewoman. Princess Anne solved this problem for Biron and Empress Anna in August 1740, when she produced a son, Ivan. Ironically, two months later the empress fell gravely ill. Hours before her death, Anna named her sister's grandson, the infant Ivan, as her successor. She then appointed the faithful Biron to serve as Ivan's regent.

Empress Anna's deathbed wishes were thwarted by the Imperial Guard regiments, which she had not attempted to win over to her selection. Biron compounded this during the first few days of his regency. Attempting to dilute the power of the Imperial Guard, he transferred several regular army units into St. Petersburg and incautiously let slip his intention to recruit peasant soldiers into the Imperial Guard, which had traditionally been chosen exclusively from the gentry class. A mere 22 days after becoming regent of Russian, Biron was seized by Guards officers and deported to Siberia. He was replaced as regent by Princess Anna, the mother of three-month-old Emperor Ivan VI.

Anne's regency survived only a year, and little changed except that a few of the Germans at the imperial court were sent away and replaced by others. The Germans in the court then began an internal struggle to control the government, which led the few Russians left at court, including officers of the Imperial Guard, to begin a search for a more acceptable ruler. Tired of a court tainted by German influence, leading Guards officers looked for a Russian candidate to replace the infant Ivan VI and his mother. They would find that person in Elizabeth, the daughter of Peter the Great and Catherine I. A handsome, charming, and probably nymphomaniacal woman of 31, Elizabeth was spending most of her time in pursuit of pleasure and had no interest in ruling the country.

❖ ❖ ❖

In some ways the Imperial Guard was not unlike the old Streltsi it had replaced as the czar's palace guards. It enjoyed comfortable quarters and generous rations in St. Petersburg, which it was unwilling to leave, and was both pampered and feared by the ruling class. Its decision to replace Regent Anne with Elizabeth would be motivated at least in part by Sweden's unexpected declaration of war on July 27, 1741. The Swedes saw an opportunity to capitalize on the chaos in St. Petersburg and regain the Baltic coast territories they had lost to Peter the Great.

Ominous reports of the Imperial Guard's dissatisfaction reached Anne, who attempted to avoid a coup against her and her son by signing an order to be issued on November 24, instructing the Imperial Grand to prepare to go to Finland to halt the Swedish invasion there. Reacting predictably, the Guardsmen beseeched Elizabeth to take the throne, but Elizabeth remained hesitant, not wishing to give up her pleasurable lifestyle to assume the burdensome responsibilities of the crown. When on November 23 the regent used veiled threats to demand to know her position on the rumored Guard's revolt, Elizabeth abruptly threw her support behind the Guard.

The confrontation between Anne and Elizabeth took place on November 23, 1741. Anne told Elizabeth that she had been informed that the French ambassador and Elizabeth's personal physician, a Frenchman named Lestocq, were part of a conspiracy to overthrow the infant Ivan VI and place Elizabeth on the throne. The regent announced that she planned to arrest Lestocq. Elizabeth denied any knowledge of the alleged plot, and ostensibly the two parted amicably. But Elizabeth realized that the time had come to act. If the Imperial Guard regiments were sent to Finland, she would be at the regent's mercy and would undoubtedly be forced into a convent.

The following day, Elizabeth began preparations for the coup that would place her on the throne of Russia. In the early evening of the 24th, she prayed for guidance and vowed before a holy icon that if she were granted the throne she would never condemn anyone to death. Then, accompanied by Lestocq and two others courtiers, she rode to the Imperial Guard barracks. Arriving at about midnight, she held aloft a large cross before which the assembled officers knelt. Reminding them that she was the daughter of their patron, Peter the Great, she made an impassioned plea for their support: "I swear to die for you, will you swear to die for me?" Answering with a resounding "yes," the entire Guard swore an oath of allegiance to Elizabeth, thereby sealing the fate of Regent Anne, her infant son Ivan VI, and the German officials and hangers-on at the Russian court.

On November 25, 1741, Elizabeth, escorted by a party of Guards officers, rode unopposed to the Winter Palace and made her way to the regent's bedroom. Elizabeth gently shook the sleeping Anne awake, telling her, "Time to get up, sister." The regent and her infant son were arrested, the boy to become for his entire life a prisoner of the crown known simply as Prisoner Number One. The Germans were arrested or banished, but in keeping with her pledge, Elizabeth refused to order the usual executions.

As word of the coup spread, great celebrations erupted among the Russian people, who fully believed that the Germans, whom they blamed for everything from taxes to fires, were finally being driven from power.

Although she could not match Peter the Great's intelligence and energy, Elizabeth was otherwise every bit her father's daughter. Like him, she was a restless soul who traveled freely around the country. She was disorganized and a bit of a slob, with her living quarters often appearing as if a Tartar army had ransacked them. Her reign, which lasted until 1761, was marked by an unending series of official functions, balls, theatrical performances, operas, and other diversions. The empress regaled her court with these events while official state documents that awaited her signature accumulated on her desk for months. She had a notorious lack of interest in the rest of the world, except for the latest fashions and court gossip from Paris. She is said to have expressed surprise when told that England was an island and not part of the European continent.

Swedish agents in Russia had urged Elizabeth to accept the throne, anticipating that she would return at least part of her father's conquests. The Stockholm government was therefore shocked when she sent units of the regular army to Finland to drive out the Swedish forces. Although Sweden had played no direct role in Elizabeth's coup, the Swedes had hoped that she would reverse Russia's policy of alignment with Austria and join the alliance headed by Sweden and France, both of which had supported her claim to the throne. Elizabeth knew their support amounted to little more than lip service and was prompted more by anti-Austrian sentiment than by any genuine affection for her. As far as she was concerned, Sweden could show its support for her by stopping the war it had begun by invading Finland, a Russian territory. The war with Sweden would continue until 1743, when a string of Russian victories forced the Swedes to sign the Peace of Åbo, wherein they ceded to Russia portions of Finland as well as the entire coastlines of the Gulf of Finland and the Gulf of Riga up to the Dvina River at the border of Courland.

Meanwhile, at Elizabeth's court the German accents introduced by Anna gave way to French fashion and the French language. Elizabeth was responsible for the expansion of the Winter Palace at St. Petersburg, with its allusions to Versailles, and for making French the official language of the Russian court. She began construction of the Catherine Palace as a summer residence outside the capital, and of a large number of buildings in St. Petersburg, all in the baroque style of her favorite architect, Bartolomeo Rastrelli. She ordered thousands of dresses from the most popular designers in Europe. When she died, her personal wardrobe included some 15,000 dresses, most of them very costly.

Several of the largest fashion houses in Paris refused to extend her credit when word spread that she habitually failed to pay her bills.

Like most of her predecessors, Elizabeth relied not on professionals but on personal favorites to run the country. She delegated a great deal of authority and power to the two Shuvalov brothers, Alexander and Peter, and to their cousin Ivan. Alexander ran the secret police, which by now had become a fixture of the Russian government. Peter took charge of government administration and finances, and Ivan, who was the empress's favorite, directed educational reform. Unfortunately for Russia, Peter Shuvalov's financial policies were a disaster. He won Elizabeth's approval for devaluing the currency and for levying a tax on vodka. These were Elizabeth's two most unpopular measures. Ivan, on the other hand, was a humble servant of the empress, declining even to accept the title of count. His efforts at improving the education and enlightenment of her subjects included founding the University of Moscow. A grateful empress appointed Ivan the university's first rector in 1755. Two years later, Ivan founded the Academy of Arts in St. Petersburg.

Under Ivan Shuvalov's influence, and through Elizabeth's personal example, the nation entered a new age of enlightenment. Russia's first theater was built for the performance of plays and operas, schools for the children of the wealthy began teaching German and French, and French literature—in the form of novels and works of science and philosophy—was read by the upper classes. French became the preferred language in many wealthy households, with Russian reserved only for speaking to servants.

When Alexis Razumovsky, a Cossack from the Ukraine, visited St. Petersburg as part of a choir that sang for the empress, Elizabeth was immediately attracted to him. She quickly made the tall, handsome, muscular peasant her lover. Razumovsky had no interest in governing Russia and avoided any responsibilities that the empress tried to thrust on him. In payment for his services, she made him a field marshal, although he had no military experience, and awarded him a large estate in the Ukraine and some 50,000 serfs. Although Elizabeth never officially married Razumovsky, it is widely believed that they were secretly wed.

Once Peter the Great had exposed Russia to Western influences, it was inevitable that the empire would become entangled in the muddled and ever-shifting European alliances. Although Russia did not intervene in the War of the Austrian Succession (1740–1748), in which the Austrian empress Maria Theresa defended the throne she had inherited from her father against France and other countries at the cost of ceding Silesia to Prussia, it did participate in the war's resumption, known as the Seven Years' War (1756–1763). Maria Theresa saw an opportunity to recover Silesia in 1756 when Austria and Prussia became locked in a struggle for control of the vast German-speaking portion of Europe. France joined the war on Austria's side while England supported Prussia. Hostilities between the French and the British spilled over into England's American colonies in what has become known as the French and Indian War, which was fought mainly in the upper Ohio River Valley, territory claimed by both European powers.

Since Russia had signed treaties with both Austria and England, Elizabeth at first hesitated to commit to either side. Eventually, her loathing for the Prussian king, Frederick the Great, settled the issue and Russia entered the war on Austria's side. Unfortunately, the appointment of Russian army officers had again reverted to selection on the basis of family ranking rather than ability, and the army was poorly led. Had it not been for the tenacity of its troops, Russia would have fared badly in the conflict. Despite heavy losses, the Russian forces conquered East Prussia, and by the summer of 1760 they were preparing to attack Frederick's capital, Berlin. For a brief period during September and October 1760, Russian and Austrian troops occupied Berlin, but they withdrew after extracting an enormous ransom from the Prussian government.

In 1761, England, Frederick's strongest ally, withdrew from the war when Prime Minister William Pitt fell from power. The Prussian king desperately cast about for a new ally and even attempted to win the support of the hated Ottoman Turks. Frederick was abruptly rescued from disaster when Empress Elizabeth died unexpectedly on December 25, 1761, and was replaced by her designated heir, her nephew Peter III, an ardent Prussian sympathizer. Hearing of Elizabeth's death, Frederick wrote to his brother, "Thanks be to Heaven."

❖ ❖ ❖

In 1742, the childless Elizabeth prepared a will intended to perpetuate Peter the Great's dynasty. She named her nephew Carl Peter Urlic as her heir. Peter, as he is more commonly known, was the son of Elizabeth's sister Anna, the duchess of Holstein; he was born in 1728, which is also the year his mother died. After selecting Peter as her heir, Elizabeth brought the 14-year-old, a rather simple-minded youth, to St. Petersburg, where she had him converted to the Orthodox faith and raised as the future czar of the Russian Empire. Three years later, against the counsel of her own advisors, Elizabeth arranged for Peter to marry Sophia Augusta, the princess of Anhalt-Zerbst, a tiny German principality. Sophia, who converted from Lutheranism to marry Peter, was one year younger than the future czar. Her mother was a Holstein princess who had supported the political aspirations of Frederick the Great; her father was a field marshal in the Prussian army. When she converted to Orthodoxy, Sophia changed her name to Catherine.

When she arrived in Russia, Catherine found an insolent prospective husband who clearly did not savor the idea of marrying the German princess, although the empress was committed to the marriage. Catherine was a jovial, slender beauty with sparkling blues eyes, chestnut hair, and an irresistible smile that captivated everyone except Grand Duke Peter. The two were actually distant cousins and had first met as children. Soon after Catherine's arrival, the thin, pale, sickly Peter confessed to her his love for one of Elizabeth's ladies-in-waiting, whom the empress had banished from court. Nevertheless, the mismatched pair were married on August 21, 1745, in an extravagant, spectacular ceremony combining French elegance and Oriental splendor. For the next 18 years, Catherine endured the grand duke's abuses and the humiliation of his refusal to consummate their marriage; only later did Catherine learn that her mean-spirited husband was physically unable to consummate it. Peter's unrestrained boasting about his many sexual conquests were mere fabrications behind which he hid his sexual problem. In her memoirs, Catherine wrote of these years:"I led a life from which ten others would have gone insane and twenty in my place would have died of melancholy." She spent much of her time during this period hunting and reading, activities to which she was strongly devoted.

As for Peter, he hated Russia and everything Russian. He had hoped that his connection to Swedish royalty, through a sister of King Adolphus Frederick of the House of Holstein-Gottorp, would earn him Sweden's crown, but Elizabeth's selection of him as her heir precluded any possibility of his aspiration being realized.

When on December 12, 1761, Peter III took the throne of Russia, he was despised by everyone. His demeaning attitude toward Russia was widely known, and the country reciprocated in full measure. He promptly withdrew Russia from the war against Frederick the Great and recalled the Russian army from Prussia, thereby saving Frederick from certain defeat: Had Russia not withdrawn, all of Prussia would have been overrun by Cossacks and regular Russian army troops, and Frederick would have been forced to flee his country or die defending it. On February 25, 1762, Russia signed a peace treaty with Prussia. This document, which was written by Frederick's ministers, returned to Prussia all the territories it had formerly possessed while giving Russia nothing in return for the five years of war it had fought. Peter then declared war on Denmark in an effort to win Schleswig for his homeland of Holstein; Russia had nothing to gain in this war.

Peter's premature ending of what could have been a successful war against Prussia, and his starting of the senseless war with Denmark, which few outside the court understood, aroused great indignation among the population. The public outrage intensified when Peter weakened the future effectiveness of the army, especially the Guards regiments, in a February 18, 1762, decree relieving the landed gentry of their obligation to provide 25 years of service to the crown in return for the land that they held in trust. Many servitors celebrated their new freedom from military service, but others saw it as both an attempt to destroy the Guards and a threat to the existence of a reliable national army.

Peter soon announced that he was restructuring the army along the lines of the Prussian army, which had only recently sustained a decisive defeat at the hands of Russian forces, even equipping several of the Guards regiments with new Prussian-style uniforms. He made it clear that he did not trust the Imperial Guard regiments and intended to replace them with several Holstein Guard units that he planned to form. Immediately, stirrings of unrest appeared among the Guards regiments.

Some of Peter III's policies were actually beneficial to the general population. Had he not displayed such obvious hatred for the Russian people, his reign might have lasted longer than a brief six months. Several of his more popular decisions included abolishing the secret police, granting the Old Believers amnesty from Elizabeth's earlier prosecutions, and significantly reducing import duties and the official price of salt. However, when he rescinded the prerogative of serf owners to sell their peasants to industrial enterprises, and began confiscating Church and monastery lands and placing priests and other clergy on annual government stipends, the majority of churchmen joined with the czar's opponents.

Peter III's reign ended quietly on the night of June 28, 1762, in a bloodless coup that made Peter's wife, Catherine, empress of Russia. Peter, who suspected his wife of using the Imperial Guard to plot against him, discovered that he had been dethroned when, after finding that Catherine had disappeared in the middle of the night, he fled to the naval fortress of Kronstadt on an island in St. Petersburg's harbor. When an officer challenged him at the fortress, Peter responded that he was the emperor. The officer's reply, "There is no emperor, only the empress Catherine II," sent Peter in full flight back to his palace. Within hours he was arrested.

CHAPTER 17

FROM CATHERINE THE GREAT TO NICHOLAS I

SPONSORED BY THE IMPERIAL GUARD REGIMENTS, Catherine II was crowned "Empress and Sole Autocrat of Russia" by the metropolitan of St. Petersburg on June 28, 1762. The church leader needed little persuasion. Most of the clergy had turned against Peter III: They knew he remained at heart a Lutheran and that he had mocked the rituals and customs of the Orthodox Church. Shortly before he was deposed, Peter had decreed that all Orthodox priests must shave off their long beards and exchange their traditional black robes for the simple, short vestments worn by German Lutheran ministers. It was a blasphemy that even Peter the Great would never have committed. Peter III had also banned icons and images of saints from the churches, and had closed all private chapels. These were foolish actions by an obviously unbalanced foreigner who had failed to realize that by attacking the Orthodox Church he was attacking the very foundation of his throne.

During the evening following her assumption of power, Catherine determined to legitimize her claim to the throne. Astride a Guards mount and wearing a borrowed Guards lieutenant's uniform, she led 14,000 troops from St. Petersburg to the emperor's winter palace at Peterhof, bringing with her a declaration of abdication for Peter's signature. Catherine knew she might be risking a confrontation with forces loyal to the emperor, especially his personal regiment of Holsteiners stationed at Peterhof, but when Peter had learned of the Guards' revolt and of their proclamation of Catherine as empress, he was reduced to a whimpering, helpless man incapable of organizing a defense of his throne.

As Catherine approached Peterhof, her husband sent her several conciliatory messages; the first, offering to share the throne with her as an equal, she ignored. A later messenger brought word that Peter was prepared to abdicate. Catherine refused to meet with her husband, evidently distrusting her own inclination toward leniency, but instead sent her lover Alexis Orlov to the palace with the document. Peter III, the emperor and autocrat of Russia, signed it without so much as glancing at it. He was immediately arrested, stripped of his decorations and his Russian military uniform and sword, and confined to his quarters under armed guard to await the empress's orders. The czar of Russia had been unseated without a single shot being fired, for by the time Orlov reached Peter's palace, Peter had lost all support, including that of the Holstein regiment, which was quietly disarmed when Orlov promised that it would not be attacked.

After Peter abdicated, he was taken to a small estate at Ropsha, 15 miles from St. Petersburg, and confined under close guard. In the week that followed, he wrote Catherine three letters, addressing her as "Your Majesty." Each letter begged her permission for he and his mistress to return to Holstein. Catherine responded by sending him his violin, a favorite dog, and several servants, but not his mistress. She monitored daily reports about the ex-emperor's health, which were prepared by Peter's head jailer, none other than Alexis Orlov. Already bordering on a complete breakdown, Peter's mental stability collapsed entirely when he was informed that he was to be moved to the infamous Schlüsselburg Fortress prison, at the mouth of the Neva River near Lake Lagoda. His unexplained death on July 7, 1762, probably at the hands of Alexis Orlov, spared Catherine the distasteful task of condemning her husband to one of Schlüsselburg's notoriously dark, dank dungeons.

At age 33, Catherine was attractive, regal in her bearing, and kindhearted and generous. Unlike her husband, she loved Russia and the Russian people and had learned to speak the language fluently, without Peter's harsh German accent. She was also a devoted mother of three children, none of whom had been fathered by Peter III.

❖   ❖   ❖

Catherine had been a neglected wife who never won Peter's affection, partly because of his own physical incapacity and partly because his aunt had forced her on him. Humiliated by a husband who refused to sleep with her and flaunted his paramours before her, Catherine had been pursued by several would-be lovers, despite the punishment that awaited them had Empress Elizabeth learned of their attentions. Although she too had feared the empress's wrath, Catherine had taken as her lover Count Sergei Saltykov, an aristocratic chamberlain in the minor court that Peter and she maintained — the "Young Court" as opposed to the court of Empress Elizabeth. Whether Catherine took this handsome young man as her lover out of genuine affection, or to satisfy Elizabeth's constant pressure on her for an heir, is unclear. Unless her relationship with Peter changed, which was unlikely, Catherine had realized that she would never produce an heir to the throne and could face the possibility of the dissolution of her marriage by Elizabeth and her removal from the court.

On September 20, 1754, following two miscarriages, Catherine gave birth to a boy. Although the child was actually Saltykov's son, Empress Elizabeth did not know this, and Peter, terrified that his aunt would disinherit him, simply acknowledged the boy as his own. No sooner had the baby been born, the empress whisked him away and took complete charge of his life. He was immediately moved into a nursery in the empress's private apartments, where she lavished such loving attention on him that some thought the child was actually hers, and not Catherine's. It was Elizabeth who named him Paul, the name of Peter the Great and Catherine I's first child, who had died at the age of 3. Historians have long speculated that Elizabeth knew Paul was not her nephew's son but accepted the boy in the interest of preserving dynastic succession. Before her death, Elizabeth reportedly considered transferring the succession from Peter to Paul, but she never followed through. Her intense dislike for her nephew also fostered speculation that she seriously considered naming Catherine her heir and exiling Peter to Holstein.

Catherine's second child, a girl, was born on December 9, 1757. This child's father is unknown; Peter reportedly had had a minor operation that allowed him to engage in sexual intercourse. But whether he ever actually consummated his marriage to Catherine is not known. The infant girl's father is widely believed to have been Count Stanislas Poniatowski of Poland, who had become Catherine's lover after Saltykov was sent abroad. Empress Elizabeth again took charge of the baby, moving her into the nursery with her brother, Paul. Despite Catherine's protestations that the girl be named Elizabeth, the empress named her Anne after her own sister, Peter's mother. A thoroughly disinterested Peter, who had said earlier, "Heaven alone knows how my wife becomes pregnant," again accepted the child as his own. The little grand duchess Anne lived less than two years and, like her brother Paul, was a virtual stranger to her parents, whom she saw only on rare occasions. Anne died in March 1759.

On April 11, 1762, Catherine secretly gave birth to a son she named Alexis. Except for a few trusted friends and servants, no one, including the emperor Peter, had even been aware that she was pregnant. Her isolation from her husband and the deft use of flowing clothes had hidden the pregnancy well. The boy's father was Gregory Orlov, the Guards lieutenant who had made a name for himself when after receiving three wounds, he had led his troops in a furious assault, during the Battle of Zorndorf, in Prussia, in 1758. The following year, while in St. Petersburg recovering from his wounds, Orlov came to Catherine's attention, and the two became lovers during 1761. In accordance with Russian custom, the infant Alexis was given his father's name as his middle name, but being a bastard and having been born in secret, Alexis Gregorevich (son of Gregory) had no surname. Catherine rectified this situation by giving Alexis the name Bobrinsky, meaning "bearskin" in Russian. A prodigious reader, Catherine had read of the American Indian custom of naming children after animals, events, or objects relating to their birth, and Catherine evidently thought of her lover as a great bear of a man. Wrapped in a soft bearskin blanket, the child was spirited from the palace by Catherine's loyal friends.

❖   ❖   ❖

Taking Gregory Orlov as her lover was propitious from a political standpoint, although Catherine may not have realized it when their affair began. Gregory was one of five sons of a provincial governor, all of whom became fiercely loyal to Catherine. It was Gregory's older brother, Imperial Guard Captain Alexis Orlov, who quietly slipped into Catherine's bedroom at six o'clock in the morning on June 28, 1762, to awakened her with the words, "Little Mother, wake up, the time has come." The Orlov brothers had been at the center of the conspiracy that deposed Peter III and put Catherine on the throne, easily winning for her the support of the Guards regiments.

The Russian people did not embrace Catherine's ascent to the throne with the same jubilation as that of the guardsmen who placed her there. Her right to the Russian crown was questionable, and the fact that she came to power through a coup against one of Peter the Great's heirs, hated as he was, raised suspicions in many influential quarters. Few Russians cared for Peter, and most applauded his downfall, yet many felt the crown should have gone to Catherine's son, Paul, who most people assumed was Peter's son and heir. Catherine would have been welcomed as regent during Paul's childhood.

Others believed the throne should have reverted to Ivan VI, the infant czar that Empress Elizabeth had deposed in 1741 and who remained a crown prisoner. However, only his jailers were aware that Ivan had never matured emotionally or mentally, possibly as a result of his confinement, and that he was incompetent to rule. Catherine's position remained vulnerable until two years later, when a group of soldiers led by a young officer named Basil Mirovich attempted to free Ivan from his prison and put him back on the throne. The attempt not only failed, but the former czar's guards, following long-standing orders, promptly executed him when the attack began. Predictably, Mirovich was executed when the coup collapsed.

Anxious to reverse her unpopular image, Catherine wisely adopted measures calculated to win favor with the people, especially those in the nobility who conceivably could unseat her. Catherine's reign is heralded as a golden age for the Russian nobility, and a time of opulence at the imperial court, yet Catherine ruled a largely backward nation. Illiteracy remained the plight of most Russians below the level of those at court. To win favor with the nobles, Catherine expanded their holdings with massive land grants and extended the hated system of serfdom, which enslaved millions of peasants, into the southern regions of the Don Cossacks, the Ukraine, and the Caucasus.

Catherine II ruled for 34 years. She brought to her reign uncommon understanding of European power politics, and like Peter the Great, she sought to make her adopted country a part of Europe's culture. She initiated a public-relations campaign that earned her the respect of many influential Europeans as well as a reputation as an enlightened, liberal reformer.

A conscientious ruler who relished the responsibilities of an autocrat, she was, unlike many of her predecessors, actually up to the task. On her first day as empress, she instructed her secretaries to prepare detailed reports of all dispatches arriving in the palace each day, and to present them to her every morning, together with the daily agenda for each government ministry. Catherine's mornings began at five o'clock, when she rose and quickly began working after lighting her own fire. Her workday usually lasted 15 hours. She organized her work on a series of tables, each containing material dealing with a particular subject. With four secretaries trailing behind her, she worked her way from table to table, digesting the information and dictating responses, instructions, or correspondence. Rarely was a subject too trivial for the empress's attention.

Catherine fully appreciated that the army, particularly the Imperial Guard regiments, had placed her on the throne when others had favored Ivan VI or her own son, Paul. Realizing that she also depended on the military to defend her against enemies that might attempt to depose her, she lavished special consideration on the army. Peter III's unpopular war against Denmark was abandoned. Also, despite having denounced Frederick the Great as Russia's "bitterest enemy," she confirmed the ludicrous peace settlement that Peter had negotiated with Prussia. Her primary concern was to consolidate her position; for this she relied on strong military support, which precluded sending forces to fight outside Russia at least until her monarchy was secure.

Everyone who participated in her coup against Peter, no matter how insignificantly, was rewarded. A list of nearly 500 individuals, of whom more than 300 were members of the Imperial Guard, was prepared, and each person on it was rewarded with money, estates, or both, as well as with promotions and other royal favors. The soldiers at the St. Petersburg garrison were given a bonus of a half-year's pay for their support. Empress Catherine became an instant favorite of the soldiers stationed in the capital.

Catherine planned to legitimize her hold on the title by an elaborate coronation. She arranged to have herself crowned in Moscow, the traditional site of coronations, rather than in St. Petersburg, which many Russians still considered an alien city. The coronation was set for Sunday, September 22, 1762. Nine days before the event, Catherine, accompanied by her son Paul, made a dazzling entry into the old capital; they were followed by a wagon train laden with 120 oak barrels of gold coins totaling 600,000 rubles, which she distributed among the Muscovites in celebration of her coronation. If Catherine could not inspire the people's loyalty, she would purchase it.

Moscow's Cathedral of the Assumption was again the coronation site. After the religious ceremony, Catherine crossed the square, which was thronged with thousands of onlookers, to pay the obligatory visits to the icons in the nearby Cathedrals of the Archangel and of the Annunciation. Cannons roared in salute, and the masses in the square cheered their approval as Catherine stood in regal purple robes, the ribbon of Saint Andrew across her chest, and held the scepter in one hand and the imperial globe in the other. She wore on her head the crown she had placed there herself, just as Empress Elizabeth had done before her. A week of festivities and public feasting followed the coronation.

The celebrations were marred by two events that shook Catherine's administration. First, her son and heir Paul became delirious with a high fever, his third such attack in a month. Catherine, concerned for her son, also feared that his untimely death could strip away her bond with the Romanov dynasty and jeopardize her claim to the throne. Paul was bedridden for two weeks and apparently suffered some mild permanent damage to his memory on account of his high fever, but he survived the illness.

The second disturbing event was the discovery of an alleged conspiracy among several Imperial Guard officers to remove Catherine from the throne and replace her with a Romanov. Although the conspiracy proved to be nothing more than loose chatter during a drunken party, five "conspirators" were stripped of their rank and exiled. During the following year, several other similar incidents arose when Guardsmen openly criticizing the empress, usually after they had drunk excessively. Knowing that the Imperial Guard viewed her as being dependent on it for her authority, and fearful that it might someday turn on her and champion a new monarch, Catherine reinstituted the secret police organization that Peter III had disbanded. She invested the revived government agency with broad investigative powers and renamed it the Secret Branch. The Secret Branch kept every potential troublemaker in the capital under surveillance, especially those who were members of the Imperial Guard regiments on the royal household staff.

❖ ❖ ❖

Following Peter the Great's lead, Catherine set out on a journey across Russia almost immediately after her coronation. But, unlike Peter, her purpose was not so much to move about as to give the people a chance to see her and accept her as their rightful monarch. She hoped to create a bond between herself and the masses that would strengthen her monarchy even as she learned more

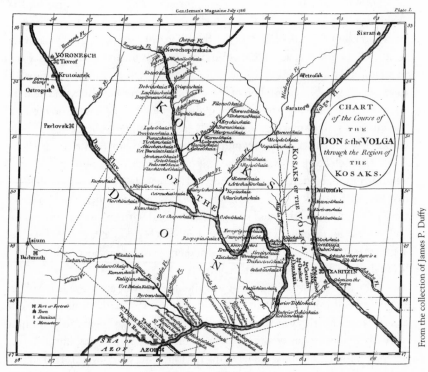

Map of the Don and Volga Regions

From the collection of James P. Duffy

about her adopted country. From Moscow she sailed down the Volga to Kazan, then traveled to Yaroslavl, then to Rostov. Everywhere, Catherine was greeted by large cheering crowds of her subjects, most of whom had never seen a reigning monarch.

Catherine's forte was international affairs. Her grasp of the balance-of-power politics practiced in Europe enabled her to influence the selection of the king of Poland. Internal strife had reduced Poland from a power rivaling Europe's leading empires to a weak nation at her neighbors' mercy. Polish kings were elected by a parliament of nobles called the Diet, which effectively ruled the country. Turmoil within the Diet was the cause of Poland's decline. Each member had the power to veto a law or government action, a power that encouraged graft and corruption. The crown frequently was given to the candidate who was rich enough to offer the highest bribes.

In 1763, Augustus III, who had been king of Poland since 1734, died. With the Diet stalemated on the selection a new king, and Prussia, Austria, and even Turkey making ominous noises on the sidelines, Catherine stepped into the breach and let the Diet members know she wanted her former lover Count Stanislas Poniatowski elected king. The Diet accepted this implied ultimatum from Poland's powerful neighbor and dutifully elected Poniatowski the last king of Poland on August 26, 1764.

Catherine's decisive influence on the seating of the new Polish king, and her use of Russian troops in Poland to put down an uprising against Poniatowski, provoked the Ottoman sultan to declare war on Russia on September 25, 1768. The empress privately embraced the confrontation as an opportunity to avenge Peter the Great's humiliating defeat near Pruth in 1711. She also welcomed the opportunity to bedeck herself with military regalia and ride at the head of a column of her troops.

Meanwhile, in her first major attempt at domestic reform, Catherine called for an elected Legislative Commission to codify a new set of laws for Russia. This gathering was part of Catherine's plan to modernize her backward empire. It was also part of her continuing effort to win popular support.

The commission, which convened its first sessions in the summer of 1767, was an amalgam of representatives from the government and almost every level of society. Of the 564 deputies on the commission, 28 represented state institutions. The other 536 members were elected deputies: 208 were towns-people from throughout the empire, 161 came from the landed gentry class, 88 represented the Cossacks and other national minorities, and 79 were elected by the peasants who worked the vast government-owned estates. Conspicuously absent from the commission were representatives of the serfs, who by now had lost most of their rights and were considered little more than slaves owned and freely sold or traded by the nobles, clergy, factory owners, and landed gentry. Even official documents treated serfs like property by referring to them not as people but as "souls." The clergy were permitted just one token deputy on the commission, signifying the Church's declining importance in Catherine's court.

Despite the problems in teaching the people the meaning of an election, and that they were not to choose a local government official but one of their peers to represent them, the Legislative Commission was a fair cross section of the Russian population, excluding the several million serfs. Because Catherine had instructed the deputies to bring to St. Petersburg their constituents' recommendations for changes, the commission brought thousands of suggestions to the capital. High on the lists of priorities were requests for more local government control, reduced taxes, punishment for corrupt officials, and clearly defined rights and obligations for each class of society.

In advance of the meetings, the empress prepared a document of nearly 500 paragraphs called the Instruction, which outlined the rules of procedure for the commission. The document also contained the empress's personal wishes that masters stop abusing their serfs, that capital punishment be abolished (which had already been accomplished by Empress Elizabeth), and that more efforts be made toward crime prevention. The document also outlined other liberalizing policies that Catherine had borrowed from the works of leading writers of the European Enlightenment.

During 203 sessions over one and one-half years, the commission wrestled with the problems of the empire, but the class differences among its members doomed it to failure. The peasants' representatives clashed with those of the landed gentry over the issue of serfdom, while the representatives of the landowners fought with those of the merchants for the rights to engage in industries and trade. Finally conceding that the commission would never accomplish anything of importance, Catherine used the Turkish declaration of war as an excuse to disband the experiment in democracy and send the deputies home to join their regiments for the coming war.

The Turks found allies among Poles who resented foreign interference, especially that of the Russians, in their internal affairs. These Poles formed themselves into confederations and fought several unsuccessful battles against the Russian army, at Bar and then at Cracow. When the Ottoman sultan, at the urging and bribery of both France and Austria, promised to send 200,000

men into Poland and the Ukraine to fight the Russians, the Polish confederations pledged an additional 100,000 troops.

Inexperienced in military planning and strategy, Catherine created an
advisory council of nine members with either military or foreign relations
experience. They all agreed that Russia must fight an aggressive offensive war
and not permit the Turks or Poles to occupy Russian territory. Actual fighting
began in January 1769, when the khan of the Crimean Tartars led 70,000 troops
into southern Russia and struck out for Poland. Local Russian garrisons were
overwhelmed by the Tartar horsemen, and the first campaign of the war
appeared to be lost when the Tartars, after extracting huge tributes and looting
the towns in their path, suddenly withdrew and returned to the Crimea.

In April, General Prince Alexander Golitsin crossed the Dniester River
and drove the Turks out of Khotin. In quick succession, during the spring of
1769 Russian forces recaptured Azov, Peter the Great's earlier expansionist
prize, and a Turkish invasion was repulsed. In the fall, Catherine's armies
occupied the Ottoman provinces north of the Danube, and in the spring of 1770
she launched a bold naval operation that electrified the world.

Catherine's lover, Gregory Orlov, who was also a member of her council
of advisors, had proposed sending a Russian fleet from the Baltic around Europe
and into the Mediterranean Sea to surprise the Turkish navy from the rear.
Virtually everyone opposed the idea, particularly the minister of war, Zachary
Chernichev, who called the scheme mad and dangerous. But Catherine liked
it. Not only would a successful voyage and engagement in the enemy's home
waters stun Europe, it would also revive Peter the Great's dream of making
Russia a major sea power. The plan was approved. By luck, Catherine had in
her service a number of senior British officers on loan from the Royal Navy.
Several of these men enjoyed ranks, such as rear admiral, and rates of pay that
they could not dream of attaining at home; they also had a strong liking for
service in Catherine's navy. Anxious for the opportunity to fight the Turks, the
traditional allies of Britain's historical enemy, France, the British officers gave
Orlov's plan their enthusiastic approval.

On July 26, 1769, a squadron of Russian warships set out from Kronstadt,
in the St. Petersburg harbor, on a circuitous route through the Baltic Sea to the
Atlantic Ocean, and finally into the Mediterranean. Transporting a landing
force of 5,500 soldiers, the squadron was under the nominal command of Alexis
Orlov, but its actual commander was an Englishman, Rear Admiral John
Elphinstone. The long, perilous journey compromised the seaworthiness of
several of the Russian ships. Arrangements had been made to use port facilities

in Britain and Gibraltar, where the squadron stopped for needed repairs. Once in the Mediterranean, Tuscany offered winter quarters for the Russians and welcomed them with great celebrations.

Admiral Elphinstone wanted to force his way through the Dardanelles Strait, bombard Constantinople itself, and link up with the Russian armies along the northern shore of the Black Sea. But because Orlov had dreamed of freeing the Greeks from Turkish oppression, the Russian squadron instead attacked several Turkish forts along the Greek coast in the hope of starting a Greek insurrection. When the Greeks, badly divided among themselves, failed to respond with the anticipated revolt, Orlov abandoned the mission and the fleet sailed on toward the Dardanelles.

Once in the Aegean Sea, the partially crippled Russian squadron, with several ships badly needing repairs, confronted the vastly superior Turkish fleet on June 24, 1770. Orlov and Elphinstone were both aggressive warriors. Although outnumbered and outgunned, the Russians launched a relentless attack that drove the Turks into the sanctuary of Cesme Bay. But the bay's security proved to be short-lived when a young British naval lieutenant named Dugdale led a small fleet of fire ships into the bay and set the Turkish warships aflame. For days after this disaster, the bodies of hundreds of Turkish sailors washed up on the nearby beaches.

Elphinstone again wanted to attack the Dardanelles and gain access to both Constantinople and the Black Sea, where another Russian fleet was pursuing the remnants of the Turkish Black Sea Fleet following a monumental battle, but Orlov insisted on further attempts to arouse the Greeks into revolting against the Turks. By the time Orlov gave up in frustration, French engineers, led by Baron Tott, had blocked the entrance to the Dardanelles, frustrating Elphinstone's plan to attack Constantinople.

Meanwhile the land war was progressing brilliantly, with one great Russian victory following another. An elated Catherine awarded decorations and accolades to her generals on all fronts. Her correspondence with Voltaire, who was one of her greatest admirers, overflowed with praise for the Orlovs and her other commanders. One letter began by telling the French writer, "At the risk of repeating myself or becoming a bore, I have nothing to report to you but victories." For his part, Voltaire waxed eloquently about Catherine's victories over the Turks, calling her "the avenger of Europe." To all who would listen, the philosopher-writer referred to Catherine as the new empress of Byzantium.

Russian victories in the Balkans were matched by others in the Crimea, as Prince Basil Dolgoruky led the Second Russian Army to a stunning victory against the Crimean Tartars and sent the khan into flight. Pressured by Dolgoruky, the beaten Tartars elected a new khan and formally surrendered to the Russians.

The speed and decisiveness with which the Russians crushed the Turks not only surprised Europeans, it also caused in them consternation that the Russo-Turkish War would escalate and involve all of Europe in the conflict. Wary of Russian designs in the Balkans, where she had her own plans, Austria's Empress Maria Theresa moved closer to her old rival, Turkey, as did France, long the preeminent Christian ally of the Islamic Ottomans. France's historic foe, Britain, was already aligned with the Russians, yet none of the other European powers wanted to be dragged into the war, especially the Prussia of Frederick the Great. Frederick most feared a French-Austrian alliance against Prussia, which, on paper at least, was Russia's ally. While Catherine worried about the rumblings coming from the great powers of Europe, a new threat captured her attention: the plague.

❖ ❖ ❖

Early signs of the bubonic plague began to appear in the Russian garrison at Jassy, the capital of Moldavia, in the early spring of 1769. On May 30, the Russian commander, General Christopher von Stoffeln, suddenly died of the illness. The Turkish army having suffered an epidemic of the pestilence, the plague had evidently spread from Turkish prisoners to their captors. On September 9, 1770, the governor-general of Kiev reported the plague in his city, and Catherine responded with measures to isolate Kiev and other danger points in the south where the pestilence was likely to enter the country. Despite heroic efforts along the southern and western borders to prevent infected people from entering Russia, Moscow reported its first plague victims in December 1770.

At first the plague was confined to only a few buildings used by the Infantry Hospital in Moscow, where 25 people died. The onset of cold weather in January 1771 checked the spread of the disease, and it was thought that the danger had passed. Suddenly, in early March, Moscow authorities discovered that 113 people had died of plague at a large textile factory complex in the center of the city. Police investigators found 16 more people with the telltale symptoms, dark spots on the skin and swollen glands, and quickly isolated the complex and its workers and families, some 2,500 people. By August the disease was beyond control, claiming lives indiscriminately. At her September 5, 1771, council meeting, the empress learned that the pestilence was taking up to 400 lives each day in Moscow alone. Only nine days later, Moscow authorities placed the daily death toll at 800.

Desperate to stem the rising death rate, Catherine sent her lover, Gregory Orlov, to Moscow on September 21. Before Orlov arrived, however, the old capital was rocked by rioting in which Archbishop Ambrose was murdered for forbidding the kissing of icons as a means of stemming the spread of the plague. Ignorant of medical preventive measures, the mobs attacked doctors and others who tried to contain the plague. Massed troops and cannon fire were finally used to disperse the mobs. When Orlov reached Moscow with a military detachment, he established himself as the virtual dictator of the city and instituted strong measures to stop the spread of the pestilence. Before the epidemic abated that winter, more than 100,000 persons had died.

Throughout the plague episode, Catherine remained an inspiring leader, determined that her people should forget their old superstitions and learn more about modern medicine. Three years before, on October 12, 1768, Catherine had publicized her faith in medicine by being among the first in Russia to be inoculated against smallpox. The inoculation was performed by a Briton, Dr. Thomas Dimsdale, and Catherine said it was done "to save from death the multitude of my subjects who, not knowing the value of this technique, frightened of it, were left in danger."

While Catherine was busy battling the plague, the war with Turkey ground to a halt. Diplomatic negotiations were opened at the urging of Frederick the Great in July 1772. That same month, Russia, Prussia, and Austria agreed on the partitioning of Poland. Catherine gained everything she had wanted from Poland: those sections inhabited by ethnic Orthodox Russians, including White Russia, Polish Livonia, and three territories that had originally belonged to the ancient Kievan grand principality, Mstislavl, Polotsk, and Vitebsk. Austria took the province of Galicia, and Prussia took what was known as East Prussia, leaving the Polish city of Danzig isolated from the rest of the country. Poland lost one-third of its land and nearly half its population, but the Polish Diet had no option but to ratify the agreement already reached by her three powerful neighbors. It was the first of three partitions that would eventually remove Poland from the map of Europe.

Negotiations with Turkey dragged on for months, making slow progress. Catherine's representatives, including her soon-to-be-estranged lover, Gregory Orlov, found the Turks intransigent on the empress's key demand: no independence for the Crimea. The Ottoman sultan understood that if he agreed to Crimean Tartar independence, Russia would quickly move in and claim the entire Crimean Peninsula as its own. As a result, the Turks refused to accept the Russian demand, even when Russia offered to withdraw from Wallachia and Moldavia, two coveted Ottoman territories in the Balkans. Before the year was out, hostilities between Russia and Turkey resumed, to be interrupted periodically by attempts to negotiate the countries' differences.

While the war continued, in Russia popular unrest manifested itself in a series of localized revolts. Most were squelched with relative ease, except for the one led by a Don Cossack named Emelian Pugachev. Pugachev's revolt is important to an understanding of the fabric of Russian society at the time because he received widespread support from diverse elements of Russian society.

Pugachev had served as a private in the Russian army during the Seven Years War, and had been singled out as a potential leader, but his undisciplined independence caused him to be knouted several times and finally discharged. In May 1773, he was arrested for helping a relative flee from the authorities and for attempting to foment a revolt against the government. Exiled to Siberia, he escaped, and in September of that year he took part in a Cossack uprising along the Ural River against conscription of troops for the Turkish war. Somehow, Pugachev managed to make himself the leader of the rebels. He also claimed he was Peter III; Pugachev said that the late czar had actually escaped the death his wife Catherine had planned for him. The revolt grew quickly, fueled by a wide variety of interests displeased with Catherine's reign: Cossacks who resented her earlier arrest of the Don Cossack hetman; Tartar tribes in the lower Ural region; several national minorities, such as the Bashkiri; and thousands of Russian serfs who envisioned freedom in revolution.

Pugachev led his followers north along the Ural River and captured several lightly defended river fortresses. Reaching Orenburg, the capital of the Ural region, he laid siege to the city. Each day that the siege continued, the rebel army grew larger as more serfs and local factory workers joined its ranks. Catherine dispatched a relief column that broke the siege, and Pugachev began his legendary odyssey around the eastern part of European Russia, changing the objective of his campaign from a Cossack insurrection to a serf rebellion against the landowners. Throughout the region, landowners were murdered by their serfs, and numerous towns fell to the rabble army.

On July 12, 1774, Pugachev captured the city of Kazan, where he established his headquarters. Proclaiming himself Emperor Peter III, he organized a mock court and pronounced death sentences for landowners and anyone else who opposed him. The revolt swelled to such proportions that officials in

St. Petersburg feared for Moscow's security and sent troops to reinforce the city's garrison.

Finally, in August 1774, Catherine commissioned General Peter Panin to remove Pugachev. Panin drove the Cossack leader from Kazan and pushed him south, recapturing the region from the rebels. Pugachev tried to rally the Don Cossacks around him once again, but after the rebellion evolved into a serf uprising, the Cossacks lost interest and backed out. On September 14, 1774, the remnants of Pugachev's army turned him over to the pursuing Russian army, hoping to buy its freedom with his life. Catherine had Pugachev publicly executed in Moscow on January 10, 1775.

The early success of Pugachev's revolt had confirmed a hard truth for Catherine. It showed her that she lacked support among the lowest ranks of her subjects and that there was little she could do about it. She owed her crown to the support of the landowners and the military, and despite the liberal views she shared with such luminaries as Voltaire, she could never do anything that would be contrary to their interests.

Peace with Turkey was finally achieved in July 1774, after overwhelming Russian military victories at Kozludzha and Shulma on the western side of the Danube River. The peace treaty, signed on July 10 at the village of Kuchuk Kainarji, granted independence to Crimea, gave Russia the coast of the Sea of Azov, and recognized the right of Russian ships to sail in the Black Sea and through the straits into the Aegean Sea. Turkey was also assessed a war indemnity of 4.5 million rubles and, perhaps most important, it acknowledged Russia as the protector of the Christians living under Ottoman rule, thereby indirectly granting Russia the authority to intervene in internal matters affecting the Ottoman Empire's Christian population.

No longer encumbered by the Turks, Catherine could devote more time to her private life. She and Gregory Orlov having tired of each other, Catherine took a new lover, the dashing cavalry officer Gregory Potemkin, who would work tirelessly to earn his mistress the title "the Great." Potemkin first came to Catherine's attention during the palace revolt that put her on the throne, when the young Horseguards officer stepped from the ranks and offered the new empress his sword knot for her to wear. Potemkin was the empress's lover for 15 years. Their relationship, which some suspect may have included a secret marriage, was somewhat capricious. Potemkin was dissatisfied with simply sitting around the palace awaiting Catherine's pleasure. He remained an active military commander and accepted assignments that regularly took him away from St. Petersburg. Wherever there was fighting, Potemkin wanted to be there.

In 1775, Empress Catherine proposed new, sweeping governmental reforms. Shocked by the swift collapse of governmental authority when Pugachev's rebel army overran the eastern provinces, she borrowed concepts from Blackstone's discourse on law and copied the localized administrative practices of the Baltic provinces that Sweden had introduced during its occupation of the region. Catherine spent five months developing her plan for decentralization of the administration of government. The plan went through a series of revisions as she solicited advice from officials who thought the same way she did. More than 600 of the nearly 2,000 pages in the original draft were in the empress's handwriting, clearly indicating that she was the principal author of the reforms. By the end of her reign, Russia had been divided, more or less along population lines, into 50 departments called either *guberniias* or vice-regencies, depending on their size, and many functions of administration and justice previously handled in the capital had been transferred to the local level.

Other reforms were to follow. In 1785, Catherine issued two important documents, the Charter of the Nobility, and the Charter to the Towns. The nobility charter enumerated the privileges and responsibilities of the nobles, and established in each government department a council of nobles that could express opinions on existing or proposed laws. The nobles were given broad powers over their own lands and serfs, and continued to be exempt from service in the military. Catherine found a way around Peter III's policy that had hindered the development of qualified military leaders from among the landed classes by making voluntary service to the state a prerequisite for participation in the elections of local noble councils. If a noble did not volunteer for state duty, which usually meant military duty, he could not even vote in the local elections.

The Charter of the Cities established municipal legislative bodies that were elected by the local urban population. The only qualification for voting was ownership of land, a business, or an industrial enterprise in the city.

None of Catherine's reforms benefitted the serfs who lived in bondage to the landowners. In fact, some of her reforms actually worsened the serfs' existence. Despite Catherine's devotion to the liberal doctrines of the Enlightenment, she believed in serfdom and did nothing to relieve the misery of the millions of serfs in her realm. In fact, she helped tighten the landowners' control over the serfs. During her reign, landowners were granted the right to punish serfs as they saw fit, including exiling them to Siberia, and to sell them as they pleased. The census of 1794–1796 identified more than 53 percent of the peasants as serfs, which meant that a startling 49 percent of the Russian population lived in bondage. Catherine also extended serfdom into the new territories conquered by Russia or acquired at the negotiating table. She freely awarded hundreds of thousands of serfs to nobles and gentry as rewards for service to the state, thereby multiplying the number of peasants transferred from state lands, where they enjoyed a reasonable degree of freedom, to privately owned estates, where they had no rights of any kind.

❖ ❖ ❖

Although her efforts at governmental reform were sincere, Catherine felt most comfortable dealing with foreign affairs. Internationally, Russia was now respected as a powerful equal and was no longer viewed as an underdeveloped, backward nation. Catherine involved Russia in various international affairs undertakings, including the creation of an international maritime law aimed at protecting the ships of neutral nations during times of war on the basis of the doctrine of armed neutrality. Russia promoted this doctrine in 1780 to protest British naval actions against noncombatants during the American Revolution. (In September 1775, the British government reportedly requested that Catherine loan the British crown 20,000 infantry troops to help put down the revolt in the American colonies. Catherine refused the request, remarking that she expected America to achieve independence during her own lifetime.)

Turkey continued to trouble Catherine. The pact signed with Turkey in 1774 had merely provided a brief respite while the combatants prepared for the next round of war. Poland also remained a problem, with both Russia and Prussia pressuring the Poles to extend full religious freedom to the Orthodox and Protestant populations. In January 1793, Russia and Prussia contrived to partition Poland a second time. Prussia took Danzig, Thorn (another Baltic seaport), and a generous slice of western Poland, transferring some 1 million people to Prussian control. Catherine, unconcerned about her ex-lover, the Polish king Stanislas Poniatowski, annexed additional territory of the former Lithuania and most of the western Ukraine, bringing an additional 3 million people under her jurisdiction.

In March 1794, the Polish general Tadeusz Kościuszko, who had served with great distinction in the Continental Army during the American Revolution, initiated a rebellion against the Russians, driving them out of Warsaw and other cities and killing several thousand in the process. The Russian army, reinforced by Prussian troops, counterattacked and retook the city of Cracow in May. The fighting subsided as each side maneuvered for an advantage, but

Warsaw finally capitulated on October 29, and the Polish leaders, beginning with King Stanislas, were all arrested. A year later, in 1795, Russia, Prussia, and Austria divided among themselves what remained of Poland, and the once powerful Polish state ceased to exist. The Poles's strongest hatred was directed at the Russians and would later haunt Catherine's successors.

❖ ❖ ❖

Throughout her reign, Catherine excluded her son Paul from all government activity. The grand duke (Paul's title until Catherine's death), who despised his mother's many lovers—especially Gregory Orlov, whom he considered an accomplice in his father's murder—was estranged from Catherine almost from the start. When his first wife died in childbirth in 1776, Catherine wasted no time finding a replacement, a Württemberg princess named Sophie. Taking the name Maria Fyodorovna, Sophie converted to Orthodoxy and married Paul six months after his wife's death. The following year, Maria gave birth to a son, Alexander, whom Catherine immediately took from his parents in order to supervise his education. She did the same thing in 1779, when Konstantin was born. It appears that Catherine was determined to exclude her son, who consistently opposed her policies, from the line of succession, and to groom one of her grandsons to inherit the throne when she died. When Alexander married Grand Duchess Elizabeth in September 1793, Paul very nearly did not attend the ceremony because he was by then estranged not only from his mother, but through her, from his own sons. He was a man virtually without a family and nearly without a country.

According to legend, in late 1796 Catherine was preparing to announce the deposition of her son in favor of her grandson Alexander when she suddenly died, leaving Paul's succession intact. At nine o'clock on the morning of Wednesday, November 5, 1796, the empress's chamberlain, Zakhar Zotov, found Catherine sprawled on the floor of one of her rooms. She had by then, at age 67, grown so obese that it took six men to drag her across the room toward her bed. Never regaining consciousness, she died that night at 9:45, gasping for breath. An autopsy showed that she had suffered two cerebral hemorrhages. Her son Paul, now 42 years old, her daughter-in-law Maria, and her two grandsons, Alexander and Konstantin, were with her when she died. Within hours, a proclamation announced Empress Catherine's death and Emperor Paul I's accession. While Catherine lay in state, Paul had his father's body exhumed. On December 5, 1796, the late czar Peter III and his deceased wife Catherine II were entombed together in the Cathedral of Peter and Paul in St. Petersburg.

The new czar immediately set about undoing as much of his mother's work as he could. He abrogated the Charter of the Nobility, revoking many of the nobles' privileges. He also reinstated corporal punishment for nobles, which the charter had abolished. Many of Catherine's senior officials were retired and replaced by Paul's associates. Within hours of his coronation on April 5, 1797, Paul instituted a new law of succession, repealing Peter the Great's 1722 decree permitting a sovereign to select a successor. Paul's new law required that the crown automatically pass to the autocrat's eldest son, a change motivated by his own experience.

❖   ❖   ❖

Czar Paul I, who had waited 34 years for the crown his mother had seized from his father, Peter III, firmly believed it should have passed directly to him and that his mother had denied him his birthright. As a young child separated from his parents by his grandaunt, Empress Elizabeth, Paul had scarcely known his mother. After taking the throne from Peter, Empress Catherine had remained aloof from her son, entrusting his education to a tutor. After her original choice for tutor, the French philosopher d'Alembert, had declined the post, Catherine had placed the boy with Nikita Panin.

Panin came from a distinguished family: His father was a renowned general, and his brother, Peter, was a brilliant young officer destined for general's rank in the Russian army. Nikita had served as Russian ambassador to Sweden during Elizabeth's reign. Educated in Russia and abroad, he was widely traveled and urbane. Catherine felt Nikita Panin was the best choice for tutor that was available, and she could not have known the danger in selecting him to educate the future emperor, namely, that he was dedicated to the doctrine of direct succession. Although Panin had supported Catherine's coup that dethroned Peter III in 1762, he had expected that she would serve as regent only until Paul reached his majority. Panin had barely managed to mask his reprehension when Catherine seized the throne he knew belonged to Paul. His own disappointment and frustration must have affected the young boy in his charge, as Paul grew to manhood despising his mother for destroying his father and usurping the throne that was rightfully his. Paul's dislike for Catherine was also fueled by her promiscuity with a succession of lovers. Now in full command, Paul I determined to rectify what he saw as the errors of the past, but his reign would last only five years.

Paul's physical bearing hardly suggested that he was emperor of a vast empire. Somewhat sickly, he looked like a man turned in on himself. A snub nose and protruding eyes gave him a farcical appearance, yet he rarely exhibited a smile, suggesting an inner sadness born of his estrangement from his parents and psychological abuse from a mother who had seen him as a potential rival for her crown. Although Paul was intelligent and inquisitive, one of his professors had described his mind as a machine hanging by a thread: should the thread break, the machine would begin spinning out of control, "and then, farewell to reason and intelligence."

Paul alluded to the monocratic despotism reserved for the reigning sovereign in his often quoted comment that no one was of any importance in Russia except the man with whom the czar was speaking, and that importance lasted "only while I am speaking with him." He scorned nobility as incompatible with autocracy, and struck out at the nobles and landed gentry whom his mother had coddled to keep their support. In 1797, he instituted a law restricting their control over their serfs. He declared Sunday a day of rest for serfs, and they were obligated to work no more than three days each week for their masters, allowing them to work the three remaining days for themselves. Although this completely unenforceable law was aimed at diminishing the power of the nobles and the gentry, not at improving the condition of the serfs, it marked the first time that the government stipulated any rights at all for the millions of enslaved Russian peasants.

Catherine's magnificent Tauride Palace was stripped of its art treasures and assigned to the Horse Guards Regiment for use as a barracks and stable. In a macabre act of temper, Paul had the body of Catherine's favorite lover, Potemkin, dug up and thrown into a canal from which it floated into the Neva River and then into the Baltic, never to be seen again. Many of Catherine's friends and advisors were jailed or exiled, and those who had suffered the same fate during her rule were freed and all their property returned to them. Paul was determined to eradicate all remnants of Catherine's reign.

Although by Catherine's own admission Paul was not Peter III's son, he did share the late emperor's love of everything Prussian. Frederick the Great was Paul's idol. The czar personally helped design new Prussian-style uniforms for the Russian army and demanded that the entire army be reorganized in the Prussian mold.

During his brief reign, Paul was an erratic leader who issued orders and decrees one day and countermanded them the next. He suffered such severe paranoia that he dismantled Empress Elizabeth's New Summer Palace, one of the most beautiful buildings in St. Petersburg, and replaced it with a gothic-style fortress, complete with battlements, a moat, and a drawbridge. Intending to live in the security of this private prison, he granted entry to only a few trusted intimates. The Michael Palace, as he called it, was completed in 1801, but czar Paul's fate was already sealed by then.

❖ ❖ ❖

Paul's greatest impact as emperor was in the arena of international relations. Shortly before her death, Catherine had indicated that she planned on joining the Anglo-Austrian–led coalition against France. Although Paul had the same contempt for revolutionary France as his mother, almost immediately upon his accession he declared Russia's neutrality in the war raging in Europe.

Paul's neutrality was more accurately an anti-French policy. He hated the revolution for having eradicating the French monarchy, and he viewed Napoleon as the embodiment of all republican evil in Europe. Paul's hostility toward the French revolutionary government was clearly reflected in his own actions: He offered refuge in southern Russia to 10,000 French expatriates who had escaped the mobs and executioners, but he refused entry to any Frenchman not carrying a passport issued by the old Bourbon monarchy. The czar banned clothes inspired by revolutionary Paris, and prohibited the public use of the words "citizen" and "society," two provocative terms co-opted by the French revolutionists.

Napoleon would end Russia's neutrality by seizing the island of Malta in the Mediterranean. On May 19, 1798, he sailed from the French port of Toulon with an expedition of 400 transport ships loaded with troops and supplies and escorted by 17 warships. His destination was Egypt, but to appease French naval and commercial interests that insisted they needed port facilities in the central Mediterranean, Napoleon paused to secure Malta. The island was also a potentially important link in communications between Napoleon's Egyptian campaign and France.

In November 1797, the Litta brothers—Lorenzo, the papal nuncio to the Russian court, and Count Julio, a former admiral in the Russian navy and a high-ranking member of the Knights of the Order of St. John of Jerusalem—had convinced the czar to accept the title of "protector" of the Order. The Knights had ruled Malta since they drove out the Turks in 1565. Consequently, Paul followed closely reports of the French landings on Malta in June 1798. The Knights were able to mount little more than token resistance against the overpowering French invasion. Napoleon required only one week in Malta to garrison his occupation force and organize a military government before continuing on to Alexandria. The Litta brothers, assisted by Russian members of the Order, elected Czar Paul I grand master of the Order on October 27, 1798. As grand master, the Russian czar would be responsible for the security of the Knights' possession of Malta. The election meant Russia would oppose the French occupation. At first Pope Pius VI refused to recognize Paul's election, which placed a fervent member of the Russian Orthodox Church at the head of a Roman Catholic order of knights, but the Litta brothers, pointing to the election as a potential opportunity to reunite the two branches of Christianity, won the pontiff's approval.

When he learned that Napoleon had successfully occupied Malta, Paul became enraged; he declared war on France and immediately opened negotiations with members of the anti-French alliance, Britain, Austria, and Naples. As Napoleon's victorious forces swept across Egypt, which was part of the Ottoman Empire, Paul also opened a dialogue with the Turks. The alliance that emerged from these negotiations, the Second Coalition, included Russia, Britain, Austria, Naples, Portugal, and Turkey. Russia quickly flexed her muscles in July 1798 by sending a naval squadron from St. Petersburg to Yarmouth, to cooperate with the British Royal Navy along the French-controlled Dutch coast. The following September, a second Russian squadron, augmented by the Turkish Black Sea Fleet, drove the French from the Ionian Islands off the west coast of Greece.

Russia's naval presence helped to establish the czar's empire as a major partner in the war against France, but the main theater of operations was on land. In April 1799, 18,000 Russian soldiers commanded by General Alexander Suvorov and supported by a larger Austrian contingent drove the French, sans Napoleon, who was still in Egypt, out of northern Italy. Suvorov's combined Russian-Austrian army scored major victories at Cassano, Milan, and Novi and took 80,000 prisoners. The Russian general wanted to drive straight through to Paris, but his Austria allies were reluctant to take the gamble and, as a result, Suvorov was forced to make a spectacular withdrawal through the French-controlled Swiss Alps.

Paul was furious with his allies, particularly Austria, which refused to exploit Suvorov's hard-won victories, and Britain, which offered only lukewarm support to the Russian-led campaign in the Low Countries, where an Anglo-Russian army was forced to capitulate to the French. Finally, in January 1800, fed up with his allies' inaction, Paul recalled Suvorov and his army from its winter quarters in Switzerland and Bohemia. The final break between Russia and its Second Coalition partners occurred when the British invaded Malta in September 1800, after having prevented the Russians from landing there earlier.

The British persisted in their occupation of Malta, refusing Russian demands that the island be turned over to the czar as grand master and protector of the Knights.

Faced with the prospect of imminent defeat by Napoleon's Army of the Rhine, Austria signed a peace treaty with France in February 1801. Impressed by Napoleon's successes, Czar Paul began to regard the Frenchman less as a revolutionary and more as the harbinger of the return of a monarchy to France. The overthrow of the Directory that governed revolutionary France, and Napoleon's subsequent election as first consul in December 1799, confirmed Paul's impression. Russia now repudiated its ties to Britain and switched its affiliation to the French. Paul also resolved to acquire Britain's colonies in India as compensation for Malta. In an ill-conceived campaign that had little hope of success, he sent General Basil Orlov with 23,000 Cossacks in the general direction of India. The Russian force set off without maps of the area it was supposed to conquer and with inadequate supplies. For weeks the Cossacks battled numbing cold and blinding blizzards, until Orlov received orders to return to Russia in early March 1801. A new emperor had taken the throne and had canceled the campaign. The new czar of Russia was Paul's son, Alexander I, the beloved grandson and favorite grandchild of Catherine the Great.

❖ ❖ ❖

Paul I's reign ended abruptly during the night of March 11, 1801. The czar's erratic behavior, especially his sudden switch of allegiance in the war against France, had added to the hostility toward him. The wealthy merchants resented the fact that war with Britain meant an almost complete cessation of trade through the Baltic, and formerly powerful nobles lived in fear of being exiled for some imagined offense. These resentments led inevitably to a plot against the czar.

Paranoid about conspiracies, Paul had sequestered himself in the Michael Palace under heavy guard. The emperor's security was in the hands of the military governor of St. Petersburg and commandant of the Imperial Guard, Count Peter Pahlen. Unknown to Paul, Pahlen was a major force in the plot to depose him. Pahlen was also one of the few men in whom the emperor had implicit trust.

That trust was put to a severe test on March 10, 1801, when Paul received an anonymous letter detailing a planned coup. The letter accused Pahlen of having full knowledge of the plot but doing nothing to apprehend the conspirators. Paul invited the governor-general to dinner that evening, and after filling him with several glass of drink, told him of the letter and its charge that he knew about the plot. Unperturbed, Pahlen readily acknowledged that he not only knew of the plot, but was actually a coconspirator.

Shocked by Pahlen's admission, Paul demanded to know how he could take part in a plot against his rightful sovereign. Calmly, Pahlen explained that he had infiltrated the conspiracy to identify its members so he could order their arrest. He artfully declined to name them until he could arrange the arrest. The emperor appeared satisfied with this explanation, but he insisted on knowing whether his wife and two oldest sons, Alexander and Konstantin, were involved. Pahlen craftily denied their complicity, but in a way calculated to arouse Paul's suspicion, thus provoking the czar to order his wife arrested and his sons placed under close surveillance. Both orders suited Pahlen's plans perfectly. Paul provided him with the ammunition he needed to win Grand Duke Alexander over to the plot against his father.

In a second masterful deception, Pahlen told the czar that several officers of the Chevalier Guards regiment, then on duty guarding the emperor and the Michael Palace, were involved in the plot. He urged the incredulous ruler to replace them with the Semenovskii Guards regiment, which Pahlen assured him was loyal to a man. Paul acted on Pahlen's advice, and by displacing his personal guards, virtually signed his own death warrant.

Leaving the badly shaken emperor with assurances that he would protect him from the plotters, Pahlen assembled the conspirators, explained what had happened, and told them they must move immediately, before the emperor had an opportunity to think more clearly about the governor-general's outrageous story.

Pahlen then visited Grand Duke Michael, who was aware that a plot was afoot but had attempted to stay above it. Pahlen showed Alexander Paul's order to arrest his mother and watch the two older sons for possible treasonous activities. Pahlen then told the grand duke something he probably already knew, that Paul reportedly intended to marry his young and favorite daughter, Catherine, to the German prince Eugen von Württemberg, and to name the prince as his successor. Alexander, after obtaining Pahlen's pledge that his father would be deposed because of insanity and would not be murdered, appears to have agreed with the governor-general's plans.

The following night, March 11, the conspirators, many of whom had taken courage from drink, quietly made their way past the guards and into Paul's bedchamber. Although Pahlen was the leader, he lagged slightly behind the others, prepared in case anything went wrong to claim that he had followed them into the palace and was about to arrest them before they could carry out their plan. Emperor Paul awoke and, finding the group of men in his room, put up a furious struggle before he was beaten to death so brutally that his body was barely recognizable.

Pahlen then immediately took charge, he being the only one with a clear understanding of what needed to be done to effect a peaceful transition of power. He ordered the dead emperor's body removed and prepared for embalming. Shaking Grand Duke Alexander from the lethargy brought on by the realization that he had contributed to his father's murder, Pahlen told him that he must present himself before the regiments of the Imperial Guard to take their pledge before anyone attempted to avenge Paul's murder.

Seeing that Alexander, who had a well-deserved reputation for laziness and malingering, was making no effort to leave with the governor-general, Pahlen took him by the arm and told him in the strongest terms it was possible for someone to speak to a czar, "You have played the child long enough. Go and reign."

Pahlen assembled the Imperial Guard. Telling them that Paul had died from a stroke, the governor-general introduced Alexander as the new emperor and cried "Long live Czar Alexander I." The soldiers responded with an ominous silence. Pahlen and the other officers who had executed the coup were dumbfounded. Alexander simply stood facing the guards, still unable to cope with all that was happening. Apparently, the one group of Russians who had admired Paul were the rank-and-file soldiers who liked the way he had berated their officers in front of them, and who had invariably expressed a personal interest in them. A few among the assembled troops actually asked to see the dead emperor's body, while others wondered aloud about the circumstances of his death. Rumors of the coup plot had not gone unreported in the St. Petersburg garrison. The soldiers remained truculent and defiant until Pahlen announced that they would all have the day off to celebrate the accession of the new emperor and promised them extra rations of vodka. With that the soldiers broke into cheers of "Long live Czar Alexander." The Guard regiments' loyalty assured, Pahlen allowed Alexander to retreat to his palace apartment, where the new emperor slept until late afternoon.

❖ ❖ ❖

Alexander I was 23 years old when he came to the throne of Russia in 1801. He was physically attractive, tall, courteous, and elegant in manner. His

Czar Alexander I

father's murder would haunt him for the rest of his life, and he never ceased protesting his complicity in Paul's death.

Alexander had come in for considerable abuse from his father because he exhibited too many liberal tendencies. Actually, Alexander's political philosophy was a mix of the liberalism he had learned from the Swiss humanitarian philosopher Frédéric César la Harpe, who had guided the young grand duke's education, and the militarism he had inherited from his father. Until Catherine the Great's death, Alexander had lived in two worlds, the grand court of the empress, and the tight-knit little military court that Paul had kept around him in his place outside the city. Alexander had perfected a balance between these two societies, changing his demeanor, chameleon-like, when ever he moved from one to the other; uncomfortable in both worlds, he nonetheless was sufficiently talented to appease both his demanding grandmother and his demanding father.

Alexander I's reign can be divided into two distinct periods. The first was marked by the liberal enlightenment of an activist emperor; the second was clouded by mysticism and reversal. Although his coronation did not occur until September 1801, Alexander, through his advisors, immediately began issuing decrees that revealed the focus of the new regime. With dizzying speed, the new emperor seemed to be attempting to reverse the many wrongs his father had inflicted on Russia and the Russian people. On March 13, civilian officials and military officers whom Paul had summarily dismissed were informed that they could begin the process of requesting reinstatement. The following day, Alexander lifted Paul's export embargo. On the 15th, all political prisoners and political exiles received amnesty while the nobility regained the right to elect judges. March 17 brought an order for the restoration of the local government institutions that Catherine the Great had created but Paul had abolished. Two days later, the police agencies were warned not to harass people or to overstep their authority. On March 22, Russia's borders, which Paul had virtually closed to foreign travelers, were reopened, and on April 2 the secret police was abolished and the Charter of the Nobility and the Charter of the Cities were reinstated.

The country was elated as the repression of five years was dissolved in a few weeks. People celebrated the arrival of a new czar as they had never done in the past. Paradoxically, Alexander was as much a parade-ground drill martinet as his father. He loved dress uniforms and spending long hours drilling troops. What, then, inspired his sudden appetite for reform?

As a young grand duke and heir to the throne, Alexander had surrounded himself with a group of liberal-minded, cultivated, articulate young men. Among them he had expressed ideas that his father would surely have considered treasonous. Alexander professed opposition to the hereditary monarchy, calling it unjust, and spoke openly with his friends of abdicating the throne, introducing an American-style constitution, and retiring to a quiet life along the shores of the Rhine to study nature with his wife, Elizabeth.

Could Paul I's son, the grandson whom Catherine the Great had groomed to succeed her, seriously contemplate such radical changes? Actually, he did not. Alexander's liberal views were merely a veneer; they generated ideas that prompted lively conversation in the salons of St. Petersburg and Paris but offered no practical application. He spoke as a liberal, but his birthright as heir to the autocratic Russian dynasty carried more weight than the abstract ideas contained in Voltaire's works.

The emperor's dysfunctional lethargy immediately following his father's murder had been obvious to Count Pahlen. Correctly assessing Alexander's lassitude, Pahlen had appointed himself surrogate monarch until Alexander could pull himself together. It was Pahlen who recalled the Cossack army from its senseless march toward India, thereby preventing certain disaster. The governor-general also quietly negotiated a settlement with British Admiral Horatio Nelson, whose fleet, anchored in the Gulf of Finland, was prepared to destroy the Russian naval base at Kronstadt. As Pahlen assumed greater personal authority, Alexander began to suspect that his father's murderer was planning to replace him as well. The emperor quietly arranged to have Pahlen and his lieutenants watched closely.

Alexander's initial reforms cost him nothing. They did, however, earn him the reputation of a benevolent reformer. The Russian people greeted his changes with enthusiasm, convinced they were harbingers of a new era of enlightenment. Russians again began wearing the stylish clothing that Paul had banned, and crowds enjoyed strolling the avenues of the capital without fear of police harassment. The imperial family quickly abandoned the forbidding Michael Palace and returned to the Winter Palace.

Alexander's talk of living a peaceful, quiet life with Elizabeth was a charade. As much as the German princess loved and idolized her husband, he ignored her to the point where she sought affection in the arms of one of her ladies-in-waiting, Countess Varvara Golovin. Alexander himself had taken several lovers during the years in which he waited for the throne, drawing farther from Elizabeth with each new love interest. Yet it was Elizabeth who, with Pahlen, had jarred him from his lethargy following Paul's brutal murder, and who had exhorted him to act like a czar. Countess Golovin, who witnessed the scene, later reported that Alexander had appeared pale and shaken when Pahlen told him he was now the emperor, and had sobbed that he did not have the strength to rule Russia. "Let someone else take my place," she reported him having said. Elizabeth had urged Alexander to dedicate himself to his people. It was probably at that point that Pahlen took the czar's arm and commanded him to stop acting like a child.

Once the family had settled into the Winter Palace, Alexander's mother, Maria, began asserting her authority over him, pushing Elizabeth into the background. She played on Alexander's guilt over Paul's murder by crying about having lost her husband, completely ignoring his poor treatment of her and his plans to imprison her and her children and take his mistress as his wife and new empress. Maria was evidently determined that, if she could not be empress, she would be at least the matriarch of the nation.

When Alexander took the throne, he was without personal confidants. The bright, young liberals of Alexander's youth had been dispersed abroad by Paul, who distrusted their influence over his son; they had been scattered, some with official appointments, to Italy, Britain, and Germany. Alexander had no advisors who could remind him of his youthful enthusiasm, no matter how superficial, for the Enlightenment. Although the new emperor recalled his old friends to Russia, he remained alone, without trusted advisors. The men responsible for his father's death and for Alexander's own accession could not be dismissed lightly, for they had already killed one czar and he feared their taste for imperial blood. Alexander retained them, but in time they were quietly withdrawn from public life and retired to their country estates. Count Pahlen was among the first to go. Pahlen had confronted Empress Maria with the news of her husband's death within minutes of Paul's murder, and when she demanded to be recognized as the reigning empress, it was Pahlen who had refused her, asserting that her son, Alexander, would reign. Maria never forgave this affront, and she worked tirelessly to remove Pahlen as St. Petersburg's governor-general. Pressure from his mother, and his own private suspicions that Pahlen was scheming to depose him prompted Alexander to exile Pahlen to his country estate.

By June 1801, Alexander's liberal friends had returned from abroad, and on the 24th of that month they held a reunion. The emperor now began meeting with them almost daily, usually over coffee. Variously referred to as the Unofficial Committee or the Committee of Friends, the group included Count Paul Stroganov, Count Victor Kochubey, Nicholas Novosiltsev, and a former Polish prisoner of war, Prince Adam Czartoryski. Unknown to this group, Alexander was also regularly meeting with another group, one that more clearly represented the thinking of the upper nobility.

The members of the Unofficial Committee were all young men enthralled by the Enlightenment, and most were Anglophiles, but they were little more than a debating society earnestly discussing a variety of reforms that none had the courage to attempt to implement. Even when Alexander asked them to review a list of reforms proposed by Semyon and Alexander Voronstov, two brothers whom the emperor deeply respected, the Unofficial Committee proved too timid to support them. The Voronstovs had proposed that Alexander issue a Charter of the Russian People, which would codify citizens' rights. The Voronstovs' plan died before it could receive serious consideration, in part because the Unofficial Committee was unable to stop debating its details and urge Alexander to move forward with it.

Although Alexander spoke of many more reforms, the few he actually contemplated were usually blocked or reversed by the opposition of the nobility and the landed gentry. Count Stroganov tried to get him to emancipate the serfs, whom Stroganov compared to the slaves in the American South. Stroganov also called for improving education through a system of public schools, and pay raises for government officials to reduce graft and corruption. The debates of the Unofficial Committee were endless, but little was accomplished. Overwhelmed by the magnitude of his problems in trying to bring his empire into the community of civilized nations, the czar took comfort from Czartoryski's observation that Russia was like a great ship, and that it would take time to alter her course without capsizing her.

Although a small yet significant improvement in the serfs' status occurred during Alexander's reign, it was not initiated by the emperor or the Unofficial Committee but by a minor nobleman in a distant province. In 1802, Count Serge Rumyantsev, the German-educated son of a former Russian field marshal, requested permission, as required by law, to sell a large number of his serfs their freedom and a sizable division of his land. The request was the catalyst for a February 1803 decree called the Law Concerning Agricultural Workers. Despite opposition from many great landowners, Alexander signed the decree, which granted landowners the right to free their serfs under certain conditions. The emancipated serfs became a new class of citizen, the "free farmers." They were granted broad rights over the land they received at the time of their emancipation, including the right to buy more land or sell some of their own. They also acquired many obligations formerly reserved for the gentry, including paying taxes and supplying recruits for the army.

During Alexander's reign (1801–1825), only 37,000 serfs received their freedom under the new law, but during the reign of Nicholas I (1825–1855), another 67,000 would be emancipated. Although these numbers were relatively insignificant when compared with the millions of serfs still owned by nobles and the gentry, Alexander's action was a first step toward complete emancipation and raised hopes for a better future among a class of people who had never before had hope.

❖ ❖ ❖

The first few years of Alexander's reign were peaceful, as Russia withdrew from Paul's war against Great Britain and slipped into an isolationist posture.

Alexander watched with admiration as Napoleon led France to a steady succession of military victories, but then Napoleon began moving east in search of additional conquests. Envisioning himself as the master of Europe, Napoleon trampled on the rights of smaller and weaker nations, especially the German principalities. He already controlled Holland and Switzerland, and Austria had been forced to sign a humiliating treaty. Following a brief respite resulting from the Treaty of Amiens, signed in 1802, war once again erupted between France and Great Britain in May 1803. Wary of that event, Alexander prepared his army for war, placing special emphasis on the production of new, more advanced artillery. At the end of May, he appointed Alexander Arakcheyev, a former close advisor to Paul I, as inspector general of artillery, with instructions to make Russian artillery at least the equal of Napoleon's vaunted artillery.

The rift between Russia and France began in March 1804, when French agents invaded neutral Baden and kidnapped the duke of Enghien, who had joined a group of French émigrés who favored the restoration of the Bourbon monarchy. Taken to a fort at Vincennes, the duke was tried and executed despite the absence of evidence to support the charge that he had taken part in a conspiracy against Napoleon's life.

Emperor Alexander was incensed by the duke's execution. His own wife, Elizabeth, was a princess of Baden, the daughter of the reigning prince, and the czar considered himself a protector of the rights of the independent German states. Strenuously denouncing the violation of a neutral country and the execution of a duke, Alexander declared the Russian court in a state of mourning for the duke of Enghien. When he next saw the French ambassador, Count d'Hédouville, the emperor ignored his presence and refused to speak to him.

A furious czar sent a strong note to Paris, protesting the duke of Enghien's execution. Napoleon replied caustically through the French foreign minister, Talleyrand, reminding Alexander that Emperor Paul I's assassins were never prosecuted. Alexander became even more infuriated. The French upstart had touched a raw nerve with his veiled accusation that the czar was complicit in his own father's murder. Count d'Hédouville was recalled to Paris, and Alexander's representative in the French capital, Peter Oubril, demanded the return of his passport; he left Paris in August.

In May 1804, Napoleon exploited the exposure of an assassination plot engineered by Britain as his excuse for having himself proclaimed emperor. Pope Pius VII was coerced into participating in the new emperor's coronation ceremony, which took place in December. Alexander railed against the revolutionary commoner who presumed to take the title of emperor without a hereditary claim. He warned that Napoleon aspired to be emperor of all Europe and had delusions of becoming another Caesar or Charlemagne. Alluding to the only other European emperor, Francis II of Austria, Alexander proclaimed that "Europe is too small for a third [emperor]."

Russia began to negotiate an anti-French alliance with Britain in late 1804. In mid-May 1805, Napoleon shocked Europe again when he declared himself king of Italy. The following month, Russia and Great Britain formed the Third Coalition and determined to liberate Italy, Holland, northern Germany, and Switzerland from French domination. Britain agreed to provide Russia with financial assistance in the form of an annual payment of £1,250,000 for every 100,000 Russian soldiers committed to the war against France. Fearing Napoleon's designs on the entire continent, Sweden and Austria soon joined the alliance.

The Russian czar had several additional motives for joining in a war against France. Alexander shared his father's and grandmother's ambition for a dominant Russian presence in European affairs; conducting a victorious war against the self-proclaimed French emperor would help Russia achieve international recognition. In addition, Napoleon's rumored intention to recapture the Ionian Islands off the coast of Greece, which his forces had relinquished to the Russians in 1798, and his installation as king of Italy posed serious problems for achieving Russia's objective of dominating the Balkans, an area that Alexander considered within his sphere of influence. If Napoleon was not stopped now, Russia herself might one day be the target of a French offensive.

Meanwhile, Napoleon had formed his Army of England, which appeared poised to cross the English Channel and attack Britain. In August 1805, after ordering his fleet to prepare for the invasion, Napoleon acknowledged that the preparations had been a ruse to lull the Austrians into thinking he was ignorant of their designs on the French-controlled German states; the Austrians had expected Napoleon to be tied up with his foolish plan to invade Britain. Instead, Napoleon rechristened his army the Grand Army and marched 200,000 men into Germany. A Russian army immediately went to Austria's defense.

Alexander had little respect for his allies. He thought Great Britain's King George III bordered on insanity, and considered the Austrian emperor, Francis II, "a fool in full dress." At home, the war shelved all plans for internal reforms, which, as far as the emperor was concerned, were happily forgotten.

Expecting the French to concentrate their efforts in Italy, the Austrians had sent 90,000 troops south, led by their best military commander, Archduke

Charles. General Karl Mack von Leiberich proceeded to Germany, which was Napoleon's true objective, with 70,000 Austrian troops. Archduke John supported Mack with a 25,000-man reserve army in the Tyrol. Russia contributed 120,000 men to the war effort; 20,000 were sent to bolster the Swedish army in operations against Stralsund, and Marshal Michael Kutuzov rushed 40,000 troops to assist Mack along the Rhine. The main Russian army of roughly 60,000 men followed Kutuzov's force and was joined by Emperor Alexander, who was anxious to achieve personal military glory and the concomitant approval of the Russian people.

The allies faced Napoleon's 200,000-man Grand Army which included seven corps, each commanded by a battle-tested marshal, a 40,000-man reserve cavalry, and the elite 8,000-man Imperial Guard. France's German allies, primarily Württemberg and Bavaria, supplied an additional 50,000 well-trained troops equipped with the latest weapons.

Not expecting the French to attack before mid-October, Mack had decided to deal first with Napoleon's German allies. On September 13, without waiting for Russian support, he invaded Bavaria. The Bavarian army withdrew northward and waited for the appearance of the French before engaging the Austrians. Mack proceeded up the Danube River, halting at Ulm, on the Württemberg border, where he waited for the Russians to arrive.

Meanwhile, the French army had crossed the Rhine on September 25 and began crossing the Danube, east of Ulm, on October 8. Mack, realizing the danger of entrapment by Napoleon's superior numbers, ordered an attack along the Danube against the French flank while the Grand Army was engaged in crossing the river. However, Mack was hampered by the incompetent Archduke Ferdinand, who was the nominal commander of the allied forces because the Russians had insisted that their aristocratic field officers were above taking orders from a mere general and could answer only to a prince of the Austrian royal family. Failing to recognize the opportunity to cripple Napoleon, Ferdinand countermanded Mack's orders and unsuccessfully pressed him to fall back to the Tyrol and await additional support.

On October 14, Ferdinand gave up trying to get Mack to withdraw, and left Ulm with 6,000 troops; he claimed he did not want Napoleon to capture a Hapsburg prince, but in truth he was terrified of the coming battle. Mack was glad to see him go. French cavalry pursued the fleeing prince, killing half his troops, but Ferdinand made good his escape. Two days later, Napoleon began a relentless artillery bombardment of Ulm that compelled Mark, already under pressure from his own generals, to surrender his army of 27,000 men.

Meanwhile, Alexander, fearing that Prussian neutrality might collapse if Napoleon pressured King Frederick William III, traveled to Berlin in an attempt to bring Prussia into the alliance. Despite a dramatic ceremony at the tomb of Frederick the Great, where both monarchs swore an oath of eternal friendship, the Prussian king declined to commit his 80,000 men to the coalition unless Napoleon refused his offer to mediate the dispute between the alliance and France. Frederick, who feared Napoleon more than any other potential adversary, decided to remain neutral until the balance had tilted decisively toward one side. Only then would he decide whether Prussia would enter the war, and on which side.

At about the time Mack was surrendering at Ulm, the first part of the Russian army, under Marshal Kutuzov, reached the Inn River on the Bavarian-Austrian border. Learning of Mack's surrender, Kutuzov, whose army was augmented by several Austrian units that had escaped Ulm, retreated to the northeast toward Moravia, where he hoped to link up with the main Russian army under Marshal Friedrich Buxhöwden. Kutuzov planned to unite the Russian forces and wait for Austrian support from Archduke Charles's army. When Napoleon was told of the Russian withdrawal, he sent his cavalry in pursuit with orders to keep "your swords up their asses."

On November 27, having taken personal command of the Russian army, Czar Alexander led an attack against the French forces at Brünn, ignoring Kutuzov's advice to delay. The marshal had wanted Alexander to wait until the Austrians had joined them, thereby creating an army in excess of 175,000 men to face less than 70,000 French and allied troops. Kutuzov had also wanted to wait until the morning mist had burned off the proposed battlefield in order to get a better view of the enemy forces and to judge Napoleon's intentions before committing his troops. Alexander, resplendent in his red and green uniform and mounted on a splendid bobtailed chestnut stallion, had disregarded the marshal's advice; he was convinced that his already superior numbers alone would win him military glory to rival his imperial predecessors.

At seven o'clock on the chilly, mist-shrouded morning of December 2, 1805, Emperor Alexander I committed 40,000 men to the opening battle against the forces of Emperor Napoleon. Another 46,000 Russians were held in reserve or were approaching the scene of the battle, near the town of Austerlitz. By 10:00 A.M. the advantage had tipped in Napoleon's favor. By 4:00 P.M. the Russian army, except for the Imperial Guard, had virtually disintegrated, scattering in all directions. French cavalry pursuing the fleeing enemy could not find tracks large enough to indicate units of a size worth chasing. The Russian army was in full flight with no hope of being regrouped. More than 25,000 Russians were lost in the battle, 10,000 of them killed by the French or drowned in a large, lightly frozen swamp to which they had been driven by Napoleon's army. French casualties were 2,000 dead and 7,000 wounded. Humiliated, Alexander refused to discuss peace terms with Napoleon and simply gathered up what forces he could find and marched east. Emperor Francis of Austria, whose capital, Vienna, was occupied by French forces, sued for peace.

The Russian army was in such disarray that for three days the czar and his small entourage—which included Czartoryski, who was now Alexander's foreign minister, and three Cossacks—wandered eastward without finding any Russian troops. Alexander desperately sought to avoid capture by Napoleon's patrols. Although much of the Russian army was wandering aimlessly around the countryside, Marshal Kutuzov, despite being wounded, kept his head. He gradually slowed the retreat and reorganized several units, turning the rout into a more orderly withdrawal.

On December 21, unnoticed under cover of darkness, the humiliated Russian czar slipped quietly into the Winter Palace at St. Petersburg. He told Elizabeth of the disaster and accused the Austrians of failing to fulfill their part of the bargain, a brazen untruth because the Austrian forces had been fully committed to the battle. Alexander swore he would raise another army of at least 250,000 men and take revenge "on this damn upstart from Corsica." For the next nine years, until Napoleon's own marshals forced him to abdicate, Alexander would be consumed by the war against France.

Disregarding his oath of eternal friendship with the defeated Russian emperor, Prussia's King Frederick William III concluded a treaty with Napoleon before Alexander had even returned to St. Petersburg. As payment for his perfidy, Napoleon gave the Prussian king control of the French Empire's German province of Hanover.

During the spring and summer of 1806, Napoleon consolidated his victories against the Third Coalition with incredible swiftness, setting the stage for a renewal of the war against Russia. In May, he sent a new ambassador to Constantinople with instructions to induce the Ottoman sultan to join a proposed triple alliance of Turkey, Persia, and France to conquer Russia. In July, Napoleon completed the creation of the Rhine Confederation, which included almost all the German states, except Prussia, under French protection and control. Because France's hegemony over the German states ended the illusion of the continued existence of the Holy Roman Empire that Charlemagne had founded in 800, the Austrian emperor, Francis I, abdicated his second title of "Holy Roman Emperor" (as which he was known as Francis II).

Technically, Russia was still at war with France, but Alexander, sulking after his humiliating defeat at Austerlitz, had no appetite for continued warfare, at least not right away. Napoleon was the master of Europe. Alexander expressed his grudging admiration for his opponent when he confided to Czartoryski during their flight from the disastrous battle, "We are babies in the hands of a giant." The czar's efficient propaganda campaign convinced the Russian people that had he and Marshal Kutuzov not been encumbered by the cowardice and perfidy of the Austrians, they would have defeated Napoleon at Austerlitz. Russians greeted Alexander as a hero and believed that his return heralded an era of peace.

Despite his great victories, Napoleon's position remained precarious. In Austria, a thoroughly humiliated and vengeful Emperor Francis I turned over control of his decimated forces to his best military commander, Archduke Charles, who quickly set about building and equipping a new Austrian army. Planning to style the new army along the lines of Napoleon's successful armies, Charles eased out of service the extremely old men who had held on to most of the top ranks.

Napoleon continued to solidify his control over most of Europe. He acquired additional Prussian territory in Germany and Switzerland when he pressured Frederick William III to sign a revised treaty. Meanwhile, Czar Alexander envisioned a Russian-Prussian alliance that could defeat France without the help of the Austrians. In early March 1806, he wrote to the Prussian king, urging him to declare war on France. Alexander promised to support Prussia against Napoleon, although he lacked the equipment and the trained troops to effectively do so. Frederick William's wife, Queen Louise, a desirable, flirtatious woman who held her husband in low regard, taunted him to take action against Napoleon. Having confirmed rumors that Napoleon had offered Hanover to Great Britain in return for a peace settlement, Frederick William threatened war against France in July 1806. The king actually had little choice because his own nobles were threatening to withdraw their support if Prussia gave up Hanover. The Prussian army, which Frederick William liked to call the army of Frederick the Great, numbered roughly 250,000 men, 145,000 of them combat troops assigned to field armies. To fulfill his commitment, Czar Alexander began assembling two armies of 60,000 men each.

Prussia's threat of war enraged Napoleon. Using the ensuing diplomatic exchanges to mask his intentions, Napoleon quickly maneuvered his armies into position to seize the Prussian capital of Berlin, and on September 21 he left Paris to take personal command of his Grand Army. Five days later, the Prussian king sent Napoleon an ultimatum to evacuate Germany or face war with Prussia. In truth, Napoleon was worried about facing the Prussian army. Although he held the Prussian commanders, including the king, in contempt, he was concerned about the inspirational potential of Frederick the Great's memory on the troops who would do the fighting. As it turned out, he had little to fear.

In late September, without waiting for Russian reinforcements, the duke of Brunswick, with constant prodding from King Frederick William, led the Prussian army toward the border with the Rhine Confederation. Frederick William hoped to prove he was a true Prussian military commander, a worthy successor to Frederick the Great, by defeating Napoleon. But poor communications and inept leadership compounded by the king's interference, and the enmity between the duke of Brunswick and Prince von Hohenlohe, who directed one of the three armies in Brunswick's command, allowed Napoleon to trap the Prussians near the villages of Jena, Auerstädt, and Friedland. The campaign began on October 6, and by the 14th, Napoleon had decimated the Prussian army.

❖ ❖ ❖

On October 24, 1806, Marshal Louis-Nicolas Davout, one of Napoleon's most courageous and effective commanders, occupied Berlin. The next day, Napoleon himself arrived in the Prussian capital. When city officials offered him the sword of Frederick the Great, he refused it, saying he had one of his own. The remaining Prussian forces took flight to the east, or sought refuge in fortresses, which French artillery and infantry assaults reduced to rubble. A series of love letters that Czar Alexander had sent to Queen Louise were found in Berlin's royal palace by French agents. Alexander had been captivated by her beauty during his visit to Berlin the previous October, and had corresponded with her ever since. Napoleon had the French press publish the letters to embarrass the czar before the world. From Prussia, Napoleon marched into what had once been Poland. Wildly cheering crowds greeted the French emperor; most Poles saw him as the savior who would restore Polish nationhood and regain the territories taken by Prussia, Russia, and Austria. Napoleon did not disappoint them. On November 17, 1806, he declared Prussian-controlled Polish territory the Duchy of Warsaw, and named the former elector of Saxony, Frederick Augustus, temporary head of the new Warsaw government. Napoleon apparently planned to restore the Polish monarchy and to make his brother, Jerome, king of Poland, but that never took place.

In December 1806, an army of 100,000 Russian and 15,000 Prussian troops invaded Poland. It was commanded by General Leon Benningsen, who had taken part in the murder of Emperor Paul I. A series of battles ensued between the invaders and the French army garrisoned in the Duchy of Warsaw, with neither army gaining a clear advantage. On February 8, 1807, near the East Prussian town of Elyau, the armies clashed in a blinding snowstorm. Heavy losses were suffered on both sides, but the outcome remained inconclusive even though Benningsen was the first to withdraw from the field. The snow caused much confusion, and Napoleon himself was nearly captured by Russian infantry when they overran his headquarters. Both sides claimed victory and retired to winter quarters to heal their wounds and reequip.

In June, the armies fought again, at Friedland. Benningsen had planned to surprise the French by attacking across the Passarge River with 90,000 men, but a breakdown in communications lost the day. The original plan had called for simultaneous pincer attacks on June 4, but at the last minute the attacks were postponed until the next day. Because word of the delay failed to reach the commander of the Prussian forces, General Lestocq launched his assault according to the original timetable and was easily driven back by Marshal Jean-Baptiste Bernadotte's superior forces. The tactical blunder alerted Napoleon to the Russians' presence and cost them the advantage of surprise.

On June 14, the Battle of Friedland decided the war. In a day of bloody assaults and counterassaults, Napoleon's 80,000 seasoned veterans overwhelmed their 60,000 Russian foes, driving them from the field. At least 15,000 Russians were killed, 15,000 more were wounded or taken prisoner, and those remaining were turned into a demoralized mob that fled back to Russia. The French lost only 1,400 dead out of 10,000 total casualties.

Czar Alexander now faced Napoleon's Grand Army alone. He could muster barely 30,000 troops to defend Russia against the French, and was only momentarily cheered when a reconstituted Prussian army of nearly 25,000 crossed into Russian territory to escape the pursuing French forces. General Benningsen told the emperor's brother, Grand Duke Konstantin, that the time had come for the czar to stop "the effusion of blood." Alexander acceded to his military leader's advice and on June 19 sought a truce with Napoleon. With his army exhausted from the campaign and a long way from its bases of supply, the French emperor was happy to agree, although he expressed the desire to meet the czar face to face to finalize the truce.

Napoleon met Czar Alexander on June 25, 1807, on a large raft anchored in the center of the Niemen River near Tilsit, on the border between Russia and French-conquered territory. The emperors greeted each other with warm smiles and embraces. Following their talks, each inspected the other's army, and both blamed the war on the king of Prussia, who stood on the river bank as a mere spectator to the historic meeting. Alexander masked his contempt for the little Corsican whom he now had to call "emperor" rather than "general." Napoleon wore a similar mask and later called Alexander a sphinx. When Napoleon offered him the Grand Cross Order of the Legion of Honor, Alexander declined, protesting that he did not deserve such an honor in defeat. Napoleon, ever the master of the scene and the flamboyant showman, replied that to be defeated by Napoleon was "almost equal to victory."

Alexander's resistance to the French emperor crumbled before Napoleon's charm and friendliness, especially when Napoleon made no territorial demands in return for a truce. As a condition of the treaty they signed at Tilsit, Alexander abandoned his Prussian, British, and Swedish allies and agreed to join Napoleon's Continental Blockade, thus closing Russian ports to British trade. The French emperor hoped to strangle Britain by cutting off trade between the "nation of shopkeepers" and the continent.

Returning to St. Petersburg, Alexander rationalized his signing of the treaty by explaining that it recognized Moldavia and Wallachia as within the Russian sphere of influence, opening the way to Russian control of the mouth of the Danube, and freed his army to challenge Sweden's claim to Finland. The treaty also bought Russia time to recover from the Friedland disaster and to bolster her defenses in case Napoleon decided to cross the Niemen River.

The people greeted Alexander's return to his capital with little enthusiasm. Many blamed the twin military disasters at Austerlitz and Friedland directly on the czar. Austria might share responsibility for Austerlitz, but it was almost entirely Russian arms and Russian leadership that had performed so pitifully at Friedland. The merchant class, and the nobles who sold England raw materials, were incensed by the provisions of the Tilsit agreement that forbade all commerce with Great Britain. Many predicted it would cripple the Russian economy: Well over one-half of the 30 million rubles in Russian exports shipped from St. Petersburg annually went to Britain, while less than 1 million rubles worth of goods went to France.

Even Alexander's own family opposed him on the Tilsit treaty. His mother, the dowager empress, railed against her son for allowing Napoleon to make Russia a "province of France." His wife, Empress Elizabeth, thought that her husband must have been hypnotized or placed under some magic spell by the French emperor. Whatever the treaty's faults, Russia was stuck with it, and Alexander would have to make the best of it.

In November 1807, Russia broke diplomatic relations with Great Britain, charging that the British ambassador, Sir Robert Wilson, had circulated a document attacking the treaty and the czar. The following February, Russian troops swept across the border into Finland and quickly defeated the small Swedish garrisons stationed there. In March 1808, Alexander officially incor-porated Finland into the Russian Empire, although the Finns would wage an unsuccessful guerrilla war against the Russians for most of the next year. Ultimately, as a form of compromise, Finland became an autonomous Grand Duchy, with Alexander I holding the title of grand duke.

❖ ❖ ❖

Although Russia engaged in occasional small conflicts along her ex-tended border, during the five largely peaceful years between the signing of the treaty at Tilsit and the outbreak of renewed war with France, Alexander refocused his attention on the internal reforms that he knew were essential to Russia's becoming a modern European state. Unfortunately, his old comrades from the Unofficial Committee no longer advised him, having abandoned him for agreeing to a trade embargo against Britain. Two figures dominated this period of Alexander's reign: Michael Speransky, the son of a priest from Vladimir, and Alexander Arakcheyev, a former official at Emperor Paul I's minor military court at Gatchina and Alexander's inspector general of artillery.

Arakcheyev, a crude, sadistic bully with spartan habits and lifestyle, was elevated to the position of minister of war and assigned to rebuild the Russian army. Alexander seriously erred when he decreed that orders from Arakcheyev were as binding as if they had come from the czar himself. Virtually everyone disliked Arakcheyev for his callous manner, but the officer class hated him, especially after his cowardice at Austerlitz, where he fled from the battlefield, crying that the bloodletting harmed his sensibilities. Behind his back he was routinely referred to as the Gatchina sergeant-major. In Arakcheyev's vision of order in Russia, the czar lived in an armed camp protected from his enemies, internal and external, by his loyal troops.

Arakcheyev's archrival was the cultured, intellectual Speransky, who first came to the emperor's attention while employed on the private staff of the minister of the interior, Count Victor Kochubey. The czar was impressed by Speransky's reports, which the count forwarded to him. In 1806, Alexander appointed young Speransky minister of justice, and two years later he accompanied the czar to Erfurt, Germany, for a conference with Napoleon. Asked by Alexander what he thought of Germany, Speransky replied that although Russia had better men, they, the German states, "have better institutions than we." The czar, who respected Speransky's gift for honest, intelligent observations, replied, "we will speak further of this after returning home."

Soon after, Alexander instructed Speransky to draft a proposal for a new constitution for the Russian Empire. The following October, Speransky laid before the czar a comprehensive plan for restructuring the entire government, a plan that included a framework for a legally constituted legislature and that would convert the autocracy into a constitutional system. Speransky's plan called for a balance of power between the government and the people, elections to fill public offices, the abolition of serfdom, and the creation of a national Duma, or legislative body, that would approve all new laws by majority vote. His plan acquired a great many powerful enemies for Speransky from among the nobility, especially in 1809, when he sponsored two apparently insignificant reform laws. Under the first one, promotion within the expanding civil service would no longer depend on favoritism but on length of service and academic qualifications; government employees who had not attended one of the growing number of universities would be required to take a series of examinations to qualify for promotion. This reform caused an uproar in the civil service, where attention to one's superior's needs were as important, perhaps more important, than qualifications and performance.

Speransky targeted the nobility and the landed gentry in his second reform law, under which men holding court rank would no longer be exempted from serving the state; they would have to serve in either the government administrative branch or in the military. Repercussions from these two laws ultimately led to Speransky's downfall. His simple lifestyle as a high-ranking courtier who refused imperial favors and accepted no bribes despite his proximity to the czar fueled the hatred of corrupt opponents who never understood the existence of an honest man.

Indications are that Alexander may have shared many of Speransky's ideas, but he acted on almost none, except for creating the State Council in 1810 and naming Speransky state secretary. The czar feared widespread opposition from the powerful classes, including his own family, and dilution of his personal authority if he allowed Speransky's constitutional reforms. Speransky's enemies finally ousted him by starting a rumor campaign that he was Napoleon's paid agent. Alexander, who used Speransky as a liaison in secret correspondence

with French officials, knew the accusations were false; however he was compelled to dismiss Speransky to demonstrate that the czar's confidants were
untainted by suspicion. In March 1812, he sacrificed Speransky to pacify the
rumormongers, sending him into exile at Nizhni Novgorod, along the Volga
River, with as much financial resources as the czar could secretly provide.
Speransky's grand design for enlightened reforms remained locked away in the
archives, and Alexander's golden age failed to live up to its promise.

❖ ❖ ❖

In 1809, Alexander was once more occupied with war. Still smarting from
the defeats at Ulm and Austerlitz, Austria saw an opportunity to avenge her
humiliating losses while Napoleon's forces were suffering in Spain and Portugal.
When the British invaded Iberia and began the bloody peninsular war by joining
Spain and Portugal in driving out Napoleon's army of occupation, it cost the
French emperor dearly in men, equipment, military leaders, and prestige. It
forced him to transfer large numbers of troops from Germany to Spain, and
encouraged the war party in Vienna to believe Austria could finally defeat
Napoleon. Austria's Archduke Charles, despite having increased the size of the
army to 300,000 men with a national guard reserve of 150,000 men, knew his
poorly trained and ill-equipped army was not ready. He was among the few
high-ranking Austrians who opposed the renewal of war.

Over the archduke's objections, Austria declared a war of German liberation against France, and Charles led 200,000 mostly raw recruits into Bavaria
on April 9, 1809. Although Charles had little confidence in reports from
Vienna about a German uprising in support of the "liberators," he was surprised
when the Germans failed completely to respond to his call to arms. The
Germans exhibited no faith in Austria's ability to defeat Napoleon.

The renewed hostilities between Austria and France presented Czar
Alexander with a dilemma. He had signed a treaty with Napoleon at Erfurt the
previous year, promising to help him if Austria initiated a new war against
France. Alexander did not want to join with the French in a war against Austria,
but he did want to destroy the Duchy of Warsaw and gain control of Austrian
Galicia. He neatly avoided the horns of his dilemma by assuring Napoleon's
envoy that Russia would "march boldly" against the Austrians while at the same
time informing Vienna's representative that he would do everything possible
to avoid a confrontation with Austrian forces.

Pressured by Napoleon to honor his commitment, Alexander sent 60,000
men into Galicia, but his expedition carefully avoided contact with Austrian

forces. Alexander's real enemy was the Polish army commander, Prince Ponia-towski, who rallied to the French side. Poniatowski complained to Napoleon that Russian losses during the campaign amounted to "two Cossacks killed and two officers wounded, one of them accidentally, as a result of a drunken brawl." After receiving this message, Napoleon screamed at Alexander's representative that more Russians died "in one of your peasant weddings than [in] your entire campaign in Galicia."

Napoleon personally assumed command of his army in Germany, a composite of 150,000 French troops and 50,000 Germans that required only four months to defeat the Austrians. In May the French took Vienna, driving the imperial government into exile. Following a series of indecisive battles, the armies clashed in a climactic battle on July 5 and 6 near the town of Wagram on the Russbach River. By 4:00 P.M. on the second day, Archduke Charles, realizing that the battle, and probably the war, was lost, quit the field and withdrew his forces north into Moravia. On July 12, facing an advancing French army, and with 45,000 Poles threatening his rear, Charles appealed to Napoleon for a truce. A treaty of surrender was signed in Vienna the following October.

Napoleon rewarded the ally that actually fought on his side, the Duchy of Warsaw, by expanding its territory at Austria's expense. Western Galicia was annexed to the Polish duchy. Russia, which failed to deliver its promised assistance, received the tiny district of Tarnopol in eastern Galicia. This was a deliberate insult to the French emperor's false ally. Napoleon further under-scored his disdain for Russian perfidy by granting the Poles a Napoleonic constitution that entitled them to maintain a permanent national army and that freed the serfs within the duchy's territory.

Alexander was horrified and threatened by Napoleon's actions in Poland. He thought of resurrecting an old plan developed by Czartoryski, in which the Polish state would be reestablished under Russian protection, making the czar the savior of Poland, but it was too late: Napoleon had already assumed that role, and the Poles were eternally grateful to him. Napoleon became increas-ingly angry with his reluctant ally when he learned that Russia was circumvent-ing the continental blockade by allowing British goods to enter St. Petersburg on ships flying the American flag.

The Polish situation gained prominence again when Napoleon, who required a son to inherit his empire, in 1809 divorced Josephine, who had failed to produce a son, in order to remarry. Czar Alexander rebuffed Napoleon's overtures for the hand of his 15-year-old sister, Anne. Alexander hinted that he might change his mind if the French emperor agreed to erase Poland from the map of Europe forever. Offended by Alexander's audacity, Napoleon instead sought the hand of the daughter of Austrian Emperor Francis I, the archduchess Marie Louise.

Relations between the French and Russian empires continued to deteriorate. The Russian economy was in a shambles due to the dramatic drop in trade with Great Britain. Alexander was under constant pressure from his nobles to sever relations with Napoleon and reopen trade with the British. He was reminded that before the defeat at Friedland and the meeting at Tilsit, his own representatives had denounced Napoleon as the Antichrist and the messenger of the devil. During 1810 and 1811, the Franco-Russian relationship steadily worsened. Napoleon sought to cripple Britain by sealing off Europe to her goods, including those shipped in neutral holds, especially ships flying the American flag. He considered the American shipping companies as little more than agents of the British merchants. In December 1810, Napoleon annexed several Baltic Sea ports, including Bremen, Hanover, and Lübeck, to ensure compliance. The following month, the French took over the Duchy of Oldenburg, an act that directly affected Alexander. The heir to the throne of Oldenburg, Duke George, was married to Alexander's sister Catherine, with whom the czar had carried on an incestuous relationship for several years. Alexander had specifically included in the Treaty of Tilsit a guarantee of the independence of his brother-in-law's future domain. Napoleon disregarded this part of the agreement. A letter of protest from St. Petersburg was refused by Paris.

On December 31, 1810, Alexander issued a decree removing Russia from Napoleon's Continental System. At the same time, the czar withdrew from the alliance with France. In April 1812, he concluded a treaty with Sweden, which had refused to join France's war against Britain. In return for the security of Russian-controlled Finland, the Swedish government received St. Petersburg's support for its claim to Norway. Two months later, Alexander signed a peace treaty with Turkey. In return for the withdrawal of Russian claims on Moldavia and Wallachia, the Turks gave Alexander Bessarabia. Russia was now at peace with her northern and southern neighbors, and could concentrate on the danger posed by the French, who were obviously preparing for war.

While mending his fences, Alexander had also honed his defenses. He focused on rebuilding his army, transferring troops to his western borders as quickly as they could be trained and shipped. Napoleon, whose army was now more foreign than French, kept a steady stream of troops moving into Prussia, and arms into the Duchy of Warsaw to help expand its army. In February and March 1812, France signed military alliances with Prussia and Austria, although the two secretly informed Alexander that they would not actively participate in a war against Russia.

In May, Napoleon, accompanied by Marie Louise, met with his bevy of subservient German princes in Dresden. From there he proceeded to the Russian border. Napoleon was no longer the lean, quick-thinking, fast moving general of earlier campaigns. In recent years he had spent most of his time at home with his new family. He had grown fat and was fatigued by years of combat. Embarrassed by his appearance, he kept to his tent, rarely making the rousing rides through the lines that had inspired his armies to great victories in the past. His army now was also substantially different than those of the past. Of his 740,000 men, only 200,000 were French. The remainder were Germans, Poles, Dutchmen, Lithuanians, Belgians, Swiss, Italians, Neapolitans, Illyrians, Spaniards, and Portuguese. Austria sent 30,000 men, and Prussia a mere 20,000. Czar Alexander, meanwhile, massed 130,000 of his 450,000 troops to meet the threat of invasion.

Shortly after dawn on the morning of May 24, 1812, several small boatloads of Napoleon's light reconnaissance infantrymen rowed across the Niemen River near the Russian town of Kovno. Their mission was to establish a bridgehead across the river so French engineers could lay their pontoon bridges in place without interference from enemy forces. Once on Russian soil, the soldiers were confronted by a single mounted Cossack officer who rode up to them and asked who they were. "French" came the reply. The Cossack spun his horse around and rode off, chased by a few random musket shots. Another Cossack was sent to give the alarm while the officer and his small patrol watched from the safety of a nearby hill as three bridges were hastily assembled and the invaders quietly marched across. The crossing continued day and night for three days. What followed became known as the Patriotic War; the name would also be applied to another war 129 years later when a German army invaded Russia.

Napoleon's army swept across the western reaches of Russia. Vilna, the capital of Lithuania, fell on June 26 without a shot being fired. Polish lancers were the first to enter the city, which the czar himself had vacated only the day before. Alexander had been attending a ball at the estate of General Benningsen just outside the city when he received the shocking news from a Cossack courier that the French invasion had begun. The Polish lancers, and the troops who followed, were greeted as liberators by the cheering population of Vilna.

The day after Vilna fell, Alexander issued a proclamation calling on his soldiers to recall the glory of Peter the Great when he defeated the Swedish invaders at Poltava. It was the 113th anniversary of that event. Outnumbered by at least three to one, and not realizing that most of Napoleon's army consisted of foreign troops, not the dreaded French forces, Alexander decided to withdraw his army and draw Napoleon deeper into the vast empty spaces of Russia. According to legend, Alexander showed a map of Russia to a French officer who had been sent by Napoleon with the message that the latter still hoped for a peaceful settlement. Pointing to the Kamchatka Peninsula on the eastern edge of Siberia, Alexander told the Frenchman: "The Emperor Napoleon will have to pursue me as far as this to obtain peace." It was a grand gesture that won the admiration of the Russians in the room.

Napoleon's invasion of Russia was ill-fated from the beginning. Typically, Napoleon had developed no long-range plan, nor had he decided on the exact objectives of his three-pronged assault once inside Russia. The French emperor had hoped, and perhaps expected, that the sheer size and power of his army would frighten the Russian emperor into submission. The old Napoleon would have personally led his army in pursuit of the retreating Russians, but the new Napoleon, tired before the campaign had even begun, remained in Vilna for three weeks, untangling the morass of Polish-Lithuanian politics. Finally, deciding not to incorporate Lithuania into the Duchy of Warsaw, he established a provincial government in Vilna instead.

Meanwhile Napoleon's army was trudging along behind Marshal Murat's cavalry, which was hotly pursuing Prince Michael Barclay de Tolly's retreating Russian forces. Alexander and his marshals and generals had no real policy for defending against the invasion other than to retreat until, hopefully at some point, they could muster enough troops to turn back the Grand Army. The retreating Russian soldiers did not practice the scorched-earth policy later cited by Soviet historians as a precedent to justify Stalin's scorched-earth policy more than a century later in World War II: most Russian soldiers were peasants who were loath to destroy the homes and crops of other peasants. But that did not matter because the villages were widely scattered, and the countryside offered little in the way of forage for men or horses. With more than 100,000 horses to maintain, Napoleon's need for forage was extreme, yet he had brought supplies for only one week for both men and beasts. As in previous campaigns, his army was to live off the land. Although this policy had worked well in the forested and cultivated countries of western and central Europe, it was disastrous in Russia.

For endless days the infantry and artillery of the Grand Army struggled to keep up with the fast-moving cavalry as the foot soldiers marched in a blinding dust cloud of their own making. Hundreds of men and horses began dropping almost immediately. Unlike the earlier Mongol invaders, Napoleon's troops were accustomed to a more temperate climate and a more populated environment, with villages and towns in closer proximity to each other. After Napoleon's forces had endured the dust raised by marching troops, mounted horses, and horse-drawn wagons for days on end, a chilling rain offered a brief but dubious respite. The weather, always extreme, exacted a terrible toll on the men and horses. Each night hundreds of men, usually not the Frenchmen, would silently slip away, preferring capture by one of the Cossack bands that regularly sniped at the army's flanks to a slow death in the intense daytime heat and piercingly cold nights. As more artillery horses died of starvation, an increasing number of cannons were abandoned along the road. Bands of soldiers would leave the line of march in search of food, but the Russians had taken all the livestock with them, and there was little or no grain in the deserted villages. Instead of finding food, Napoleon's troops usually fell prey to the Cossacks.

As the Russian army withdrew toward Moscow with the French in close pursuit, the citizens of the old capital became frightened of the approaching invaders. In July, Alexander visited the city to assure the people of his determination to keep the French out of the city. His trip was an enormous success. The population cheered the czar everywhere he went. When he vowed that the fate of Moscow was linked to his own, the people began calling him Alexander the Blessed.

Alexander left Moscow and traveled to Tver to visit his sister Catherine, who was pregnant with her first child. Seeking comfort, the czar was shocked when she chided him for thinking he was qualified to lead the army and reminded him of the Austerlitz debacle. When he asked who should lead the army, she advised him to dismiss the foreigners, the Barclays and Benningsens, and to place a true Russian in charge. Her candidate was Field Marshal Kutuzov. Returning to St. Petersburg, the czar found his mother the Dowager Empress Maria directing the packing of her possessions, which were to accompany her to Kazan, where she hoped to be safe from Napoleon. Empress Elizabeth was the sole member of the imperial family to show genuine courage in the face of a threatened French attack on the capital. She worked tirelessly, nursing wounded soldiers returning from the front and helping the orphans of dead soldiers. Unknown to the public, she donated almost all her state allotment to charitable endeavors. She also comforted and supported her husband as he monitored the ominous news of the invasion's progress.

The main body of the Russian army continued to retreat eastward to Smolensk, where it was joined by an army from the south led by General Prince

Peter Bagration, bringing the Russian combined strength to 180,000 men. The czar and the supreme Russian army commander, Barclay de Tolly, disregarded the recommendation of Alexander's military mentor, the Prussian General Karl Ludwig von Phull, to make a defensive stand at Drissa on the Dvina River. Instead, they opted to continue their withdrawal.

In the first week of August the Russians withdrew from Smolensk, leaving behind General Nicholas Rayevsky with a small rear guard to harass and delay the enemy. Following a bitter, bloody battle, the French seized the city on August 13. Yet before the Grand Army had reached Smolensk and fought its first major battle, it lost nearly half its men to sickness, desertion, casualties, or the need to leave troops behind to garrison occupied towns and keep open communication and supply lines.

The collapse of Smolensk caused widespread indignation in Russia. Alexander's brother, Grand Duke Konstantin, charged Barclay de Tolly with treason, calling him a traitor and an outsider who was leading the enemy directly to Moscow. The aristocracy wanted a Russian to lead the army, not a foreigner. Despite his approval of Barclay de Tolly's performance—Alexander had given him overall command with the admonition that this "is my only army, I have no other"—the czar yielded to the pressure and replaced him with the 67-year-old Kutuzov. The czar had disliked the old field marshal since the defeat at Austerlitz, even though it was Alexander who had failed by ignoring Kutuzov's advice.

When Kutuzov assumed command, he quickly discovered that he had little option but to follow his predecessor's schedule of deliberate retreat. Although arrival cheered the troops, who were gloomy over the constant retreat and looked forward to being led by a Russian, some of the general officers feared Kutuzov had grown too old and too fat for command. Many questioned his mental capacity and eyesight. He had been shot in the head twice, costing him an eye, but the wounds had evidently not affected his brain, although many suspected he was rapidly losing sight in his other eye. The cagey old marshal understood the concerns of his officers and quickly set about proving that his one eye was as good as their two, which was far from true. After secretly sending a Cossack patrol out to stand guard along a road a short distance from his headquarters, Kutuzov took a large group of generals and other high-ranking officers for an inspection tour of the area. Suddenly he reined in his horse and asked who those horsemen off in the distance were. When one of the generals replied that he could not see them clearly, but that he thought they might be a French patrol, Kutuzov answered confidently that no, they were not French, they were Cossacks. His companions were surprised when, as they rode forward, the Cossacks came clearly into view. The marshal's eyesight was not questioned after that.

In early September, Marshal Kutuzov decided it was time to stand and fight a major battle against the invader. His army had increased in size as new recruits and units joined it, while Napoleon's army had rapidly diminished. Kutuzov did not make the decision to fight without relentless pressure from his own generals and the nobles in the imperial court at St. Petersburg. When the armies finally clashed at the little town of Borodino, 74 miles west of Moscow, they were of equal size, roughly 120,000 Russians and 130,000 French and allies, although the Russian troops may have been in slightly better physical condition. On the eve of the battle, Napoleon fell ill with a high temperature and a bad cold, which confined him to his headquarters a mile behind the front line.

Napoleon and his French troops had been elated when Kutuzov replaced Barclay de Tolly. They held all Russian commanders in low esteem, particularly Kutuzov, whom they mistakenly thought responsible for the Russian debacle at Austerlitz. When he saw that Kutuzov intended to make a stand at Borodino, Napoleon decided to give the Russians time to build their fortifications, in order to reduce the chances that the old marshal might end the fighting and withdraw if the tide turned against him. The French emperor, tired of chasing the Russians across the "damnable country side," wanted desperately to fight a decisive battle with the shadowy Russian army; he fully expected to win.

The battle began at 6:00 A.M. on September 7, 1812, with more than 100 French guns firing a relentless bombardment on the Russian lines. The fighting lasted all day, with numerous fortified positions changing hands so often that no one could keep count. Marshals asked Napoleon to commit his Imperial Guard to the battle. At first he hesitated, then flatly refused, fearing that if he committed the Guard and the battle lasted into a second day, he would have nothing in reserve. The Guard commander, Marshal Jean-Baptiste Bessières, had startled Napoleon by reminding him that he was 800 leagues from Paris, a long way to retreat without the Guard's protection if it were to suffer heavy casualties.

At day's end, the battle that Napoleon called the worst of his life had taken a devastating toll on both armies. Russian casualties were at least 45,000, including 23 generals, one of whom was Prince Bagration, who died of his wounds a few days later. French losses were roughly 30,000, including 47 generals. Although the Russians quietly slipped away during the night, uncharacteristically leaving their wounded behind, both sides claimed victory. But if any side could claim victory in this useless battle, it was the Russians, who could replenish their losses in men and equipment more easily than Napoleon, who was so far from his supply bases that they might as well not have existed.

Kutuzov retreated through Moscow, then turned southeast toward Ryazan. He considered Moscow indefensible and refused to expend lives fighting for it. His strategy to preserve his army and chip away at Napoleon's forces depended heavily on the Cossacks. The popular, fearless Cossack hetman, Prince Matvei Platoff, was everywhere, his penetrating dark eyes flashing wordless orders to his practiced cavalry. Under Platoff's skilled leadership, the Cossacks had been harassing the Grand Army since the day it crossed into Russia, and never ceased beleaguering the weary troops and their slow-moving supply wagons and ambulance carts, which had to negotiate miles of open roads stretching from Napoleon's field positions back to Smolensk and Vilna, and finally to Kovno. The attacks became so numerous and effective that Napoleon had to assign as many as 1,500 men and a battery of artillery to defend a single wagon train.

In St. Petersburg, Czar Alexander I was ecstatic with the early reports of the Battle of Borodino. He fully expected to hear that Napoleon himself had been captured. But then gloom set in as additional, more accurate reports arrived, including one from Marshal Kutuzov. The old man knew how the emperor felt about him, but he also knew there was no competent general in Russia to replace him. He simply told the czar, "I venture to say to your majesty that the coming of the enemy to Moscow will not mean the subjugation of the Empire."

On September 14, 1812, Emperor Napoleon entered Moscow. From Sparrow's Hill he had observed the vast city through a field glass, admiring Moscow's thousand churches and monasteries, each with glittering golden domes flashing in the bright sunlight. As his advance guard chanted "Moscow! Moscow!" Napoleon whispered to one of his aides, "So this is the famous city." As the first French and allied troops marched in, they found Moscow deserted, except for its poorest citizens, who had taken advantage of the exodus to loot homes and shops for food and treasures they could never afford to own.

Life in the newly conquered city was hell for the invading force. Moscow's governor-general, Count Fedor Rostopchin had released the city's prison population and granted it amnesty on the condition that it remain in Moscow and set ablaze every building and home occupied by enemy soldiers. These criminals were joined by police agents who had been left behind, disguised as beggars, both to spy on the French and to help set fires.

Napoleon was appalled when he learned that the Russians planned to burn the city to the ground. He ordered the arrest and execution of anyone caught setting fires, but was unable to stem the tide of arson that devoured entire sections of Moscow. Rostopchin had taken with him the city's fire-fighting force, as well as the water pumpers it used, so there was little the French could do to halt the larger fires. With the city facing destruction by its own inhabitants, Napoleon's soldiers began looting for food, then for valuables to take home. Because it had been Napoleon's wish not to cause any destruction in Moscow, most of his troops were camped outside the city, especially the non-French regiments, but once they saw that the Russians were burning everything, they moved swiftly to "rescue" what they could from the flames.

When news reached St. Petersburg that the enemy occupied Moscow, court officials and imperial family members urged Alexander to seek a truce. His mother, the dowager empress, pressed him to write to Napoleon, but he refused. A "truce party," which including Alexander's brother, Konstantin, soon grew up around her. But Alexander stood firm, refusing to even discuss the possibility of a truce.

In Moscow, Napoleon, convinced that the fall of the former capital would bring the Russians to the peace table, waited impatiently for word that never came. During the first two weeks of the occupation, he heard nothing of the Russian army; it seemed to have disappeared. When scouts finally brought news of Kutuzov's army, the French emperor understood what had happened. The "old fox," as Napoleon called him, had placed his army out of harm's way, to rest and recuperate in a part of the country untouched by the ravages of war. Napoleon was trapped in the city he had come to conquer. With winter drawing near, it was too late to pursue Kutuzov or to march on St. Petersburg. Yet Napoleon feared that if he withdrew and marched west, his allies, especially the untrustworthy Austrians and Prussians, would take it as a sign of weakness and not only desert him but attack his columns once they were free of Russia. He simply could not understand why the stubborn czar would not come to terms.

Life in Moscow remained anything but grand for the Grand Army. Although the troops confiscated an abundance of luxury items, such as furs and jewels, they found little food. Nor was there any supply of such important items as boots or shoes. What foodstuffs had been left behind by the fleeing Russians was destroyed in the first fires. Freezing wet weather began to take a heavy toll, and malnutrition had become endemic. Soon soldiers were dying in large numbers from diseases associated with the weather and the food shortage. Without forage, the horses that had been used to pull artillery and supply wagons perished: perhaps as many as 20,000 died in the month Napoleon was in Moscow. Cavalry units began slaughtering their mounts for food. The army was quickly disintegrating within the walls of the vast, ancient city, and its commander in chief could do nothing but withdraw and try to get back to Poland.

The only contact the French forces had with the Russians was between Marshal Murat's cavalry and Hetman Platoff's Cossacks. At one point a casual truce existed between the two mounted forces, which mingled and ate together. Murat was delighted to learn that he was held in high regard by the famous Cossack leader and his men, and that Platoff had once ordered that Murat should not be killed. Captured if possible, but not killed. The Cossacks admired the daring marshal who rode ahead of his troops, wearing his colorful uniform and plumed hat and leading them bravely, with no apparent regard for his own safety.

Meanwhile Napoleon busied himself with mundane chores, time weighing heavily on his hands. He spent long hours reading novels or histories, or playing blackjack, while waiting for word from St. Petersburg that Alexander was willing to discuss a truce. Still, no word came.

In St. Petersburg, Alexander was adamant that he would never communicate with Napoleon; the czar claimed the people were on his side, and he was right. However, his popularity had started slipping in September, with the taking of Moscow, when the Russian population began exhibiting less patience than their czar with the lack of action against the invader. While Napoleon locked himself in the Kremlin, Alexander locked himself in his palace on Kamenny Island in the Neva River, taking long, solitary walks during which he meditated on his and his nation's problem.

That "problem" remained secluded in the Kremlin as September turned into October and Napoleon could no longer ignore the coming of winter. It was ironic that he was quartered in one of the oldest and largest cities in the world, but he could neither feed nor clothe his army properly. There was no food to be had at any price because the peasants refused to enter the city to sell produce, and the Cossacks forced foraging parties to remain close to the city's walls.

The stand-off between the two emperors finally ended on October 17, when Napoleon issued orders to prepare to leave Moscow. One final attempt to offer a truce to Alexander through Kutuzov failed to even bring a reply from the czar. Instead, Alexander sent his soldiers a message telling them: "Either Napoleon or me. We can no longer rule together." The war would continue until every French soldier had been driven from Russian soil.

Napoleon plunged into the preparations for departure. He intended to take every soldier, including the wounded, with him. His plan called for a march to the south, where he could anticipate finding both food and forage, then a turn west toward Smolensk, where he expected to find sufficient supplies to maintain winter quarters. His plan might have worked had he left two weeks earlier, or if the Russian winter had held off for several more weeks.

At dawn on October 19 the Grand Army marched, in some disarray, out of Moscow. Before leaving, the French blew up several Kremlin buildings and set others aflame. It meant little, however, because the city had been all but gutted by the Russians themselves. Although some army units maintained a semblance of discipline, too many soldiers were concerned with taking their booty with them, dragging carts or pushing wheelbarrows full of furs, jewels, and silverware along as they marched. The southwesterly route offered the opportunity of finding food and forage, and also might enable Napoleon to maintain the appearance of advancing against the enemy and not retreating.

Marshal Kutuzov, determined not to engage in another large-scale battle with the French, shadowed the Grand Army's retreat. His Cossacks and army cavalry harassed the enemy, taking thousands of lives as Napoleon's force fought horrible weather conditions, local partisan groups, and internal discord in its struggle to reach safety. Kutuzov only wanted to allow the enemy to leave Russia with as little loss of Russian lives as possible. Too many of his countrymen had died fighting the invader; he merely wanted Napoleon to leave Russia.

In St. Petersburg, Alexander and many of the nobles in his court, few of whom had ever fired a shot in anger or experienced combat, denounced the old marshal. But Kutuzov remained impassive to the cries for revenge from his czar. The Russian army was in only slightly better condition than the retreating enemy, having suffered as much as the French from the subzero weather and food shortages. When the Russian army reached Kovno, where the invaders had first entered Russia and were now departing, it was down to 30,000 men, although reinforcements were on their way from St. Petersburg.

On December 14, the last remnants of Napoleon's army crossed the Niemen. Although perhaps as many as 100,000 men escaped Russia, only 30,000 to 50,000 resembled anything like an organized army. As they retreated through central Europe, their former allies heaped more misery on them, killing many and robbing the rest of the loot they had managed to carry from Moscow.

On December 23, a jubilant Czar Alexander I entered Vilna to a triumphant welcome from his armies, which had converged on the former Lithuanian capital. Alexander distributed countless medals and awards to his victorious forces, including the field marshal who had chased the invaders from Russia. Although the czar disliked few men as he did Kutuzov (Alexander never forgave himself for refusing the marshal's advice at Austerlitz), he nevertheless bestowed numerous honors on the old warrior. The overconfident Alexander now wanted to pursue Napoleon all the way to Paris, but Kutuzov instead recommended that Napoleon be left to the British and the Prussians, who had changed sides, to finish off. "Our men need a good rest," Kutuzov told his resentful emperor, who still chafed at accepting advice. His pride wounded because he had made no genuine contribution to the Grand Army's defeat, Alexander resented Kutuzov even more vehemently. He wrote to an aide in St. Petersburg that he was having difficulty in his attempt "to get rid of the Field Marshal, but it is absolutely necessary to do so."

Alexander was determined to exact a costly penalty from the French for what had happened at Smolensk and Moscow, and in order to salvage his own reputation from the defeats at Friedland and Austerlitz. He had sought to improve his personal image as Russia's leader in the same way as Peter the Great had, but he was no born leader of men who could mount his horse and lead an army into battle.

Napoleon's invasion and the nearly complete destruction of Moscow had changed Alexander. Always somewhat of an introvert, during the months that Napoleon was in Russia the czar had turned to religion and mysticism for comfort. He revealed as much when he said: "The fires of Moscow lit up my soul. I came to know God and became another man."

Over Kutuzov's objections, the Russian army crossed the Niemen and, joined later by the Prussians and Austrians, initiated a war against the new army Napoleon had raised following his return to France. Things again went badly for the French emperor. He lost Spain to the British, his army fleeing Madrid in panic before the duke of Wellington's onslaught. In early 1814, three armies allied with the Russians—the Germans, Prussians, and Austrians—pushed the remains of the French army back toward Paris. When Napoleon, showing flashes of his old brilliance, counterattacked and won several significant victories, the allies wavered and spoke of negotiating a truce with him, but Alexander's determination held them together, and on March 21, 1814, Alexander I, the czar and emperor of Russia, entered Paris at the head of an army of 30,000 men. A representative of the Austrian emperor, who out of respect for his daughter, Napoleon's wife Marie Louise, had decided not to join the parade, rode next the czar. On Alexander's other side was the king of Prussia.

Alexander's younger brother, Grand Duke Nicholas, who had distinguished himself as a military engineer, followed close behind.

❖ ❖ ❖

After Napoleon's first fall, Alexander became more active in European affairs. Influenced by a Baltic mystic named Julie de Krudener, he forced his allies to form a fraternal order of Christian monarchs that he called the Holy Alliance. Many European princes and statesmen paid lip service to the czar's religious coalition, but they privately denounced it as little more than "sublime mysticism and nonsense."

At home, Alexander came under the influence of Prince Alexander Golitsin, a former avowed atheist who professed to have found God and had become a dedicated mystic. Soon the czar himself was absorbed in mysticism and spirituality. Through his influence with Alexander, Golitsin rose to the powerful position of procurator of the Holy Synod, presiding over the Russian Orthodox Church's Supreme Council of Bishops. Alexander also appointed him minister of education. In this influential position Golitsin did Russia serious harm. An educated aristocrat, Golitsin was also the president of Russia's Bible Society; he believed the Bible contained all essential knowledge, and that all other sources of knowledge and education were either useless, untrustworthy, or both. Under his direction, education in Russia, which had been making slow but steady progress among the upper classes, suffered a devastating setback. University library shelves were stripped of their books, and students were given Bibles to study instead. University students were subjected to severe discipline, forced to live in monastic-style barracks, harassed by an extensive network of spies and informers, and required to attend religious services. A Golitsin henchman, Michael Magnitzky, actually accused the czar's brother, Grand Duke Nicholas, of being a freethinker.

After Napoleon's defeat, when Alexander forced King Louis XVIII, whom the allies had seated on the French throne, to accept a constitutional monarchy rather than rule as an absolute monarch, the czar and autocrat of Russia instantly became the darling of European liberals. But Alexander's popularity began to slip when he chose not to aid a Greek rebellion against the Turks.

In March 1821, Prince Alexander Ypsilanti, a Russian army officer and aide-de-camp to the czar, led a Greek revolt against the weakened Ottoman Empire. The rebellion spread rapidly and gained thousands of followers who saw the opportunity to throw off the Turkish yoke. When the sultan's men dragged the patriarch of Constantinople from his church during mass and hung him as he still wore his vestments, Russia was swept by demonstrations demanding that the Russian army revenge the persecution of its Orthodox brothers. Alexander would have been within his rights, contained in the treaty of 1774, had he wanted to rescue the Greeks from the terrible atrocities the Turks were perpetrating on innocent men, women, and children. In fact, the czar flatly rejected a personal plea from Ypsilanti for help. Alexander stood by his decision not to help the Greeks. Europeans and Russians looked on in horror as the vaunted Holy Alliance did nothing to help the Christians against their Muslim tormentors.

Alexander, mesmerized by the mysticism and occultism he studied for endless hours, soon became isolated from his own people. His popularity, which had reached a peak following the defeat of Napoleon, all but disappeared as many of his appointed officials restored repressive policies that had not been seen in Russia for generations. The architect of these reactionary policies was the feared and hated Alexander Arakcheyev, whose official title was minister of war but who functioned more as vice-czar. During the last years of Alexander's reign this cruel, uneducated man was in some respects the actual Russian ruler. He was the czars closest collaborator and the administrator of Alexander's restrictive policies. Alexander apparently slipped into paranoia, imagining conspiracies where none existed, and suspecting plots against him which where never substantiated. In the end, he trusted only Arakcheyev.

Alexander I died of what many believe was cholera during the night of November 19, 1825, at Taganrog, on the coast of the Sea of Azov. He was 48 years old. Only his wife, Empress Elizabeth, who died a short time later, viewed the body before his coffin was sealed. When Soviet authorities opened the coffin a century later to search for valuables to sell on the world market, they reported that it was empty.

Alexander's mysticism, his discussions with his brother Nicholas about abdicating in order to live out his life in meditation with Elizabeth, the mysterious circumstances of his sudden death far from St. Petersburg, and the fact that his coffin was sealed—barring the traditional viewing of the body—gave rise to rumors that the czar whom the people had once called "the Blessed" had not died but had slipped away to the Holy Land to devote himself to the work of God. Eleven years later, a peasant named Fedor Kuzmich appeared in the Siberian town of Tomsk without a passport or other means of identification. Many believed he was actually Alexander I, returned from the Holy Land. The mystery surrounding Alexander's death remains unresolved.

❖ ❖ ❖

Alexander's untimely death created a new crisis for Russia. Because he had no sons to inherit the throne, it should have been passed to his oldest brother, Konstantin, but he had married a Polish woman not of royal birth and had renounced his right to the throne. When Konstantin repudiated his claim to the throne, Alexander had prepared documents naming his second brother, Nicholas, his successor. These documents were sealed and locked away, to be opened when Alexander died. Although Nicholas had some advance warning from his brother that he was to be the next czar, he had no direct knowledge of the documents. Therefore, when the papers were opened, Grand Duke Nicholas was not yet certain whether he wanted to assume the burdens of the office his brother had left him. He hesitated.

Disregarding Alexander's wishes, Nicholas took an oath of allegiance to his brother Konstantin, who was then living in Warsaw with his Polish wife. He also made the members of the Imperial Council and the Imperial Guard regiments swear allegiance to Konstantin. He then wrote to Konstantin, urging him to return to St. Petersburg and assume the throne. Konstantin informed his younger brother that he had already renounced his right to the throne, a fact that had been kept secret until then, and that he stood by that earlier decision. Konstantin made it clear that he recognized Nicholas as the new czar. For two weeks the brothers corresponded, each reluctant to accept the throne. Nicholas's reluctance to take his brother's crown eventually caused a revolt in the capital.

The Russian army's experience in western Europe had sown among liberal-minded guards and regular army officers the seeds of a rebellion that historians have blown out of proportion. The Decembrist revolt of 1825, by liberals who thought they could create a constitutional monarchy, was short-lived; it ended on December 14, when loyal artillery units mowed down demonstrators in St. Petersburg.

Rumors of an impending revolt among Imperial Guard units had prompted Nicholas to stop trying to convince his brother to take the throne. Instead, he had asked Konstantin to return to St. Petersburg and make his renunciation public. Nicholas was not popular with the Imperial Guard, and he feared that if Konstantin's repudiation did not appear to be genuine, the Guard might accuse Nicholas of being a usurper. But Konstantin refused to return to the Russian capital, perhaps fearing that, once there, the pressure to accept the crown would be overwhelming. In fact, he threatened to move even farther from Russia unless Nicholas stopped bothering him about the throne.

What Nicholas probably did not know at the time was that when Konstantin divorced his Russian wife and married Countess Jeanne Grudzinska, czar Alexander had issued a secret manifesto stating that Konstantin's wife and any children she had with him could not be considered members of the imperial family because the countess was not from a reigning family. So, even if Konstantin became czar, any sons he had could not inherit the throne from him. Besides, Konstantin appears to have been very happy living in Warsaw as viceroy of Poland, a post to which Alexander had appointed him.

The revolt, or more accurately the coup, was initiated by men of noble birth who sought a more democratic form of government. Unfortunately, they were less resolute about action than they were about principles. They lacked real support from both the rank and file of the Guard and the St. Petersburg garrison. And from the civilian population they had no support. The plotters had kept their conspiratorial societies so secret that few people even knew they existed or what they represented. They were able to assemble enough troops to mount a serious demonstration by falsely telling the soldiers that Nicholas had tricked his brother into remaining in Warsaw so that he could take the throne for himself. The troops then went into the streets to support Konstantin. Some

Czar Nicholas I

From the collection of James P. Duffy

were told to shout "Long live the constitution," which, through some mental stretch, they thought referred to Konstantin's wife.

No real action was taken against the government, such as it was, and the revolt amounted to little more than a demonstration by some military units showing a preference for Konstantin over Nicholas. When loyal troops fired artillery on the insurgents, the latter immediately dispersed and returned to their barracks. Several leaders and instigators of the revolt were executed immediately, while others were exiled to Siberia. Several smaller demonstrations in other Russian cities were also quickly quashed, and the infamous Decembrist Movement expired having accomplished nothing. The abortive coup ended all discussion regarding who would occupy the throne. On the same day as the fruitless demonstrations in St. Petersburg, the army swore its oath of allegiance to the new czar, Nicholas I.

The 30-year-old czar who ascended the Russian throne in December 1825 was over six feet tall. He had a slightly aquiline nose, his mouth and chin were firm beneath a light mustache, and he possessed an imposing stature with his head always held high. He would wear the crown that he so reluctantly accepted, for 30 years. Nicholas was thoroughly trained as a military engineer and considered himself a soldier, not a statesman. To him, the army embodied the best features of society: order, structure, an absence of contradiction, and clearly defined lines of command.

Perhaps it was his own inclinations, or perhaps it was the liberal revolt that marked the first day of his reign, but whatever the cause, Nicholas was a consummate autocrat. Fluent in English, German, French, and Russian, he had also studied Latin and Greek and was contemptuous of many theories of enlightened education, including those of political economy, public finance, and jurisprudence. He held constitutional law in low regard, viewing "sound morals" as the best theory of law. His reign would mark the high point of absolutism in Russia and see the start of a Russian police state that would outlast his family's dynasty.

In 1826 Nicholas formed the Third Section of the Imperial Chancellery; ostensibly, its purpose was to protect the rights of orphans and widows, but it was actually a political police organization. Its members included large numbers of informants, agents provocateur, and men specially trained in surveillance. Its function was to uncover plots against the czar and conspiracies against the government. Nicholas spent much of his reign discouraging progressive ideas from western Europe from taking root in Russia. His secret police arrested hundreds of students and professors who embraced Western ideas, and earned him the hatred of the intelligent, cultured forces in his society.

The year he organized the Third Section, Nicholas I also introduced a strict policy designed to prevent publication of journals and books that his censors judged to be morally unsatisfactory or seditious. His central committee of censors was also instructed to encourage the circulation of journals and books that were morally uplifting or supported the existence and superiority of autocracy as a form of government.

Nicholas feared the masses, and rightly so. During his reign Russia experienced nearly two dozen peasant uprisings a year, usually fomented by disgruntled peasants who had been denied emancipation from the bondage of serfdom. Nicholas shared Alexander's revulsion for the system, calling serfdom "a flagrant evil." Yet, just as his predecessors, he dared not abolish it for fear of alienating the gentry and nobles whose support was vital to the preservation of the dynasty.

Although history portrays Nicholas I simply as a martinet who wanted to restructure society along the lines of a military organization, he was actually a complex individual with contradictory convictions about government. Despite his having labeled the Decembrists "monsters" whose ideas were in opposition to the basic nature of the Russian people, in private he found their views interesting. He revealed as much in 1828 when he brought back from Siberian exile one of their leaders, the historian Alexander Kornilovich. The czar imprisoned him in relative comfort in the Peter and Paul Fortress and provided him all the books and newspapers he desired. In return, Nicholas requested his views, in writing, on just about any subject Kornilovich chose to discuss. Twenty-two of Kornilovich's memoranda were preserved in the czar's archives; they dealt with a wide variety of subjects, including foreign trade, local administration, and education reform.

Nicholas, like his brother Alexander, inherited from Paul I a "parade ground" mentality. Each of them found routine, close-order drill, in which troops respond as one to their officer's command, exhilarating. Paul, Alexander, and Nicholas loved being on the parade ground, watching their favorite troops drill. However, Nicholas carried this obsession a step further: He wanted to govern Russia as a military colony, with everyone marching as one to a cadence called out by himself as drill sergeant.

❖ ❖ ❖

Nicholas's reign was influenced by an ideology called Narodnost, which, although not directly translatable, is broadly rendered as Official Nationality. Count Sergei Uvarov, Nicholas's minister of education, proclaimed it official government policy in 1833. Based on the three principles of Orthodoxy, autocracy, and nationality, this concept of society imposed severe restraints, especially in education, on the Russian people. In a letter to local officials in charge of education districts, Uvarov said their obligation was to see to it that the education of the people was based on these three principles. "I am convinced," he wrote, "that every professor and teacher, being permeated by one and the same feelings of devotion to the throne and fatherland, will use all his resources to become a worthy tool of the government."

Orthodoxy referred to the unique and important role of the official church in the lives of all Russians, who in return were obliged to give complete obedience to the rituals of that church. Autocracy meant total devotion to the czar as both the absolute ruler of Russia and the foundation on which the state stood. Nationality described the unique Russian mystique that made the people truly dedicated supporters of the dynasty and the Church.

Orthodoxy, autocracy, and nationality were articles of faith for the most reactionary elements of society. The doctrine soon moved beyond the scope of education and became the guiding dogma of the nation. Throughout the land, the cry of "faith, czar, fatherland" was used as a defense against any and all liberal ideas, especially those that challenged the czar's right to rule as an absolute monarch.

The reactionary principles embodied in Official Nationality also determined Russian foreign policy. As most of Europe embraced enlightened liberal thinking, which emphasized national self-determination, Nicholas was increasingly distanced philosophically from his peers elsewhere on the continent. His insistence that international policies could be decided at meetings of monarchs, and that the personal views of statesmen were paramount, would never earn him the respect that his brother Alexander had once enjoyed among the European community of nations.

Alexander had left Nicholas with the problem of deciding Russia's position on the Greek rebellion against the Turks. Despite the treaty that expressly granted Russia the right to protect the Christians living in the Ottoman Empire, Alexander had refused to do so, even though his own army probably could have defeated the Turks in less than two months. The problem festered like an open wound, with most Russians favoring strong military assistance to the Greeks.

Nicholas was unsympathetic toward the Greeks, calling them "rebels" who should obey the sultan's lawful rule. He was motivated more by his affinity for another crowned head of state than by any desire to deliver brother Orthodox Christians from the Turkish infidels. In April 1826, the duke of Wellington, world famous for his defeat of Napoleon at Waterloo, visited St. Petersburg and convinced Nicholas to reconsider, arguing that the czar's abandonment of the Greeks would leave the defense of Christendom to others. The czar now joined Great Britain in demanding that the Turks grant the Greeks full autonomy if they agreed to pay the sultan an annual tribute. When the Turks refused, France, Russia, and Britain declared war on Turkey. On October 20, 1827, a combined allied fleet annihilated the Turkish Egyptian Fleet at the Battle of Navarino, off the Peloponnesus Peninsula. Following the battle, the French and British, perhaps fearing Russian expansionism, lost interest in the cause and withdrew from further action. Nicholas, though, was now committed to the conflict, at least in terms of Russian public opinion, and could do nothing less than prosecute the war to victory.

On April 26, 1828, responding to the forced expulsion of all Christians from Constantinople, Russia declared war on Turkey, and a Russian army invaded Moldavia and Wallachia. It then crossed the Danube and rolled over Turkish defenses, capturing several cities en route to Adrianople, the gateway to the Ottoman capital. Adrianople itself fell to the Russians on August 19, 1829. With Constantinople now menaced by the czar's army, the Turks called for a truce, and in September they signed the Treaty of Adrianople. The treaty gave Russia uncontested access to the Black Sea and the Bosporus and Dardanelles Straits, as well as control of the mouth of the Danube; it also granted autonomy to the Greeks.

In Russia, Nicholas focused his attention on the problems of the crown peasants, the serfs who lived and worked on land owned directly by the czar. Disturbed by the conditions under which they lived, Nicholas removed tens of thousands from local police jurisdiction, under which they had been widely abused, and put them in the care of the Imperial Domains Ministry, under Count Paul Kiselev, which greatly improved their lot, and established the first schools to educate their children.

Nicholas also reached back into Alexander's reign, bringing Michael Speransky out of exile and commissioning him to develop a new code of laws for Russia. Speransky never had time to accomplish this task because he first had to identify and record all of the country's existing laws, many of which had never been written down. This monumental task, which was a great step forward for Russian jurisprudence, produced 45 volumes, plus an index.

Another incident, in Persia, further demonstrates Nicholas I's conviction in the legitimacy of dynastic rule. In 1826, a war broke out between Russia and Persia, the result of several border incidents that had gotten out of control. The Russian army was generally successful, and after it captured a large portion of Persian-controlled territory, a treaty was signed in 1828. The Treaty of Turkmanchai ceded part of Armenia to Russia and gave the Russian navy exclusive rights to the Caspian Sea. When Nicholas was pressed by his advisors to aid an uprising against the Persian shah, who was a member of the long-ruling Kajar dynasty, the czar refused. He insisted that Persia be preserved, and that he would oppose any revolt against the shah.

When news of the French revolution of July 1830 reached Russia, and was soon followed by details of the revolt in Belgium, Nicholas was shocked. Failing to win Prussian support for action against the "infamous" rebels, he decided to act alone and prepared an army stationed in Poland to march west to put down the revolutions and restore Charles X to his throne. Charles was the brother of Louis XVIII, whom Alexander I had been instrumental in placing on the throne in Paris. Nicholas considered it his obligation to sustain the Bourbon dynasty, which had been deposed in the revolution of 1789 and had regained its rightful place after Napoleon's downfall. But before Nicholas could act, the European states, including Prussia and Austria, recognized Louis Philippe, the so-called Citizen King, and so the Russian-led troops never marched. Nicholas withheld Russian recognition for four months, and to demonstrate its displeasure with the way the last Bourbon king had been deposed and replaced by a minor noble who had fought in the republican army, Russia would not resume normal diplomatic relations with France until 1852. The czar's decision to use the Polish army as part of the force he had intended to send to France, however, caused much unrest in Poland, where constitutional government had established a firm foothold.

The successful revolutions in France and Belgium in 1830 inspired another revolt, this one closer to home. Russia and Poland had never enjoyed good relations, especially following the three partitions, which gave Russia control over Polish affairs. Relations had become more embittered when, on May 12, 1828, Nicholas had himself crowned king of Poland. Although he had insisted on using a Russian crown for the ceremony, Nicholas yielded to Polish pride by taking an oath to uphold the Polish constitution. The incongruity of Nicholas ruling in Russia as an absolute autocrat, and claiming the Polish throne as a constitutional monarch, caused widespread indignation in Russia, where his subjects perceived that the Poles enjoyed more rights than they did. Nicholas was not at all happy about being Poland's constitutional monarch—he was a staunch autocrat—but he had accepted the compromise to avoid war with Poland.

The following March, Nicholas reprimanded the Polish senate for giving what he considered to be light sentences to a small group calling itself the Polish Patriotic Society, which was shown to have had links to one of the Russian groups that participated in the Decembrist revolt. Resentment of his treatment of their senate ran high among the Poles, and it eventually lead to serious trouble.

In late November 1830, a group of cadets from the Polish Military Academy forced its way into Belvedere Palace, Grand Duke Konstantin's Warsaw residence with plans to assassinate the grand duke. Simultaneously, a young instructor from the academy, Lieutenant Peter Wysocki, lead another party of cadets in an attack on the Warsaw barracks housing Russian cavalry. Although both groups failed—the cadets did not kill Konstantin and the Russian cavalry drove the attackers off—the rebels did manage to occupy a portion of the city with the help of large numbers of citizens to whom they had distributed weapons. Had Konstantin acted decisively, he might easily have put down the rebellion; instead, he withdrew from Warsaw, taking with him Russian and Polish troops loyal to the government.

Initially, the conservative forces within Poland, including Prince Adam Czartoryski, Alexander I's close friend and onetime foreign minister who opposed Nicholas, saw the revolt as futile and opposed it, fearing that it would bring harsher policies from St. Petersburg. But their trepidation vanished as the revolt spread throughout the country. Although Czartoryski was made head of a provisional government, the radical Patriotic Society held the most important seats.

Konstantin attempted to negotiate with the rebel government. He withdrew across the border, refused to call up Lithuanian army units to put down the rebellion, and recommended amnesty for the rebels. But he refused to endorse the provisional government's demand to reincorporate the Lithuanian provinces into the Polish kingdom.

Nicholas would not compromise with the rebellious Poles. Near the end of December 1830, he mobilized the Russian army and issued a manifesto offering amnesty to the Polish rebels only if they surrendered immediately. The following month, the Polish Diet lashed back at the czar, removing him from the Polish throne and forming a new national government under Czartoryski's leadership. The Diet, which had already proclaimed the rebellion a national movement, demanded the return of Lithuania.

Field Marshal Baron Ivan Diebitsch led a 120,000-man Russian army into Poland in February 1831, to put down the revolt and arrest the leaders of the new government. The Russian force, meeting strong resistance from a courageous Polish army, suffered several defeats and large losses in men killed and wounded. Despite these victories, the Polish cause was doomed, however, because no other country would come to Poland's aid. Without widespread support from their large peasant population, the Poles found themselves often friendless in their own country.

In April 1831, some members of the Diet attempted to win support for the coming war with Russia by improving the condition of the Polish serfs, but the landowners in the Diet prevented passage of a bill they perceived as damaging their interests. The dissension within the Polish Diet and government stifled their ability to function in Poland's best interests as war loomed closer.

Nicholas's response to the Diet's attempt to win the peasants' favor was to issue a proclamation lightening the tax burden on all peasants in the Russian-occupied provinces. The result was that the new Polish government's call to arms against the Russians failed to rally the peasants to the cause.

When Diebitsch died of cholera in June, he was replaced by the notoriously brutal Marshal Ivan Paskievich. Warsaw fell to Paskievich on September 8, 1831 and most of what remained of the Polish army fled across the border into Prussia and Austria, where it was disarmed. The irregular insurgent forces fought on for several months, conducting hit-and-run operations from the sanctuary of Poland's dense forests, but for all practical purposes the revolt ended when the Russians recaptured Warsaw.

As reward for their victory, Paskievich was made prince of Warsaw, and his generals were awarded the estates confiscated from the Polish nobles who had supported the rebellion. Because most of the rebel leaders had escaped abroad, beyond his reach, Nicholas generously commuted 258 death sentences to perpetual banishment. The short-lived Polish constitution, written in 1815, was replaced with the Organic Statute in February 1832. Although the statute included several high-sounding phrases about civil liberties, its true purpose was to make Poland a permanent part of the Russian Empire.

Despite references to elected officials and to a system of checks and balances in the Organic Statute, Poland now was an autocracy ruled by Paskievich in the name of the Russian czar. Paskievich's official title was soon changed to viceroy, and he ruled as the dictator of Poland until his death in 1856. In the interim, Poland, under the direct control of the czar, was Russified. The Russian language was used in secondary schools and government administrative bodies. Estates belonging to the Catholic Church were seized, and Catholic clergymen were put on a regular salary paid by the state. The works of most leading Polish writers were banned, and stringent censorship was imposed.

Support for Russia began to fade in western Europe oven its treatment of Poland. The revolt against Charles X, and his replacement by the so-called Citizen King, Louis Philippe, culminated in France's withdrawal from the Holy Alliance. A creation of Alexander I, the alliance was the vehicle by which the Russian court hoped to maintain a high degree of influence over European affairs. Great Britain stepped in and uncharacteristically joined its archrival, France, in an "alliance of constitutional states." The alliance also included Spain and Portugal, both of which had been freed from Napoleon's domination by the British. The British prime minister, Lord Palmerston, made it clear that the alliance was intended to be a "powerful counter-balance to the Holy Alliance," which was made up exclusively of states still ruled by hereditary monarchies: Russia, Prussia, and Austria.

As his international prestige declined, Nicholas I turned even more intently toward internal affairs. To isolate his people from Western, democratic influences he expanded censorship to mammoth proportions. Virtually every government ministry had censorship powers. Subjects considered seditious or harmful were banned from publication, including philosophy and logic. Books on anatomical and physiological subjects were forbidden to include anything that might "offend the instinct of decency." Authors were not permitted to finish a sentence with ellipsis points, which might indicate there was something more that had to remain unsaid. Books and articles approved by a censor before publication could be questioned again after publication, and the author could be punished even though his work had been approved.

The czar was omnipresent. He made unannounced visits to schools, factories, and barracks, or simply walked the streets of St. Petersburg, not only to observe the people but to control them. He was determined to shield his dynasty from foreign influences by controlling every detail of the lives and thoughts of his subjects. His motto was "obey without discussion." At a time when liberal ideas were gaining ground in even the most conservative countries of Europe, Nicholas created an intellectual barrier between Russia and the West; he was determined to keep his people ignorant.

Czar Nicholas I

During his surprise visits, Nicholas sometimes ordered people dismissed from their jobs for minor infractions of laws or customs that were often known only to the czar. Hundreds of accounts exist of government officials, school teachers, and factory managers having been fired for insignificant transgressions. One account tells of the time Nicholas walked into a classroom while a teacher was giving a lecture. The czar ordered the teacher dismissed because one of his young pupils, although listening intently to the lecture, was leaning on his elbows. People who disagreed with him, or who challenged the concept of autocracy, were imprisoned in institutions for the insane. But there were also examples of the czar's kindness, such as the time when Nicholas entered a building and discovered an old porter asleep, slumped over his desk. On the desk was a message the man had been writing: "I am in despair. Who will pay my debts?" Nicholas leaned over the man and wrote below the message, "I, Nicholas I."

The autocrat relaxed his guard only when he was at home with his family. Although he may have transgressed on occasion, Nicholas was a devoted husband, deeply in love with his wife, Alexandra. He begrudged his time away from her, and complained of being homesick if they were separated even for a few days. He was equally devoted to his children, especially Alexander, his heir apparent. When Prince Alexander married a beautiful Hessian princess, Marie, the festivities lasted nearly two weeks and included a gala ball at the Winter Palace attended by 42,000 people. On quiet evenings with his family around him, the czar of all the Russias liked to have Sir Walter Scott's novels read to him, or to play his cornet. He admired Scott's style so much that he once recommended that Alexander Pushkin rewrite the opera *Boris Godunov* as a novel, "in the manner of Scott."

In 1848, a series of cataclysmic events in Europe confirmed Nicholas's fears. Successful revolutions against monarchies erupted in rapid succession across the face of Europe, beginning in France, where Louis Philippe was replaced by a provisional government dedicated to giving all citizens the right to vote. When news of the success of the Paris revolt reached Vienna, people took to the streets to demonstrate against the government, but their real target was the widely despised reactionary chancellor and foreign minister, Prince Klemens von Metternich. Forced into retirement by Emperor Ferdinand I, who feared the violent demonstrations would bring down the Hapsburg dynasty, Metternich was replaced by a succession of liberal-minded ministers. Each in turn tried to keep the empire intact but failed to balance the demands of various nationalities for autonomy.

On March 5, Hungary acquired autonomy by threatening revolution. Immediately thereafter, the Croats demanded their freedom from Hungary. Later that same month, revolts in Italy replaced the empire's governing bodies with republican forms of provisional governments in Milan, Venice, and Sardinia-Piedmont. On April 13, Hungary declared its total independence from Austria.

As the Austrian Empire reeled from these blows, in June the Czech leader František Palacký opened the Prague Pan-Slav Congress, which demanded equality for Slavs in the German-dominated empire. When the government finally responded to the threatened disintegration of the empire, Austrian troops quashed the Czech revolt and retook Milan.

Meanwhile, in March a bloody six-day confrontation between demon-strators and loyal troops on Berlin's streets forced Prussia's King Frederick William IV to call for a national constitutional assembly. Other German states, fearing mob demonstrations in their own capitals, hastily followed his lead.

In St. Petersburg, Nicholas I watched the chaos with horror and dismay. Having appointed himself the champion of legitimacy in Europe, the czar was determined to defend the Prussian and Austrian dynasties. On March 14, 1848, he issued a personal manifesto informing the Russian people that riots and disorders had broken out throughout Europe and would soon threaten the Russian Empire's own borders. He urged the Russian people to rally around the cry of "for faith, czar, and fatherland" and defend the empire's frontiers.

Nicholas conceded that France was lost to the revolutionaries; although he had briefly considered sending an army to Paris to reinstate Louis Philippe, and had actually assembled an army of more than 300,000 men for this purpose, he quickly discarded the thought. Prussia and Austria, with their borders along Russia's western frontier and with their long-reigning dynasties, were another matter. He offered their monarchs military assistance to put down the rebel-lions. To his credit, Frederick William IV declined the proposal to use Russian troops against his own subjects. But Ferdinand I, realizing that he could not preserve the multinational Austrian Empire without Russian help, gratefully accepted Nicholas's offer.

In June, Russia loaned Austria 6 million rubles, and through the czar's ambassador in London, made it clear to the British government that any attempt by a third party to come to the aid of the rebellious Italian republics would provoke Russia to enter the conflict as a combatant on the side of the Hapsburgs. The following month Russian troops entered Moldavia and Wal-lachia, which were formally parts of the Ottoman Empire but under Russian protection, to put down nationalist uprisings. In August, 1849, the Austrian government invited Russian participation in helping to put down the revolt in Hungary. Marshal Paskevich led 200,000 men into Hungary and defeated the rebels, ending the brief Hungarian independence. That same month, the Austrian army reclaimed its former territories in Italy.

By the following spring, 1850, Frederick William had dissolved the constitutional assembly he had called under pressure. He created a Prussian constitution favoring the wealthy classes on which he relied for support. Even in France, events went badly for the revolutionaries. The middle classes had taken control of the French assembly away from the radicals, and had voted to establish an American-style republic. Needing a strong leader who could contain the numerous mini-insurrections of fringe groups such as the Red Republican anarchists, the French chose as their first president Charles Louis Napoleon Bonaparte, the late emperor's nephew. Following in his uncle's footsteps, Louis Napoleon eventually changed his title to first consul, then finally, in 1852, to emperor of the Second Empire.

The failed revolutions of 1848 left Russia as the most powerful ally of the hereditary dynasties. Nicholas, whom Europeans began calling the "gendarme of Europe," considered himself the guardian of European legitimism and master of central and eastern Europe's destiny. The reality was that after the 1848 revolutions Russia's isolation from Europe intensified and many former friends eventually joined an alliance against the czar's empire. France and Britain viewed Russia as an anachronism, a throwback to pre-republican days. Prussia resented Russia's attempt to interfere in its internal affairs. The animosity between the two countries intensified when Prussia, late in 1848, tried to provoke a conflict with Denmark over control of Schleswig and Holstein. Nicholas defended Denmark's claim to these principalities and threatened to occupy East Prussia if Frederick William IV did not back down. Even Austria, whose empire Russia had helped preserve, resented Nicholas's imperious attitude. The new Austrian emperor, Francis Joseph I, whose mother had induced her husband to abdicate in favor of their son in December 1848, disliked Nicholas, even though they shared similar ideologies. Francis Joseph restored the empire, centralizing control in Vienna.

The collective antagonism against Russia and its czar culminated in Nicholas's greatest catastrophe, the Crimean War. Like many others, the war started over a relatively minor incident: since 1840 a dispute had been smoldering between Orthodox Christians and Roman Catholics over control of some of the most revered Christian shrines in the Holy Land. In 1852, when Louis Napoleon, who was now called Napoleon III, defended the Roman Catholics, Nicholas overreacted. In February 1853, the czar sent an emissary to Constantinople with a demand that the Ottoman sultan, Abdul-Medjid I, who ruled the Holy Lands, settle the dispute in favor of the Orthodox Christians. The sultan, who feared the Russian czar more than the distant French emperor, agreed. However, the sultan rejected a second demand—that he grant explicit rights to all Orthodox citizens living in the Ottoman Empire—which he viewed as interference in the empire's internal affairs.

In June 1853, Russian troops occupied Moldavia and Wallachia to demonstrate the czar's displeasure with the sultan. Nicholas realized that if war came, Turkey likely could depend on French support, and he did not wish to precipitate hostilities with France. However, he was ignorant of the strong anti-Russia sentiments in Vienna and Berlin, and incorrectly assumed he could count on both Prussia and Austria for backing. Although a few peace overtures offered hope that war might be averted, in the end it was unavoidable.

The first preliminary military maneuvers occurred at sea. When Napoleon III learned that Russia had occupied Moldavia and Wallachia, he ordered the French fleet stationed at Toulon into the eastern Mediterranean. Great Britain then sent her Malta fleet into Turkish waters, and warned Nicholas that if a Russian army crossed the Danube, or if the Russian Black Sea Fleet attacked a Turkish port, the Royal Navy would sail into the Black Sea. Strengthened by this support, in September the sultan demanded that Nicholas withdraw his forces from Moldavia and Wallachia. Using bad judgement, however, the sultan failed to wait until his ultimatum had expired before attacking the Russian army.

The early fighting went well for Russia. The Turkish assault against Russian forces in the two Danubian provinces was defeated, although at heavy cost to the lightly armed occupation force. In mid-November, two more Russian victories followed in quick succession. On the 18th, the Russian Black Sea Fleet, under Admiral Paul Nakhimov, was patrolling along the coast of Asia Minor when it surprised a Turkish fleet preparing to sail from the port of Sinop with war supplies. The Russians entered the harbor and destroyed all but one of the enemy's vessels. The next day the Russian army scored a spectacular victory against a superior Turkish force at Bash-Kadiclar.

The sinking of the Turkish fleet in the Black Sea was the catalyst that finally brought Great Britain and France into the war. French and British fleets entered the Black Sea with instructions to protect Turkish ports. The allies warned Admiral Nakhimov that any Russian action against a Turkish port would provoke a response from the combined British and French fleets. This threat left Nakhimov in a quandary. Because he had already destroyed the only Turkish naval presence in the Black Sea, the only option left to his warships was to attack Turkish ports, but the allied threat forced him into inaction.

Britain and France formally entered the war in March 1854. Nicholas announced to his subjects that France and Britain had joined with the "enemies of Christendom" to wage war against Russia, and that the czar and his people were the defenders of the Cross. Soon thereafter, Austria, which remained neutral, demanded that the Russians withdraw from Moldavia and Wallachia, which bordered the Austrian Empire to the east, so as to prevent the war from spilling over into Austrian territory. Not wanting to provoke the Austrians into joining the growing alliance against him, Nicholas acceded to the Austrian demand. When the Russians withdrew, Austria's perfidy was made clear when its forces moved in to occupy both provinces.

The war stalled for a time, as if the protagonists were searching for a place to fight. The Austrian occupation of the two Danubian provinces had driven a wedge through the only European border between Russia and Turkey. The remaining common border was the rough, mountainous terrain of the Caucasus, on the eastern end of the Black Sea, a treacherous region totally unsuited for modern warfare, as the Germans would learn nearly a century later.

When the spring thaw opened Russia's icebound White Sea and Baltic Sea ports to the British, the Royal Navy made short work of the obsolete Russian warships stationed there. Finally, in September 1854, the allies chose the Russian province of Crimea as the location to begin pursuing the land war. A large peninsula protruding south into the center of the Black Sea, Crimea seemed a logical place to start. At the peninsula's southwestern tip was the fortified city of Sevastopol, the largest Russian port on the Black Sea and home to Admiral Nakhimov's Black Sea Fleet.

In mid-September, a combined Turkish, French, and British force of 60,000 men landed at Eupatoria, on the western coast of Crimea, and drove south toward Sevastopol. Prince Alexander Menshikov attempted to stop them with 30,000 troops, mostly raw recruits, but the Russians were badly mauled, in part because they were armed primarily with flintlock muskets, which were no match for the 30,000 modern carbines that the allies had brought. The carbines allowed for more rapid and accurate firing from greater distances.

Meanwhile, Sevastopol prepared for its defense. Most of the Black Sea Fleet's ships, which were useless because the allies controlled the sea, were sunk in the harbor to prevent entry. Some 10,000 sailors moved the ships' guns ashore to defend against the invading army. In December 1854, the allies laid siege to the Russian port. The siege lasted until the following September, when the Russians withdrew.

Although the Crimean War was fought by some of the most powerful nations in Europe, almost all of its military action was concentrated around Sevastopol, as if control of that single port was paramount to victory, which ultimately it was. Westerners remember the Crimean War for the October 25, 1854, battle for Balaklava, south of Sevastopol. In that battle, a British light cavalry brigade made a heroic but useless charge against well-placed Russian artillery and lost more than a third of its men. The action was immortalized in Alfred Lord Tennyson's "The Charge of the Light Brigade."

In Russia, the Crimean War exposed the inadequacies of the autocracy. With all power in the hands of one man, the country was ill-equipped to fight a war. Transportation for troops and supplies barely existed, in part because the czar had built no roads. The troops were poorly trained and, except for the naval commanders, even more poorly led. The Russian army, in desperate need of modernization, was commanded by officers chosen mostly for their ingratiating attitude toward superiors rather than for their qualities of leadership. Corruption among war matériel suppliers was rampant, and the supplies that actually reached the Crimea were woefully inadequate. Russia's defeat in the Crimean War, and the war's impact on the country's future, was a direct result of Nicholas I's incompetency. He had imagined that he could rule his country and conduct its foreign relations simply through the power of his own will, but history showed that he was tragically mistaken.

Czar Alexander II

CHAPTER 18

THE LAST CZARS

NICHOLAS I, CZAR AND EMPEROR OF ALL the Russias, died on March 2, 1855, in the midst of the Crimean War. During the third week of February, the czar had caught a bad cold, which in his usual manner he neglected. Left untreated, the illness progressed into pneumonia, and on March 1, his personal physician announced that Nicholas had only a short time to live. From his deathbed, the czar sent his regrets to the military forces holding out in besieged Sevastopol, and to his son and heir, Alexander, he explained that he had attempted to resolve the difficult problems of the empire in order to leave him a "peaceful, orderly, and happy realm" but had failed. For this he apologized.

"Now," he told Alexander, "I shall pray for Russia and for you. After Russia, I loved you above everything else in the world. Serve Russia." Moments later, holding the hands of his wife Alexandra and his son Alexander, Nicholas quietly slipped away.

When news of the czar's death was made public, the inevitable rumors spread almost immediately. His detractors said that he had been despondent over the failure of his personal autocratic leadership, and that the Crimean fiasco was the last straw that drove him to suicide, although no evidence exists to support this conclusion.

When Alexander II came to the throne at age 37, Russia was in total disarray. The empire's ensnarement in a desperate war against the mightiest powers in Europe was an invitation to others, including Austria and Prussia, to begin rattling sabers, and that had compelled Nicholas to maintain costly defenses along the western border. Alexander knew he had to withdraw from these international entanglements and remedy the internal wrongs wrought by his father if the country was to recover its lost status. In 1855, Russia was a spent country ruled not by a dynasty but by an engorged bureaucracy so openly corrupt that every element of society accepted it as a fact of life. Before his death, Nicholas had acknowledged as much when he commented that Russia was governed more by "bureau chiefs" than by its monarch.

Alexander first had to deal with the countries allied against Russia. Their siege of Sevastopol appeared destined for success, with supplies from Paris and London reaching allied forces more quickly than supplies from Moscow were reaching the Russian defenders. After the fall of Sevastopol on September 8, 1855, and the summing up of the horrendous loss of life suffered by both sides in what amounted to a military sideshow, the Russians and the allies were ready to talk. The allies had lost approximately 100,000 men, the Russians, twice that number. The terrible conditions in the military camps of both sides had spawned a series of epidemics, including typhus, which took more lives than the actual fighting.

Beginning on February 25, 1856, and continuing until the end of March, an international congress met in Paris to settle the peace terms. The resultant Treaty of Paris was unkind to Russia, but the czar had little choice but to accept its terms. Russia relinquished control of the lower Danube, which included the southern part of Bessarabia, the territory around the mouth of the Danube. In addition, Russia surrendered its role as protector of Moldavia and Wallachia to the allied powers, and the treaty declared the Black Sea neutral, thereby barring warships from its waters. Alexander also waived the claim that Russia was the protector of Orthodox Christians living in the Ottoman Empire. The young czar maintained that the price Russia paid for peace was fair.

Freed from the international conflict that had drained Russia's treasury and workforce, Alexander concentrated on domestic reform. A top priority was improving the lives of the serfs. Alexander was not a liberal, as many chroniclers have described him, but he was a practical man. He realized that serfdom would present Russia's progress in the European community. Alexander's pragmatism led to a series of reforms since the time of Peter the Great. Alexander's subjects quickly realized that a new, more tolerant era had come to Russia. In the manifesto announcing his coronation, the young czar granted sweeping amnesties to the Decembrist insurgents and forgave back taxes and unpaid fines. In March 1856, Alexander issued another manifesto declaring an end to the Crimean War and outlining his plans for widespread reform; it concluded with this promise: "May Russia's internal welfare be established and perfected; may justice and mercy reign in her law courts; and may everyone enjoy in peace the fruits of honest labor" under laws "equally protecting all." Between December 1855 and mid-1857, Alexander relaxed the onerous system of censorship, although the applicable laws remained unchanged. He lifted restrictions on foreign travel, and police spies disappeared from university campuses. University lecture halls were opened to everyone, and they soon filled with adults hungry for the knowledge denied to them in their youth. Army officers began teaching peasant soldiers how to read and write. Reform was in the air, and the people, with few exceptions, welcomed it.

Before a meeting of nobles in Moscow in March 1856, Czar Alexander II denied that he wished to emancipate the serfs, but he admitted that emancipation was inevitable and said "it would be much better if it came from above rather than from below." The unspoken word was "revolution." Peasant uprisings had become common occurrences, with hundreds taking place each year. The slaughter of noble families by rebelling serfs had ceased to shock society. The czar recognized, as did most thinking people, that forced bondage was the least productive social structure for farming. Slaves would never produce as much as free men working their own land.

Although he became known as the Czar-Liberator, Alexander undertook his reforms halfheartedly, always torn between his father's traditional policies and the need to change the empire before it collapsed under the weight of its internal oppression. Standing behind the czar, gently prodding him toward reform, was Empress Marie, the beautiful Hessian princess who manipulated what her critics called the "petticoat government."

❖ ❖ ❖

Six years after he ascended the throne, Alexander II took a first, intrepid step to set free millions of serfs. His manifesto of February 19, 1861, released them from their masters' control "in perpetuity." Alexander's original intent in freeing the serfs was to help Russia escape its feudal chains, but reactionary elements among the nobles short-circuited this admirable purpose.

At a time when Russia was developing a money economy amid pressing domestic competition for markets for the agricultural and industrial products produced by serf labor, the idea of holding people in bondage was an aberration. Smaller landowners could no longer afford to pay for the upkeep of serfs who failed to produce on a par with free labor. Prior to the manifesto of February 1861, many landlords, deep in debt from trying to feed and clothe their serfs, welcomed talk of emancipation. Large estate owners, who could be counted on to oppose their own best interests in favor of maintaining the status quo, resisted the czar.

Back in 1856, faced with opposition from the powerful nobility, Alexander had initiated the process of emancipation by first easing press restrictions that had prevented public examination of the question of serfdom. But the catalyst that began the actual process of emancipation came from landowners in the three provinces that had formerly been Lithuania. They proposed to free their serfs without giving up their land holdings. Although this proposal was a step in the right direction, it presented a fresh problem. How would the freed serfs, most of whom tilled the soil, earn a living if they had no land to work? Alexander's solution was to free the serfs "with land."

In 1856 the czar established a series of committees to settle the details of emancipation, but they failed to reach a solution. They wrestled unsuccessfully with such questions as how land would be distributed to the emancipated serfs, who would own the livestock presently on the land, and who would pay the landowners for the land given to the freed serfs. In December 1856, Empress Marie complained about the flagging progress toward emancipation, blaming the resistance on the ignorance of those "in high places." Calling the situation serious, she wrote to her brother: "the czar's position [is] very difficult, since people show little or no sympathy with him. But thank God he is not losing courage."

Taking hold of the situation in late 1857, Alexander finally got the process moving by ruling that serfs would have the right to buy land, along with the livestock and houses on it, at the time of their emancipation. The following year, committees of landed gentry were established in all the provinces to help develop procedures for the emancipation. The committees sent recommendations to a central committee in St. Petersburg, which finalized how and when emancipation would take place.

On February 19, 1861, two months before the opening salvos of the American Civil War, which abolished slavery in the United States, Alexander II proclaimed an end to serfdom in Russia. News of the proclamation was greeted by cheering crowds throughout the country, and Alexander was hailed as the Czar-Liberator. Unfortunately, the new freedom for Russia's peasants was not without drawbacks. The procedures for ending serfdom were cumbersome and complex, and it was some time before the peasants realized that their new freedom was illusory.

In 1857, Alexander II had decreed that once freed, serfs would have the right to own land. He foresaw a system whereby the government would purchase plots for them from landowners. This idea died when it became clear that the government did not have the money to do so. As the framework for emancipation evolved following Alexander's manifesto of 1861, it was decided that the serfs could not own land individually, but only as members of communes. These communes were governed by the landed gentry, who once again controlled their former serfs. It soon became clear to everyone that the czar had merely altered the feudal system, not abolished it.

An assembly of nobles in Tver, having considered the potential consequences of partial emancipation (notably, continued rebellions), wrote to the czar in 1861, offering to forgo some of the rights and privileges accorded them in the proclamation in favor of a genuine emancipation. The peasants eventually realized that the proclamation, which had been read to them because they could neither read nor write, did not guarantee the freedom they had been led to expect. Unrest spread rapidly across the countryside; in one rebellion, at Bezdna, in Kazan province, 150 peasants were killed or wounded before Cossack troops put an end to it.

The peasants did not criticize the czar because they wrongly believed that he truly intended to free them. Instead they blamed government bureaucrats and the landowners themselves. The serfs, who made up 45 percent of the population, had expected to be freed from their servitude, and when they learned they had been deceived, they were angry. Disappointment with the emancipation, and anger over the installment payments and taxes that the peasants owed for the land, spawned an unrest that would plague the Russian Empire for the next 56 years, until the Romanov dynasty was brought down.

❖ ❖ ❖

Having accomplished what he thought he could do for the serfs, Alexander turned his attention to improving the efficiency of local governments. Local
administration continued to depend on the central government in all matters.
The czar meant to correct this by instituting a form of self-government based
on an assembly of local elected members, called the zemstvo, meaning "of the
land—the community." The law he signed in January 1864 was based on
proportional representation, and the zemstvo system of local government was
the closest thing to a democracy that had been seen in Russia in a long time.
Each local zemstvo was empowered to select a board to govern its own district.
The board, which could hire professional advisors, was responsible for providing
a range of services, including medical and veterinary services, education, road
construction and upkeep, and maintenance of food reserves for emergencies.
The zemstvo system in rural Russia lasted until 1917, and was instrumental in
delivering improved social services to the peasant population.

In November 1864, Alexander II addressed judicial reform by introducing
a series of laws that dramatically changed the administration of justice in Russia.
Until then, Russian courts had been riddled with corruption and cumbersome,
semisecret laws and practices that enabled the wealthy to buy justice but denied
equal treatment to those who could not afford to bribe court clerks or judges.
Alexander's reforms created an entirely new judicial system modeled on that of
France. Landowners, who had been judges in the old system, were removed from
that post. New lower courts were created, and a system of appeals was instituted.
Antiquated prejudicial procedures were replaced with a uniform system of
prosecution and defense, and everyone was assumed to be equal before the law.
Criminal cases were no longer investigated by the police, but became the
responsibility of an examining magistrate, and juries were introduced to insure
that defendants received a fair trial. With few exceptions, court trials were
opened to the public. Although the principles embodied in Alexander's judicial
reform acts were not uniformly applied, and equality before the law was rather
inconsistent (some bureaucratic practices from the old system carried over to
the new), the basic principle of an independent judiciary would survive until
the Bolshevik Revolution.

The year 1864 also saw a new approach to education. Secondary schools
were opened to students of all social classes, work began on a system of primary
schools, and universities were given a large measure of autonomy. But education
reform, which got off to a halting start under Education Minister Alexander
Golovnin, who was appointed to the post in 1861, did not last long after
students began demonstrating against laws governing their activities. An

abortive attempt on the czar's life on April 14, 1866, brought education reform to a complete stop.

The attempted assassination took place as the czar was returning to his carriage following a walk in the Winter Garden in St. Petersburg. A crowd, anxious to catch a glimpse of Alexander, had gathered around the carriage. In the crowd was a young nobleman named Dmitri Karakozov, who was a member of a small communist student group. Evidently, some members of the group had discussed assassinating the emperor but rejected the idea. Allegedly mentally unbalanced, Karakozov decided to take it up on himself to eliminate the Czar-Liberator out of fear that Alexander's reforms would deradicalize many students.

As Alexander approached his carriage, Karakozov raised his arm and was about to fire a pistol when a young peasant man saw the gun and struck Karakozov's arm, sending the shot harmlessly into the pavement. Alexander heaped many rewards on the peasant, including enough money to sustain him in luxury for life. Karakozov was arrested. Weeks of interrogation produced no evidence of a conspiracy, only the perpetrator's admission that he had attempted to kill Alexander in order to draw attention to the plight of the peasants. Declared "unbalanced of mind," Karakozov was tried under the new system of justice, found guilty, and eventually hanged.

The assassination attempt, although probably nothing more than the act of an "unbalanced mind," as the court had found, changed Russia's direction. Those reforms already in effect could not be undone. However, Karakozov's single shot frightened Alexander into slowing the reform movement almost to a halt. The incident was the first attempt on an autocrat's life by someone other than a family member or a pretender who sought to usurp the throne. Karakozov's bullet introduced a new form of citizen protest—assassination.

Before the would-be assassin fired his bullet, Alexander II had undertaken one other critical reform. The Russian army had proved to be an inefficient bureaucracy incapable of winning a war, even one as limited in scope as the Crimean. Russia's enemies had thrown less than 70,000 men against Sevastopol. Alexander should have been able to send 10 times that number to Crimea and destroy the allied army, but the antiquated bureaucracy that ran the army was too reactionary (i.e., rank was based not on merit but on family connections and politics) and corrupt (with money for contractors funnelled into officers' pockets) to meet the challenge. The czars were partly to blame for failing to place more emphasis on the construction of roads and railroads, which could have sped supplies and reinforcements to the beleaguered city, but it was the army high command and its bureaucrats who had hampered every attempt at modernization. The individual Russian soldier had been courageous in the face of the enemy, but his equipment and training had been badly outdated, and his leadership inept. Russia should never have lost the Crimean War. Had the country had anything resembling a modern army, the allies would have been driven into the Black Sea within weeks of their arrival in Crimea. That this did not happen was due in part to the army's command structure, where old men held their posts long after their skills had deteriorated. Many had grown wealthy dealing with corrupt suppliers who filled their pockets while sending the troops inferior equipment.

Moreover, until the reforms of 1874, the army had relied on conscription among the peasants and serfs for most of its soldiers. A serf could buy his freedom by serving 25 years in the army. In addition, criminals were regularly sentenced to a term of enlistment in the army as their punishment. Treatment of these men from the lower classes was harsh, with corporal punishment a regular part of life. Few joined the army out of a sense of duty. Most enlisted to escape the dreary life of a serf, others to avoid prison, and still others for the opportunity to receive a regular meal and clothes. Russian society regarded the army as a vast penal colony.

Czar Alexander tried to make conscription practices fair. Previously, a village or estate had been assigned a quota of conscripts, based on the size and tax base of the estate on which it was located. The nobility and the gentry had been exempt from conscription, and members of some other classes, such as merchants, had been able to buy their way out of the army by paying someone to take their place. The new system reduced the term of a conscripted soldier's enlistment to six years of active duty, followed by nine years in the reserves, and then five more in the militia. Conscription was made universal for every able-bodied male who had reached the age of 20. Graduates of primary and secondary schools were allowed to "volunteer" instead of waiting for conscription, and they served less time on active duty. University graduates served even shorter terms of active duty, provided that they also "volunteered" their services.

Alexander improved living conditions in the new army, and he drastically curtailed corporal punishment, except in punishment battalions. Under his reform-minded war minister, Count Dmitri Miliutin, privates were introduced to classes in reading and writing. Alexander planned to replace his large, costly, and poorly trained army with a smaller, more professional, and better led force that could call on trained reserves in times of emergency. In some ways the army, through universal conscription and the efforts at rudimentary education for the peasant soldiers, became the forerunner of social and equality in imperial Russia. The officer corps was stripped of the very old and infirmed, and new military schools began the process of educating future officers.

Except in the army, where reform continued to make slow progress, all reforms ceased when Karakozov tried to shoot Alexander II in April 1866. The czar, who had embraced reform not out of principle but because of selfish motivation to preserve the empire and the autocracy, reexamined his decision. Convinced that the would-be assassin was part of a student plot against his life, Alexander removed Golovnin as education minister and replaced him with the tyrannical, reactionary Count Dmitri Tolstoy. The new minister reintroduced oppressive controls on university students' activities, including supplanting the study of the natural sciences with study of ancient Greek and Latin. The universities were seething with radical revolutionaries, and the fact that the would-be assassin was from a noble family, which was purely coincidental, chilled Alexander's relations with the nobles.

❖ ❖ ❖

It is ironic that the system developed to facilitate the emancipation of the serfs, complex and unworkable as it was, was the brainchild of the Russian intelligentsia. Because the men who created it had little understanding of the peasant mind, they could not foresee that the former serfs would look on the new system, which placed them in debt to their former masters for decades to come, as merely another form of bondage. As a result, the millions of newly freed serfs disdained the communal system; they demanded their own property but refused to buy it from the landowners. They expected the czar to take land from their former masters and give it free of charge to the peasants. The intelligentsia never understood that this was the peasants' concept of freedom, not long-term financial obligations to their former masters. The peasants' disillusionment with emancipation stirred sporadic violence around the country, and the Cossacks were kept busy putting down their uprisings. Instead of analyzing what had gone wrong, and working to correct it, the intelligentsia reflexively opposed the czar, refused to credit him for reforms already in place, and identified (or at least tried to indentify) with the peasants.

With their rather romanticized vision of peasant life, and with their false assumptions about the democratic aspirations of the peasants, radical intellectuals and university students in 1874 organized themselves into secret societies, where they sought to nurture the spark of revolution. They imagined that the assemblies at the heart of a peasant village could form the basis for revolution against the autocracy. Their failure to incite large-scale revolt was in part due to the fact that most peasants remained absolutely loyal to the czar, their "little father"; they condemned government bureaucrats and landowners, who they believed failed to follow the czar's orders.

It was this idealism, coupled with a populist belief that revolution would come from the masses, that drove nearly 3,000 young male and female radicals to join a crusade called "going in among the people" beginning back in 1873. Although a few young people moved into remote peasant villages with pure motives, such as bringing medical and veterinary services to the peasants, most were determined to radicalize a population that they believed was waiting to hear their call for freedom from the autocracy. They proved to be badly mistaken, for the peasants generally distrusted these newcomers and often reported their activities to the police. Peasant loyalty to the czar held firm against the radicals' high-minded talk of democratic institutions and socialism. Disillusioned by their failure, those who managed to avoid arrest returned to the cities and, by 1877, turned to violence to achieve their goals. Assassination became one of the chief political weapons of the time. Opposition to the government was centered in groups with names such as People's Will and Land and Freedom, which were dedicated to political assassination.

Early in 1878, a woman named Vera Zasulich shot and seriously wounded General Dmitri Trepov, the St. Petersburg chief of police. Rather than fleeing after firing the shot, Zasulich gladly surrendered and confessed that she had shot Trepov because he had ordered the flogging of a prisoner who had refused to remove his hat in Trepov's presence. Despite her confession, a jury acquitted her of attempted murder. When the police attempted to rearrest her, she was spirited away by a revolutionary group and later surfaced in Switzerland.

Emboldened by the Zasulich case, other radicals turned to politically inspired murders. In quick succession, chiefs of police and governors in at least a half-dozen cities were killed. By 1879, the terrorist groups, which had grown in number despite the fact that their memberships never reached more than a few hundred, had decided to focus all their assassination efforts on the Czar-Liberator himself. On April 2, a member of the Land and Freedom group, Alexander Solovev, fired five shots at the czar, none of which struck their target. In November, members of People's Will, operating from a building alongside the Moscow railway, tunneled under the tracks and set off a large explosive as the czar's train passed above. Alexander II, who was returning from a tour of Crimea, escaped injury because he was not in the car directly above the bomb. In February 1880, a carpenter named Khalturin obtained employment at the

Winter Palace. Over several weeks, he smuggled sticks of dynamite into the palace and hid them. He later placed the explosives in the dining room; a timer was set to detonate the explosives after the czar had entered the room during a state dinner. The blast killed 11 guests and wounded 55 others, but Czar Alexander, who was delayed in another room by a guest, was unharmed.

Faced with repeated attempts on his life, Alexander II increasingly turned to repressive measures to stop the terrorists. But the security forces appeared helpless in protecting the czar, who remained alive purely by luck. The abortive railroad sabotage, the explosion in his own dining room, and the blasé attitude of the educated classes toward the attempts on his life shook Alexander to his core. He was despondent because hardly any of his subjects cared whether the assassins succeeded or not.

Convinced that repressive measures would not remedy the problem, Alexander reverted to reforms and more liberal ministers. Soon after the explosion in the Winter Palace, he appointed General Count Michael Loris-Melikov to head a special commission charged with both suppressing terrorism and recommending reforms that would get at the root cause of the attacks and the public's apathy toward them. The commission, largely composed of liberals and moderates, recommended that an elected body representing all classes of the population should serve the czar in a consultative capacity. This was the kind of reform that might lead to the creation of a representative legislature. But it was never tested, for on March 13, 1881, the very day Alexander signed the documents implementing the recommendation, the few remaining People's Will activists made a final and successful attempt on the czar's life. The revolutionaries feared that the special commission's recommendation would find widespread support among Russia's more moderate liberals. By allowing local assemblies to send representatives to a nation council, the czar would be giving the people a voice, no matter how small, in the government.

It was Sunday, and the czar had attended the parade at the Michael Riding Academy. He was returning to the Winter Palace in his armored coach, which was escorted by six Cossacks and accompanied by two sledges containing police and court officials. Because Alexander was late for a 3:00 P.M. meeting, his coach driver chose a shortcut: leaving the protected route patrolled by plainclothes policemen, the czar's coach rushed along the Catherine Canal. A man suddenly stepped into the nearly deserted roadway and threw a parcel in front of the horses pulling Alexander's coach. The explosion reverberated for blocks, drawing citizens and police to the scene. A gasp rose from the gathering crowd as

From the collection of James P. Duffy

Czar Alexander II

Czar Alexander emerged, uninjured, from the smoking wreckage. A small boy and two Cossacks lay in a large pool of blood in the street.

The police officials and the Cossacks urged Alexander to mount one of the sledges and continue the trip to the palace, but the czar hesitated out of concern for the wounded. After Alexander was assured that they would be cared for, an officer remarked, "Thank God your majesty is safe." The czar, gesturing toward the wounded, responded, "Yes, thank God, but look at these. . . ." He never finished his sentence, for just then another assassin stepped from the crowd and shouted "Too early to thank God" as he hurled his bomb directly at Alexander. When the smoke and blown snow cleared, nearly two dozen people lay dead or dying. One of them was Alexander II. His abdomen blown open, both legs crushed, and his mutilated face streaming blood, the czar managed to implore a Cossack officer, "Quickly, home to the palace, to die there." In the freezing rain outside the palace, more than 10,000 people soon gathered to await news of their czar. Many, bareheaded in the snow, knelt and prayed for his recovery. Within two hours the Czar-Liberator was dead, and Russia's last hope for a constitutional government died with him. Although the many failed attempts on Alexander's life had drawn little sympathy from the urban population, his assassination was a different matter. Suddenly, thousands of upturned faces saw Grand Duke Vladimir step out on a balcony to announce that the czar was dead.

The news spread rapidly throughout the country, plunging Russia into a state of shock. Nearly every segment of society mourned the czar. The liberals sought to distance themselves from the revolutionaries, including those who earlier had brightened the salons of high-society matrons with their titillating talk of revolution. The peasants, even those who had been cheered by the terrorists' daring escapades against local police officials, were horrified by the murder of their "little father." The more conservative elements called for additional repressive measures against the radical groups, and for death sentences for anyone found to be connected with the assassination.

The assassination of Alexander II brought to the Russian throne his son, Alexander III. The revolutionaries had killed the czar in order to stop the reforms that might cost them what little support they had among the population. Although almost all of those connected to the assassination were arrested and executed, they did achieve their primary goal. The son of the Czar-Liberator opposed most of his father's reforms.

Alexander III was a powerfully built, honest, decisive man whose conservative leanings were fortified by a clear mind and a singular confidence. His views had been reinforced by the failure of his father's reforms to settle the violence in the country, as well as by the numerous attempts on his father's life and the brutality of its ending.

❖ ❖ ❖

Born in 1845, Alexander III was the second son of Alexander II and Empress Marie, the former Princess Dagmar of Denmark. His older brother, Nicholas, died of spinal tuberculosis when the latter was 22, leaving the broad-shouldered Alexander, who entertained his son and his nephews by tying fireplace pokers into knots, as the heir apparent. Alexander III, who often has been called the last autocrat, set the tone for his reign just minutes after his father died, when the chief of police asked him if he had any orders. The new czar replied: "Orders? Yes, of course. The police have apparently lost their heads. The army will take charge of the situation."

His father's assassination changed forever the empire that Alexander III's forebears had ruled for generations. Fifty years later, Grand Duke Alexander, the cousin of Alexander III and a close member of the imperial family, reported how he, as a boy of 15, had felt about the future at the time of the assassination.

> We knew that something immeasurably greater than a loving uncle and a courageous emperor had receded with him into the past. Idyllic Russia, the country of the ruling father and obedient sons, ceased to exist on March [13], 1881. Never again would a Russian czar be able to think of his subjects in terms of boundless confidence; never again would he be allowed to give his undisturbed attention to the cares of the state. The romantic traditions of the past and the sentimental conceptions of sovereignty followed Alexander II to his tomb in the Fortress Peter and Paul. They too were mortally wounded by the explosion that tragic Sunday, and nobody could have denied that the future of the empire, possibly of the entire world, depended upon the issue of the coming contest between the new czar of Russia and the fast increasing forces of destruction.

In 1866, Grand Duke Alexander, the future Czar Alexander III, had married a Danish princess, Sophie Frederica Dagmar, whose sister, Alexandra, later married the future king of England, Edward VIII. The couple led a happy life, one free of the romantic affairs that had plagued the marriages of earlier czars. Alexander had preferred the quiet life of his country estate to the pomp and ceremony of St. Petersburg, and once there as czar he surrounded himself with a small group of family members and friends, for whom he occasionally played the trombone in a quartet. He was a devoted husband to Princess Dagmar, now Empress Maria, and a doting father to their five children, all born between 1868 and 1882.

Alexander III was not a man of great imagination, but he was a hard worker and a conscientious monarch whose most outstanding characteristic was his straightforward manner in handling problems. He was a firm believer in the almost forgotten policies of his grandfather, Nicholas I: Orthodoxy, autocracy, and nationality. To him the crown was Russia, and Russia was the crown. Recognizing, as his father had not, the dangers of remaining visible in St. Petersburg, Alexander moved himself and his family to Gatchina Palace, an estate some 40 miles west of the city. Although the police were unable to protect the imperial family in the sprawling capital, at Gatchina the czar could isolate

himself not just from assassin's bombs but also from the never-ending round of
balls and dinner parties he found so tiresome. There he could work in peace.

Within hours of his father's entombment, Alexander announced sweeping changes in the government. He replaced virtually every high official of the
former reign, including Count Michael Loris-Melikov, whose special commission was disbanded and its recommendation forgotten. At first, there had been
speculation that Alexander might embrace the commission's recommendation
as a part of his father's legacy, but these hopes were dashed when Constantine
Pobedonostsev stepped forward as the new czar's primary advisor. Frequently
called the Black Czar, Pobedonostsev was a former professor of civil law at
Moscow University and the procurator of the Holy Synod. He had also been
Grand Duke Alexander's tutor. Pobedonostsev hated the West, distrusted
liberal institutions such as parliaments, and thought Russia should be governed
on the principle of autocracy and the devotion of the peasants to the throne.
Pobedonostsev was also the principal tutor to Alexander III's son and heir,
Nicholas. His would exert immeasurable influence on the regimes of both men.

By the summer of 1881, a set of regulations tantamount to martial law
was put into effect. The Temporary Regulations were intended to remain for
three years in order to allow the government to deal with terrorists. In fact, they
would stay in effect until the dynasty fell. A series of "counterreforms" followed,
most conceived and drafted by Pobedonostsev and all designed to correct the
"errors" of the previous czar. At the end of April 1881, an imperial manifesto,
probably written by Pobedonostsev, proclaimed that Alexander would rule
Russia with "complete faith in the strength and truth of absolute power." That
absolute power was manifested in a return to harsher times in Russia. In 1884,
the University Statute abolished the autonomy of the universities and forbade
students to form or join any kind of organization. In 1889, the laws governing
the election of local assemblies were amended to favor the nobles and the
gentry. The following year, a new law established the position of land captain;
the person holding that title would serve at the pleasure of the minister of the
interior and exercise control over the activities of the peasants, thereby indirectly restoring the old form of centralized government in the countryside.

❖ ❖ ❖

Alexander III's reign was distinguished by two principles that dominated
much official thinking: Russification and anti-Semitism. The czar was totally
committed to the idea that Russians were superior in every way to the other
nationalities that lived within his empire. At the time, there were more than

150 different nationalities in Russia, many with their own distinct languages, religions, and customs. Alexander established Russian as the empire's official language, and Russian settlers were sent to various regions with the objective of making indigenous populations minorities in their own provinces. The Catholic Poles and the Lutheran Baltic Germans came in for special treatment at the hands of St. Petersburg's nationalistic bureaucrats.

Jews in particular were singled out for harsh treatment during Alexander III's reign. Discrimination against Jews was not, of course, restricted to Russia, nor was it introduced by Alexander III. According to Grand Duke Alexander, the czar's cousin, "the Jews began to suffer persecution in Russia only with the advent of the rulers whose blind obedience to the dictates of the Church proved stronger than their understanding of the spirit of a great empire." One of the few rulers who disregarded the anti-Semitism of the Orthodox Church leaders was Nicholas I, who had turned back a churchman's anti-Semitic project with the comment, "The czar of Russia cannot divide his subjects into Gentiles and Jews."

Under the reign of Alexander II, Jews, especially wealthy ones, had welcomed the czar's efforts to "fuse this people with the native inhabitants." Many of these Jews had desired to move out of the Pale of Settlement, a collection of 15 provinces in southwest Russia and Poland that had been redefined in 1825 as the only place within the empire where Jews could live. (In 1791, Catherine II had set up the original Pale of Settlement in the same area, then a group of 25 provinces where Jews were allowed permanent residence.) Jews were not permitted to own or work the land, they could not employ Christians as servants, they were not permitted to speak Hebrew, and, except for a small number of the wealthiest merchants, they were restricted from traveling to St. Petersburg.

The first few years of Alexander III's reign were marked by an increase in official anti-Semitism and by numerous pogroms against Jews. The czar summed up his attitude toward Jews in a comment he made after reading a police report about violence against them: "I am glad in my heart when they beat the Jews, but it cannot be permitted." Restrictions on travel and employment of Jews increased. In 1886, Jews were removed from all posts in the judiciary and excluded from all government administrative positions. The same year, the number of Jews permitted to enter universities was restricted to 10 percent of the student population, even at universities located in the Pale of Settlement. The Jews would fare no better when Alexander's son, Nicholas II, came to the throne.

Jews struggled as best they could in Russia. They considered themselves as Russian as the average Orthodox peasant, but in the end, many who could afford to do so left the empire, emigrating as far away as the United States. Others, especially the young men and women, were welcomed into revolutionary groups.

❖ ❖ ❖

As a young man, Alexander III had come under the influence of the ideology of Pan-Slavism, which promoted a worldwide Slavic nationalism. Despite the fact that he was almost purely German and had scarcely a drop of Russian blood coursing through his veins, as czar, Alexander harbored an intense dislike for Germany and the Germans. He often proclaimed, "Russia for the Russians." Alexander, who loathed the emperor of the recently formed German Empire, flatly rejected the efforts of Kaiser Wilhelm and Chancellor Otto von Bismarck to persuade the czar to join in a Russo-German alliance when they visited St. Petersburg in 1885.

Although much of Alexander's attention was focused on internal affairs, the czar could not ignore international tensions. After all, Russia was a vast empire that had participated in European affairs for decades. Alexander proved to be as single-minded concerning Russia's sphere of influence in international affairs as he was with domestic issues.

Bulgaria, which was in the Russian sphere of influence as defined by Alexander, was ruled by his cousin, Prince Alexander of Battenburg. In 1881, following the murder of Czar Alexander II, the prince had maneuvered to change the Bulgarian constitution and make himself an absolute monarch. He had to constantly parry the intrigues of Russia and Austria, for those empires coveted his small nation. For some time, the Bulgarian army had been controlled by Russian officers, with Bulgarians restricted to the lower officer ranks. Prince Alexander ultimately wearied of the Russians' interference in his internal affairs and expelled two leading Russian generals.

In 1885, Eastern Rumelia, a province of the Ottoman Empire, overthrew its Turkish administration and requested union with Bulgaria under Prince Alexander's rule. Expecting the Turks to retaliate against Bulgaria, Czar Alexander III immediately recalled all 600 Russian army officers still attached to the Bulgarian army; he thought the Turks would humble the prince and his army without Russian leadership. An attack came a short time later, but not from the Turks. The king of Serbia, Milan I, feeling threatened by Bulgaria's expansion through its incorporation of Eastern Rumelia, invaded Bulgaria at the instigation of Vienna. Czar Alexander, bemused, waited for the Bulgarian army to be crushed by the Serbs. At first the Bulgarians faltered, suffering an early defeat, but the popular Prince Alexander rallied his forces and drove the Serbs back into Serbia. In recognition of his victory, the Ottoman sultan recognized the prince's rule of the wayward province by appointing him governor general of Eastern Rumelia.

Czar Alexander was furious. Determined to punish his cousin, he engaged in one of the most ill-conceived and clumsy attempts at a coup in history. The czar's agents infiltrated Bulgaria's capital, Sophia, and bribed a handful of disgruntled Bulgarian army officers who had not received their expected promotions. The officers, using a regiment of troops who had no idea they were taking part in a coup, surrounded the prince's palace in the middle of the night of August 20–21 and kidnapped him. He was taken aboard the royal yacht and transported to the Russian Black Sea port of Reni, where the conspirators attempted to turn their prisoner over to the ranking Russian officer, a captain of the cavalry. When the captain learned who the prisoner was, he threatened to arrest the Bulgarian officers, who had expected a more congenial reception. The cavalry officer forced everyone to remain aboard the yacht while he wired St. Petersburg for instructions. When his instructions arrived, the captain released Prince Alexander from his captors and allowed him to leave for wherever he wished to go, in order to limit the appearance of Russian involvement. The yacht and its occupants were ordered to return to Bulgaria.

Word of the coup circulated in Bulgaria. The rumors were confirmed when the conspirators announced the formation of a provisional government on August 22, 1885. Within days, however, the populace and the army rose up against the new government. Most of the conspirators fled the country, never to be heard from again. A new government was established, and telegrams urging the prince, whose whereabouts were unknown, to return were sent throughout Europe.

When Prince Alexander returned to Bulgaria on August 29, he was greeted at every town by cheering citizens who welcomed him as their monarch. Unfortunately, he had been "shattered" by the coup and especially by the treachery of several army officers whom he had trusted. Within a few months he abdicated in favor of a regency.

All of Europe was scandalized by what had happened in Bulgaria. England's Queen Victoria, never an admirer of the Romanovs, called the coup the work of "these Russian fiends." Austria and Germany, although fearful of angering the czar, aired their negative feelings about the incident. Czar Alexander and Russia were thoroughly humiliated by the laughable coup attempt. The czar compounded his problem by sending an army general to Sophia to demand that the regency be dissolved and the reins of government be handed over to him. The Bulgarians contemptuously rejected the demand. Alexander then sent the Russian Black Sea Fleet into a Bulgarian harbor as a show of force, but he finally had to back down from his blatant attempt to take over Bulgaria.

Humiliated and isolated from Europe, Alexander turned toward the southeast for conquests. There he fought several brief but unproductive wars with Persia and Afghanistan.

Alexander III died suddenly on October 20, 1894, at the age of 49. The mantle of autocracy fell on the shoulders of his 26-year-old son. At his father's death, Nicholas II took his cousin Alexander by the arm, and with tears flowing down his cheeks, cried: "What is going to happen to me, to you, to Xenia, to Alix, to mother, to all of Russia? I am not prepared to be czar. I never wanted to become one. I know nothing of the business of ruling."

❖   ❖   ❖

Nicholas Alexandrovich Romanov was not alone in his belief that he was totally unsuited to be czar of Russia. The future prime minister, Sergei Witte, recorded a conversation with Empress Marie about her son Nicholas shortly before Alexander III's death, in which she admitted that the heir apparent lacked the strong will and character to rule Russia. Nicholas was not the empress's first son, nor was he her first choice to follow her husband to the throne. Alexander Alexandrovich had been the imperial couple's first son, but he died in infancy, so the title of czarevitch, or heir to the throne, had fallen to the second son, Nicholas. Marie loved Nicholas, but her favorite was Michael, her youngest son, who was 10 years younger than Nicholas. Evidently, Marie preferred having Nicholas abdicate his right to the throne in favor of Michael, but she never pressed the issue. In one of those ironic twists that populate so much of Russia's history, Marie's wish would be granted 23 years later when the fate of the dynasty and the empire were already sealed.

At the time of Alexander III's death, the imperial family was staying at its palace at Livadia in Crimea. Ten days before the huge czar died, a train brought Princess Alexandra (Alix) of Hesse-Darmstadt, the granddaughter of Queen Victoria, to Livadia at Nicholas's urgent request. Nicholas wanted his beloved fiancée close by as his father slipped toward death. Their betrothal was not yet official, but Czar Alexander remedied that soon after her arrival by giving the couple his blessing.

When Alexander III died, the imperial family agreed that Nicholas and Alexandra should wed as quickly as possible in order to give Russia a new imperial family with a new empress. Nicholas had taken the oath as czar the afternoon following his father's death, and now he needed a wife to complete his family before he was officially crowned. Dowager Empress Marie and the new czar wanted the marriage ceremony performed in the Livadia Palace before Alexander III was entombed, but the late czar's four brothers, Grand Dukes Vladimir, Alexei, Paul, and Sergei, argued that the wedding was an event too important to take place in virtual isolation. The four senior grand dukes being extremely powerful and influential members of the royal family, the wedding was scheduled for shortly after the funeral of Alexander III.

Alexander's body waited a full week in Crimea until all the arrangements for a czar's funeral could be made. It was then brought to St. Petersburg, where it lay in state at the Cathedral of the Fortress of Peter and Paul. Tens of thousands watched in silence, many on their knees praying for the late czar, as the funeral procession slowly wound through the city to the dirge of muffled drums. The body lay in view for 17 days, as thousands silently filed past for a final look at the giant czar. Among the dignitaries attending the funeral were the kings of Serbia, Greece, and Denmark; two future kings of England, Albert, the prince of Wales, and his son George; Prince Henry, the brother of the German kaiser; dozens of other members of European royalty; and hundreds of officials from throughout Russia.

On November 26, 1894, one week after Alexander was laid to rest, Nicholas and Alexandra were wed in a ceremony marked by subdued joy. The religious ceremony was not followed by a reception, nor did the couple take a honeymoon, on account of the czar's proclamation of a year of mourning for his father. The new czar and czarina moved in with the dowager empress until a suitable palace could be arranged. Their first child, Olga, was born in November 1895. Despite the national mourning that clouded their wedding, Nicholas and Alexandra would remain a totally devoted couple until their joint deaths in 1918.

❖ ❖ ❖

Nicholas's reign got off to a bad start, and in a country populated by superstitious people who saw omens in almost everything, that was especially unfortunate.

Czar Nicholas II's coronation was delayed because of the period of mourning for his father, but the date was finally set for May 16, 1896. The day before, the imperial couple, the dowager empress, and hundreds of royal family members and officials entered Moscow, the site of coronations, in a triumphant procession escorted by thousands of members of the Imperial and Cossack Guards. Virtually everyone was arrayed in their finest, with the men wearing dress uniforms, polished helmets, and tunics covered with decorations. In contrasting simplicity, the new czar stood out among all this finery. He rode alone on a white horse, displaying no decorations and no extravagant uniform. Wearing a simple army tunic buttoned to the neck, he raised his right arm in a salute to the thousands who had gathered to witness the coronation of the last czar.

The following day, Nicholas and Alexandra were installed in a five-hour-long coronation in the Kremlin's Cathedral of the Assumption. Nicholas sat on the jewel-encrusted Diamond Throne first used by Czar Alexis, the second Romanov czar, while Alexandra occupied the Ivory Throne, which had been brought to Moscow from Byzantium by the Greek princess Zoe Palaeologus, the wife of Ivan the Great and mother of Basil III.

The third day of coronation ceremonies, May 18, was traditionally dedicated to the public. The new czar would usually appear before the people and supervise the distribution of gifts commemorating the coronation. Beer and food would be dispensed to the gathered crowds. In anticipation of seeing the new czar and czarina, of possibly receiving a souvenir, and of participating in the free festivities, nearly 500,000 people gathered along the streets of Moscow leading to Khodynka Field, where the activities were to take place.

Grand Duke Sergei, the czar's uncle and Moscow's governor-general, having failed to accurately assess the size of the crowds, had assigned only a squadron of Cossacks to keep the crowd out of the field before the czar's party arrived. As dawn slowly crept across Khodynka Field—actually a practice ground for army engineers, it was bisected by numerous trenches and bomb craters—those at the head of the crowd caught sight of a number of stands that had been set up for the event, each covered with a stack of porcelain cups bearing the imperial double-eagle monogram. The cups were gifts for the men, and kerchiefs, also bearing the imperial monogram, were to be distributed to the women. Soon a false rumor spread through the crowd: the government had failed to produce enough souvenirs. As the rumor reached the rear of the vast crowd, those in back began to press forward, anxious not to return home without one of the gifts. Suddenly, almost in unison, the crowd surged forward, literally lifting some of the mounted Cossacks and their horses off the ground. In an effort to prevent the onrushing crowd from reaching the trenches, the Cossack officer in charge waved his arms frantically, but the crowd either ignored him or misinterpreted what he was yelling and kept rushing forward.

People at the front of the crowd, who were carried along by the momentum, saw the trenches first but were helpless to avoid them. Thousands of men, women, and children fell into the long ditches, hundreds piled on top of hundreds and were crushed into the dirt by thousands of feet as the crowd swept over them. It was only the arrival of Cossack reinforcements that halted the mob, giving the people in the field time to look around and learn of the great tragedy in which they had taken part. Nearly 2,000 people died, most of them crushed to death. Hospital wards quickly filled with thousands more who had been injured in the stampede.

The czar learned of the catastrophe at 10:30 that morning and was shocked. In his diary, he called the day a "sad national holiday." A few of the gifts were distributed to the survivors, but Czar Nicholas ordered most of the items destroyed. The porcelain cup, now a treasured collector's item, is commonly called "the cup of sorrows."

Nicholas' first impulse was to rush to Khodynka field, but he was restrained by his family, especially his mother. The dowager empress viewed the tragedy as the result of Grand Duke Sergei's ineptitude, and she wanted her son to keep as far away from it as possible. She demanded that Nicholas create a commission to determine who was responsible for the tragic event, knowing full well that Sergei, her late husband's brother, was guilty of failing to prepare Moscow appropriately for the tens of thousands of people who had swelled the city's population for the coronation. Nicholas agreed. The inquiry would trigger a succession of intrafamily feuds and intrigues that persist even after Nicholas's death.

The incident on Khodynka Field might have slipped from memory had Nicholas listened to his mother's other advice. Marie, wise in the ways of the superstitious Russian peasant, wanted to distance Nicholas from the catastrophe in order to dissuade people from viewing it as a bad omen for his reign. She wanted him to cancel all coronation-related entertainments at which the czar and czarina were scheduled to be present. Marie wanted him to appear, at least in public, to be in a state of mourning for the victims. Nicholas did agonize for the dead and injured. From his private funds, he sent the family of each victim 1,000 rubles, and he paid for coffins for the dead instead of allowing them to be buried in mass graves, which was the usual practice following such a calamity.

Marie was opposed by Alexandra and Nicholas's uncles, the senior grand dukes. Alexandra, who had a touch of the mystic in her, feared that their wedding immediately following a czar's funeral and the catastrophe at Khodynka Field were bad omens, and she hoped the joyous coronation celebrations would erase their memory. The grand dukes, who had little regard for public opinion, feared that canceling the celebrations would create a larger scandal; they urged Nicholas to continue with his schedule. In his memoirs, Alexander Izvolsky, who later served Nicholas as foreign minister, wrote that Nicholas's first thought on learning of the catastrophe was to cancel all festivities and "retire to one of the monasteries." It might not have changed history, but had Nicholas followed through on this impulse, his ill-starred reign might have gotten off to a better start.

Although the czar and czarina spent the next two days visiting the injured in Moscow's hospitals, distributing gifts and money to the survivors and the families of the dead, all the people remembered was that on the evening of the tragedy the imperial couple attended a ball given in their honor by the French ambassador, and that they danced and acted as if nothing had happened. Muscovites began referring to Grand Duke Sergei as the "Duke of Khodynka," and to the czar as "Bloody Nicholas."

Examining the character of Russia's last czar is extremely important because it played a vital role in the eventual collapse of the dynasty. The noted British historian Bernard Pares has described Nicholas as "deficient of will." Nicholas began his reign with the pledge that he would continue his father's policies; he resolutely believed in the autocracy, but he lacked the decisiveness to rule autocratically. Habitually described as "gentle, kind, and friendly," Nicholas too often yielded to those who disagreed with him, or whose policies failed to provide for the national interest. Foremost among these were his uncles, the senior grand dukes. These four men, driven by greed for power, had little fear of their nephew the czar. In fact, Nicholas feared them and their volatile tempers, which they frequently and skillfully vented on him. When Nicholas appeared unwilling to concede on some matter of importance to them, the uncles resorted to loud shouts that intimidated the mild-mannered czar.

Nicholas's second cousin and brother-in-law, Grand Duke Alexander Mikhailovich, provided an insight into the czar's fear of his uncles. Nicholas and Alexander were discussing the miserable condition of the Russian navy, which was controlled by Grand Duke Sergei, when Alexander recommended a complete reorganization of the service. The czar thought it was a good idea but expected that "uncle Sergei" would not stand for it. When Alexander reminded him that he was the czar, and that the navy badly needed to be reorganized according to 20th-century standards, Nicholas replied that he could do nothing about it because "uncle Sergei would be acting up terribly. Everybody in the palace will be certain to hear his voice." The czar was tacitly admitting that although he held the throne, others, specifically his father's brothers, controlled the affairs of state. Nicholas did everything possible to avoid confrontation with them.

Nicholas II longed to be as firm as his father, but he simply lacked the capacity. He wanted people to like him, as he openly liked people. Although on occasion he could be stubborn, he was incapable of taking a stand on an issue without massive support. He required reinforcement from someone he respected before making a decision he wanted to make all along. The czar's relationship with the German kaiser, Wilhelm II, which would determine to a large extent Nicholas's fate, illustrates the difference between his style of autocracy and that of his father. Alexander III despised Wilhelm and demonstrated this repeatedly by refusing to speak to the kaiser face to face, preferring instead to turn his back on him and speak over his shoulder. Nicholas was both enthralled and fearful of Wilhelm; he was captivated by the kaiser's bellicose manner, which he interpreted as representing strong leadership qualities but in truth was a facade masking the German's tortured uncertainties about his talents and his physical handicap. Wilhelm's left arm had been wrenched from its socket at birth and failed to develop properly, leaving him with a withered arm and hand that were noticeably smaller than those on his right side. All his life, Wilhelm worked at hiding his deformity with specially designed pockets or inside gloves.

In their private correspondence, which was conducted in English, the kaiser usually addressed the czar as "Dearest Nicky" and signed his letters "Your affectionate Willy." Wilhelm used this private communication channel to push Nicholas in directions that were favorable to Germany's foreign policy objectives. One of these directions was east, away from the affairs of Europe and the Middle East and toward China and Korea. Wilhelm was not the only person to encourage Nicholas to enhance his own and Russia's prestige with Asian conquests, but he was one of the most influential. Moving east could put Russia in direct confrontation with the Japanese Empire, and possibly even with the colonial empire of Great Britain. Such confrontations would distract the Japanese and the British from German designs in Asia.

❖ ❖ ❖

Russia's first clash with Japan, which would ultimately lead to a historic naval disaster, occurred in 1895, following Japan's invasion of China and occupation of several important ports, including Kinchow and Port Arthur. The

Russians had long coveted Port Arthur as an alternative to Vladivostok, Russia's only Pacific port, which was ice-bound for at least three months of the year. The Japanese also invaded Korea, which had long been isolated from outside influence and was the target of both Japanese and Chinese expansionist policies.

The April 7, 1895, treaty between the defeated Chinese and the victorious Japanese ceded Port Arthur, Formosa, and the Pescadores to Japan, along with a large indemnity. Declaring the Japanese occupation of Port Arthur a menace, Nicholas, along with France and Germany, threatened war if Japan continued to occupy the port. Japan withdrew and the Russians moved in. Japan was also forced to give up the concessions it had won on the mainland and to recognize Korea's independence. The following year, China conceded to Russia the right to build the East China Railway.

Buoyed by his success, Nicholas cast about for another victory to enhance the reputation he craved—that of a fearless warrior. Although Nicholas had no military credentials, he shared with his Romanov predecessors an enthusiasm for military parades, with flags flying and drums beating while he wore his colonel's uniform. The opportunity appeared to present itself when the Russian ambassador to Constantinople approached the czar with a scheme to conquer the Ottoman capital. The provocation for this action was a renewed series of massacres of Christians, this time Armenians, by the Turks. Ambassador Alexander Nelidov claimed that 30,000 Russian soldiers smuggled aboard naval vessels could land on both sides of the Bosporus Strait and, at his signal, fall on the city. The plan was purely amateurish. Had Nicholas proceeded, his troops probably would have been wiped out by the forces defending Constantinople. Landing 30,000 troops so near the city in secret was virtually impossible. Although Nicholas easily won the support of the minister of war, minister of the navy, and president of the Ministerial Council for the plan, it was only through the efforts of the powerful and respected minister of finance, Count Sergei Witte, that the ill-conceived plan was shelved.

Nicholas was pleased when in the summer of 1900 a Russian force, operating as part of an allied relief army, rescued the foreign nationals besieged in Peking by the Boxer rebels, who had been supported by the imperial Chinese government. Unfortunately, the Russians immediately set upon the city, engaging in widespread looting. Following the defeat of the Boxers, Russia occupied Manchuria.

Meanwhile, Russia's relations with Japan remained strained. The tension between the two countries increased dramatically when, in 1903, Nicholas supported the plans of an adventurous former cavalry officer named Bezobrazov to create an enterprise called the Yalu Timber Company, whose avowed intention was to harvest trees along the Korean border. Bezobrazov's real goal, endorsed by the czar, was to disguise Russian troops as lumber workers and smuggle them into Korea, where they would be reorganized for a campaign to control the Korean Peninsula. It was a dangerous ploy because the Japanese considered an independent Korea vital to their national security. At home, the Russian foreign minister, Count Vladimir Lamsdorf, who opposed the czar's meddling in Far Eastern affairs, was kept in the dark when Russian troops moved into Korea. When Witte learned of the plan, he objected and was dismissed from his finance post. The Japanese ambassador in St. Petersburg made several fruitless attempts to gain an audience with Nicholas and went home on February 3, 1904. War was in the air.

On February 8, without a declaration of war, Japan attacked the Russian-held port of Chemulpo, later called Inchon. As the Japanese fleet approached, two Russian cruisers, the *Koriets* and the *Varyaga*, steamed out to meet them. In the ensuing battle, the two outnumbered cruisers were sent to the bottom. Several thousand Japanese soldiers landed and marched north to take positions on the Korean-Chinese border along the Yalu River. The following day the Japanese fleet attacked Port Arthur, which is located on a narrow peninsula across the Yellow Sea from the west coast of Korea. Commanded by Japan's renowned Admiral Togo Heihachiro, the Imperial Navy badly damaged two Russian battleships and one cruiser, and sent a squadron of small torpedo boats into the crowded harbor to wreak havoc on the bottled up Russian Far Eastern Fleet.

When the war began, Japan was better prepared than Russia. Both the Japanese Imperial Navy and Imperial Army had kept abreast of the diplomatic efforts to reach a settlement and knew that war was inevitable. Japan had the ability to quickly put 150,000 combat troops into action against the Russian army, and its navy had already developed contingency plans for establishing Japanese control of the seas around Korea and Manchuria. The 80,000-man Russian field force, spread throughout eastern Siberia and Manchuria, was supported by 23,000 garrison troops as reserves and another 30,000 railway and frontier guards whose primary job was protection of the Trans-Siberian and East China railroads. The two navies were more or less equal in overall size, but the Japanese had an advantage in smaller craft, destroyers, and torpedo boats, which proved invaluable in the close combat that the fleets fought. With control of the sea, Japan would have the ability to rapidly provide supplies and reinforcements, while Russia would have to rely on the nearly 6,000-mile Trans-Siberian

Railroad, which was not designed to handle the extra weight of heavy artillery. In addition, the railroad consisted of a single rail line for roughly 4,000 miles, further reducing its strategic value.

The Japanese quickly isolated Port Arthur from the mainland, and the highly prized fortress ceased to be of any military value to Russia. Meanwhile, the war raged across Manchuria. The Russian army fought gallantly but vainly as it was slowly pushed back into Siberia. Field commander General Kuropatkin's orders to subordinate commanders were routinely countermanded by officials in far-off St. Petersburg, including the czar himself. Nicholas remained confident that the Russian bear would crush the "monkey" troops of the mikado, as Japan's emperor was called. Gradually, St. Petersburg and the rest of the nation came to realize the enormity of the conflict that many had predicted would be a "short victorious war."

In a truly desperate move to do something to satisfy public demands for effective action to relieve Port Arthur, the decrepit Baltic Fleet was sent around the world to battle the modern, European-trained Japanese Imperial Navy. Nicholas had vacillated for weeks over whether to send the fleet to the Pacific, first issuing orders to prepare the fleet to sail, then canceling them days later, then reissuing them only to cancel them once again. His indecision convinced everyone around him of his inability to face the fact that the war was lost and to deal with defeat. Finally, under the command of Admiral Zinovi Rozhdestvensky, who considered his assignment a suicide mission to satisfy demands for a victory at any cost, and who had earlier expressed the belief that "we haven't a chance against the Japanese," the fleet embarked in October 1904.

Before the Baltic Fleet had even reached the Atlantic Ocean it almost started a war with Great Britain. The Russian captains all knew about the small Japanese torpedo boats that had infiltrated the Port Arthur harbor and sunk or severely damaged larger warships with near impunity, and they feared the same fate. There were rumors that Japan had already established in European waters a fleet of these boats flying foreign flags as disguise. During the night of October 21, and while in the North Sea, the Russians suddenly found themselves surrounded by a large number of small boats and fired. Unfortunately, the boats turned out to be a British fishing fleet. Luckily, only one British boat was sunk and only two lives were lost, but Britain was outraged. Nicholas expressed his regrets to King Edward and eventually paid £65,000 in damages to the boat's owners and the crew's survivors.

The incident was a bad omen for the Baltic Fleet, which continued its journey. The fleet steamed through the North Atlantic, the South Atlantic, around Africa's Cape of Good Hope, and north through the Indian Ocean toward Japan and disaster.

As the world watched the spectacle of a 19th-century fleet struggling to reach a battleground halfway around the world, Port Arthur surrendered in January 1905. The siege had cost the Russians more than half of the 28,200 men in the garrison, while the Japanese lost nearly 58,000 men. The capitulation of the fortress freed 100,000 additional Japanese troops, who rushed north into Manchuria to join the war against the Russian army. The decisive land battle was fought near Mukden, along the South Manchurian Railroad. For 14 days the Russian soldiers fought heroically against the Japanese, whose bravery and daring equaled their opponent's. Finally, after each side had lost over 70,000 men, the Russians, exhausted and unable to receive supplies and reinforcements, withdrew on February 25, 1905.

Meanwhile, Admiral Rozhdestvensky's creaky old fleet worked its way north along the Asian coast. Admiral Togo waited for him near the north end of the Tsushima Strait. At two o'clock on the afternoon of May 27, 1905, the modern Japanese battleships swept across the path of the oncoming Russian fleet sailing in single file, firing on it from 7,000 yards. Russian vessels were picked off one at a time from a range that their guns were unable to match. In 45 minutes the battle was over, with most of the Russian ships either sunk, sinking, or drifting out of control. Japan's infamous torpedo boats closed in on the stricken Russian fleet and completed the job. All eight Russian battleships were sunk, as were most of the dozen cruisers and nine destroyers. Only two cruisers and one destroyer managed to reach Vladivostok intact. Admiral Rozhdestvensky was taken prisoner when the Japanese rescued the crew of his sunken flagship.

News of the disaster reached the czar while he was attending a family picnic in celebration of the ninth anniversary of his coronation. After reading the communiqué he fell silent. The fate of the fleet seemed to signal the destiny of the empire, and perhaps Nicholas at that moment realized it.

❖ ❖ ❖

Bad news about the war 7,000 miles away compounded bad news at home. The country was coming apart. Throughout the empire workers were rising up against the factory owners, demanding better wages. Peasants renewed the old tradition of violent rebellions against landowners, whose homes were burned and lives forfeited at an increasing pace.

Life in Russia was becoming cheap, especially the lives of government officials who were targeted by the numerous revolutionary groups that had sprung up on campuses and in factories. The revolutionaries, who for the most part sought to replace the autocracy with a socialist government, were soon joined by average citizens who, enraged by the news from Manchuria, blamed the government, and now even the czar himself, for the debacle.

Matters had come to a head in St. Petersburg on Sunday, January 9, 1905. Following news of Port Arthur's surrender, a huge crowd of demonstrators estimated at 120,000, led by a Ukrainian priest, Father George Gapon, who had been a secret police informant, marched on the Winter Palace, demanding to see the czar. Reports of what happened next are confusing, often tainted by the political leanings of the reporter, but the basic fact is that the troops sent to protect the palace fired on the mob. Several dozen men, women, and children were killed before the crowd scattered. The event became known as "Bloody Sunday" and provided the revolutionaries with a rallying cry to incite the people.

Czar Nicholas, who was not in the city at the time, was deeply distressed. In his diary he wrote that it was "a difficult day. Lord, it is so painful and hard." The shooting turned the people against the czar. Because he had failed to protect them when they only wished to petition him, many ceased to considered Nicholas II their czar. The old inviolate belief that the czar and the people were one was gone forever.

Now the autocracy really began to unravel. The following month, Grand Duke Sergei, the czar's uncle, was killed by a bomb thrown by a young anarchist. Political assassinations and labor unrest spread like wildfire across Russia. The czar meanwhile listened to all sorts of advice, and as usual he wavered from one extreme to the other on what to do. He remained a staunch autocrat, but the autocracy was collapsing around him. Finally, on October 17, 1905, the czar issued what became known as the October Manifesto, which called for elections to a national assembly, the Duma.

An elected National Assembly was not what he wanted, but Nicholas's desire to rule as the monarch of a peaceful nation populated by citizens whose loyalty and devotion to the czar was unquestioned was beyond his reach. Most of Russia's population was illiterate and did not understand such terms as republic, democracy, and representative government, which were used by the revolutionary speakers who crisscrossed the country, but the people knew there had to be change. A soldier best expressed the widespread ignorance of revolutionary goals when he said, "yes there must be a republic, but there must also be a good czar to be head of it." Nicholas and most of his advisors failed to understand that what the people really wanted was not so much a change in the type of government that ruled Russia, but rather an improvement in their own lives and the hope that their children could do better. The revolutionaries understood this and twisted it to their own ends. One official who did understand was Peter Stolypin, whom Nicholas appointed minister of the interior in April 1906 as part of an extensive government reorganization. Stolypin had been a provincial governor, the only one who was able to maintain peace in his province during the preceding stormy months.

Also in April 1906 the first elected Duma was inaugurated in an elaborate ceremony at the Winter Palace. The Duma's 524 deputies represented 26 political parties and 16 nationality groups. Although the Constitutional Democratic Party, with between 170 and 180 members, dominated the Duma, it by no means controlled the assembly as different groups frequently voted together on specific issues. Of the 200 peasants in the Duma, 100 were not affiliated with any party or group, although they usually voted with the more radical groups, especially on land reform questions.

The Duma got off to a bad start when, by almost unanimous vote, it petitioned the czar for universal suffrage and a land reform act based on the expropriation of large estates. Nicholas refused to see the deputies or to read their petition. The Duma then demanded that the government resign, which it refused to do, and the matter rested there, with neither side budging. In July, when the prospects of winning government cooperation appeared hopeless, the Duma published its petition to the czar, who promptly dissolved the assembly. Along with dissolving the Duma, Czar Nicholas appointed Stolypin president of the Council of Ministers. He would be the last head of the government to attempt to negotiate a settlement between the government and the leaders of the liberal opposition.

Stolypin called for elections for a new Duma, which would meet early in the following year. He also instituted policies aimed at pacification and reform. His first goal was to eliminate the revolutionaries who were killing thousands of people—high and low government officials, police officers, and innocent bystanders—each year. Once this had been accomplished, he would seek real reforms that would go far to prevent the revival of revolutionary groups. Using draconian measures, including military courts to try terrorists, he very nearly succeeded in wiping out the underground terrorist groups. The most ardent bomb-throwers were arrested and executed (a few managed to escape abroad), but not before they struck back at Stolypin by blowing up his home, killing 32 people and badly injuring a score more, including his children. Nevertheless, Stolypin persevered. Although he did not believe in constitutional government, Stolypin recognized the need to improve the condition of the peasants as a way to achieve peace. He promulgated laws giving land-owning peasants the right to dispose of their land as they saw fit, and made government lands available to peasants at low cost.

The next few years witnessed a series of Dumas that were largely ineffectual because of a weighted voting system that kept them from reaching consensus. All were unable or unwilling to come to terms with the government. For their part, the government and especially the czar flatly refused to cooperate with the Dumas. The conflict fueled the engine of revolution. Peter Stolypin's policies—including those that made large tracts of land available to peasants and revived the Peasant Land Bank, which loaned peasants the money to buy land—were significant steps forward. Even Nicholas, who still hoped somehow to return to the days when the czar ruled supreme, could not fail to recognize the beneficial impact of these policies. But Stolypin's work ended abruptly on September 1, 1911, when he was fatally shot by a revolutionary while attending an opera in Kiev and within sight of the czar and his family. Stolypin's successors lacked both his drive and his interest in reform to sustain his programs.

❖ ❖ ❖

In August 1904, an event that would have a dramatic impact on the imperial family and the nation occurred: Czarina Alexandra gave birth to an eight-pound baby boy with curly yellow hair and bright blue eyes. The boy was named Alexis in honor of Nicholas's favorite czar, the second Romanov ruler, and as Nicholas himself said, to "break the chain of Alexanders and Nicholases." The boy inherited hemophilia from his mother's family. Carried by females and infecting males, the disease had been transmitted to the royal families of Europe by the daughters of Queen Victoria, who herself was a carrier. Victoria's daughters and granddaughters had married into most of the royal courts of Europe, and the disease became the scourge of royalty. Soon it became obvious to the parents of the heir to the Russian throne that he had been chosen by nature's random selection process.

Alexis's hemophilia became a state secret, guarded from the public by the imperial family and those who were closest to it. The boy had to be protected from the slightest injury because it could cause bleeding that might not be stopped. The need to protect their little boy drew the members of the royal family closer together. Always a bit of a mystic and drawn to ardent prayer,

Alexandra now prayed constantly for a miracle for Alexis. Although the boy's ailment remained largely a family secret, indirectly it would have a profound effect on Russia, and eventually on the world. Alexandra's search for a miracle to cure her incurable son led her to a figure whose very name conjures dark images, Gregory Rasputin.

❖ ❖ ❖

The mysterious, unwashed, hypnotic Rasputin will forever be linked with the weak czar and his wife.

In many respects, especially through her powerful influence over her husband, Alexandra was in effect the last ruler of imperial Russia. Imperial family life revolved around young Alexis and the need to keep the "little treasure," as the czar called him, safe. Grand Duke Alexander Mikhailovich reported that life for the imperial family had lost all other meaning, after the discovery of Alexis's hemophilia. Visiting family members feared even smiling in the empress's presence, and the royal couple's residence was little more than a house in mourning. Nicholas, although he buried himself in work, was increasingly divorced from events beyond the family and its immediate circle.

Alexandra's religious fervor became fanaticism as she pressed everyone in and around the imperial court to spend their time on their knees praying for a miracle to cure her son. Then in November 1905, she was introduced to a "miracle worker" named Rasputin, who came from a small peasant village in Siberia. Rasputin quickly became a darling of St. Petersburg society, which was always attracted to someone or something different that might brighten its otherwise boring existence. Rasputin was part of a Russian phenomenon, the "starets" or unordained holy man who roamed the vast Russian landscape, where he preached all sorts of religious dogma and was usually supported by the more ignorant among the peasant population.

Many people found Rasputin repulsive because of his unkept appearance. His long black hair, parted in the middle, hung over his ears in a stringy mess; the droppings of past meals were often embedded in his thick beard; and his body and clothes remained unwashed for extended periods of time. Yet many St. Petersburg's society women found him interesting, even erotic. The mysterious monk preached a kind of sex-based religion that promised his followers, especially the ladies, the path to true eternal salvation by submitting themselves to him.

Rasputin was promoted to Alexandra as a miraculous healer, and in him she saw the potential to cure Alexis's hemophilia. During the next few years,

Rasputin did work near-miracles. Inexplicably, he could stop the bleeding, and he even was able to relieve the boy's pain by simply speaking to him on the telephone. Was Rasputin a true miracle worker, or simply a charlatan who was extremely lucky? The truth probably will never be known. What *is* known is that this curious man gradually infiltrated the imperial family and eventually dictated almost every move it should make to the empress, who in turn easily manipulated the czar.

Outside the imperial court and society circles, Rasputin was a dreaded, contemptible figure who, propelled by an overpowering sex drive, spent much of his time in debauchery. Nicholas appears to have been less convinced of Rasputin's holiness than his wife, but he made the equally fatal error of seeing the starets as a symbol of the common people with whom the czars had traditionally bonded. The people, however, were more perceptive. Rasputin was judged to be a despicable character by most of the population.

Rasputin's domination of Alexandra and, through her, the czar was so great that prior to the start of World War I he influenced court appointments and had men removed from important posts simply because they offended him. Given the circumstances, talk that Rasputin was sleeping with the empress was inevitable, but the holy man did everything he could to encourage it, going so far as to confide to a number of journalists that "I do what I want with her." When Rasputin's enemies brought stories of his late-night debaucheries to the palace, they were invariably labeled as liars by Alexandra and either dismissed from their positions or isolated and made useless. When World War I started, Nicholas decided to join the Russian army in the field. He in effect left the governing of Russia in Alexandra's hands, which was tantamount to placing Rasputin in charge.

The Great War began in July 1914, when Austria declared war on Serbia following the June 28 assassination of the Austrian heir apparent, Archduke Franz Ferdinand. Russia responded by partially mobilizing its army. On August 1, Germany, Austria's ally, countered the mobilization with a declaration of war against Russia. Two days later, France, Russia's ally, ordered a general mobilization that caused Germany to declare war on France. Austria then issued her own declaration of war against Russia. Within weeks, most of the European nations had entered the conflict. At first, because the war stirred great patriotic fervor in Russia, the revolutionary groups were driven even farther underground. Initially, there was no serious opposition to the war; in fact, the Duma met on August 8 and voted to endorse the government's war policy without dissent.

The German strategy, which the kaiser enthusiastically endorsed, was to first crush the French army and its ally, the British Expeditionary Force, and then turn the German army's might against Russia. On August 4, the Germans crossed into Belgium and attacked the mighty fortress at Liège. Under fire from giant howitzers designed to crumble fortress walls, Liège fell on the 16th. Four days later, the invaders occupied Brussels. Although the French and the British mounted a gallant defense, the German advance continued for several weeks. Suffering one defeat after another, the French and the British called on their Russian allies to relieve some of the German pressure. But the vaunted "Russian steamroller" was merely a figment of the imaginations of several Russian generals and editorial writers.

The Russian army was totally unprepared for war. In a move that stunned the leading figures in Russian military circles, Nicholas appointed his cousin, Grand Duke Nicholas, commander in chief. When Nicholas learned of his appointment, he burst into tears because he had no idea of how to command the vast army placed under his leadership.

Barely 30 percent mobilized, the Russian army marched off to war. The Russian soldiers, as they had for generations, responded without hesitation to the call of their czar. Many loyal troops went into battle bare-handed, needing to wait for a comrade to fall before obtaining a usable weapon. At first, with the main part of the German army occupied on the Western Front, the Russians successfully invaded East Prussia and Galicia, but as German units were moved east, the tide of battle turned and the Russians absorbed massive losses in a series of disastrous engagements. The most demoralizing was a three-day battle near the town of Tannenberg: from August 26 through the 29th, 125,000 Russians were killed, wounded, or taken prisoner. German casualties were less than 14,000 men. Devastated by the loss, the Russian army was pushed out of East Prussia and into Russian territory.

The appeal to fight for the czar and Holy Russia eventually drew 15 million Russians into the war, but the number is deceiving. Supporting this primitive army was a backward nation unable to produce sufficient weapons, ammunition, uniforms, and the myriad other items an army requires to survive in the field. Russia's inefficient railroad system also hampered the Russian troops, who were always short of everything.

After a year of almost constant setbacks inflicted by the German and Austrian war machines, Czar Nicholas demoted his cousin and took personal command of the army. Incompetent but decisive leadership was replaced by incompetent and indecisive leadership. Nicholas had no military experience and tended to defer to staff officers who were mostly ineffectual courtiers. The czar took command of an army that bore no resemblance to the force that had marched off to war only a year earlier. In less than a year, the Russians had lost hundreds of thousands of troops, and the core of the regular army had been decimated. Nicholas now led an army of conscripts, almost 80 percent of whom were peasants who had little understanding of what the war was about and were for the most part poorly trained and ill-equipped. Desertions numbered in the tens of thousands each month as the desperate men fled for home to be with their families.

Meanwhile, in Petrograd (the name of the capital having been changed from the German-sounding St. Petersburg), the empress unofficially ruled in her husband's absence. On matters she could not manage directly, such as major appointments to governmental posts, Alexandra wrote to the czar with her recommendations. The devoted husband invariably acquiesced to her. But Nicholas failed to understand the consequences of these appointments in the new scheme of things. Since the advent of the Duma, he was no longer the absolute ruler of Russia whose decisions were unquestioned. Therefore, it was essential that talented men be placed in high posts, but unhappily, Alexandra based many of her decisions on advice received from Rasputin. The holy man had no interest in ruling Russia, only in preserving the autocracy that sheltered him and tolerated his notorious lifestyle. He used his influence to remove officials whom he disliked, or who had spoken against him, and had them replaced by those who bowed to his wishes. Therefore, at the most critical time in its history, Russia was run mostly by men who were selected by a sex-crazed peasant with little understanding of, or regard for, what he was doing to the country.

As the war continued to go badly, and as deserters brought back tales of the horrendous losses at the front, the people's patriotic spirit waned. Conscripting millions of peasants from the fields and sending them to war had caused critical food shortages in the cities. In part, the problem was caused by a decline in the production of more efficient, larger farms, which were left short of workers, but an overtaxed, antiquated distribution system further strained by the war effort contributed heavily. Food riots erupted spontaneously in many cities, including Petrograd.

Early indications that the end of the dynasty was near surfaced in November 1916, when the Duma met in Petrograd amid widespread popular disaffection. The month before, striking industrial workers had won over to their side two regiments of soldiers who had been sent to disperse them. The soldiers fired on the police, and only the timely arrival of loyal Cossacks had prevented the mutiny from spreading. The Duma's members, furious at the way the government was being run, wanted to end Rasputin's influence. In November 1916, members of virtually every political party took to the Duma platform to attack Rasputin and the government ministers he had helped to appoint. The czar was compelled to yield to the Duma majority, which insisted on the dismissal of Rasputin's most infamous protégé, Boris Stürmer, who served as both president of the Council of Ministers and minister of foreign affairs. Stürmer had failed dismally in both positions, and he was rumored to have treasonous liaisons with German agents. Although Rasputin tried halfheartedly to save at least one of Stürmer's posts, the czar removed this "red flag" for the opposition from both jobs.

The following month, December 1916, Rasputin was murdered by a small group of conspirators, including two members of the extended imperial family who recognized the destructive influence of the starets. They had first tried poison. When that failed, they shot Rasputin and bound him and threw him into the Neva River, where he drowned. The effect of this crime on Alexandra was devastating. To her, the death of Rasputin was tantamount to a death sentence for Alexis.

❖ ❖ ❖

Toward the end of 1916, change at the top levels of the government appeared inescapable. Soldier revolts had become commonplace, especially after the officers who might have kept the rebellious peasant soldiers in line had been killed by the thousands in combat. The world had been made aware of the unrest in Russia by reports filed by foreign diplomats, but the troubles became a stark reality in France in 1916 when a Russian brigade passing through Marseilles on its way to fight in Greece turned on its officers and killed the colonel in command. French troops put down the mutiny, and 20 Russian soldiers were executed. Almost every member of the Duma recognized that the autocracy, even in the guise of a constitutional monarchy, was doomed. The burning question was, What kind of government would replace it? Members of the imperial family saw the end coming and tried to make Nicholas understand the condition of the nation and the peril to his dynasty and himself, but he refused to listen. When they collectively sent him a letter asking for clemency for Grand Duke Dmitri for his role in Rasputin's murder, and for the creation of a reconstituted ministry that would be answerable to the Duma, his fateful response was, "I allow no one to give me advice."

Everyone in Russia acknowledged that the government was rapidly disintegrating and verging on collapse, except the czar and the czarina. Repeated attempts by the family to make them realize what was happening met with continued rebuffs, especially from Alexandra, who was convinced that this crisis, like the one in 1905, would blow over and her dear Nicky would continue to rule as czar.

The catalyst for the revolution that destroyed the dynasty was not a plot of some revolutionaries, or a conspiracy of the Duma; it came directly from the people, specifically, from the women of Petrograd. Exhausted by long hours spent on lines in the freezing cold, hoping to purchase a loaf of bread, they listened intently to reports of food supplies rotting in far-off railroad stations because there were no trains to bring them to the capital. These truthful reports were compounded by suspicions that the shortages were created by government officials who were lining their own pockets by selling the food on the black market. On March 8, 1917, the women waiting in line to buy bread were told there was no bread left. The women began screaming at the bakery spokesman, and someone threw a rock through the shop window. It was followed by another, then another and another. The following morning, a Friday, the women returned to the streets to demonstrate for bread. Stores with supplies of food were looted. The women were soon joined by workers from nearby factories, and cries for peace mingled with demands for bread. By Saturday, Petrograd was paralyzed as huge crowds swept through the city, calling for an end to the war, for more food supplies, and, most ominous of all, for the end of the autocracy.

Troops sent into the city, especially those from the Petrograd garrison, refused to fire on the people and instead joined them. Even the feared Cossacks declined to fire on the crowds or to even use their dreaded whips to restore order to the streets. The crowds' fever was spurred by revolutionaries and the numerous German agents who had been sent into the capital to stir up revolution. Especially active were the members of the tiny Bolshevik Party. The only armed force still loyal to the government was the police, but it was quickly overwhelmed and some of its members were killed by the mobs that roamed the city.

By Monday evening, March 12, the still leaderless mobs had seized control in the capital. Few rioters had political aspirations, and most of them trusted the Duma. At his military headquarters at Baranovichi (a Polish railway junction on the main line from Moscow to Warsaw), the czar refused to believe the reports arriving from Petrograd, and he ordered that troops from the front be sent to the city to put down the demonstrations. The Duma overruled him, however, and no troops were sent. Nicholas also dissolved the Duma, but the members ignored the order. In recognition of the fact that the czar had no clear understanding of what had actually happened in the capital, the Duma created a Provisional Government.

When Nicholas attempted to return to Petrograd, the Duma ordered his train stopped en route. He was held in isolation until Thursday, March 15, when two members of the Duma arrived with a demand that he abdicate. All but one of the leading Russian generals that the czar could reach through the army's telephone and telegraph system agreed that he must abdicate. Even the czar's cousin, the former commander in chief of the Russian army, Grand Duke Nicholas, advised Czar Nicholas to step down.

Meanwhile, the German High Command, apprised by its spies of events in Russia, ceased all military operations on the Eastern Front in order to give the Russian army the freedom to focus on the revolution. German leaders reasoned that helping to bring the Russian government down might lead to military victory. Soon, Russian revolutionaries hiding in Germany and Switzerland, including the Bolshevik leader Vladimir Lenin, were put aboard trains and returned to their homeland to contribute to the chaos.

In Petrograd, a second force had emerged as an alternative to the Provisional Government from the most left-wing members of the Duma, the Petrograd Soviet (Council) of Workers and Soldiers. It eventually would be dominated by the small but violent Bolshevik Party.

On March 15, 1917, seated in his imperial railroad car, Czar Nicholas II, the last in a long line of Russian monarchs, wrote out his own abdication manifesto. In it, he called for continued efforts to crush the Austrian and German forces, and, not wishing to be separated from his son, Alexis, he abdicated in favor of his brother, Grand Duke Michael. Michael, who understood the situation in Petrograd better than Nicholas, refused to accept the crown unless he was requested to do so as a constitutional monarch by a duly elected constituent assembly. Thus ended the Romanov dynasty.

Around the country people were stunned, especially those in the towns and villages of the countryside, where there was little understanding of the events in the capital. Few Russians had expected the czar to abdicate, not even those most vehemently opposed to the government. People met in church to pray for the country and for their "little father."

Nicholas spent the next five days visiting the front and bidding farewell to his former army. He was treated with respect wherever he went, and many officers cried at the sight of their fallen leader. Fearful that the lives of the former czar and czarina were in danger from extremists (many Russians considered

Alexandra a German agent who had undermined the czar), the Provisional Government voted to "deprive the deposed emperor and his consort of their liberty."

On March 22, the czar was brought to his family at the Alexander Palace in Tsarskoye Selo, outside Petrograd, where they remained prisoners for five months. There, they were subjected to the whims of surly revolutionary soldiers who periodically invaded the palace to make sure the Romanovs had not escaped. Nicholas, released at last from the burdens of governing, appeared calm and tranquil to the few visitors he was permitted to see.

At the end of March, members of the Provisional Government secretly requested that Great Britain provide asylum to the imperial family, which the government of Lloyd George reluctantly granted, but the Petrograd Soviet learned of the plan and attempted to stop it. Even King George V, Nicholas's cousin, eventually turned against him, fearing that granting the former czar sanctuary in England would arouse English public anger. Ironically, the allies that Nicholas II had gone to war to help, the allies to whom he was so devoted, abandoned him in his time of need.

Unable to guarantee the family's safety so near the capital, the Provisional Government, and especially its leading figure, Alexander Kerensky, sought a safe harbor for the Romanovs. At first it was thought that Nicholas should be moved to Crimea, but the long train ride—more than 1,000 miles—would expose the former czar and his family to the whims of numerous revolutionary groups and Soviets in the industrial cities through which the train would have to pass. Finally, Kerensky settled on Tobolsk, a commercial center in western Siberia. Escorted by a squad of Cossacks, the family was spirited out of the Alexander Palace and put aboard a train that flew Japanese flags and bore the markings of the Japanese Red Cross.

The family, along with a few trusted servants who had volunteered to accompany it, spent eight months in Tobolsk. There, Nicholas read in the newspapers that the Provisional Government had been overthrown by the small, well-armed Bolshevik Party, and that Kerensky himself was now in flight from the new government. The much heralded Red Revolution of November 1917 had actually been a virtually bloodless coup against a weak government that lacked even the ability to defend itself. The new government was under the direction of Lenin, one of the revolutionaries who had been returned to Russia by the Germans.

The final destination of the last czar and his family was Ekaterinburg, in the Urals. The city, a hotbed of antimonarchist feelings, had a special hatred for the Romanovs. Nicholas and his family remained imprisoned there until the night of July 16, 1918, when, at the order of the Bolshevik Central Committee in Moscow, or more specifically Vladimir Lenin, they were awakened and taken to a basement room where they were murdered.

EPILOGUE

Ten days after the bloody slaughter of Nicholas II and his family and servants, the city of Ekaterinburg fell to the forces of the "Whites," who were engaged in a civil war against the "Red" Bolshevik government. An investigation conducted by the Whites determined that the corpses had been moved to a nearby wooded area, where they were dismembered, soaked in gasoline and sulfuric acid, and burned. The remains had been shoveled into an abandoned mine shaft, and hand grenades had been dropped around the opening in a clumsy attempt to close the mine.

Throughout Russia, members of the Romanov family were rounded up and executed by the Bolsheviks. A few family members managed to escape abroad, but most died at the hands of Russia's new rulers. One of those who managed to flee Russia with Bolshevik agents at their heels was Dowager Empress Marie, the wife of Alexander III and mother of Nicholas II. The 72-year-old former czarina was taken from Crimea by a British battleship in April 1919 as Red Army units approached. She lived the remaining nine years of her life as a guest of her nephew, King Christian X of Denmark.

Imperial Russia became Soviet Russia, and the imperial czars were replaced by the Red czars, who were every bit as powerful and bloodthirsty as the worst of Russia's ancient rulers. Vladimir Lenin and Josef Stalin cast as black a shadow over the Russian landscape as any Russian ruler before their time. Today, nearly eight decades after Lenin seized power, Russia's new, democratic rulers are as busy erasing the traces of the Soviet past as the Soviets were in eliminating the Romanov past.

Appendix

GENEALOGICAL TABLES

THE GRAND PRINCES OF KIEV

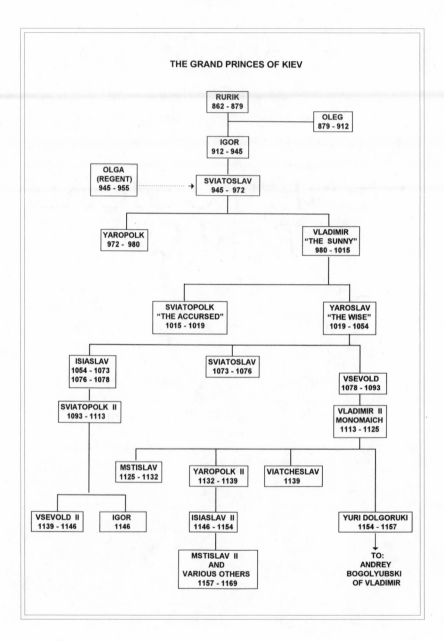

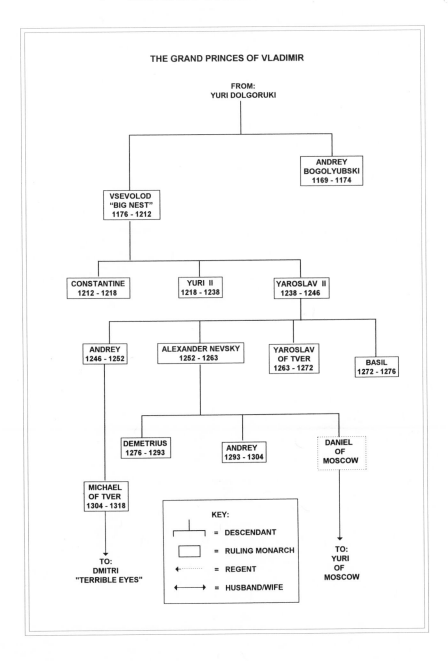

THE GRAND PRINCES OF VLADIMIR

FROM:
YURI DOLGORUKI

ANDREY
BOGOLYUBSKI
1169 - 1174

VSEVOLOD
"BIG NEST"
1176 - 1212

CONSTANTINE
1212 - 1218

YURI II
1218 - 1238

YAROSLAV II
1238 - 1246

ANDREY
1246 - 1252

ALEXANDER NEVSKY
1252 - 1263

YAROSLAV
OF TVER
1263 - 1272

BASIL
1272 - 1276

DEMETRIUS
1276 - 1293

ANDREY
1293 - 1304

DANIEL
OF
MOSCOW

MICHAEL
OF TVER
1304 - 1318

KEY:

⌐ = DESCENDANT

▭ = RULING MONARCH

◄········ = REGENT

◄─────► = HUSBAND/WIFE

TO:
DMITRI
"TERRIBLE EYES"

TO:
YURI
OF
MOSCOW

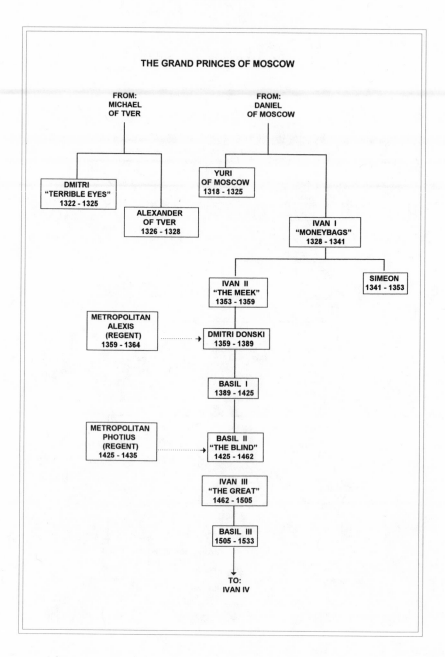

THE GRAND PRINCES OF MOSCOW

FROM:
MICHAEL
OF TVER

FROM:
DANIEL
OF MOSCOW

DMITRI
"TERRIBLE EYES"
1322 - 1325

ALEXANDER
OF TVER
1326 - 1328

YURI
OF MOSCOW
1318 - 1325

IVAN I
"MONEYBAGS"
1328 - 1341

SIMEON
1341 - 1353

IVAN II
"THE MEEK"
1353 - 1359

METROPOLITAN
ALEXIS
(REGENT)
1359 - 1364

DMITRI DONSKI
1359 - 1389

BASIL I
1389 - 1425

METROPOLITAN
PHOTIUS
(REGENT)
1425 - 1435

BASIL II
"THE BLIND"
1425 - 1462

IVAN III
"THE GREAT"
1462 - 1505

BASIL III
1505 - 1533

TO:
IVAN IV

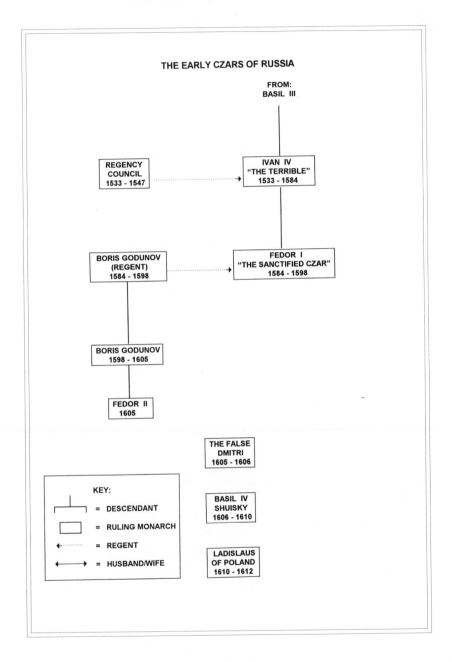

THE EARLY CZARS OF RUSSIA

FROM:
BASIL III

REGENCY
COUNCIL
1533 - 1547

IVAN IV
"THE TERRIBLE"
1533 - 1584

BORIS GODUNOV
(REGENT)
1584 - 1598

FEDOR I
"THE SANCTIFIED CZAR"
1584 - 1598

BORIS GODUNOV
1598 - 1605

FEDOR II
1605

THE FALSE
DMITRI
1605 - 1606

KEY:

= DESCENDANT

= RULING MONARCH

= REGENT

= HUSBAND/WIFE

BASIL IV
SHUISKY
1606 - 1610

LADISLAUS
OF POLAND
1610 - 1612

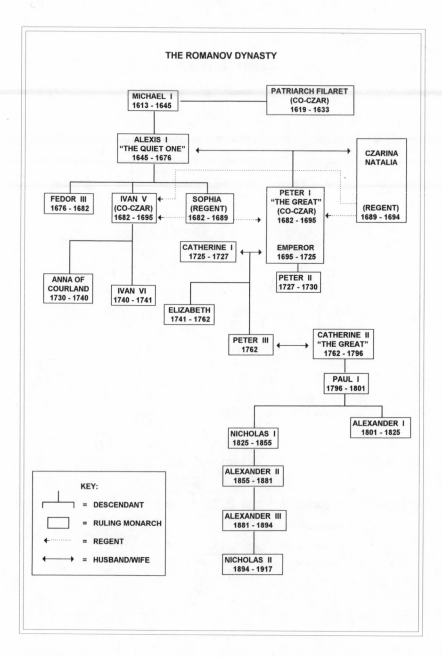

THE ROMANOV DYNASTY

MICHAEL I
1613 - 1645

PATRIARCH FILARET
(CO-CZAR)
1619 - 1633

ALEXIS I
"THE QUIET ONE"
1645 - 1676

CZARINA
NATALIA

FEDOR III
1676 - 1682

IVAN V
(CO-CZAR)
1682 - 1695

SOPHIA
(REGENT)
1682 - 1689

PETER I
"THE GREAT"
(CO-CZAR)
1682 - 1695

(REGENT)
1689 - 1694

CATHERINE I
1725 - 1727

EMPEROR
1695 - 1725

ANNA OF
COURLAND
1730 - 1740

IVAN VI
1740 - 1741

PETER II
1727 - 1730

ELIZABETH
1741 - 1762

PETER III
1762

CATHERINE II
"THE GREAT"
1762 - 1796

PAUL I
1796 - 1801

ALEXANDER I
1801 - 1825

NICHOLAS I
1825 - 1855

ALEXANDER II
1855 - 1881

KEY:

= DESCENDANT

= RULING MONARCH

= REGENT

= HUSBAND/WIFE

ALEXANDER III
1881 - 1894

NICHOLAS II
1894 - 1917

BIBLIOGRAPHY

Alexander, Grand Duke of Russia. *Once a Grand Duke*. Garden City, N.Y.: Garden City Publishing Company, 1932.

Alexander, John T. *Catherine the Great*. New York: Oxford University Press, 1989.

Almedingen, E. M. *The Emperor Alexander I*. New York: Vanguard Press, 1966.

Anthony, Katharine. *Catherine the Great*. New York: Alfred A. Knopf, 1925.

Atkin, Muriel. *Russia and Iran, 1780–1828*. Minneapolis: University of Minnesota Press, 1980.

Barker, A. J. *The War against Russia*. New York: Holt, Rinehart and Winston, 1970.

Billington, James H. *The Icon and the Axe*. New York: Alfred A. Knopf, 1966.

Blum, Jerome. *Lord and Peasant in Russia*. New York: Atheneum, 1967.

Bobrick, Benson. *Fearful Majesty*. New York: G. P. Putnam's Sons, 1987.

Buchanan, Meriel. *The Dissolution of an Empire*. London: John Murray, 1932.

Cate, Curtis. *The War of the Two Emperors*. New York: Random House, 1985.

Chambers, James. *The Devil's Horsemen*. New York: Atheneum, 1985.

Charques, R. D. *A Short History of Russia*. New York: E. P. Dutton, 1956.

Cherniavsky, Michael, ed. *The Structure of Russian History*. New York: Random House, 1970.

Clarkson, Jesse D. *A History of Russia*. New York: Random House, 1961.

Connelly, Owen. *Blundering to Glory*. Wilmington, Del.: SR Books, 1987.

Coughlan, Robert. *Elizabeth and Catherine*. New York: G. P. Putnam's Sons, 1974.

Cowles, Virginia. *The Russian Dagger*. New York: Harper & Row, 1969.

Cross, Samuel Hazzard. *Slavic Civilization through the Ages*. New York: Russell & Russell, 1963.

Custine, Marquis de. *Empire of the Czar*. New York: Doubleday, 1989.

D'Encausse, Hélène Carrère. *The Russian Syndrome*. Translated by Caroline Higgitt. New York: Holmes & Meier, 1992.

Dvornik, Francis. *The Slavs in European History and Civilization*. New Brunswick, N.J.: Rutgers University Press, 1962.

Dziewanowski, M. K. *Alexander I: Russia's Mysterious Tsar*. New York: Hippocrene Books, 1990.

Florinsky, Michael T. *Russia*. 2 vols. New York: Macmillan, 1965.

Fredericks, Pierce G. *The Sepoy and the Cossack*. New York: New American Library, 1971.

Gooch, G. P. *Catherine the Great*. London: Longmans, Green, 1954.

Graham, Stephen. *Boris Godunof*. New Haven: Yale University Press, 1933.

Grouset, Rene. *The Empire of the Steppes*. Translated by Naomi Walford. New Brunswick, N.J.: Rutgers University Press, 1970.

Gurney, Gene. *Kingdoms of Europe*. New York: Crown Publishers, 1982.

Harcave, Sidney. *Russia: A History*. Philadelphia: J. B. Lippincott, 1964.

Haslip, Joan. *Catherine the Great*. New York: G. P. Putnam's Sons, 1977.

Hingley, Ronald. *Russia: A Concise History*. New York: Thames and Hudson, 1991.

Jones, Gwyn. *A History of the Vikings*. New York: Oxford University Press, 1968.

Kerensky, Alexander F. *The Catastrophe*. New York: D. Appleton, 1927.

Kirchner, Walter. *A History of Russia*. 6th ed. New York: Barnes & Noble Books, 1976.

Kluchevsky, V. O. *A History of Russia*. 5 vols. Translated by C. J. Hogarth. New York: Russell & Russell, 1960.

Klyuchevsky, Vasili. *Rise of the Romanovs*. Translated by Liliana Archibald. New York: Barnes & Noble Books, 1993.

Lamb, Harold. *The City and the Tsar*. Garden City, N.Y.: Doubleday, 1948.

Lawrence, John. *A History of Russia*. New York: Meridian/NAL, 1978.

MacKenzie, David, and Michael W. Curran. *A History of Russia and the Soviet Union*. 3rd ed. Chicago: The Dorsey Press, 1987.

Massie, Robert K. *Nicholas and Alexandra*. New York: Athenuem, 1967.

———. *Peter the Great*. New York: Ballantine Books, 1981.

Miliukov, Paul, Charles Seignobos, and L. Eisenmann. *History of Russia*. 2 vols. Translated by Lam Markmann. New York: Funk & Wagnalls, 1968.

Oldenbourg, Zoe. *Catherine the Great*. Translated by Anne Carter. New York: Pantheon Books, 1965.

Pares, Bernard. *A History of Russia*. New York: Alfred A. Knopf, 1953.

Paszkiewicz, Henry K. *The Making of the Russian Nation*. Chicago: Henry Regnery Company, 1963.

Pipes, Richard. *Russia under the Old Regime*. 2nd ed. New York: Collier Books, 1992.

Radzinsky, Edvard. *The Last Tsar*. Translated by Marian Schwartz. New York: Doubleday, 1992.

Riasanovsky, Nicholas V. *Nicholas I and the Official Nationality in Russia, 1825–1855*. Berkeley: University of California Press, 1959.

———. *A History of Russia*. 4th ed. New York: Oxford University Press, 1984.

Riha, Thomas, ed. *Readings in Russian Civilization*. 2nd ed. 3 vols. Chicago: University of Chicago Press, 1969.

The Russian Chronicles. London: Random Century House, 1990.

Saul, Norman E. *Russia and the Mediterranean, 1797–1807*. Chicago: University of Chicago Press, 1970.

Seeger, Elizabeth. *The Pageant of Russian History*. New York: Longmans, Green, 1950.

Staden, Heinrich von. *The Land and Government of Muscovy*. Translated by Thomas Esper. Stanford, Calif.: Stanford University Press, 1967.

Stephenson, Graham. *Russia from 1812 to 1945*. New York: Praeger, 1970.

Sumner, B. H. *A Short History of Russia*. New York: Harcourt, Brace and Company, 1949.

Szamuely, Tibor. *The Russian Tradition*. New York: McGraw-Hill, 1974.

Ulam, Adam B. *In the Name of the People*. New York: Viking Press, 1977.

Vernadsky, George. *A History of Russia*. New York: New Home Library, 1944.

Vryonis, Speros, Jr. *Byzantium and Europe*. New York: Harcourt, Brace & World, 1967.

Wallace, Robert. *Great Ages of Man: Rise of Russia*. New York: Time-Life Books, 1967.

Walsh, Warren B., ed. *Readings in Russian History*. Syracuse, N.Y.: Syracuse University Press, 1950.

INDEX

Names in **boldface** indicate czars or czarinas. Page numbers in *italic* indicate illustrations or captions. An "m" following a page number indicates map; "g" indicates glossary.

David, Prince of Kiev 48
Davout, Louis-Nicolas 272
Dazhbog (Slavic nature god) 7
Decembrist Revolt (1825) 292–293, 311
De la Gardie, Jakob 164, 165
Demetrius (r. 1276–1293) 67, 351g
democratic freedoms 41–42
"democratic revolution" 48
Denmark 117, 136, 137, 211, 235
Deulino, Armistice of (1618) 176
Devlet Gerey (Crimean leader) 218
d'Hédouville, Count 266
Diamond Throne 329
Diebitsch, Baron Ivan 300
Dimsdale, Thomas 248
Dionys, Metropolitan 145
Dionysus, Abbot 168
Dir (Viking chieftain) 11, 14
"divine right" 110
Dmitri ("Terrible Eyes") (r. 1322–1325) 71, 352g
Dmitri ("the False") (r. 1605–1606) 152–161, 153, 353g
Dmitri (Cossack nominee for czar) 173
Dmitri (grandson of Ivan III) 110
Dmitri (son of Ivan IV and Maria Nagaia) 135, 144, 147
Dmitri, Grand Duke 344
Dmitri, Prince (pretender) 163–167
Dmitri Donski (r. 1359–1389) 79, 81, 81–88, 93, 352g
Dmitri of Suzdal 81–82
Dolgoruky, Prince Alexis 226
Dolgoruky, Prince Basil 226, 246–247
Dolgoruky, Catherine 226
Dolgoruky, Prince Ivan 225
Dolgoruky, Prince Michael 189–190
Domostroi (Home Management) (how-to manual) 131–132
Don Cossacks 178, 212
Dorystolum, Siege of (971) 27–28
Drevlyane (Slavic people) 20–22
"druzhina" (princely retinue) 40
Dugdale, Lieutenant (British naval officer) 246
dukes *see specific names (e.g.,* Charles Frederick)
Duma 122, 125–126, 132, 166, 337–339, 341, 343–344
Dutch East India Company 204

E

Eastern Orthodox Church 23–24, 32–35, 92–93, 146–147
Eastern Rumelia 325, 326
Eastern Slavs 5, 7
East Prussia 233
education 40, 290, 296, 311, 314, 317
Edward VIII, King of England 322, 335
Eisenstein, Serge 66
Elizabeth (r. 1741–1762) 222, 225, 226–227, 229–234, 237–238, 354g
Elizabeth (wife of Alexander I) 253, 274, 282, 291
Elizabeth I, Queen of England 141
Elphinstone, John 245–246
Elyau, Battle of (1807) 273
emporors *see specific names (e.g.,* Francis I)
Enghien, Duke of 266
England *see* Great Britain
Estonia 116m, 218
Eudoxia Lopukhin (wife of Peter I) 196

F

False Dmitri *see* Dmitri ("the False")
famines 152
Fedor I ("the Sanctified Czar") (r. 1584–1598) 137, 141, 142–149, 353g
Fedor II (r. 1605) 157, 158, 353g
Fedor III (r. 1676–1682) 184–186, 354g
Ferdinand, Archduke of Austria 268
Ferdinand I, Emperor of Austria 303, 304
Finland 116m, 218, 219, 231, 275
fires 130–131, 148
France *see also specific rulers (e.g.,* Louis XVIII)
    Crimean War 306, 307
    Holy Alliance withdrawal 301
    Napoleonic Wars 267–288, 289
    Revolutionary Wars 256, 257, 258, 266
    Revolutions of 1848 303, 304
    Russo-Turkish War 247
    Seven Years' War 233
    war against Turkey 297
    World War I 341, 342
Francis I, Emperor of Austria (Francis II, Holy Roman Emperor) 267, 270, 271, 279
Francis Joseph I, Emperor of Austria 305
Franz Ferdinand, Archduke of Austria 341
Frederick III, Holy Roman Emperor 110
Frederick Augustus, Elector of Saxony 272

❖ CZARS ❖

Philaret, Patriarch (Fedor Romanov) (co-czar) (r. 1619–1633) 151, 159, 163, 166, 176–178, 354g
Philip, Metropolitan 140
Philip, Prince of Sweden 167, 172
Philippopolis, Bulgaria 26
Phocas, Bardas 31
Phocas, Peter 27
Photius, Metropolitan (regent) (r. 1425–1435) 90, 352g
Phull, Karl Ludwig von 283
Pitt, William 233
Pius VI, Pope 257
Pius VII, Pope 266
Platoff, Hetman 287
Platoff, Prince Matvei 285
Pobedonostsev, Constantine 323
"pogosty" (tax collection depot) 23
pogroms 324
Poland 56m, 116m
  influence in False Dmitri's court 159–160
  king chosen by Catherine II 243
  Napoleonic Wars 272–273, 278, 280, 281
  Novgorod treaties with 97–98
  occupation of western Russia 167
  partitioning of 248, 252, 253
  revolt against Russian rule 299–300
  Russian rule of 298–301
  Ukraine lost by 182–183
  wars and conflicts with Russia 35, 39, 46, 176–177, 245, 252–253
  war with Ottoman Empire 199
Polish Patriotic Society 299
political reforms 132, 251, 262, 276
Polotsk (principality) 50
Poltava, Battle of (1709) 216–217
Polyeuctus, Patriarch of Constantinople 27
Poniatowski, Count Stanislas *see* Stanislas Poniatowski, King (Poland)
Port Arthur 333–336
"possessors" (religious group) 108
Potemkin, Gregory 250, 255
Pozharsky, Prince Dmitri 168–170, 173
"Preobrazhenskii" (regiment) 193–194
princes/princesses *see specific names (e.g., Berke)*
principalities *see specific principality (e.g., Moscow)*
private property 76
Provisional Government 346, 347

Prus (alleged son of Caesar Augustus) 109
Prussia 116m, 122, 234, 252, 253 *see also specific rulers (e.g., Frederick the Great)*
Pskov (city and principality) 74, 84, 113
Pugachev, Emelian 249–250
Pushkin, Alexander 303

Q
queens *see specific names (e.g., Elizabeth I)*

R
"Raskolniki" *see* Old Believers
Rasputin, Gregory 340–341, 343–344
Rastrelli, Bartolomeo 231
Rayevsky, Nicholas 283
Razumovsky, Alexis 232
Red Square (Moscow) 131, 150, 158, 161, 167, 184
reforms
  educational 311
  legal 108, 132, 151, 243, 262, 297–298, 311, 314
  military 133, 185–186, 275, 315–316, 317
  monetary 123–124
  political 132, 251, 262, 276
  religious 31, 32
Regency Council (r. 1533–1547) 121–122, 126, 353g
regents *see specific names (e.g., Boris Godunov)*
Rehnskjold, Carl Gustav 217
religion *see specific religion (e.g., Christianity); denomination (e.g., Roman Catholic Church); house of worship (e.g., Cathedral of the Assumption)*
religious reforms 31, 32
Revolutions of 1848 303–305
Rhine Confederation 270, 272
Riga (city) 2m
"right of departure" 112
Rogned (wife of Vladimir "the Sunny") 29, 30
Rogvolod (Viking prince) 29
Roman Catholic Church
  campaign for unification with Orthodox Churches 92–93, 101
  Council of Florence (1439) 92–93
  False Dmitri's conversion to 154, 155, 159–160
  Russification policy in Poland affecting 301